SCIENCE
HORIZONS

Silver Burdett & Ginn
MORRISTOWN, NJ ▪ NEEDHAM, MA
Atlanta, GA ▪ Cincinnati, OH ▪ Dallas, TX ▪ Deerfield, IL ▪ Menlo Park, CA

SCIENCE
HORIZONS

George G. Mallinson
Distinguished Professor
of Science Education
Western Michigan University

Jacqueline B. Mallinson
Associate Professor of Science
Western Michigan University

Linda Froschauer
Science Senior Teacher
Central Middle School
Greenwich, Connecticut

James A. Harris
Principal, D.C. Everest
Area School District
Schofield, Wisconsin

Melanie C. Lewis
Professor, Department of Biology
Southwest Texas State University
San Marcos, Texas

Catherine Valentino
Former Director of Instruction
North Kingstown School Department
North Kingstown, Rhode Island

Dedicated with love
to our colleague, teacher, and friend
Denny McMains
whose talent and courage
were the inspiration for Science Horizons

Acknowledgments appear on pages 574–576, which constitute an extension of this copyright page.

Science HORIZONS

Dear Students,

Welcome to SCIENCE HORIZONS! Are you looking forward to science this year? We hope so. You are learning science in an important time in history. In the past 100 years, many changes have taken place because of scientific discoveries. In the year 1900 many homes were without electricity. Only a few people dreamed of flying. Today astronauts walk on the moon. Computers can do in a few seconds what once took months or years to do.

What will the next 100 years be like? There are exciting changes on the horizon. You may travel to Mars. You may live or work in giant skyscrapers with more than 400 floors. What else may happen? In science class you will find out.

Along with changes come problems to solve. It takes large amounts of energy to keep a modern city running. Our air and water have become polluted. Many kinds of plants and animals are in danger of disappearing. In science you will learn how these things happen. You will also discover how you can help to solve these problems.

Most of all, this year you will have fun. Turn to the table of contents to see the exciting year we have planned. Then begin your journey with a trip to the bottom of the ocean. A machine called *Jason* is waiting for you.

Bon voyage,

The Authors

Contents

UNIT TWO
PHYSICAL SCIENCE

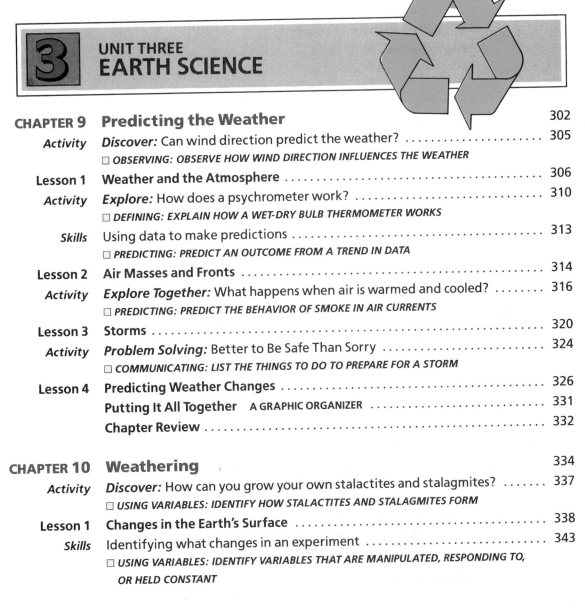

3 UNIT THREE
EARTH SCIENCE

UNIT FOUR
HUMAN BODY
4

AN EXPLORER'S DREAM

On a cold night in April 1912, the luxury ocean liner *Titanic* hit an iceberg and began to sink. *Titanic* drifted downward more than 3 km (2 miles) until it came to rest on the ocean floor.

Now for the first time since that terrible night, another ship was nearing *Titanic*. From inside the little submarine *Alvin*, Dr. Bob Ballard gazed at the ghostly ship. Dr. Ballard said he would always remember "the stark sight of her immense black hull towering above the ocean floor."

Dr. Ballard and the crew of *Alvin* spent days exploring the rust-covered *Titanic*. They were even able to explore the inside of the ship.

Jason Jr. at a porthole of *Titanic* ▶

◀ **Dr. Robert D. Ballard**

*"My lifelong dream was
to find this great ship…Now,
finally, the quest was over."*

— *Dr. Robert D. Ballard*

Alvin was too large to enter the wreck. But *Alvin* had a partner — a robot named *Jason Jr.* According to Dr. Ballard, *Jason Jr.* was their "swimming eyeball." It was attached to *Alvin* by a long cable and was operated by remote control.

Jason Jr. was small enough to get close to portholes, go down staircases, and move into small spaces. Its cameras took pictures that answered many questions about what happened on board the ship on that night in 1912.

Finding the wreck of *Titanic* was the lifelong dream of Dr. Robert Ballard. He grew up loving the ocean and everything about it. While still a teenager, he learned to scuba dive. He knew that somehow his future had to do with the ocean. Later, he would decide to become a marine geologist.

At Woods Hole Oceanographic Institution, Dr. Ballard helped to develop small ships called submersibles (sub-MUR suh bulz) to explore the deep sea. Inside the submersible *Alvin,* Dr. Ballard has seen more of the ocean floor than any other person alive.

Yet Dr. Ballard wondered if there might be a faster, safer way to explore the deep sea. Perhaps robots could be used as eyes, ears, and hands for people.

"Through such robots man could remain under the sea for weeks…extending his reach…into earth's last great uncharted frontier."

— *Dr. Robert D. Ballard*

Robots could also help to make another of Dr. Ballard's dreams come true. He wanted to share the thrill of undersea exploration with people all over the world.

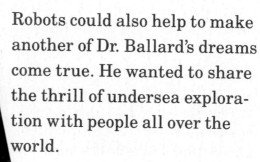

THINKING

Skills

Measuring force with a scale

A skill is something you do well. In science, you will learn many thinking skills. Whenever you do a **Skills** lesson, you will follow three steps. First, you will **practice** so that you can learn how to do the skill. Second, you will **think** about how you used the skill. Third, you will **apply,** or use, the new skill on your own.

When *Alvin* is launched, it is lifted off a large ship and placed into the water. It takes more force to lift *Alvin* in the air than to lift it in water. You can measure the force it takes to lift an object in air and in water. Measuring is an example of a skill.

Practicing the skill

1. Shape a piece of clay into a ball that fits in your hand.

2. Tie a string in a loop around the clay. Hang the clay from a scale. What is the force needed to lift the clay in air?

3. Lower the clay into a jar that is three-fourths full of water. What is the force needed to lift the clay in water?

Thinking about the skill

How could you measure the force needed to lift your body in water and in air?

Applying the skill

Show that the force needed to lift the clay does not change when you change its shape. Form the clay into a cube. Measure the force needed to lift the clay in air and in water. Measure other shapes in this way. Compare your results.

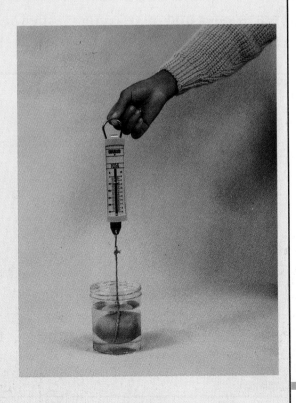

Dr. Ballard's exploration of *Titanic* gave him a chance to test an undersea robot and show how it could improve ocean exploration. Then he set his sights on building an even better robot, named *Jason*.

▲ **Scientist with "Knuckles"**

Jason is larger than *Jason Jr.,* and it has mechanical arms. A special grasping tool, nicknamed "Knuckles," can be attached to one of *Jason*'s arms. Together they can pick up objects on the sea floor. *Jason* also has color cameras that can transmit television pictures.

Suppose you were in control of *Jason* as it moves near the ocean floor. You would sit at the control panel in a large mother ship at the surface. This is safer and more comfortable than being cramped in a small submersible down below.

Control room for *Jason* and *Argo* ▼

Like *Jason Jr., Jason* has a partner. But *Jason's* partner is not *Alvin*. It is another robot, called *Argo*. *Argo* acts like a container for *Jason*.

Jason in front of carrier Argo ▼

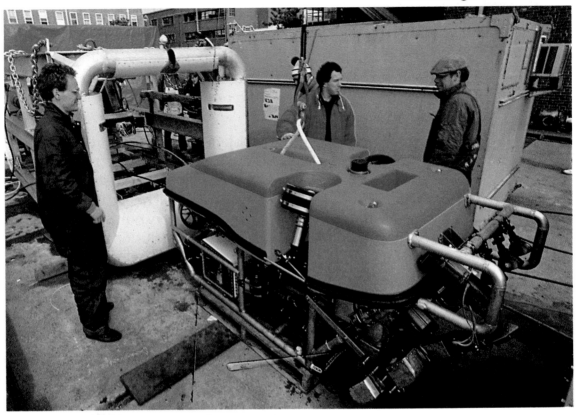

How do *Jason* and *Argo* work together? *Jason* is carried inside *Argo* on board a mother ship. *Jason* and *Argo* are lowered into the water together. Then *Jason* can be launched from *Argo*. Both robots carry cameras that take pictures of the ocean floor. As *Jason* explores, it stays attached to *Argo* by a cable. *Argo*, in turn, is connected by a long cable to the mother ship.

While scientists were building *Jason*, many problems had to be solved. One of the problems was rusting. Scientists had to find ways to stop the rusting of metal parts used to build *Jason*.

Problem Solving

Let's Arrest the Rust

Finding a way to stop rust from forming is an example of problem solving. This science book has activities in which you can practice solving problems. There are four steps to follow.

First, **think** about the problem. List facts about the problem that you already know. Gather other facts that you need. Second, use the facts to **plan** a way to solve the problem. Make a list of the things you will need. Third, gather the things you need and **do,** or carry out, what you planned. Record your results and conclusions. Fourth, **share** your results and conclusions with your classmates.

Just how well would *Jason* work? In May of 1989, *Jason* was shipped to Europe to find out. There it was placed on its new mother ship, *Star Hercules*. The scientists on board the ship wanted *Jason* to explore a shipwreck on the bottom of the Mediterranean Sea.

Thousands of years ago the Mediterranean Sea was a busy place. Greek and Roman ships carried things to and from every port in the ancient world. Some of these ships were lost during storms and battles at sea. The contents of these sunken ships are scattered on the ocean floor.

▼ *Star Hercules*, mother ship for *Jason*

How can you prevent an object from rusting in salt water?

Think Rust forms when iron or steel combines with oxygen. Salt water in the oceans speeds up the forming of rust. What can you do to steel to prevent it from rusting? What do you know about rusting? What else do you need to know?

Plan Plan to use two plain steel wool pads and a spray bottle filled with salt water. Use one pad as a control. Use the other pad for the experiment. What things can you do to the experiment pad to keep it from rusting?

Do Prepare the experiment pad as you planned. Then spray the pads with salt water and keep them wet. Compare the pads daily for a week.

Share Describe to the class how each pad looked after a week. Explain whether your plan worked.

Among the sunken objects are many large clay jars. Olive oil, wine, fish oil, wheat, and other useful things were stored and carried in these jars. Studying the jars gives scientists clues about how people lived in ancient times.

To help pick up the jars from the sea floor, *Jason* got some help from "Knuckles." *Jason* was able to lift the jars off the sea floor and place them in a netlike basket. Then the jars were brought to the surface to be studied.

▲ *Jason* **exploring the ocean floor**

21

▲ The *Jason* Project at a museum

How would you like being on board the mother ship, *Star Hercules?* In a way you can. It can happen through telepresence (tel ih PREZ uns). *Telepresence* is a word used by Dr. Ballard. It means television that shows scientific discovery as it is happening — right now, in the present. The excitement of real exploration happens right before your eyes.

Telepresence is the idea behind the *Jason* Project at museums all over the United States. In this project, thousands of school children watch television screens that show *Jason* exploring the deep sea in another part of the world.

▲ How telepresence works

sea to the museum auditorium in about half a second!

Live broadcasts are made several times a day. Students not only see what is going on. They also share in a question-and-answer period with Dr. Ballard at sea. By wearing headphones, a student can ask Dr. Ballard a question and listen to his reply. So students can discover along with *Jason*'s crew.

Jason's pictures are sent from the ocean floor to the mother ship by a special cable. The color pictures are then beamed up to a satellite. Finally, a satellite beams the live television signal to museums that are part of the *Jason* Project. What *Jason* "sees" is seen on color television screens in many museums at the same time. The signal travels from the bottom of the

"Remotely operated deep-sea…robots…could give man what I have come to think of as a 'telepresence' in the sea."

— *Dr. Robert D. Ballard*

Explore Together

How can you learn what the ocean floor looks like?

Each of *Jason's* missions takes teamwork by many scientists. Everyone on board the mother ship has a special job to do. In Explore Together activities, you will be part of a group, or team. Every member of the group has a job to do.

The Organizer gets the materials for the activity and leads the cleanup when the activity is done. The Investigator carries out the activity and makes sure it is done properly. The Manager helps the Investigator. The Manager also keeps time, makes sure safety rules are followed, and does calculations. The Recorder writes down the group's results and conclusions. The Recorder also records all the data collected. The Reporter shares the results and conclusions of the group with the rest of the class. When the Group is named, everyone helps.

Now it is your turn to work on a team. Find out how a team can learn what the ocean floor looks like.

A

Materials

Organizer   scissors • shoe box • modeling clay • masking tape • marker • metric ruler • lead sinker tied to a 30-cm piece of string

Procedure

Manager   **A.** Cut out the narrow side of a shoe box as shown in picture *A*.

Manager   **B.** Work inside the box. Use the clay to make a model of the ocean floor with mountains and valleys. Do not let the Investigator see what you are doing.

Recorder   **C.** Take a strip of masking tape that will fit across the top of the box. Place a mark every centimeter along the tape. Label the marks *A*, *B*, *C*, and so on. Place the tape on top of the box as shown in picture *A*.

Investigator   **D.** With the back of the box facing you so that you cannot see the "ocean floor," hold the string near mark *A* on the tape. Lower the sinker until it touches the clay bottom. Measure the distance from the tape to the clay bottom.

Recorder   **E.** Make a table like the one shown. Record the measurement in the column marked *A*.

Investigator, Recorder   **F.** Repeat step **D** and step **E** for each of the remaining marks along the tape.

Investigator   **G.** Using the data that you collected, draw an outline of the "ocean floor" of your shoe box. When you are finished, compare the outline to the clay model.

	Mark on Tape							
	A	B	C	D	E	F	G	H
Distance from tape to bottom (in centimeters)								

Writing and Sharing Results and Conclusions

Group, Recorder   **1.** How well does the drawing compare to the clay model? Explain your answer.

2. What are some problems in making a map of the ocean floor in this way? Why would photographs taken by *Jason* be a better way to map the ocean floor?

Reporter   **3.** How do your results and conclusions compare with those of your classmates?

Dr. Robert Ballard has spent a lifetime of hard work finding answers to his questions about the deep sea. Do you have questions about the oceans? What other things about the world do you wonder about? You can find answers to your questions just as he did. Studying science can help you.

Science is a way to ask and answer questions about the world. It is a way of learning about the world around you. Plants, animals, matter, energy, the earth, and space are all part of the world around you.

Finding answers to your questions can be exciting and fun. Once long ago, Dr. Ballard said that a teacher of his had made science come alive. There are many ways to make science come alive. Dr. Ballard uses robots as his eyes, ears, and hands. You can use this science book in much the same way. With it you can explore the oceans, climb mountains, come face to face with animals, and examine the human body.

"We must show [students] that everything hasn't been discovered, that there is a lot of the world left to explore, and that exploration can be rewarding in many ways."
— *Dr. Robert D. Ballard*

SCIENCE
HORIZONS

LIFE SCIENCE

Chapter 1

Simple Living Things

What You Cannot See

What you cannot see can hurt you—or it may very well help you. There are many types of tiny living things too small to be seen with the unaided eye. They must be viewed through a microscope.

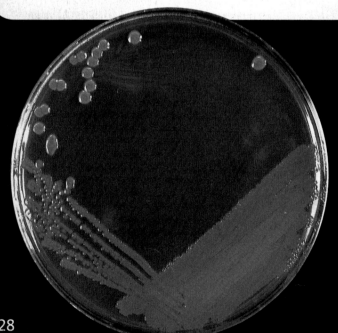

Many of the tiny living things have helped people throughout history. They are called bacteria (bak TIHR ee uh). Some types of bacteria are used to make cheese. Some are used to make yogurt. Other types of bacteria help all living things. They break down once-living things, freeing their nutrients to be used again.

One of the best uses of bacteria may be in cleaning up wastes. Some poisonous wastes are now dumped in land-fills. The poisonous substances can seep into the ground and into the water supply. But certain bacteria can break down these substances, making them harmless and keeping ground water safe.

Bacteria are also being tested in a new type of sewage treatment plant. This treatment system has two main steps. First, tanks of waste water are treated with a certain type of bacteria. As the bacteria break down the harmful chemicals, they give off a gas called methane. The methane gas can then be collected and used for fuel.

Even though the bacteria have cleaned the water of harmful chemicals, the water would still not be safe to drink. It needs more cleaning. Scientists have found that using it to water nursery plants, such as trees, roses, and shrubs, cleans the water further. Since the plants grow in tubs of water, their roots filter the water as it swirls through the tubs. Then the water can be disinfected to make it safe to drink. This two-step process produces methane gas, beautiful plants, and clean water!

ACTIVITY

Discover

What affects the growth of simple living things?

Materials slice of white bread that does not contain preservatives · 4 small sealable plastic bags

Procedure

You have probably seen simple living things around your home or school. You may have seen some on food that has spoiled, for example.

You can grow simple living things on a piece of bread Cut a slice of bread into four pieces. Seal each piece of bread in a separate bag. Think about conditions that might help things grow. Then test each piece in a different condition.

Caution: *Do not open any of the bags—you may be growing harmful living things.* Decide how you will measure the growth on the bread. Check the bags for 2 weeks. What conditions helped the growth of simple living things?

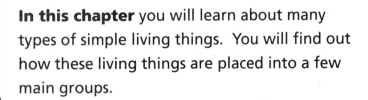

In this chapter you will learn about many types of simple living things. You will find out how these living things are placed into a few main groups.

31

1. Cells

Getting Started   How small are the smallest living things? To get an idea, try this. Tear a sheet of notebook paper in half. Then tear one of the halves in half again. Repeat this until the paper is too small to tear again. The tiny bit of paper remaining is still larger than the smallest living thing.

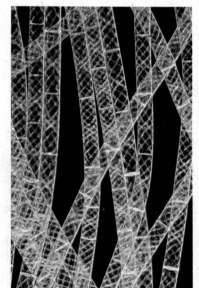

▲ Spirogyra

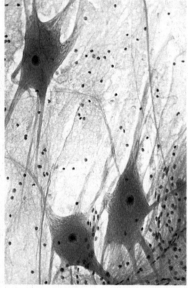

▲ Nerve cells

▲ Moss leaf cells

What are living things made of?

All living things are made up of one or more cells. The basic part of all living things is the **cell.** Most cells are so small that they can only be seen with a microscope. An **organism** (OR-guh nihz um) is any single living thing. Organisms have different sizes and shapes. Some organisms are many-celled, and some are one-celled.

You, for example, are a many-celled organism. So are trees, fish, and most other living things that you can think of. A many-celled organism is made up of various types of cells. The cells of each type carry out certain activities, and the cells depend on one another. The organism as a whole carries out the activities of life.

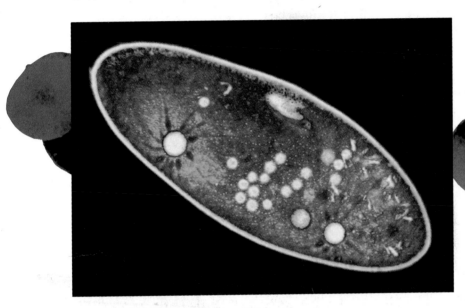

◄ Paramecium

▲ Blood cells

Some cells from many-celled living things are shown at the left. These pictures were taken through a microscope. How do the cells differ? Which of the cells are found in animals? Which of the cells are found in plants?

Look at the picture above of a one-celled living thing called the paramecium (par uh MEE-see um). This picture was also taken through a microscope. A one-celled organism is a complete living thing. It is considered complete because the cell can carry out all the activities of life. It moves, responds, and grows. It uses food for energy. It gets rid of wastes. It can also reproduce, or make more of its own kind.

What is a kingdom of living things?

Scientists classify all organisms into five large groups called **kingdoms.** Look at the chart. Each kingdom is made up of living things that have some traits in common. Animals make up the animal kingdom and plants make up the plant kingdom.

The other kingdoms are made up of simple living things. They are the protists (PROHT-ihsts), the fungi (FUN jye), and the monerans (moh NER unz). In the rest of this chapter, you will study these organisms.

Kingdoms of Living Things				
Monerans	**Protists**	**Fungi**	**Plants**	**Animals**
One-celled	One-celled	Most are many-celled	Many-celled	Many-celled
Example: bacterium	Example: paramecium	Example: mushroom	Example: dandelion	Example: chimpanzee

Earth Science
CONNECTION

Now that you have learned how scientists classify organisms, use reference books to find out how they classify rocks. What are three groups of rocks?

Lesson Review

1. What is the basic part of all living things?
2. How does a cell of a many-celled organism differ from the cell of a one-celled organism?
3. What is a kingdom of living things?

Think! Imagine you are a detective at the scene of a crime. You find some red specks that might be blood stains. How could using a microscope help you find out what they are?

Skills

THINKING

Observing how things are alike and how they are different

When you look at two living things, you can see how they are alike and how they are different. Small differences in the way two living things look can show big differences in what they do and how they grow.

Practicing the skill

Living things are made of cells. The drawings show two different cells. One is from the leaf of a water plant, and the other is from an onion bulb.

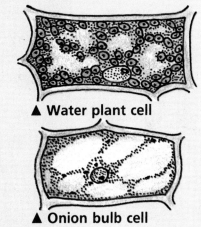

▲ **Water plant cell**

▲ **Onion bulb cell**

1. How are the cells alike? Do you see a part of the water plant cell that looks like a part of the bulb cell? What other things are alike in both cells?

2. How are the cells different? Describe the parts that the water plant cell has that the bulb cell does not have.

Thinking about the skill

How could you describe to a friend how you found the ways two living things are alike and the ways they are different?

Applying the skill

List the words you can use to describe each tulip. How are the tulips alike? How are they different?

2. Protists—One-celled Organisms

Words to Know
protists
cell membrane
nucleus
cytoplasm
cell wall

Getting Started Imagine you are the size of the dot of an *i* and you are exploring a lake in a minisubmarine. Living things of many shapes moving in different ways swim by. There are whirling "boxes" and crawling "blobs." There are spinning "slippers" and throbbing "trumpets"—and more! Welcome to the world of protists!

What are some traits of protists?

Protists make up one kingdom of one-celled organisms. Some protists are animallike—they have some of the traits of animals. Other protists are plantlike—they have some of the traits of plants. Most protists live in water or in moist

▼ Stentor

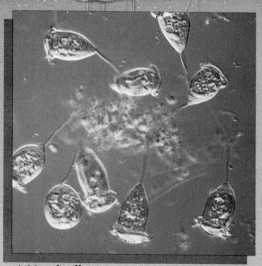
▲ Vorticella

places. Look at the pictures of protists. They include some that you met during your imaginary trip in the minisubmarine.

What is an animallike protist?

Some protists are animallike because they move about and eat other organisms. The ameba (uh-MEE buh) is an animallike protist. Look at the picture of an ameba. Find the cell membrane. The **cell membrane** surrounds and protects the cell. The cell membrane is somewhat like a fence around a house. Nothing can enter or leave the cell without going through the cell membrane.

Find the dark structure near the center of the ameba. This structure is the nucleus (NOO-klee us). The **nucleus** is the cell's control center. It controls all the activities of the cell.

A jellylike material called **cytoplasm** (SYT-oh plaz um) surrounds the nucleus. Find the cytoplasm of the ameba. Parts in the cytoplasm carry out the activities that keep the cell alive.

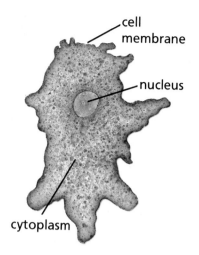

cell membrane

nucleus

cytoplasm

▲ Ameba ▼

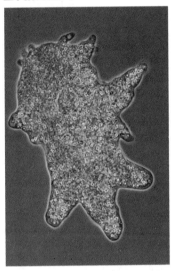

▲ A diatom

▼ A dinoflagellate

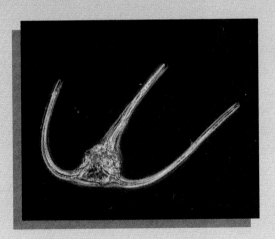

The ameba eats other tiny organisms. Look at the numbered pictures. They show how the ameba catches food. (1) The cell membrane bulges as the cytoplasm flows toward a bit of food. Pseudopods (soo do pahdz), or "false feet," start to form. (2) The pseudopods grow longer as more cytoplasm flows into them. (3) The pseudopods surround the food. (4) The food passes into the cell.

Ameba getting food ▼

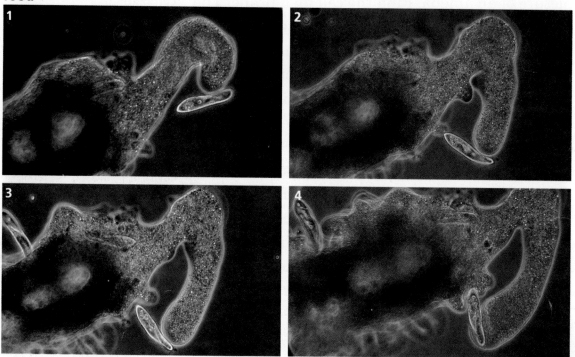

Ameba comes from a word that means "to change shape." Why is *ameba* a good name for this protist?

There's a protist missing from the zoo — or is there? Find out when you read **The Great Protozoan Mystery** in *Horizons Plus.*

What is a plantlike protist?

Some protists are plantlike because they can make their own food. Chlorophyll (KLOR uh fihl) is a green substance found in plants, which is needed for making food. Like green plant cells, plantlike protists contain chlorophyll.

ACTIVITY

Explore Together

What do the parts of a cell look like?

Organizer

Materials
iodine solution in dropper bottle · 2 microscope slides · piece of onion · tweezers · 2 cover slips · microscope · dropper · pond water

Procedure

Manager

A. Use a dropper to put a drop of iodine solution in the center of a microscope slide. **Caution:** *Iodine will stain and can be harmful if swallowed.*

Investigator

B. Bend a piece of onion back so that it breaks in two. Slowly pull the two halves apart. A thin layer of onion will peel off. Use tweezers to remove a piece of this layer.

Investigator

C. Float the layer of onion in the drop of iodine, as shown. Place a cover slip over the onion on the slide.

Group, Recorder

D. Observe the tissue under the low power of the microscope. Draw several of the cells you observe.

E. Observe the onion skin under high power. Focus on one cell. Make a drawing of the cell and label the cell parts you can identify.

Investigator

F. Place a drop of pond water on another microscope slide. Place a cover slip over the drop.

G. Observe the pond water under low power. Make drawings of any one-celled organisms you can see.

Writing and Sharing Results and Conclusions

Group, Recorder

1. What do onion cells look like?

2. List the cell parts you observed.

3. What one-celled organisms did you see in pond water?

Reporter

4. How do your results and conclusions compare with those of your classmates?

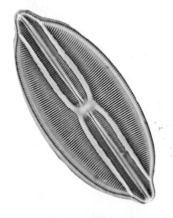

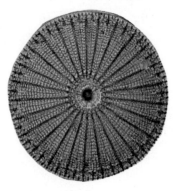

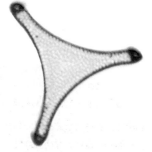

The diatoms in the pictures are plantlike protists. Notice the colors of the diatoms. Green chlorophyll is found in all diatoms. Why do some diatoms not look green?

Like the cell of an ameba, the cell of a diatom has a cell membrane, nucleus, and cytoplasm. Find these main parts in the drawing. The jobs of these cell parts in a diatom are the same as they are in an ameba. What are those jobs?

Parts of a diatom ▼

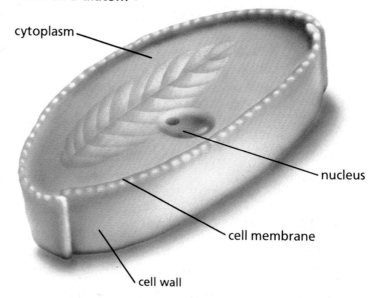

cytoplasm

nucleus

cell membrane

cell wall

A diatom also has a part not found in an ameba. It is the cell wall. A **cell wall** is a stiff structure outside the cell membrane. Find the cell wall in the drawing. The two halves of a diatom's cell wall fit together somewhat like a box and its lid.

Some diatoms live in fresh water, but most live in the ocean. Diatoms are often the food of other protists and small animals. How is the use of diatoms as food important for larger living things, including people?

▲ Diatoms

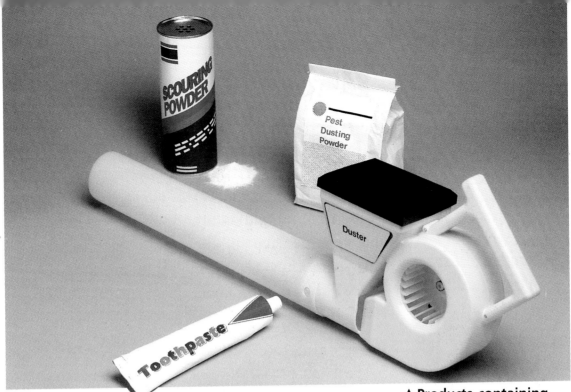

▲ Products containing diatom cell walls

When diatoms die, they fall to the bottom of the ocean. The glasslike remains of their cell walls settle there. People collect and use this material to make many products, as shown.

Some scouring powder is made from diatom cell walls. If you rub scouring powder between your fingers, you can feel rough bits of diatom cell walls. The remains of diatoms are also used in toothpaste, paint, and as a spray to fight garden pests. Why is the use of diatom cell walls better than some other ways to fight garden pests?

Lesson Review

1. How are all protists alike?
2. How are an ameba and a diatom alike, and how are they different?
3. List three products made from diatom cell walls.

Think! Another name for some protists is protozoans (proht oh ZOH unz). *Proto* means "first," and *zoans* means "animals." Which protist, an ameba or a diatom, do you think is a protozoan, and why?

Earth Science
CONNECTION

What is diatomaceous earth? *Use reference books to find out. From what organisms does this matter form? How is it used?*

3. Fungi-Nongreen Plantlike Organisms

Words to Know
fungus
spore

Getting Started How are these things alike: a mushroom, mold on bread, mildew on a towel, and the blue color in blue cheese? Strange as it may seem, they are all related living things. You will learn more about them in this section.

What are some traits of fungi?

All the living things you read about above are fungi. They are similar to plants in some ways. For example, like plants, the mushrooms shown below grow in the ground. And they do not move from place to place.

The singular of *fungi* is *fungus* (FUNG gus). A **fungus** is a plantlike living thing that does not contain chlorophyll. Some fungi, such as yeasts, are one-celled. Others, such as mushrooms, are many-celled.

Mushrooms on ground ▼

Unlike plants, fungi cannot make their own food, but to get energy for living, they must take in food. What do fungi lack that is needed for making food?

Some fungi get food from things that were once alive. Other fungi are parasites (PAR uh syts). A parasite is an organism that gets food from and harms another living thing.

What are mushrooms?

Mushrooms are one type of fungi. Some mushrooms are found growing on the ground or on fallen logs in damp, shady areas. Other mushrooms grow on living trees. Which of those shown are similar to mushrooms you have seen growing? Which one may be a parasite?

Mushrooms are made of threadlike structures. As the drawing shows, some of the threads spread under the ground. The threads take in food from dead matter in the soil.

▲ Mushrooms on fallen log

◀ Mushrooms on tree

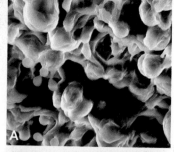

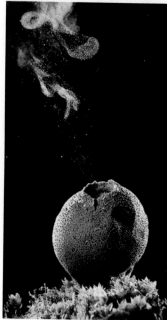

The part of a mushroom that can be seen above ground makes and releases spores. A **spore** is a single cell that can grow into a new organism. The picture at the left shows one type of mushroom bursting and releasing millions of spores. Some of these spores may grow into new mushrooms. What do you think happens to the rest of the spores?

People use many types of mushrooms for food, but some mushrooms are deadly poison. Mushrooms sold in food stores are safe to eat, but you should never touch or eat wild mushrooms. Only an expert can tell for sure which mushrooms are dangerous.

▲ (A) Mushroom spores under microscope
(B) Mushroom releasing spores

What are molds?

Molds are a second kind of fungi. These organisms may grow on bread or fruit. Look at the pictures of bread mold. Like a mushroom, the mold is made up of threadlike structures. Some of the threads grow down into the bread, which the mold uses for food.

(A) Bread mold under microscope
(B) Mold on bread▶

▲ (A) Mushrooms and yeasts used in kitchen
(B) Yeast cells

Other threads of the mold grow into the air. The dark cases at the ends of these threads contain spores. Like the spores of mushrooms, mold spores are reproductive cells. A mold spore that lands on fresh bread may grow into a new mold.

What are yeasts and mildews?

Yeasts are a third kind of fungi. Yeasts are single-celled organisms that form colonies, or groups. People use yeast to make bread. The yeast uses sugar that is in the bread dough for food. When the yeast uses the sugar, carbon dioxide gas is formed. The carbon dioxide makes the bread rise. Look at the pictures above of yeast and its use in bread-making.

Mildews are a fourth kind of fungi. Like yeasts, mildews are also single-celled organisms. You may have seen or smelled mildew growing on damp cloth or leather. Some mildews are parasites on plants. For example, mildew can damage the leaves of a tree, as shown.

Mildew on leaf ▼

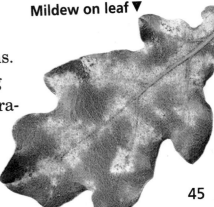

45

Problem Solving

How Sweet It Is!

Yeast needs food for energy and for growth. Molasses contains sugar, a good food for yeast. Suppose you mix yeast with warm water and molasses. After 15 minutes you will see bubbles, as the picture shows. Bubbles form from any sweet material that yeast uses for food. What gas are the bubbles made of?

What kinds of sweeteners can yeasts use for food?

Think of a way to find out what kinds of sweeteners yeasts can use for food. Plan to test artificial as well as natural sweeteners. Show your idea to your teacher and then try it. What kinds of sweeteners are good foods for yeast?

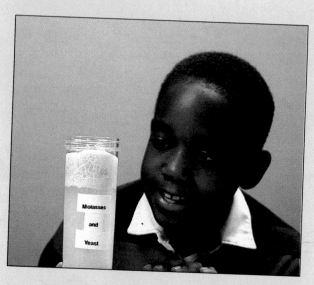

Decaying log ▼

What are some other effects of fungi?

Fungi affect other living things in many ways. One way is by helping to decay, or break down, dead organisms. Decaying matter changes to simpler materials as the fungi break it down. These materials can then be used by other living things. Look at the picture of a log. How have fungi caused the log to change?

Some types of fungi cause human diseases, many of which affect the skin. Athlete's foot is caused by a fungus that grows on the skin between the toes. Ringworm, which grows on the scalp, is also caused by a fungus.

Many products are made with fungi. Look at the picture of blue cheese. Fungi help to give this cheese its color, flavor, and texture.

What kind of antibiotic (an tye bye AHT ihk) have you taken for an illness? Penicillin (pen ih-SIHL ihn) is an antibiotic developed from a fungus. The pictures show how this fungus looks under a microscope and how it looks growing on an orange. Other fungi are used to make other medicines.

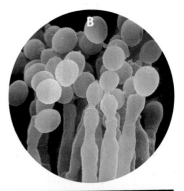

▼ Blue cheese

▲ (A) Penicillin fungus on orange
(B) Penicillin fungus under microscope

Lesson Review

1. In what ways are all fungi alike?
2. Name four types of fungi.
3. List two ways that fungi are helpful and two ways that fungi are harmful to people.

Think! Fungi need more than food in order to grow. They also need moisture and warmth. How could you use this information to prevent the growth of mold or mildew in your home?

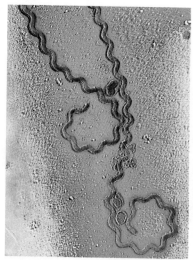
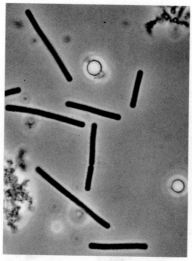
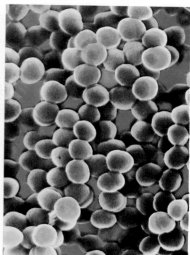

4. Monerans and Viruses

Getting Started You know that protists are very small. Can any living thing be even smaller? The ameba on page 37 is a protist. The pictures show some monerans. Over 500 monerans could fit inside one ameba!

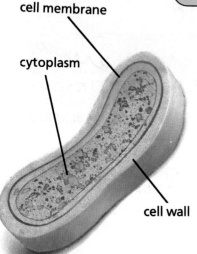

cell membrane

cytoplasm

cell wall

▲ Parts of a bacterium

What are some traits of monerans?

A **moneran** is a one-celled organism that does not have a nucleus. Another name for monerans is **bacteria** (bak TIHR ee uh). The singular of *bacteria* is *bacterium* (bak TIHR ee um).

As you can see in the pictures, bacteria may be round, rod-shaped, or spiral-shaped. Some types of bacteria live together in colonies.

Look at the drawing of a bacterium. Notice that the cell of the bacterium has a cell membrane and a cell wall. The cell also has cytoplasm. Nuclear material is spread throughout the cytoplasm.

How do bacteria get energy?

Like some protists, some monerans make their own food. Blue-green bacteria are monerans that contain chlorophyll. This means that they can get energy by making their own food.

Blue-green bacteria can survive wherever there is moisture. Some live in fresh water and others in salt water. Still others live in damp places. You may have seen colonies of blue-green bacteria growing on a rock, as shown in picture A. Imagine how many billions of single bacteria make up that colony! Picture B shows how some of these bacteria look under a microscope.

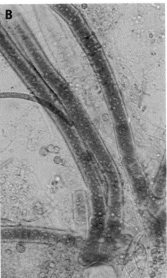

▲ (A) Blue-green bacteria on rocks
(B) Blue-green bacteria under microscope

Most bacteria do not contain chlorophyll. This means that they cannot make their own food. Like fungi, they get energy by absorbing food from other living or once-living things.

Bacteria without chlorophyll are found almost everywhere. They live in water, in soil, and in the air. They are on your desk, on your skin, and inside your body.

▲ Bacteria in yogurt

How are bacteria helpful and harmful?

Many of the bacteria that live inside your body are helpful. Some of these bacteria are in your intestines. These bacteria help to break down wastes that remain after food is digested.

As you read at the beginning of this chapter, some bacteria break down dead organisms. How is this action of bacteria helpful? You also read how people use bacteria to make products such as this yogurt.

Some bacteria are harmful to people. You may know that many bacteria can cause illness. Vaccines (vak SEENZ) contain materials that can protect the body against some diseases. To be given a vaccine is called vaccination (vak suh-nay shun). The table lists some diseases caused by bacteria. Notice that vaccination is used to prevent some diseases. What are some other ways to prevent diseases caused by bacteria?

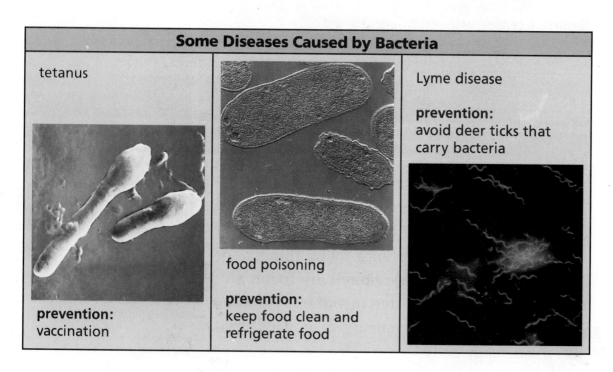

Some Diseases Caused by Bacteria

tetanus

prevention: vaccination

food poisoning

prevention: keep food clean and refrigerate food

Lyme disease

prevention: avoid deer ticks that carry bacteria

What are viruses?

You know that all living things are made of cells. **Viruses** (VYE rus ihz) are things that seem to be alive, but they are not made of cells. Viruses are even smaller than bacteria. Look at the drawing. About 700,000 viruses like this one lined up side by side could fit across the width of this page!

How is a virus like a living thing? A virus can reproduce, or make more viruses. But a virus reproduces inside a living cell.

Look at the numbered drawings. The steps describe how a virus can reproduce inside a cell. (1) A virus attacks and part of it enters a cell. (2) The virus causes the cell to make more viruses. (3) The cell becomes filled with viruses. (4) The cell bursts, setting free the viruses. These viruses can then spread to other cells. What do you think each virus may do next?

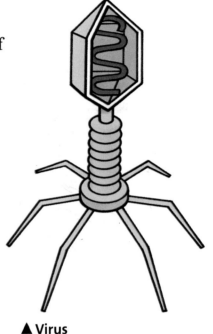

▲ Virus

▼ Virus attacking and reproducing in cell

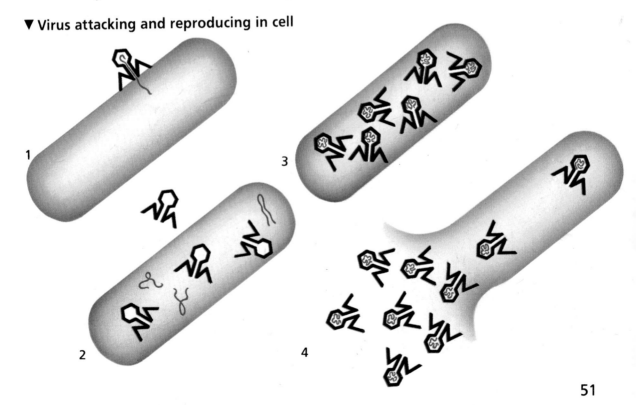

When viruses reproduce, they destroy cells. In this way, the viruses can cause disease. Look at the viruses in the chart. Which virus diseases have you had? How can some virus diseases be prevented?

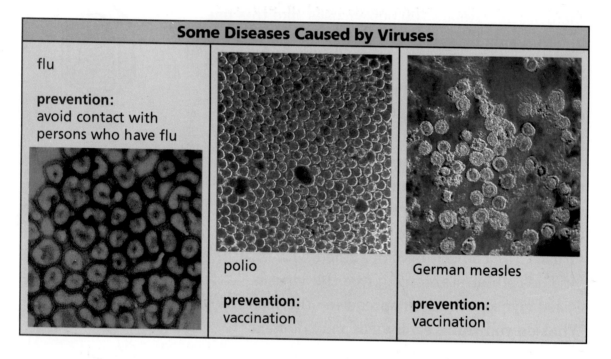

Some Diseases Caused by Viruses

flu

prevention:
avoid contact with persons who have flu

polio

prevention:
vaccination

German measles

prevention:
vaccination

AIDS is also caused by a virus. This virus destroys the body's ability to fight disease. Thus, a person with AIDS may get diseases that a healthy person could fight off. A person with AIDS can die from one of these diseases. So far, there is no vaccine or cure for AIDS.

Lesson Review

1. How are all monerans alike, and how are blue-green bacteria unlike other monerans?

2. List two ways that bacteria are helpful and two ways that they are harmful to people.

3. How does a virus reproduce inside a cell?

Think! Are viruses living things? Not all scientists think so. What do you think?

Chapter Connections

Make a copy of this graphic organizer but leave out some of the important words or phrases. Exchange papers with another student. Fill in missing words or phrases.

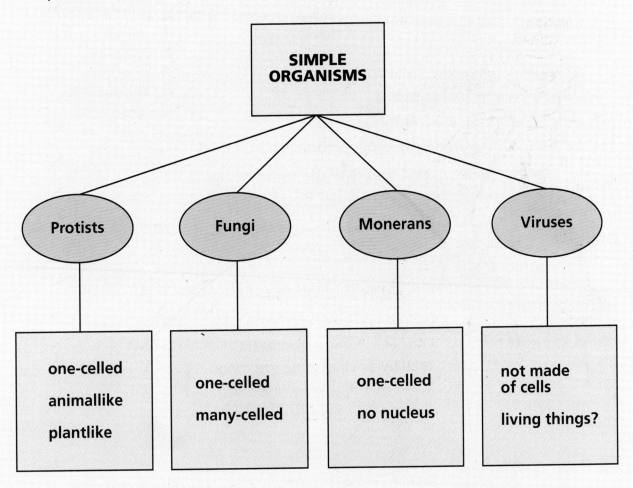

Writing About Science • Research

In this chapter you learned that vaccinations are used to immunize people against certain diseases. What is a vaccine? How is it made? What does it do to prevent illness? Read about vaccines and write a report.

Science Terms

A. Write the letter of the term that best matches the definition.

1. Basic part of all living things
2. Large groups of organisms
3. Surrounds and protects the cell
4. Control center of a cell
5. Cell that can become a new organism
6. Another name for monerans
7. Jellylike material around the nucleus
8. Stiff structure outside the cell membrane

a. bacteria
b. cell
c. cell membrane
d. cell wall
e. cytoplasm
f. kingdoms
g. nucleus
h. spore

B. Number your paper from 1 to 5. Use the terms below to complete the sentences. Write the correct term next to each number.

fungi   monerans   organisms   protists   viruses

There are five kingdoms of living things or ___(1)___. A member of the kingdom of ___(2)___ is one-celled and has a nucleus. A member of the kingdom of ___(3)___ is one-celled and does not have a nucleus. Some members of the kingdom of ___(4)___ are one-celled and some are many-celled, and none contain chlorophyll. ___(5)___ do not belong to any kingdom because they are not made of cells.

Science Ideas

Use complete sentences to answer the following.

1. In what way is the structure of all living things the same?
2. How is the cell of a paramecium different from a blood cell?
3. What three parts are found in the cell of all protists?

4. How do plantlike and animallike protists differ in the way they get energy?

5. Which protists have glasslike cell walls that people collect and use?

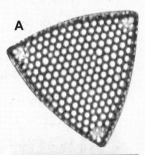
A

6. What is one way that many fungi are like plants and one way that they are unlike plants?

7. Compare the ways in which parasites and fungi that cause decay get food.

8. What type of organism causes bread to rise?

9. How is the cell of a moneran simpler than the cells of other organisms?

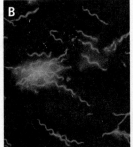
B

10. Which monerans can make their own food?

11. How are some bacteria that live inside the human body helpful?

12. What is one disease caused by bacteria?

13. How is a virus like a living thing, and how is it unlike a living thing?

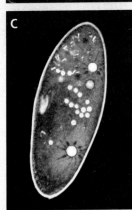
C

Applying Science Ideas

1. Study the organisms in pictures A, B, C, and D. Which is a plantlike protist, which is an animallike protist, which is a moneran, and which is a fungus?

2. Why can water in a stream look clear and clean but still be dangerous to drink?

3. Think about one-celled organisms and many-celled organisms. Why is it an advantage for a large animal to be made of many cells instead of one cell?

D

Using Science Skills

Observe the pictures of the different bacteria on page 48. Make a list of the ways they are alike. Make a list of the ways they are different.

Animals Without Backbones

Slugging It Out

If there was a contest for the most disliked animal, the slug might be the winner. Slugs have been disliked, in part, for the damage they can cause. Gardeners and farmers have found the slug to be a major pest that eats a wide range of plants. In wet years, slugs have destroyed up to three fourths of the strawberry plants in western Washington.

Slugs have also been disliked for their looks. Some people are disturbed by the banana-shaped body with its slimy coat. Other people dislike the way a slug moves. It drags along the ground very slowly. In fact, the word sluggish is used to describe something that is slow-moving.

Near the slug's head there is a gland that releases mucus (MYOO kus), a sticky liquid substance. The mucus covers the body and forms a surface on which the slug can move forward. The slug glides over this homemade highway, leaving a shiny trail of mucus in its path.

Scientists want to learn more about the slug's mucus. It not only helps the slug move but also helps to protect the slug. The mucus forms a protective layer around the thin skin of the slug. Without the mucus, slugs would have little defense against disease. Bacteria and molds would invade the body.

Knowing more about the slug's mucus may help in finding cures for some diseases of humans. Dr. Deyrup-Olsen studies slugs. She says, "I can only think of mucus as a miraculous, wonderful substance, a lifesaver and something to be terribly grateful for."

Computer scientists also want to learn more about slugs. They would like to model computers after the slug's brain. Even the most advanced computer is no match for a brain. The simple brain of a slug is being studied as a model for new computer designs.

Slugs are also popular in Elma, Washington, home of the annual slug race. Steve Morrow, the town's slug trainer, raises banana slugs especially for the race. On race day the slugs "sprint" about 1 m (3 ft) to the finish line. One super slug slid home in a record-setting 43 seconds.

Discover

How are earthworms helpful in the garden?

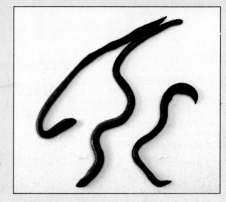

Materials   pencil · paper · reference books

Procedure

   Scientists group slugs with a large number of other animals. One animal in this group is the earthworm. Unlike slugs, earthworms are not garden pests. Earthworms are good for the soil.

   If you ever dig in the ground where earthworms live, you may notice that the soil is very loose. As an earthworm moves through the ground, it takes in soil through its mouth. It leaves behind tunnels filled with tiny balls of soil. Gardeners think it is very lucky to find earthworms in the soil. Find out why the soil in which earthworms live is good for plants. Talk to people who grow plants. Find out more about earthworms in reference books.

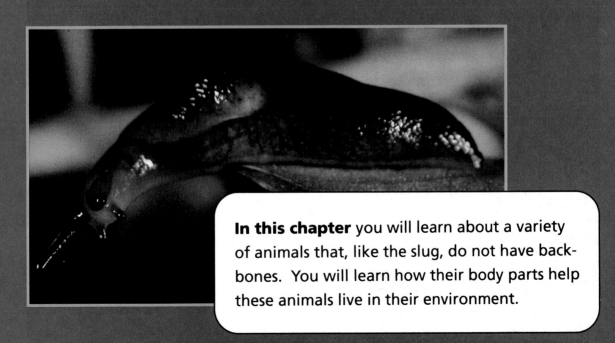

In this chapter you will learn about a variety of animals that, like the slug, do not have backbones. You will learn how their body parts help these animals live in their environment.

1. Classifying Invertebrates

Words To Know
invertebrates

Getting Started The drawing below shows many living things in the water along a rocky shore. Many of the organisms are found on the rocks. Which of these organisms, do you think, are plants? Which are animals?

How do scientists classify animals?

Rocky-shore organisms ▼

Scientists think that there are more than a million different kinds of animals. And more animals are being discovered all the time. In order to study these animals easily, scientists divide them into two major groups. The animals in one group are those with backbones. The animals in the other group are those without backbones. The animals in the drawing below do not have backbones.

Animals with backbones are called vertebrates (VER tuh brihts). Humans are vertebrates. A backbone is made of many small bones, called vertebrae (VER tuh bray). Run your fingers down the center of your back. What do you feel? Each bump you feel is one of these small bones.

A backbone gives an animal's body shape and support. But many animals do not have backbones. Animals without backbones are called **invertebrates** (ihn VER tuh brihts).

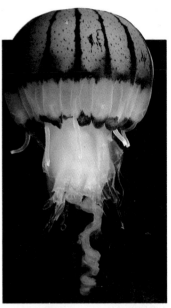

▲ Jellyfish

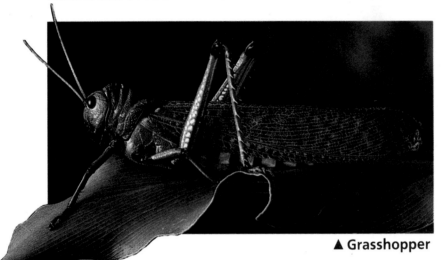

▲ Grasshopper

How, do you think, is the body of each of the invertebrates in the pictures shown supported? The jellyfish has a soft jellylike body that is supported by the water in which it lives. The grasshopper's body and the beetle's body are supported by a hard outer covering.

You may have seen invertebrates in many environments. Perhaps you have found earthworms wriggling through the soil. Of course, you have seen many kinds of insects near your home, under rocks, or even on a dog. In fact, invertebrates live almost everywhere on Earth.

▲ Ladybug beetle

How many invertebrates are there?

Look at the drawing. It shows the percentages of vertebrates and invertebrates on the earth. Scientists believe that invertebrates make up 97 percent of all animals.

Percentages of vertebrates and invertebrates ▶

3% vertebrates

97% invertebrates

To help study these many invertebrates, scientists classify them into several smaller groups. Animals that have many of the same characteristics, or traits, are classified in the same group. Suppose you found an invertebrate and wanted to know how to classify it. You would first look at its traits. Then you would place it in a group with other animals that share many of the same traits.

Lesson Review

1. What are the two major groups of animals? Identify the trait that makes these two groups different from each other.
2. What percentage of the animal kingdom includes animals without backbones?
3. Why do scientists classify the many invertebrates into smaller groups?

Think! Which of these animals would you classify as invertebrates—cat, bee, blue jay, mouse, jellyfish, worm?

Skills

THINKING

Creating ways to classify things

If you classify living things according to their traits, you can study them more easily. You know that animals can be classified into two large groups—those that have a backbone and those that do not. What trait do you use to classify animals in this way?

Practicing the skill

1. Look at the animals in the drawings. Observe the traits that some animals have in common. Notice the traits that are unique to each animal.

2. You can classify these animals into two groups. Make a two-column list. Label one column *Animals with Legs.* Label the other column *Animals without Legs.* Write the names of the animals that belong in each column.

3. Observe the animals that have legs. Choose a trait that some have and some do not. Make a two-column list as you did in step **2**.

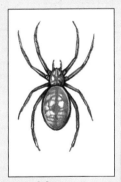  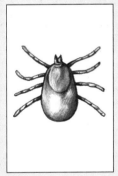  

▲ Spider   ▲ Tapeworm   ▲ Tick   ▲ Leech   ▲ Ant

Thinking about the skill

What are some other animals that you can classify the same way you did these animals?

Applying the skill

Look carefully at the animals without legs. Choose a trait that you can use to classify these animals into two groups. Write the animals that belong in each group.

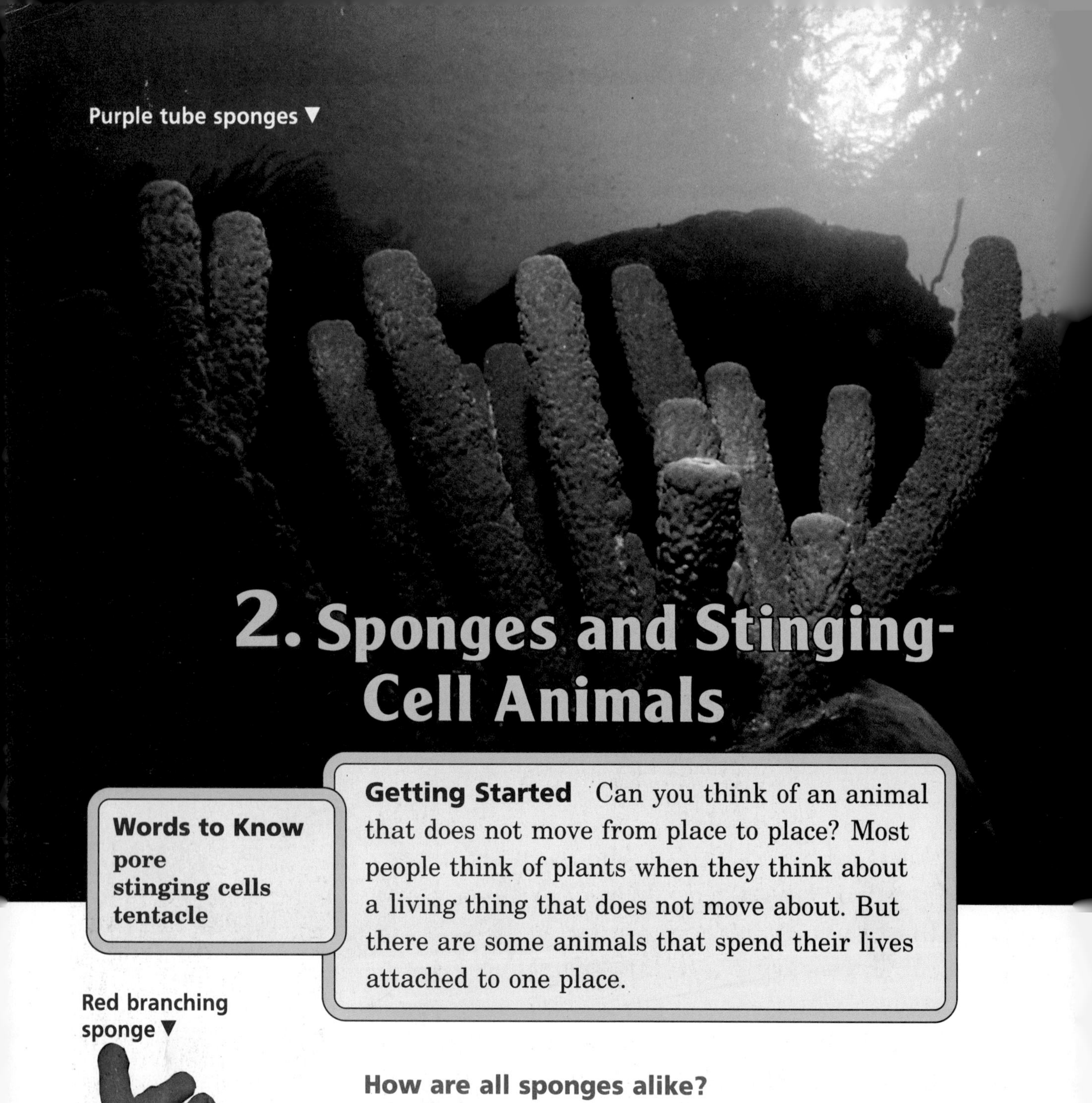

Purple tube sponges ▼

2. Sponges and Stinging-Cell Animals

Words to Know
pore
stinging cells
tentacle

Getting Started Can you think of an animal that does not move from place to place? Most people think of plants when they think about a living thing that does not move about. But there are some animals that spend their lives attached to one place.

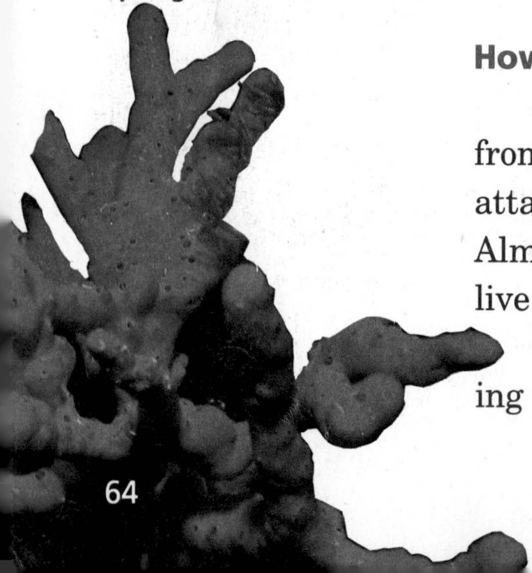

Red branching sponge ▼

How are all sponges alike?

A sponge is an animal that does not move from place to place. A sponge spends its life attached to rock or to other hard surfaces. Almost all of the 5,000 known species of sponges live in salt water.

Remember that animals are grouped according to their traits. Some sponges are microscopic in size; others are over 2 m (about 7 feet) tall. Some sponges are brightly colored; others are drab. But all sponges share certain traits.

One trait that all sponges share is an outer body layer that has many pores. A **pore** is a small hole or opening. Sea water enters a sponge through its pores. Find the pores in the drawing of the sponge.

Needlelike parts of a sponge ▼

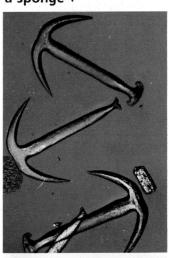

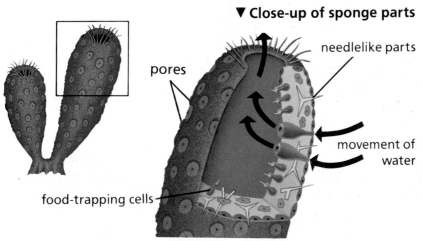

▼ **Close-up of sponge parts**

pores

needlelike parts

movement of water

food-trapping cells

Since sponges are attached to hard surfaces, they cannot hunt for food. Instead, they obtain their food by filtering the sea water that enters their pores. A sponge about the size of a hot dog can filter about 115 L (about 30 gallons) of water daily! The water carries tiny bits of food with it. Cells in the inner layer of the sponge trap the bits of food. Find these cells in the drawing.

As you can see, sponges have many different shapes. What gives a sponge its shape? What gives it support? Many sponges have needlelike parts that give them shape and support. The shapes of the needles are used to help classify sponges into different groups. Find the needle-like parts in the drawing.

▲ **Purple vase sponge**

What are stinging-cell animals?

Have you ever seen a jellyfish? All the animals shown here are in the same group as the jellyfish. They are in the same group because they have many traits in common. These animals all belong to a group of animals called stinging-cell animals. **Stinging cells** are cells that contain a poisonous thread.

The body of a stinging-cell animal is shaped like a hollow sac. The opening, or mouth, of the sac is surrounded by tentacles (TEN tuh kulz). A **tentacle** is an armlike part. Find the mouth and tentacles in the drawings of a jellyfish and a hydra.

◄ Jellyfish ▼

▼ Hydra

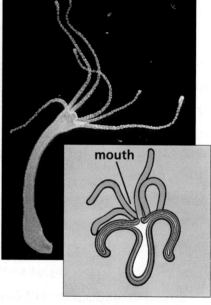
mouth

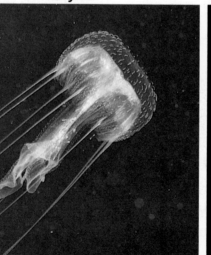
mouth

The tentacles of these animals contain stinging cells. Stinging cells help protect the animal and catch food. How do stinging cells work? When a small animal brushes against a tentacle, poisonous threads are released from the stinging cells. The poison stuns or kills the animal. The tentacles then bring it into the mouth of the stinging-cell animal. As you can see, the fish in the pictures below is about to become a meal for the sea anemone.

▼ Sea anemone eating fish

Usually the sting from a stinging-cell animal is only strong enough to kill a small animal. But some stinging-cell animals have poison powerful enough to harm or even kill a human. Suppose you were to swim into the tentacles of a Portuguese man-of-war. You would be stung by hundreds of poisonous threads. Each poisonous thread can cause intense pain and swelling.

Lesson Review

1. How are all sponges alike?
2. Explain how sponges obtain their food.
3. What body parts do all stinging-cell animals have in common?
4. How do stinging cells help a sea anemone capture food?

Think! An anemone cannot move quickly. How, do you think, is it protected from an animal that is trying to eat it?

Earth Science
CONNECTION

Have you ever held a piece of coral? Coral looks like rock. Write a report about coral and coral reefs. How is coral made? What are some different types of coral reefs?

3. Worms

Words to Know
parasite
flatworm
roundworm
segmented worm

Getting Started How would you describe a worm? You would probably say that it is round and long. You might also say that it lives in soil. Now look at the picture above. Describe this animal. Believe it or not, this also is one type of worm.

Roundworm ▶

Flatworm ▶

Segmented worm ▼

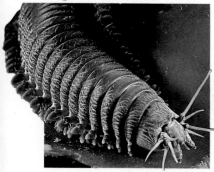

What are the three groups of worms?

The bodies of worms are different from the bodies of sponges or stinging-cell animals. Scientists classify worms into three groups. These are flatworms, roundworms, and segmented (seg-MENT ihd) worms. Compare the body shapes of the flatworm, roundworm, and segmented worm.

Some worms in each of the three groups are parasites. A **parasite** is a living thing that lives on or in another living thing. The parasite harms the living thing on which it lives. The living thing on which the parasite depends is called the host. The parasite usually depends on the host for food.

What are the traits of flatworms?

A **flatworm** is a worm with a flattened body and only one body opening. Flatworms take in food and release wastes through the one opening. The picture shows a planarian (pluh NER-ee un). A planarian is one kind of flatworm. Look at the picture to find the mouth of the planarian.

▼ Planarian

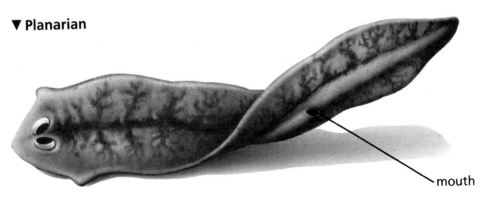

mouth

Planarians live under rocks in streams and ponds. Suppose you were to turn over a rock in a pond. You might find a small group of planarians. Each planarian is about the length of a short fingernail.

Planarians move away from light. How do they sense light? Point to the two dark eyespots on the planarian in the picture. These eyespots can sense light. Planarians look for food in dark

69

places or at night. They feed on other small animals. A planarian takes in food through the opening on the underside of its body. Wastes leave the body through the same opening.

Planarians have an unusual trait. They can regrow body parts that have been cut off. Tell what happens to the planarian in these drawings.

▼ Planarian regrowing

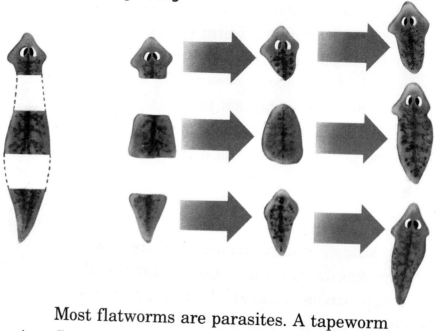

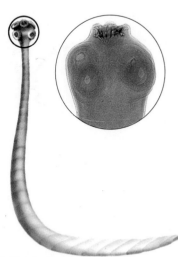

▲ Pork tapeworm with close-up of head

Most flatworms are parasites. A tapeworm is a flatworm that is a parasite. A tapeworm cannot digest food. The tapeworm lives inside the intestines of the host. The host supplies the digested food that the tapeworm needs to survive. The pork tapeworm in the picture is a parasite that can live inside pigs. If a human eats undercooked pork that contains a tapeworm, the human can become a host to the worm.

What are the traits of roundworms?

A second group of worms is the round-worms. A **roundworm** is a worm that has a round body and two body openings. Food enters through one opening, the mouth. Wastes leave through the other opening, the anus (AY nus).

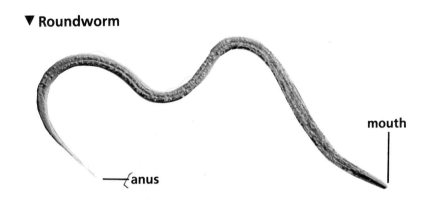

▼ Roundworm

mouth

anus

Many roundworms are parasites. Some roundworms cause diseases in humans. Hook-worms are one example. Hookworms can enter a person through the skin of bare feet. They then live in the intestines. A person infected with hookworms feels tired and weak.

What are the traits of segmented worms?

A third group of worms is the segmented worms. A **segmented worm** is a worm that has a body divided into segments, or sections. Each segment, except those at the head end and tail end, is alike. As the worm grows, new segments are added near the tail end of the worm. So the oldest parts of a segmented worm are those closest to its head.

ACTIVITY

Explore Together

How does an earthworm respond?

Materials

Organizer

three earthworms · cotton swabs · vinegar · large clear plastic jar · soil · water · cornmeal · foil · rubber band dark construction paper

Procedure

Investigator, Manager

A. Obtain an earthworm. Carefully touch the mouth end of the worm with a cotton swab. Observe what happens. Then touch the center of the worm with the swab. Record your observations.

Investigator, Manager

B. Dip a cotton swab in vinegar. Bring the swab close to the head, tail, and center of the earthworm's body. *Do not actually touch the worm.*

Recorder

C. Record your observations.

Manager

D. Set up an earthworm habitat as shown in the picture. Place three earthworms in the jar. Note their positions. Cover the top of the jar with foil. **Caution:** *Wash your hands after handling the earthworms.* Set the jar aside for 1 day.

Recorder

E. Record what you see inside the jar. Then cover the sides of the jar with a piece of dark construction paper. Set the jar aside for 1 day.

Investigator

F. Remove the foil and paper and observe the inside of the jar. Has the position of the earthworms changed?

Writing and Sharing Results and Conclusions

Group, Recorder

1. How does the earthworm respond to touch and to vinegar? Does it respond the same way in all parts of its body?

Reporter

2. Describe how the earthworm responds to light and to dark. Share your results with classmates.

◀ **Earthworm**

An earthworm is a segmented worm. Earthworms are found in soil all over the world. They burrow through the soil, feeding on dead leaves and grasses.

Some segmented worms are parasites. The leech is an example of a segmented worm that is a parasite. Leeches live in freshwater streams and ponds. They can become attached to the skin of turtles, fish, and people. Most leeches get food by sucking blood from the host animal.

Lesson Review

1. In what two ways are flatworms different from roundworms?
2. Choose one parasite. Describe where the parasite lives and how it gets its food.
3. How are segmented worms different from roundworms?

Think! You know that planarians move away from light. Suppose you had a container of planarians. How could you get all the planarians to gather in one corner of the container?

Earth Science
CONNECTION

Earthworms are important in the building of soil. Find out in what ways earthworms improve soil.

How can leeches be used in medicine?

When you get a cut, some blood leaks out, but soon the blood forms a plug called a clot. The clot keeps you from losing more blood. Meanwhile fresh blood brings food and oxygen to the cut. Without blood flowing through it, the cut would not heal.

Did you know that blood can also be food for a leech? Leeches are segmented worms. Some are parasites that live in water, and their food is the blood of other animals. The leech has a sucker on one end and teeth on the other. It clings to an animal with the sucker and bites with its teeth. Then the leech drinks blood through the bite.

STS

A special chemical inside the leech helps it get plenty of blood. If clots formed where a leech had bitten, blood would stop flowing out. So a leech puts into the animal a chemical that stops clots from forming.

Doctors use leeches to help people with serious cuts or wounds. Sometimes after an operation to reattach a person's finger, too much blood fills the finger. Blood vessels clog up, and fresh blood cannot flow through. The finger may die before it can heal. Leeches placed on the finger remove the extra blood, allowing the finger to heal.

Scientists collect the chemicals in leeches, and doctors use the chemicals as medicine. Sometimes dangerous blood clots form inside a person's body. A chemical in one kind of leech can break up such clots. But it takes many leeches to make a small amount of medicine. Today, leeches are becoming scarce because so many of them have already been collected from ponds and swamps. Also, the wetlands where leeches live are carelessly being destroyed. Scientists want to learn how to make the leech's chemicals, but until they do, we are still going to need a lot of leeches.

Critical thinking

If people destroyed all the wetlands where leeches live, what might happen?

Using what you learned

What are some medicines that come from plants? Look in an encyclopedia or ask a doctor. Make a chart showing these medicines and their uses. Draw pictures of the plants.

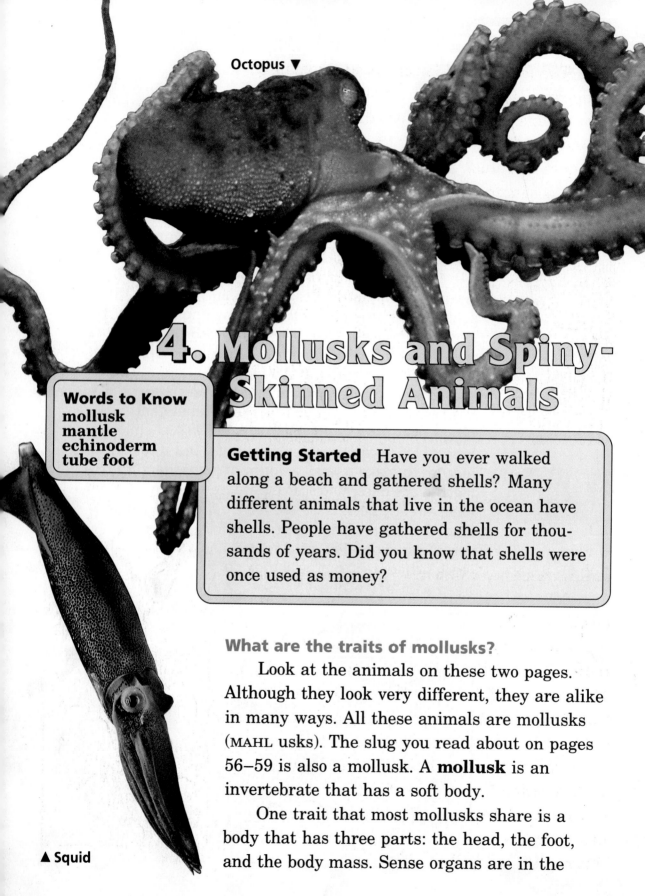

Octopus ▼

4. Mollusks and Spiny-Skinned Animals

Getting Started   Have you ever walked along a beach and gathered shells? Many different animals that live in the ocean have shells. People have gathered shells for thousands of years. Did you know that shells were once used as money?

What are the traits of mollusks?

Look at the animals on these two pages. Although they look very different, they are alike in many ways. All these animals are mollusks (MAHL usks). The slug you read about on pages 56–59 is also a mollusk. A **mollusk** is an invertebrate that has a soft body.

One trait that most mollusks share is a body that has three parts: the head, the foot, and the body mass. Sense organs are in the

▲ Squid

76

head. The foot is used for crawling, swimming, or digging. The body mass contains a heart and other organs. A mantle covers the organs. The **mantle** is a fleshy covering that protects the organs of a mollusk. In most mollusks the mantle produces materials that form one or two shells.

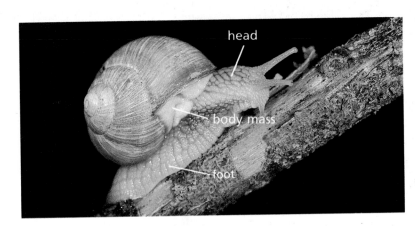

◀ Snail

What are three kinds of mollusks?

One type of mollusk, such as the snail, has one shell. The snail has a hard "trapdoor" covering the opening of its shell. The snail can pull its head back into the opening and shut the trap door. In this way the snail is protected from enemies.

Another type of mollusk has a double shell that is hinged. The clam is this type of mollusk. The clam gets its food by filtering it from the water. The tubelike parts shown in the drawing of the clam are used for feeding.

A third type of mollusk does not have a shell covering the outside of its body. Squids and octopuses are this type of mollusk. The squid has a small, thin shell inside its body. The octopus has no shell at all.

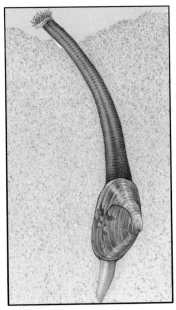

▲ Clam

Problem Solving
A Matter of Survival

Snails do not have lungs as you do. They breathe through their skins. The skin of a snail must be moist so that the gases can pass through. Therefore, snails must live in a moist environment.

How might a dry environment affect a snail's behavior?

Plan and carry out an experiment to test your ideas. How does the snail's shell help it survive?

What are the traits of spiny-skinned animals?

The animals in these pictures all belong to the group of animals known as echinoderms (ee-KYE noh durms). An **echinoderm** is a spiny-skinned invertebrate that lives in the ocean.

The sea star is one kind of echinoderm. The outer body of a sea star is made up of hard plates covered by a thin skin. The plates help protect the sea star. What if a part of a sea star is cut off? Like the planarian, the sea star can regrow missing parts.

How do echinoderms move?

Echinoderms move from place to place on tube feet. A **tube foot** is a hollow structure with a sucker at the end. Point to the tube feet of the sea star shown in the picture. How do the tube feet help the sea star move? Water is pumped into the tube feet and the feet extend. Water is

▲ Sea urchin

▲ Sea star

sucked back into the body and the feet contract. As the tube feet extend and contract, the sea star moves ahead.

The tube feet are also used for getting food. For example, sea stars often eat oysters. They wrap their arms around the shells of the oyster. The tube feet are then used to pull open the oyster shells. If you have ever tried to open an oyster, you know that a lot of force is needed to open its shells.

▲ Sea star opening oyster

Lesson Review

1. List three traits common to most mollusks.
2. Explain how the three kinds of mollusks differ from one another.
3. Identify two traits all echinoderms have in common.
4. Describe how tube feet help a sea star move.

Think! Sea stars can eat a large number of oysters. Suppose sea stars are cut into pieces and thrown into the sea. What effect might this have on the number of oysters?

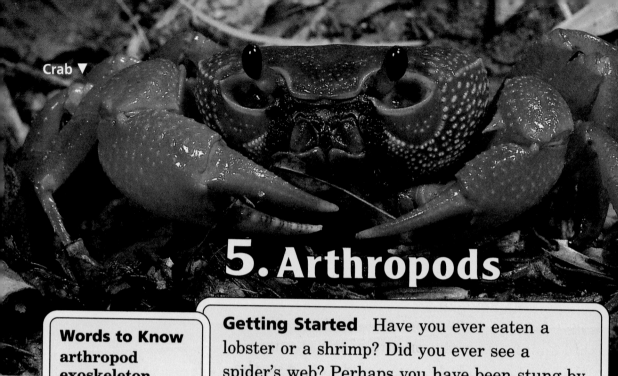

Crab ▼

5. Arthropods

Getting Started Have you ever eaten a lobster or a shrimp? Did you ever see a spider's web? Perhaps you have been stung by a bee or wasp. These animals seem to be very different. But they all belong to the same large group of animals.

(A) Spider and web,
(B) Bee ▶

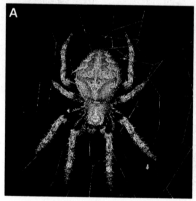

What are the traits of arthropods?

What do bees, shrimps, and spiders have in common? They all belong to the largest group of animals. They are all arthropods (AHR throh-pahdz). An **arthropod** is an animal with jointed legs, a segmented body, and a hard outer covering.

The hard outer covering of all arthropods is called an **exoskeleton** (eks oh SKEL uh tun). The exoskeleton protects the organs inside the animal's body. It also prevents the loss of water from the body. Because of this, some arthropods can live in very dry places.

The exoskeleton is different from other body parts because it does not grow. For the animal to grow, it must molt. To **molt** means to shed the outer body covering. Before it molts, an arthropod grows a new, soft exoskeleton under the old one. Look at the picture of the shrimp that has just molted. After the shrimp molts, the new exoskeleton hardens in about three days. The shrimp will molt about 15 times in its life.

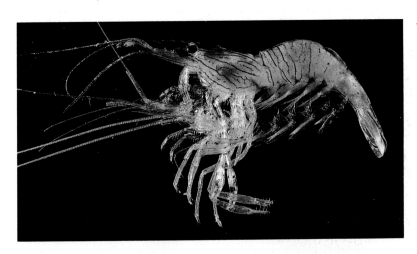

◄ **Shrimp molting**

antenna

Find the antennas on the beetle in the picture. Antennas are sense organs that help an arthropod locate food and other objects. Antennas are covered with thousands of tiny bristles. Most of these bristles detect odor. But some bristles detect air movements, tell whether the air is dry or damp, and even pick up sounds.

▲ **Harlequin beetle**

Suppose you found a segmented animal with jointed legs and an exoskeleton. From what you have learned, you should know that it is an arthropod. But what kind of arthropod is it? An arthropod's body may have two, three, or many body sections. The number of body sections is used to help classify arthropods into one of several main groups.

Which arthopods have two body sections?

Suppose an arthropod has only two body sections. There are two groups of arthropods that have this trait. The crustaceans (krus TAY-shunz) make up one group. A crustacean is an arthropod that usually has two body sections and two pairs of antennas.

Most crustaceans live in water. Lobsters, shrimps, and crabs are examples of crustaceans. Find the two body sections and two pairs of antennas on the lobster.

Two body sections of a crustacean ▼

Lobster ▶

82

Crustaceans also include very tiny animals, such as the krill. Although they are tiny, krill provide food for the largest animal on the earth—the blue whale.

Arachnids (uh RAK nihdz) make up the second group of arthropods with two body sections. Unlike crustaceans, arachnids do not have antennas. Arachnids include ticks, mites, scorpions (SKOR pee unz) and spiders. The spider in the picture has killed an insect. A spider kills an insect by biting it with its fangs. This sends a poison into the insect. Both spiders and scorpions make poisons to kill insects.

Read **One Day in the Desert,** page 156, to find out about a battle between a huge spider and a beetle that stands on its head to fight.

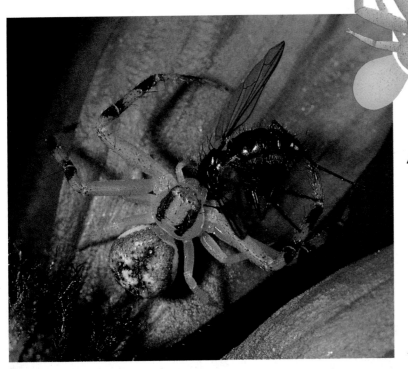

▲ **Two body sections of an arachnid**

◀ **Spider with prey**

Ticks and some mites are parasites that feed on the blood of other animals. These arthropods sometimes carry disease. For example, ticks carry Lyme disease and can pass it to humans and dogs.

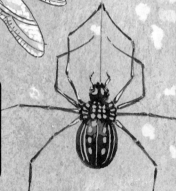

Explore

What are some traits of arthropods?

Arthropods live almost everywhere. You will find them in salt water, in fresh water, in the soil, and even on a dog. Each of these animals is very different, but they all have certain traits in common.

Materials
insect · spider · pill bug · hand lens · Discovery Scope
petri dishes or plastic jars

Procedure
Caution: *Handle live animals carefully. Do not collect animals with stingers.*

A. Make a chart like the one shown.

4. Are the legs jointed?
5. Does it have antennas?
6. Does it have wings?

D. Draw a picture of your insect.

	Animal	Exoskeleton	Number of Body Sections	Number of Legs	Jointed Legs	Antennas	Wings
1.							
2.							
3.							

B. Place an insect into a petri dish or the plastic box of your Discovery Scope.

C. Examine both the top and bottom side of your insect. Record the answers to each of these questions in your chart.
   1. Does it have an exoskeleton?
   2. How many body sections does it have?
   3. How many legs does it have?

E. Repeat steps **B-D** for each arthropod you are to examine.

Writing and Sharing Results and Conclusions
1. What traits do all arthropods have in common?

2. How do the arthropods you examined differ in the number of legs they have?

Which arthropods have three body sections?

Suppose an arthropod has three body sections. Then it would belong to the group that contains more animals than all other animal groups combined. The animals in this group are insects. There are 750,000 known kinds of insects. Scientists think that there may be three or four times that number that have not yet been identified!

All insects have the same basic body plan. The insect body is made of three parts: the head, the thorax (THOR aks), and the abdomen (AB duh mun).

▲ Three parts of an insect body

◄ Bee

The head of an insect has a mouth and most of the sense organs. The **thorax** is the middle part of an insect's body. All insects have three pairs of legs attached to the thorax. Many insects also have wings attached to the thorax. The **abdomen** is the rear part of an insect's body. It contains organs for digesting food and for reproduction. Locate the three basic parts of an insect's body in the drawing of the bee.

Which arthropods have many body sections?

Suppose an arthropod has more than three sections. Then it is placed in the group that includes millipedes (MIHL uh peedz) and centipedes (SEN tuh peedz). These arthropods live in moist places under rocks and logs.

Compare the pictures of the millipede and the centipede. As you can see, the centipede has fewer legs than the millipede. Millipedes and centipedes differ in other ways. Millipedes eat plants, but centipedes are meat eaters. Centipedes eat insects and other small animals.

Body sections of a centipede ▼

▲ Centipede

▲ Millipede

Lesson Review

1. What three traits do all arthropods have?
2. Most invertebrates must live in water. But many arthropods live in very dry environments. How is this possible?
3. Draw and label the parts of an arthropod with three body segments.
4. Compare a spider with a bee. In what ways are they alike? In what ways are they different?

Think! Why is it important for an arthropod to have a new exoskeleton before it sheds its old exoskeleton?

Physical Science
CONNECTION

Use reference books to find out how bees use different forms of light to locate things such as their hive and food.

Chapter Connections

Illustrate one animal from each of the invertebrate groups on the graphic organizer.

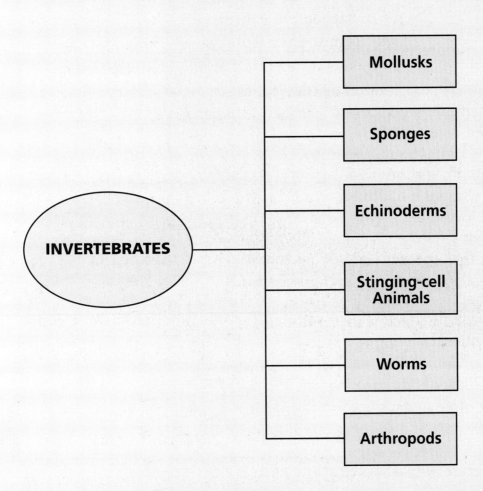

INVERTEBRATES

- Mollusks
- Sponges
- Echinoderms
- Stinging-cell Animals
- Worms
- Arthropods

Writing About Science • Create

There may be invertebrates living on the earth that have not yet been discovered. Can you imagine one? Create an invertebrate and write a paragraph about it. Describe its traits and environment. Illustrate your paragraph and name the invertebrate you created.

Science Terms

Write the letter of the term that best matches the definition.

1. Worm that has a body divided into sections
2. Opening through which water enters a sponge
3. Covering that protects the organs of a mollusk
4. Living thing that lives in or on another living thing and harms it
5. Spiny-skinned invertebrate
6. Worm with a round body, two body openings, but no sections
7. All animals without a backbone
8. Soft-bodied invertebrate with head, foot and body mass
9. Special cells that contain a poisonous thread
10. Worm with a flattened body and one body opening
11. Animal with jointed legs, a segmented body, and a hard outer covering
12. Hard outer covering of all arthropods
13. To shed the outer body covering
14. Middle part of an insect's body
15. Armlike body part of a stinging-cell animal
16. Rear part of an insect's body
17. Hollow structure with a sucker at the end

a. abdomen
b. arthropod
c. echinoderm
d. exoskeleton
e. flatworm
f. invertebrates
g. mantle
h. mollusk
i. molt
j. parasite
k. pore
l. roundworm
m. stinging cells
n. tentacle
o. thorax
p. tube foot
q. segmented worm

Science Ideas

A. Use complete sentences to answer the following.

1. What are the two main groups of animals? How do they differ from each other?
2. What are some ways that invertebrates differ from each other?
3. Briefly describe how a flatworm, a roundworm, and a segmented worm differ from each other.

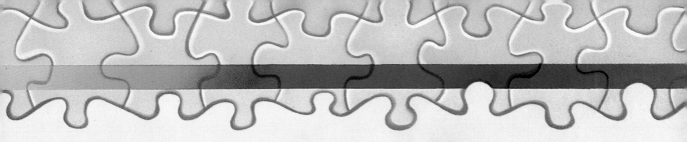

B. Copy the chart shown below on a separate piece of paper. The chart lists five animals. Across the top of the chart are traits of five groups of animals. Write *yes* in a box if the animal has the trait. Write *no* in a box if the animal does not have the trait.

	exoskeleton	soft body with shell	stinging cells	tube feet	pores
sponge					
sea anemone					
snail					
sea star					
lobster					

Applying Science Ideas

1. Why are spiders classified in a different group than that of insects?
2. Suppose you found an arthropod under some leaves. How could you quickly decide to which group of arthropods it belongs?
3. Suggest two medical emergencies in which the use of leeches could help to save a person.

Using Science Skills

Suppose a seafood market received a delivery of lobsters, crabs, shrimps, octopus, and squid. Choose a trait. Classify these animals into two groups according to this trait.

Chapter 3

Plant Growth and Adaptations

Flower Power

These flowers are orchids (OR kihdz). They can be found growing on the branch of a tree. But the flowers are not a part of the tree. They are a part of plants that live on trees.

In some regions of the world, it rains nearly every day. In those places, trees grow to be very tall. Their leaves shade the ground far below them. Instead of growing on the dark ground, some small plants like orchids grow up in the trees where there is more light.

How do these small plants get up into the tree? The seeds of such plants are dropped by birds or monkeys. Some of the seeds get stuck in the bark of a tree. There they sprout, collecting moisture from the surface of the tree. These plants also take in moisture from the air, earning the name *air plant.*

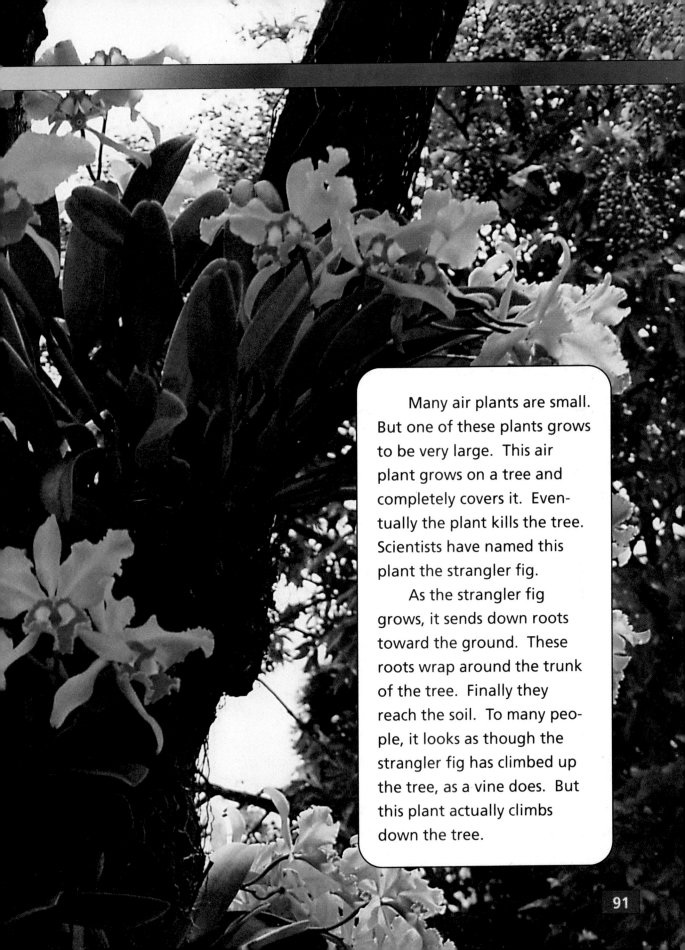

Many air plants are small. But one of these plants grows to be very large. This air plant grows on a tree and completely covers it. Eventually the plant kills the tree. Scientists have named this plant the strangler fig.

As the strangler fig grows, it sends down roots toward the ground. These roots wrap around the trunk of the tree. Finally they reach the soil. To many people, it looks as though the strangler fig has climbed up the tree, as a vine does. But this plant actually climbs down the tree.

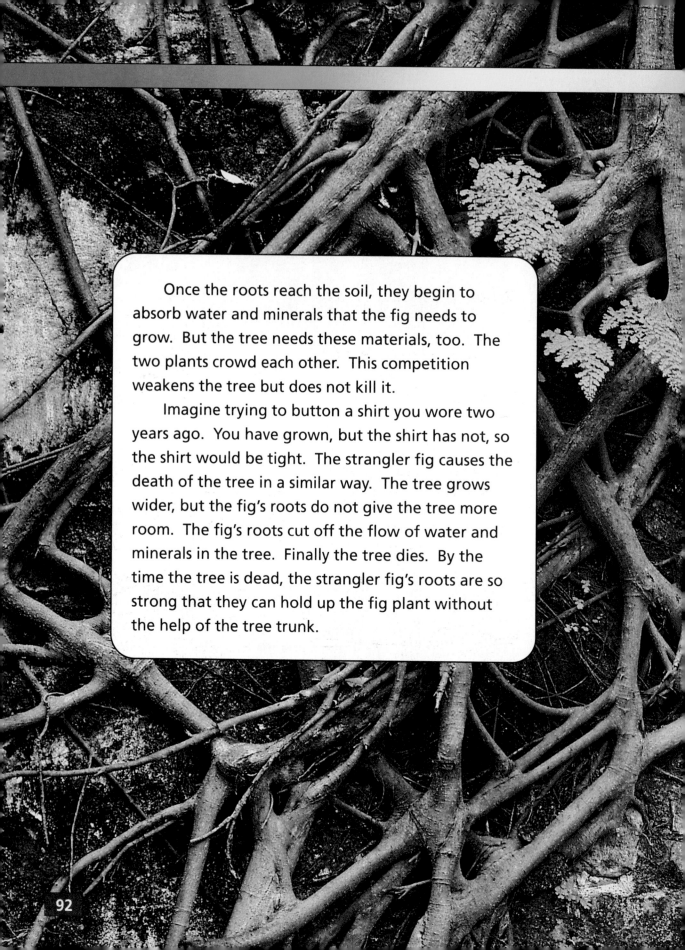

Once the roots reach the soil, they begin to absorb water and minerals that the fig needs to grow. But the tree needs these materials, too. The two plants crowd each other. This competition weakens the tree but does not kill it.

Imagine trying to button a shirt you wore two years ago. You have grown, but the shirt has not, so the shirt would be tight. The strangler fig causes the death of the tree in a similar way. The tree grows wider, but the fig's roots do not give the tree more room. The fig's roots cut off the flow of water and minerals in the tree. Finally the tree dies. By the time the tree is dead, the strangler fig's roots are so strong that they can hold up the fig plant without the help of the tree trunk.

Discover

Does overcrowding affect the growth of a plant?

ACTIVITY

Materials 2 paper cups · potting soil · radish seeds · water · metric ruler

Procedure

Often, after seeds sprout, the plants grow in little clumps. You may have wondered why gardeners thin these clumps by pulling out some of the tiny plants.

Put some potting soil in two paper cups. Plant about 30 radish seeds in one cup. Plant six radish seeds in the other cup. Give both cups the same amount of water and light. After a week, measure the heights of the plants in each cup. What is the difference? How could you help the crowded plants grow taller? Test your solution. Did it work?

In this chapter you will learn more about what plants need to grow. You will discover how plants grow taller, and you will see what makes plants grow thicker.

1. How Plants Grow

Getting Started Suppose you are in charge of caring for a plant. What will happen if you forget to water it? If a plant is not watered enough, it will stop growing and may die. But plants need more than water. What else must you do for a plant to keep it alive?

How do the growth patterns of plants vary?

Different plants grow in different ways. Look at the plants shown on these pages. The way in which a plant grows is its growth pattern. Some flowering plants are short and grow near the ground. Many of these plants grow close to others of their kind. Because of that growth pattern, people often use them as ground covers.

Trees, shrubs, and vines are three types of plants with different growth patterns. A tree is a plant that has one main woody stem, or trunk. A shrub is usually a medium-sized plant that has many trunks. A vine is a plant with a climb-

◀ **Oak tree with ivy and periwinkle as ground cover**

ing stem that may grow on the sides of a building, a fence, or a tree. Which of the plants shown is a shrub, which is a tree, and which is a vine?

▼ Japonica

▼ Forsythia

▲ Ivy on wall

What do plants need to grow?

The environment (ehn vy ruhn muhnt) of a living thing is everything that surrounds and affects it. To grow and be healthy, every living thing needs certain things from its environment. You, for example, need oxygen, water, and food. What else do you need to live?

Plants need light and water. Plants also need oxygen and carbon dioxide from the air. Plants need minerals from the soil in which they grow. And they need a proper temperature range and enough space in which to grow.

 *Plants in space? Find out how to make them grow as you try **Investigating Plant Growth.***

▲ Beavertail cactus

▲ Fern

The amounts of things that different plants need from their environments vary. For example, plants differ in their need for water. Look at the pictures. The cactus lives in a desert, where it seldom rains. The fern lives in a forest, where it rains more often. A cactus can store water for several months, but a fern must take in water every few days.

It is usually much hotter in a desert than in a forest. A plant will grow in a place where the temperature range is suited for its growth. How do the proper temperature ranges for a cactus and a fern differ?

Lesson Review

1. Describe the growth pattern of flowering plants used as ground cover.
2. How does a tree differ from a shrub? How does a vine differ from both a tree and a shrub?
3. Name seven things that a plant needs for growth and must have in its environment.

Think! Plants make their own food, yet people add "plant food" to the soil of houseplants. What does the plant food contain that plants need?

THINKING

Skills

Experimenting to find an answer

Many experiments have two sets of materials. In the experiment you make both sets of materials the same. Then you change one thing in one of the sets. The thing you want to change is related to a question you want to answer. To answer your question, you will compare one set with the other. The set that you compare the other set with is the control group. The set that you change is the experimental group.

Practicing the skill

How does salt water affect the growth of a freshwater aquarium plant?

1. Obtain two jars. Label the jars *A* and *B*. Put fresh water in both jars.

2. Change the water in jar *A* by adding a spoonful of salt. This is the experimental jar.

3. You will compare a plant in jar *A* with a plant in jar *B*. Jar *B* is the control jar.

4. Put freshwater plant pieces of the same size in both jars. Put the jars in a sunny window.

5. Compare the plants daily for 5 days.

6. How are the plants different?

Thinking about the skill

Why was it important to have a control jar in this experiment?

Applying the skill

Set up and do an experiment to answer the question: "How will acid from vinegar affect a freshwater plant?" You can grow plants in two jars. How will you set up the two jars? What will you change in one of the jars? What will the control jar be like?

2. Growth in Length

▼ Bamboo

Words to Know
growth region

Getting Started Imagine a plant that grows so fast that you can actually see it grow. About how much taller have you grown since you were born? Some bamboo plants can grow as much in 1 day as you have grown in your life!

What part of a stem increases in length?

The type of bamboo shown is one of the fastest-growing plants known. Also shown is a Sitka spruce, one of the slowest-growing plants. In 3 years the height of one Sitka spruce increased by only about 10 mm (0.4 inches). Use a calculator to find how much taller the tree would grow in 10 years.

Growth of bamboo

1 day's growth

Growth of Sitka spruce

10 years' growth

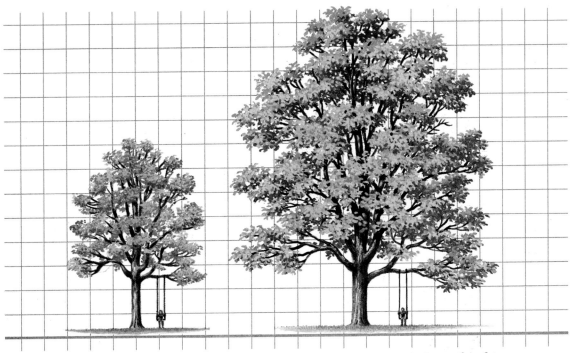

▲ **Growth of tree over several years**

Have you ever seen a swing hanging on the lowest branch of a tree? The drawings show such a swing when it was new and then several years later. How did the tree change? Observe that the distance between the swing and the ground did *not* change.

The trunks of trees are stems, and so are the branches of trees. Notice that the distance between any two branches shown in both pictures did not change. Yet the tree grew taller and the branches grew longer over the years. Why did the branches grow longer but not farther apart? A tree trunk grows in length only near its top, and a branch grows near its end.

What causes a stem to grow longer?

A **growth region** in a plant is a tissue in which growth occurs. A tissue is a group of like cells that work together. A growth region found near the tip of a stem causes the stem to grow longer. Just as there is a growth region near the tip of a tree trunk, there is a growth region near the tip of each branch.

▼ Cells in stem tip

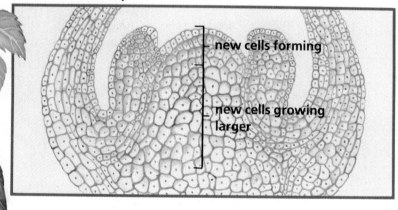

new cells forming

new cells growing larger

The drawing shows the cells inside the growth region near the tip of a stem. The small cells near the tip produce new cells. As the new cells grow, they become larger and longer. As the number and size of cells near the tip increase, the stem grows longer.

What do buds on a stem become?

▼ Stem buds

Another kind of growth region in plants is found in swellings on stems called stem buds. Examples of stem buds are shown in the picture at the left. Seed plants that live longer than one year and rest during the winter form stem buds at the end of each growing season. These buds grow into new stems, leaves, or flowers.

Most stems have one or more buds at their tips. During the winter, when the weather is cold, the plant does not grow; it is in a resting stage. In the spring, when the weather gets warmer, the buds open and begin to grow.

Explore Together

Where is the growth region that causes a stem to grow longer?

Materials

Organizer

black felt-tip pen · metric ruler · pole bean seedling, about 5 cm high, growing in soil in a paper cup · water in a spray bottle

Procedure

Investigator, Manager

A. Use a black felt-tip pen and a metric ruler to make a mark 1 cm below the top leaf of a pole bean seedling that is about 5 cm tall. Make four more marks on the stem. The marks should be 1 cm apart, as shown in the picture.

Manager

B. Make a drawing of the seedling as shown. Label the marks in your drawing *1, 2, 3, 4,* and *5.*

Group, Recorder

1. Predict what will happen to the lengths of the stem sections between the marks as the plant grows.

Investigator, Recorder

C. Every day for 5 days, water the plant with water from a spray bottle. Every day, measure the length of each section. Record your measurements.

Group

2. Which section is longest after 5 days?

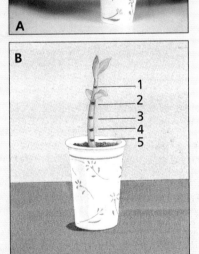

Writing and Sharing Results and Conclusions

Group, Recorder Reporter

1. Which section of the stem grew the most?
2. How do your results and conclusions compare with those of your classmates?

▲ Buds "forced" to grow in winter

You can "force" some buds to grow during the winter by bringing stems into a warm room and placing them in water. If you watch such a stem carefully, you can see the rapid growth of the end buds. In the pictures above, notice how much the buds grow from day to day.

How do roots grow longer?

Do roots grow near their tips, the way stems do? To find out, you can observe roots in seedlings. Drawing *A* shows a 1-week-old pea seedling with its root marked into sections. Drawing *B* shows the same seedling a week later. What do the drawings show about the growth region where the root gets longer?

The growth of roots in length is similar to the growth of stems. Like a stem, a root has a growth region near its tip. Look at the drawing of cells in a root tip on the next page. Find the place where new cells are being produced in the root. Now find the place where cells are increasing in length. Two processes—the making of more cells and the enlarging of those new cells—cause the root to grow longer.

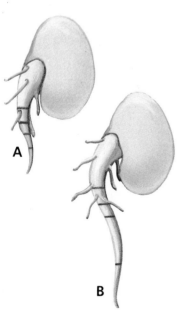

A

B

▲ Growth of a root

Compare the drawing of the cells in a root tip with the drawing of cells in a stem tip on page 100. What kinds of cells are found in both the stem and the root? Notice that the end of the root contains a structure *not* found in a stem. This structure is the root cap. Cells in the root cap protect the delicate root tip as it grows through the soil. As the root grows, some of the protective cells die and fall off. They are replaced by new cells that grow in the root cap.

▼ **Cells in root tip**

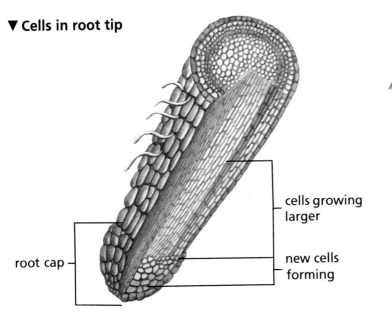

root cap

cells growing larger

new cells forming

Lesson Review

1. What changes in the cells of the growth region of a stem cause the stem to grow longer?

2. What parts of a stem produce new stems, leaves, or flowers?

3. Compare the locations of the growth regions that cause roots and stems to grow longer.

Think! In places where there are different seasons, many trees grow taller only during the spring and summer. Explain why the trees grow only during these seasons.

3. Growth in Thickness

Getting Started Can you tell the ages of the two trees shown on this page? Does it surprise you that the bristlecone pine is older than the sequoia? You cannot tell the age of a tree from its size alone. But as you will see, there is a way to find the age of a tree from a pattern that forms as it grows thicker.

Words to Know
phloem
xylem
annual rings

How do stems grow thicker?

Bristlecone pines, sequoias, and other plants not only grow taller but they also grow thicker. A woody stem grows thicker because of growth that occurs in a ring-shaped growth region. Cells in this growth region produce two kinds of tissue. One kind of tissue, called phloem (FLO-ehm), forms in a ring just outside the growth region. **Phloem** is a tissue made of tubes that carry food through a plant.

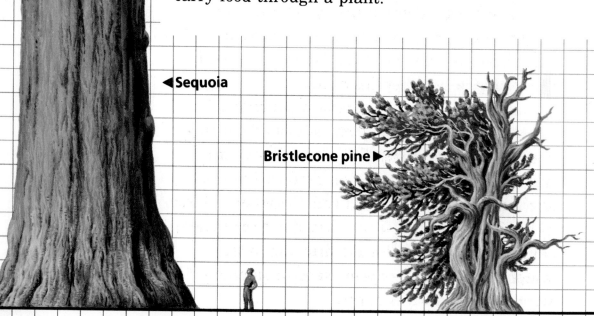

◄ Sequoia

Bristlecone pine ▶

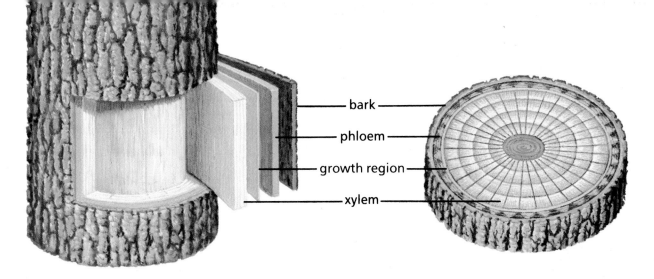

bark

phloem

growth region

xylem

▲ Tissues in woody stem

Another kind of tissue, called xylem (ZYE lum), forms from the ring-shaped growth region. **Xylem** is a tissue made of tubes that carry water and minerals through a plant. Look at the drawings above. Find the growth region, the phloem, and the xylem.

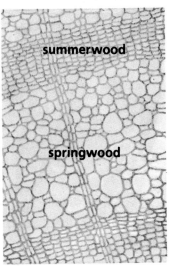

summerwood

springwood

▲ Cells in an annual ring

How do annual rings form?

Woody stems, such as those of trees and shrubs, usually grow for many years. The wood is made up of xylem cells. In places where the seasons change, many large xylem cells are produced in the spring. These cells have thin walls and are light in color. Xylem produced in the spring is called springwood.

In the summer the rate of production of new cells slows down. Xylem cells made during the summer are small. They have thick walls and are dark in color. Xylem produced in the summer is called summerwood. Together, a layer of springwood and a layer of summerwood make up 1 year's growth. Use the drawing to tell which type of wood—springwood or summerwood—forms a wider layer.

*Did you ever think you could read from a tree? Learn how in the **Skeleton Tree** in Horizons Plus.*

Each set of light and dark layers of xylem cells forms a ring. These rings of wood that are produced yearly in the stems of trees are called **annual rings.** How can you use annual rings to tell the age of a tree?   Look at the picture and drawing of a tree trunk. About how old is the tree?

By studying a tree trunk, scientists can determine more than the tree's age. They can also learn about the weather in past years from its effects on the tree. Notice that the annual rings shown in the drawing vary in width. Growth is much slower during periods of drought. A lack of water causes an annual ring to be narrow. A year in which temperatures are warmer than usual can have a long growing season. How would a longer growing time affect the size of an annual ring?

Tree trunk cut across ▼

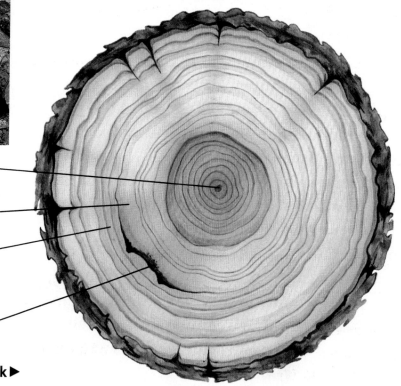

first year of growth

rainy spell

dry spell

scar from forest fire wound

Annual rings in tree trunk▶

106

How do roots grow thicker?

Like stems, roots have growth regions that cause them to grow thicker. These growth regions also produce two kinds of tissue—phloem and xylem. Recall that phloem is made of food-carrying tubes, and xylem is made of water-carrying tubes. Find the phloem and xylem of the root in the drawing.

A root also contains food-storing tissue. Find this tissue in the drawing. Compare the locations of tissues in roots and stems, as shown below and on page 105.

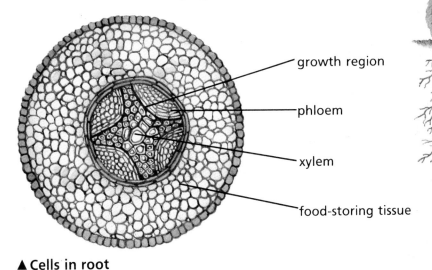

growth region

phloem

xylem

food-storing tissue

▲ Cells in root

Lesson Review

1. Where is the tissue located that causes a woody stem to grow thicker?
2. What two kinds of tissues form when a stem grows thicker? Which of these tissues carries water? Which carries food?
3. How is an annual ring formed in a woody stem?
4. Compare the locations of the growth regions that cause a stem and a root to grow thicker.

Think! Why does a tree die when a strip of bark is removed from all around its trunk?

▼ Venus' flytrap

4. Growth and Survival

Getting Started Did you ever touch a hot pan that you thought was cool? How did you react? Look at the pictures below of a Venus' flytrap. How did the plant react to the fly? How was something in the environment involved in both reactions?

How do plants respond by growing?

The reaction of a living thing to something in its environment is called a **response** (rih-SPAHNS). Pulling your hand away from a hot pan is a response. Any object or event that can cause a living thing to react is a **stimulus** (STIHM-you luhs). The plural of *stimulus* is *stimuli* (STIHM-you ly). If you touch a hot pan, the heat is a stimulus. What was the response of the Venus' flytrap? What was the stimulus?

Plants respond, or react, to a variety of stimuli, including light, gravity, and water. A plant response that involves growth is a **tropism** (TROH pihz uhm). Plants often bend toward light as they grow. The growth response of a plant to light is called phototropism (fo tah-TRO pihz uhm).

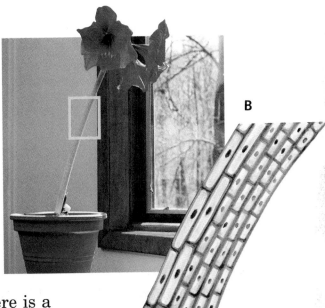

▲ (A) Cells in straight stem (B) Cells in bent stem

What causes phototropism? There is a growth substance in plants that speeds up cell growth. Drawing *A* shows cells of a plant evenly lighted on all sides. If this plant is placed where it gets light on only one side, the growth substance moves to the side *away* from the light. Then the cells on the shaded side grow faster and larger than those on the lighted side.

In drawing *B,* notice the difference in the sizes of the cells on the two sides of the stem. The larger cells on the shaded side have caused the stem to bend toward the light. What will happen if this plant is turned so the other side is shaded?

Explore

How does a plant stem respond to gravity?

When you plant a garden, you do not have to think about placing each seed "right side up." Neither do farmers, who plant many thousands of seeds at a time. Suppose plants did not "know" which way to grow. Think what effect this would have on farming!

Materials

black felt-tip pen • 3 seedlings, each in a paper cup of soil
modeling clay • water in spray bottle

Procedure

A. Use a black felt-tip pen to label three cups containing seedlings *1, 2,* and *3.*

B. Use modeling clay to make a support for each cup so that the seedlings are held in the positions shown in the picture.

B

Place the cups where the three seedlings will get the same amount of light.

1. Why should each seedling get the same amount of light?

C. Every day for 5 days, water the seedlings with water from a spray bottle and observe them.

2. Predict how the stems will look after 5 days.

3. Why should each seedling get the same amount of water?

Writing and Sharing Results and Conclusions

1. After 5 days, compare the appearance of the stems of plants *1, 2,* and *3.*

2. How did each stem respond to gravity?

▲ Jeffrey pine

How do responses help plants survive?

The survival of any living thing depends on its getting what it needs from the environment. A seed may land in a place where there is little light. As the plant grows, its stem may bend toward the light. It may bend enough for the plant to get the light it needs.

Responses to gravity and water also help plants survive. A stem responds to gravity by growing in the direction opposite to the pull of gravity. Because the stem grows upward, the leaves on the stem get light. Roots respond to gravity by growing in the direction of the pull of gravity. The downward growth of roots helps the roots reach water in the ground. Roots also respond by growing towards the water itself.

Lesson Review

1. Name three stimuli to which plants respond.
2. Define *tropism* and describe a phototropism.
3. How do responses to gravity help plants survive?

Think! Look again at the air plants at the beginning of this chapter. What adaptation of an air plant helps it survive without roots?

Physical Science
CONNECTION

Do all colors of light cause phototropism? Design an experiment to find out.

seed

5. Structure and Survival

Words to Know
adaptation
extinct

flower

Getting Started Have you ever seen a lawn that seemed to be full of dandelions? People often have trouble keeping dandelions from "taking over" lawns. Like other weeds, dandelions have a trait that makes them hard to destroy. What is that trait?

How do structures help plants survive?

Living things survive because they are well adapted, or suited, to their environment. A response or structure that helps a living thing

◄**Parts of a dandelion**

leaf

root

survive is called an **adaptation** (ad uhp TAY-shuhn). You have learned that plants have tropisms that help them survive. These growth responses of plants are one kind of adaptation.

Many plant structures are adaptations because they also help plants survive. The dandelion has many different adaptations. Look at the drawing of a dandelion. Notice that the plant's broad leaves are close to the ground. If the flower is cut off by a lawn mower, the leaves may remain and the plant survives.

The dandelion plant has a long, thick, strong root. If you try to pull it out of the soil, the top of the root breaks off. New leaves and flowers can grow from the deep part of the root, and the plant survives.

Dandelions produce many seeds. But if a seed lands close to the parent plant, the young plant that grows competes with the parent for space. For seeds to have a good chance to grow, they must travel away from the parent. How are the seeds of the dandelion adapted for travel?

What are some other plant adaptations?

Plants that live in different environments have different adaptations. Some pine trees grow where there is little rainfall. As the drawing shows, a pine tree has needlelike leaves. These leaves have a small surface area. So pine trees do not lose much water through their leaves.

◀ **Leaves of pine tree**

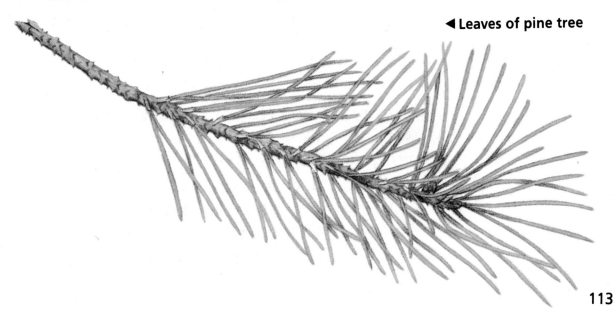

Barrel cactus ▲

A cactus lives where the weather is hot and dry. Its roots are long, and they spread out just under the surface of the soil. When it rains, cactus roots take in large amounts of rainwater. They can absorb the water before it evaporates into the air, runs off, or soaks deep into the soil. The thick stem of the cactus stores water that is used during the long dry spells. How are this plant's stems and roots adaptations?

Why should you never eat wild plants you do not know? Some plants produce poisons that help the plants survive. The leaves of the locoweed contain a substance that is poisonous to animals. So the poison protects the plant against animals that might eat its leaves.

Look at the black walnut tree in the picture. This tree gives off a substance that prevents the growth of young plants. New plants do not grow around the tree. This poison is an adaptation because there are no new plants near the tree to compete for space.

▼ Black walnut

Problem Solving

When the Growing Gets Tough, the Tough Get Growing

Producing tough, or hardy, seeds is one plant adaptation. A plant with hardy seeds has a good chance to reproduce, or make more of its kind. And a plant species that reproduces has a good chance to survive. Suppose a gardener buys a packet of radish seeds to plant in the spring. The gardener leaves the seeds in the car. The temperature overnight drops to freezing—0°C (32°F). The gardener needs to find out just how hardy those seeds are before planting them.

How does exposing radish seeds to freezing temperatures affect their ability to sprout when planted?

Plan an experiment that tests the effect of freezing on radish seeds. What information do you need to know to solve this problem? Ask your teacher to approve your plan and then try it. Do you think a radish seed is hardy?

Why are some species of plants endangered?

Sometimes the environment of a plant changes. If the plant is not adapted to the new environment, it may die. A species of animal or plant with no living members is said to be **extinct** . Species that are in danger of becoming extinct are called endangered.

Many plants are endangered. The pictures show some of these plants. Why might these plants become extinct? People often clear land for houses, roads, and farms. Then the environment changes, resulting in the loss of plants that lived in the original environment. What are some possible effects of plants' becoming extinct?

▼ Hawaiian silversword

▼ Rhododendron

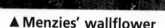

▲ Menzies' wallflower

Lesson Review

1. What is an adaptation?
2. What are three adaptations of dandelions?
3. How are the roots of a cactus an adaptation?
4. What is one thing people do that can cause plants to become extinct?

Think! One result of plants' becoming endangered is that animals can also become endangered. Explain how plants can affect animals in this way.

Chapter Connections

Explain the major ideas in this chapter to a partner. Use the graphic organizer as a guide.

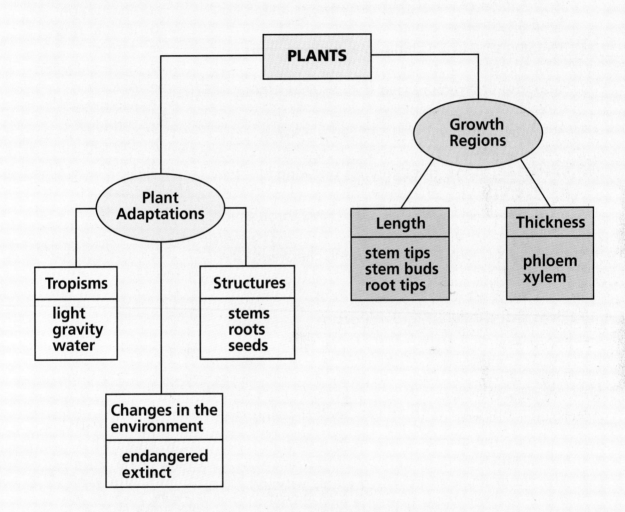

Writing About Science • Imagine

Imagine three changes that could occur in a plant's environment. Think of possible plant responses or structures that would help a plant to survive in the new environment. Write a paragraph about your plant and its environment.

Science Terms

Next to each number, write the letter of the term that best matches the definition.

1. Tissue made of tubes that carry water and minerals through a plant
2. Reaction of a living thing to something in its environment
3. Response or structure that helps a living thing survive
4. Any object or event that can cause a living thing to react
5. Species of animal or plant with no living members
6. Tissue made of tubes that carry food through a plant
7. Rings of wood produced yearly in the stems of trees
8. Plant response that involves growth
9. Plant tissue in which growth occurs

a. adaptation
b. annual rings
c. extinct
d. growth region
e. phloem
f. response
g. stimulus
h. tropism
i. xylem

Science Ideas

Use complete sentences to answer the following.

1. Compare the growth patterns of a tree, a shrub, and a vine.
2. Give an example of how two plants vary in their need for water from the environment.
3. Study the drawing of the tree. List each letter that identifies a place on the tree where growth in length can occur.
4. List three plant parts that may form from stem buds.
5. Where is the growth region that causes a root to grow longer?

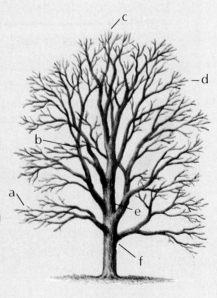

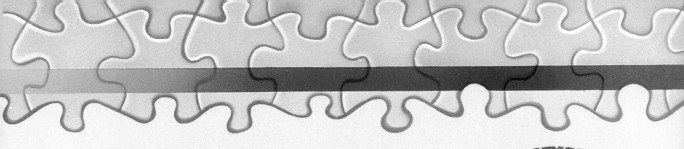

6. Study the drawings of cross sections of two plant parts. What part is shown in *A*? What part is shown in *B*? Which number indicates a growth region in each plant part?

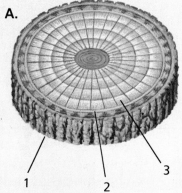

A.

7. What two kinds of tissues do the ring-shaped growth regions in both stems and roots produce?

8. Name the two kinds of woody tissue that form annual rings in a tree trunk. How do the colors of these two tissues compare?

9. How does a stem respond to the light?

B.

10. How does the way roots respond to a source of water help a plant survive?

11. Give two examples of plant leaf structures that are adaptations.

12. What activity causes many plant species to become endangered?

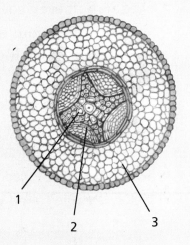

Applying Science Ideas

1. A girl nails a birdhouse to a tree trunk 1 m (3 ft) from the ground. How high from the ground will the birdhouse be after the tree has grown 2 m (6 ft) taller? Explain your answer.

2. Suppose you go on vacation to an island in the tropics. You visit a rain forest where you see the stump of a large tree. There are no annual rings in the stump. How do you explain this?

Using Science Skills

You want to find out how to make cut flowers last longer. For your experimental group, you put some flowers in a cool place. What would your control group be like?

Chapter 4

Biomes

Dusty Damage

Imagine that dust is everywhere, both indoors and outdoors. It even covers your face while you sleep. The dust stings your eyes, fills your nose, and catches in your throat. Day after day hot winds blow clouds of dust across the land. Sometimes the dust storms are thick enough to block out the sun.

Could you live in a place like this? Many people who lived on the grasslands in parts of Kansas, Oklahoma, Texas, Colorado, and New Mexico did in the 1930s. People called this area the Dust Bowl.

What caused the Dust Bowl? People helped to cause it. The grasslands once had good soil for farming and for grazing cattle and sheep. But farmers dug up large areas of the grasses to plant food crops. Ranchers let their cattle and sheep graze on the grasses until the root systems were destroyed. Then there was a drought, a long period of time with no rainfall. The grasses, which had root systems, were no longer there to hold the soil in place. Crops dried up in the sun. Strong winds blew away the topsoil. The land became a Dust Bowl.

People may have made droughts in the 1980s worse, too. In 1988 much of the United States was drier than normal. It was very hot. Many crops died in the fields. Some lakes and rivers had no water. Some forests burned. Topsoil was blown away.

Scientists who study climate say that the 1980s were the hottest 10 years on record. Some say that the heat might be a result of the greenhouse effect. This is the warming of the atmosphere caused by chemicals put into the air. These chemicals include carbon dioxide, the main chemical that causes the warming. Carbon dioxide comes from the burning of fuels such as oil, natural gas, and coal. People burn these fuels.

The Dust Bowl was a region with certain plants and animals as well as a certain temperature and a certain amount of rainfall. People in the Dust Bowl changed one thing, the grasses, and that changed everything else in the region. People in the United States burn fuels and that changes everything else in these regions. Can people live in a region and not change it?

Discover

How does grass help hold the soil in place?

ACTIVITY

Materials   small spade · clump of grass and soil · small plastic bag · hand lens

Procedure

With a spade, dig up a square portion of grass and soil. Place it in the plastic bag. Observe the root system. Draw a picture of it. Remove the grass from the bag. Carefully shake the clump of soil to remove the soil from around the roots. Observe the root system again. Sketch it again. How does the grass keep the soil in place?

In this chapter you will learn about different types of regions. You will learn about the kinds of animals and plants that live in each region.

▲ Alaska

▲ Florida

1. Zones of Life

Getting Started   Imagine that you are taking a plane trip from Florida to Alaska. What living things might you see as you get on the plane in Florida? How would they be different from the ones you might see as you leave the plane in Alaska?

What factors affect where organisms live?

Look at the pictures of Florida and Alaska. How do the organisms shown differ? Each environment has different kinds of organisms. One factor that affects where organisms live is climate. **Climate** (KLYE mut) is the average weather of a region over a long period of time.

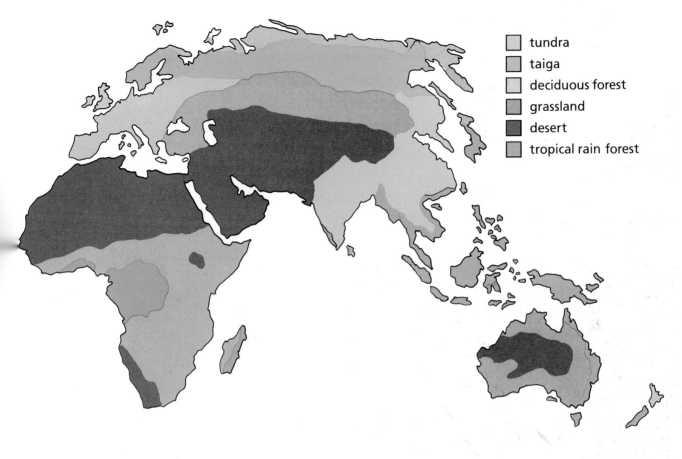

	tundra
	taiga
	deciduous forest
	grassland
	desert
	tropical rain forest

▲ Biomes map

Two basic factors determine both climate and weather. These factors are precipitation and temperature. Weather is the result of day to day changes in these factors. Climate is the average of these factors over a long period of time.

A **biome** (BYE ohm) is a large region on the earth that has a certain climate and certain kinds of organisms. Each biome is described in terms of its climate and its living things. The plants and animals that survive in a biome are adapted to the conditions in that biome.

There are six major land biomes. Look at the map of the world and find the biomes shown. In which biome do you live?

Notice on the map that the biomes are shown as specific regions. But you should remember that a biome does not end at a line. Biomes overlap each other. Each biome blends into the next one.

Average Precipitation and Temperature of Land Biomes		
Biome	Average precipitation (yearly)	Average temperature range (yearly)
Tundra	11 cm	−26°C to 4°C
Taiga	35 cm	−10°C to 14°C
Deciduous forest	115 cm	6°C to 28°C
Tropical forest	253 cm	25°C to 27°C
Grassland	90 cm	0°C to 25°C
Desert	16 cm	24°C to 32°C

 The table above lists the average yearly precipitation and temperature range for the land biomes. Which biome has the most precipitation? Which has the least? Use a calculator to find which biome has the greatest range in temperature. Which has the least range?

Earth Science
CONNECTION

Get a map that shows the world's climates. Compare the map on pages 124–125 with the climate map. How are they alike? How are they different?

Lesson Review

1. What factors determine where an organism lives?
2. How is climate different from weather?
3. How do biomes differ from one another?

Think! Do you think that the biomes on the earth today are like they were thousands of years ago? Do you think they will be the same in the future?

THINKING

Skills

Arranging things in order

You can arrange some things in order based on size, mass, volume, and number. Perhaps you have arranged books in order according to their size. Arranging things in order can help you see the relationships between them.

Practicing the skill

The table shows the average monthly temperature for five cities. The cities are arranged in alphabetical order.

Average Monthly Temperature, Degrees Celsius											
	January	February	March	April	May	June	July	August	September	October	November	December
Atlanta, GA	6	7	12	17	21	24	26	25	23	17	11	7
Los Angeles, CA	14	15	16	17	18	21	23	24	23	21	17	14
Miami, FL	19	20	22	24	26	27	28	28	28	25	23	21
Nashville, TN	3	4	9	16	20	24	26	26	22	16	9	5
San Antonio, TX	10	12	17	21	24	28	29	29	26	21	16	12

1. Use a calculator to find the average yearly temperature for each city.
2. List the five cities in order according to their average yearly temperatures, from lowest to highest.

Thinking about the skill

When might it be important to arrange things in order according to size at home?

Applying the skill

Look at the world biomes map on pages 124–125. List the biomes in order according to the area they cover. Begin with the largest biome and end with the smallest.

2. The Tundra and the Taiga

Words to Know
tundra
taiga

Getting Started The words *tundra* and *taiga* come from the Russian language. Find the tundra and taiga on the biomes map on pages 124–125. Why do you think these northern biomes have Russian names?

What is the tundra like?

The **tundra** (TUN druh) is a biome that is cold and receives little precipitation. Winters in the tundra are long, dark, and very windy. A thin layer of snow covers much of the land. Summers in the tundra are very short. There are only about eight weeks of the year when conditions are right for plants to grow. Use the table on page 126 to find the temperature range and average precipitation in the tundra.

Tundra in winter ▼

Tundra in summer ▼

Most of the soil in the tundra is frozen all year. This frozen soil is called permafrost. Water cannot drain through the rock-hard permafrost. Also, roots cannot grow through it. During the summer a thin top layer of soil above the permafrost thaws. This thin layer of moist soil is where the tundra plants grow. Muddy pools of water collect everywhere during the summer. Why do you think the pools form?

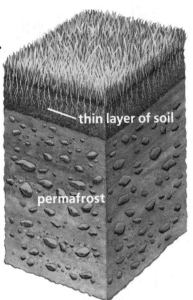

▲ Permafrost

What kinds of plants and animals live in the tundra?

Few kinds of plants can survive in the tundra. Because the growing season is so short, the plants in the tundra are adapted to grow very quickly. Many plants in the tundra grow from seeds to mature plants in only two months.

Tall trees would need deep roots to stand up against the strong tundra wind. But, because deep roots cannot get through the permafrost, there are no tall trees in the tundra. The few trees that do survive in the tundra are dwarf trees.

Most of the tundra is covered with grasses, mosses, and lichens. Lichens are actually two organisms, an alga and a fungus, that live together. The alga makes the food. But, the fungus cannot make food. The fungus can store water, and the alga uses some of this water to make food. Together as a lichen, the alga and the fungus can live in places where neither one could survive alone.

Tundra plants are food for the herbivores that live in the tundra. Herbivores are plant

Tundra lichens ▼

▲ Caribou grazing on lichens and grasses

Lemming ▼

Lemmings In snow tunnels ▼

eaters. Lemmings are small herbivores of the tundra. They eat seeds and shoots. Caribou are large herbivores of the tundra. The caribou in the picture are grazing on lichens and grasses.

Herbivores are food for other animals of the tundra. Arctic foxes, snowy owls, and wolves are carnivores, or meat eaters, of the tundra.

Animals that live in the tundra have adaptations that enable them to survive the long, cold winters. Lemmings eat and sleep in tunnels under the snow. Below the snow, they are sheltered from the wind. The temperature in their tunnels is much warmer than in the freezing air above.

Some animals, such as caribou, migrate to regions that have milder climates. Herds of caribou migrate south across the tundra. Some

Problem Solving

Water, Water Everywhere

In the brief growing season of the tundra, the frozen surface changes to ponds, bogs, and soggy soil. To understand the cause of this change, it is helpful to make a model of the summertime tundra.

How can you make a model of the summertime tundra?

Use a plastic container for your model. What can you use to represent the permafrost layer? What can you place on top of the permafrost layer? What happens when you add water to this model?

herds travel more than 2,000 km (1,200 miles) each year across the tundra. Most birds move south in the winter, too. Why do you think caribou and birds move south?

What is the taiga like?

The **taiga** (TYE guh) is a biome in which the main type of plant life is evergreen trees. This biome has long, hard winters and constant snow cover. Although it is very cold, there is no permafrost in the taiga. Without permafrost the roots of trees can push through the ground. So tall trees can grow in the taiga.

How does the climate of the taiga compare with that of the tundra? Use the table on page 126 to find out. Which biome has warmer summers? Which biome has more precipitation?

What kinds of plants and animals live in the taiga?

The most common plants of the taiga are the conifers. Most conifers have leaves all year, so they can produce food all year.

Because conifers keep their leaves all year, little sunlight reaches the forest floor. Without much light, only a few types of plants grow on the forest floor. Ferns and mosses are plants that can grow without much light.

Conifers provide food and shelter for many animals. For example, porcupines often spend the winter in one tree. They eat the needles and bark of the tree. Some birds, such as the crossbill, eat the seeds from the cones. Notice the shape of the crossbill's beak. How does this shape help the bird to get seeds out of cones?

(A) Snow-covered conifers,
(B) Crossbill eating seeds from conifer cone,
(C) Close-up of crossbill beak ▼

The moose is a herbivore that lives in the taiga all year. During the winter, moose can survive on a diet of pine needles. During the spring and summer, moose wade through the thawed lakes. The moose in the picture is eating lake plants. It can hold its head underwater for a long time while it gathers plants with its fleshy lips.

Moose feeding on lake plants ▼

Lesson Review

1. Compare the climates of the tundra and the taiga.
2. Why are there no tall trees in the tundra?
3. Describe one common plant and one common animal from the tundra or taiga. How is each one adapted for survival?

Think! During the short summer in the tundra, swarms of insects appear. How may the large number of birds that spend the summer in the tundra be related to the large number of insects?

Earth Science
CONNECTION

Oil is an important natural resource. The Alaskan Pipeline was built to remove oil found in Alaska. Find out what steps were taken to protect the tundra.

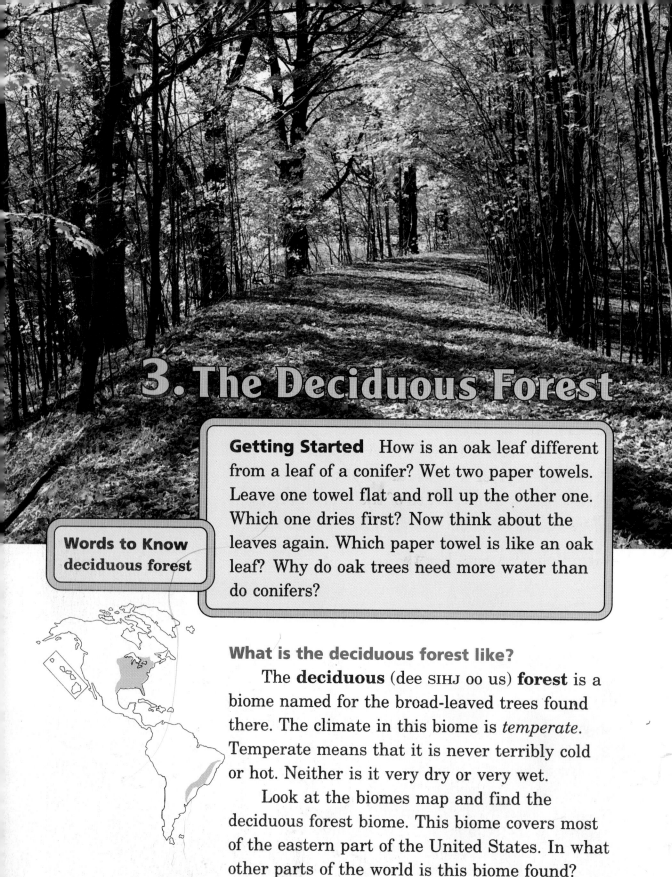

3. The Deciduous Forest

Getting Started How is an oak leaf different from a leaf of a conifer? Wet two paper towels. Leave one towel flat and roll up the other one. Which one dries first? Now think about the leaves again. Which paper towel is like an oak leaf? Why do oak trees need more water than do conifers?

Words to Know
deciduous forest

What is the deciduous forest like?

The **deciduous** (dee SIHJ oo us) **forest** is a biome named for the broad-leaved trees found there. The climate in this biome is *temperate*. Temperate means that it is never terribly cold or hot. Neither is it very dry or very wet.

Look at the biomes map and find the deciduous forest biome. This biome covers most of the eastern part of the United States. In what other parts of the world is this biome found?

What kinds of plants live in the deciduous forest?

Trees in the deciduous forest include maple, oak, and beech. Deciduous trees have broad leaves that make food during the spring and summer. The word *deciduous* comes from the Latin and means "to fall down." In the fall the leaves of deciduous trees begin to drop.

Because the trees are bare for part of the year, some sunlight reaches the forest floor. In the early spring, before the trees have all their leaves, many wildflowers blossom. Wildflowers grow quickly before they are shaded by the new leaves of the trees.

The deciduous forest is divided into several layers. Each layer has certain plants and animals. What are the names of the four different layers in the drawing?

Layers of the deciduous forest ▶

canopy

understory

shrub layer

forest floor

Explore Together

How does a Berlese funnel work?

Materials

Organizer

moist paper towel · plastic jar · tape · black paper · scissors · petroleum jelly · mesh produce bag · funnel · lamp with 60-watt bulb · leaf litter

Procedure

Manager

A. Place a moist paper towel in the bottom of the jar. Tape a piece of black paper around the outside of the jar. Place a small amount of petroleum jelly around the top of the jar.

Investigator

B. Cut a small piece of the mesh bag and place it in the funnel. Place the funnel in the jar. Place the leaf litter on the mesh bag in the funnel.

Investigator

C. Position the lamp so that it shines directly on the leaf litter. **Caution:** *Do not touch the lamp bulb because it gets hot.* Set the Berlese funnel in a safe place.

Group, Recorder

D. Check the jar in an hour. Turn off the lamp. Remove the black paper from the jar. Observe the contents of the jar. Record what you see.

E. Repeat step **D** two more times.

Writing and Sharing Results and Conclusions

Group, Recorder

1. What animals did you see in the jar?

2. Why did the animals go into the jar?

Reporter

3. How do your results and conclusions compare with those of your classmates?

What animals live in the deciduous forest?

The many plants of the deciduous forest provide food for herbivores. Squirrels, deer, rabbits, and beavers are some of the larger herbivores of this biome. These herbivores are food for the carnivores. Foxes, black bears, and hawks are carnivores that live in the deciduous forest.

There are many invertebrates in the deciduous forest. Recall that invertebrates are animals without backbones. Insects, worms, snails, millipedes, and slugs are a few of the invertebrates you might find. The invertebrates are eaten by snakes, frogs, salamanders, and birds. Find some of these animals in the drawing on page 135. Name the layer in which you find them.

Animals of the deciduous forest are adapted to the changes in the seasons. In the winter, temperatures are low and food is scarce. Squirrels store food in the fall. They bury acorns and other nuts. Bears sleep for most of the winter and survive on the fat stored in their bodies. Many birds fly south for the winter. For example, the warbler shown spends the spring and summer in the deciduous forest. It spends the winter in the warm West Indies.

▲ **Black-throated blue warbler**

It takes some quick thinking by Sara to solve the **Mystery at the Supermarket.** *Read about it in Horizons Plus and see if you can solve the mystery too.*

Lesson Review

1. Describe the climate of the deciduous forest.

2. Explain why most wildflowers grow in early spring.

3. What are the four layers of the deciduous forest? Give an example of one animal from each layer.

Think! Describe how building a highway through a forest might affect the organisms in the forest.

Layers of the tropical
rain forest ▶

4. The Tropical Rain Forest

Words to Know
tropical rain
forest

Getting Started Write down five words you
think of when you hear the word *jungle*.
Jungle is the name often given to the next
biome you are about to study. It is hot, humid,
and rainy here!

What is the tropical rain forest like?

The **tropical rain forest** is a biome that
has high temperatures and a large amount of
rain. Tropical rain forests are found only near
the equator, where there is lots of sun and rain.
The warm, humid climate of the rain forest is
ideal for rich plant growth. If you were in a
tropical rain forest, it would feel a lot like being
in a huge greenhouse.

The tropical rain forest changes very little
from season to season. The seasons vary mostly
in the amount of rainfall.

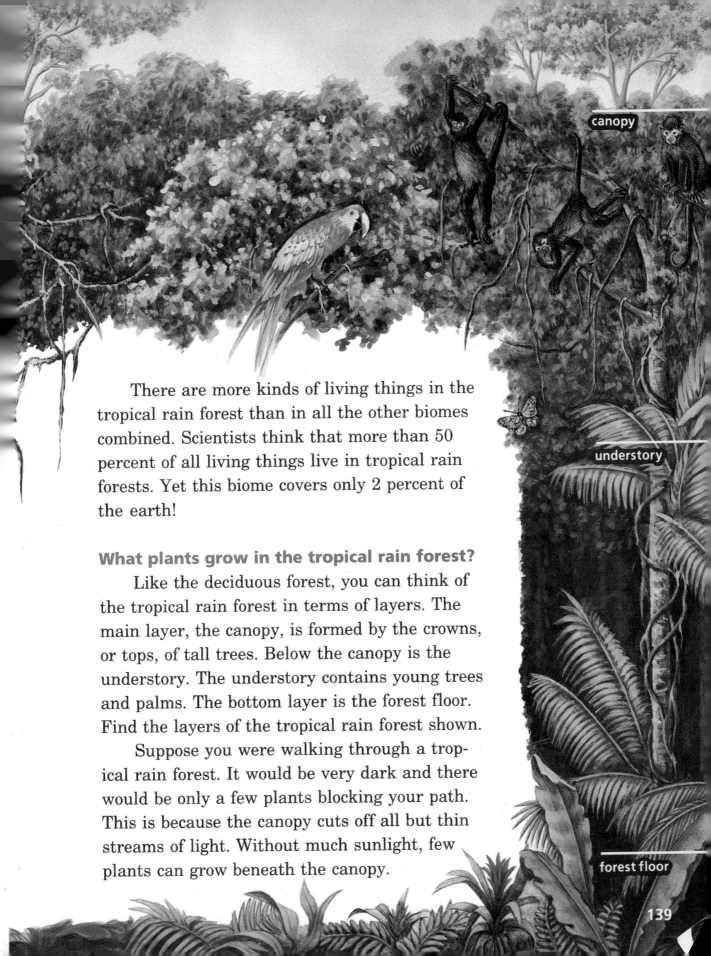

canopy

understory

forest floor

There are more kinds of living things in the tropical rain forest than in all the other biomes combined. Scientists think that more than 50 percent of all living things live in tropical rain forests. Yet this biome covers only 2 percent of the earth!

What plants grow in the tropical rain forest?

Like the deciduous forest, you can think of the tropical rain forest in terms of layers. The main layer, the canopy, is formed by the crowns, or tops, of tall trees. Below the canopy is the understory. The understory contains young trees and palms. The bottom layer is the forest floor. Find the layers of the tropical rain forest shown.

Suppose you were walking through a tropical rain forest. It would be very dark and there would be only a few plants blocking your path. This is because the canopy cuts off all but thin streams of light. Without much sunlight, few plants can grow beneath the canopy.

Some plants are found in all the layers of the forest because they climb on rain forest trees. For example, a hanging vine starts out life as a seed on the forest floor. As it grows, it climbs up a tree. Once it reaches bright light, it flowers and produces fruit.

Many trees have adaptations that protect them from animals that climb. Some trees have long thorns. The sandbox tree has sharp spikes growing out of its trunk. It also squirts out a poison sap when its bark is cut. Its sap can actually blind a person.

▲ South American hummingbird

South American toucan ▼

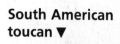

South American parrot ▲

What animals live in the tropical rain forest?

Few animals of the tropical rain forest move from one layer to the next. Each layer is a distinct habitat, each with different conditions. Most rain forest animals are adapted for life in only one layer.

More animals live in the canopy layer than in any other part of the forest. Many kinds of birds live in the canopy. Some birds feed on only

◄ Sloths clinging to branch in canopy

Spider monkey in canopy ▼

one type of plant. For example, the humming-bird drinks nectar from flowers with its long thin bill. Look at the three birds. How do you think their bills aid them in getting food?

Sloths and monkeys climb in the canopy layer. Sloths, like the ones shown in the picture, move slowly. What adaptation does the sloth have for hanging onto trees? Monkeys move rapidly. They can swing from tree to tree. Their grasping hands, feet, and tails are adaptations that help them move about in the trees.

The tropical rain forest is being destroyed faster than any other biome. Every minute, at least fifty acres of tropical rain forest are destroyed. As these forests are destroyed, the earth loses the plants and animals that live in them.

Lesson Review

1. In what way do the seasons vary in the tropical rain forest?
2. Describe the layers of the tropical rain forest.
3. Choose one animal and one plant of the tropical rain forest. Describe how they are adapted for life in this biome.

 Think! If fifty acres of tropical rain forest are destroyed every minute, use a calculator to find how many acres of tropical rain forest are destroyed each day.

141

Why are the rain forests important to all people?

Long ago, Mayas lived in the lush rain forests of Mexico. They used small areas for farms. The Mayas only cut trees that would grow back fast. If a tree or plant gave them fruit, medicines, or other things, they let it live. When they moved away, the forest grew back over their fields. The Mayas used the forest, but they protected it as well.

Today, farmers have a different way of clearing the rain forests. They burn all the trees and plants over huge areas. But the rain forest soil is poor, and crops will not grow in it for more than a few years. So the farmers must move on and clear still more land. Many people have other reasons for clearing the rain forest. Often they are poor and want better lives. They want to use the trees for fuel and to build furniture. Some want to start ranches and raise cattle. People in the United States will buy meat from the ranches to make hamburgers.

STS

Scientists know that the cutting of the rain forests is now affecting life on Earth. Trees take carbon dioxide out of the air. When trees are cut down, too much carbon dioxide is left, causing temperatures to rise everywhere on Earth. If temperatures continue to rise as the forests disappear, our planet could become too warm to live on. New deserts could form all over the earth. The ice at the poles could melt. The oceans could flood the shores. Preserving the rain forests would prevent all these disasters.

Rain forests also contain valuable medicines. Many people would die from cancer and other diseases if we did not have drugs made from rain forest plants such as the rosy periwinkle flower. Scientists think they could find many more cures in the rain forest. But soon the rain forests may disappear completely. Each year the amount of rain forest that is destroyed equals the size of Pennsylvania. At this rate the forests may be completely destroyed in 100 years.

Critical thinking

Some people want to cut down the rain forests. Other people want to leave the rain forests alone. Tell why both groups could be right.

Using what you learned

Could people today learn to preserve the rain forests while they are using it, as the Mayas did? Work with classmates to think of ways to save the rain forests. What rain forest products can people collect without harming its plants?

5. The Grassland and the Desert

Words to Know
grassland
desert

Getting Started Imagine walking over a hill and seeing herds of hundreds of bison. You could have seen a sight like that if you had lived 150 years ago. The American grassland was once the home of huge herds of bison.

What is the grassland like?

The **grassland** in temperate regions is a biome that has cold winters, warm summers, and uneven precipitation. Use the table on page 126 to find the temperature range and average rainfall of this biome.

Look at the biomes map. Notice that the grassland of North America is to the west of the deciduous forest. As you go from east to west across the United States, the climate becomes drier. Where there is not enough water for trees to grow, the forest blends into grassland. There are other types of grasslands in different parts of the world.

What living things are found in the grassland?

As you might guess, grasses are the main kinds of plants in the grassland. Each year the grasses die and decay. When plants die, they return minerals to the soil. The minerals make the soil very good for growing plants.

Many insects live in the grasslands of the United States. They include ants, locusts, and grasshoppers. Grasshoppers have mouth parts that enable them to chew grass. Other insects have piercing mouth parts for sucking out the juices of the grasses.

Grasses provide a good hiding place for small animals like insects. Other animals are too large to hide in the grass. These animals have other ways in which they are protected from enemies. Some animals, such as the prairie dog in the drawing, hide in underground burrows. Prairie dogs dig so many burrows that sometimes other animals move in. Notice the owls in an old prairie dog burrow.

Prairie dog burrows ▼

Hawks, snakes, foxes, and coyotes are carnivores of the grassland. The wolf was once an important carnivore of the grassland. However, wolves are now very rare. Why do you think this is so?

How has the grassland biome changed?

Many years ago most of the grassland biome was covered with grasses and wildflowers. Now only a few places still have the native plants. Much of the grassland is now used for growing grain. Farmers plant rye, wheat, corn, oats, and beans. The grassland of the United States has been called the Nation's Breadbasket. Why do you think this name is used?

Cattle and sheep are also raised on the grasslands. In some places there has been too much grazing. When sheep graze, they can nibble the grass down to the soil surface. Often

Farmland ▼

Explore

How can you make a desert terrarium?

If you have ever been in a desert, you know that it has unusual plants. A cactus is a common desert plant. You can grow your own desert by planting some cacti in a container called a terrarium.

Materials
large jar or 2-L soda bottle · scissors · paper towels · terrarium charcoal · sand · potting soil · cactus plants

Procedure

A. Get a large jar or soda bottle. If you use a soda bottle, ask an adult to help you cut off the top. Wash and dry your container.

B. Place 0.5 cm of terrarium charcoal in the bottom of the container.

C. Mix 1 part sand and 3 parts soil together. Put a layer 3 cm thick on top of the charcoal.

D. Fold a piece of paper towel lengthwise. Wrap this around your cactus so you do not get pricked by the needles. Grasp the cactus where you have placed the paper towel and insert the roots into the soil.

E. Place a thin layer of sand around the base of each plant to cover the soil mixture.

F. Moisten the soil. Cover your terrarium and place it in a sunny place.

Writing and Sharing Results and Conclusions

1. How is this terrarium like a real desert?

2. How often do you think you should water the terrarium?

this kills the grass. Grass roots hold the soil in place. Without the roots, wind and rain blow the topsoil away. The result of this is that in some areas of the world, grassland is becoming desert. On page 120 you read about how this once happened in the grasslands of the United States.

What is the desert like?

The **desert** is a biome that receives less than 25 cm (10 inches) of rainfall each year. The average rainfall is only about 15 cm (6 inches). The rain that does fall evaporates quickly. Find the desert biome on the biomes map.

Many people think that a desert is always hot. But this is not true. During the night, deserts are often very cold. The temperature may drop by as much as 17°C (63°F) from the daytime temperature.

Deserts in the southwestern United States are called cool deserts. Cool deserts are hot during the summer. But during the winter the temperature can drop to 0°C (32°F). Sometimes it even snows in the desert.

prickly pear cactus

rattlesnake

What living things are found in the desert?

Desert plants are adapted to survive with very little water. Some desert plants can store water. The giant saguaro (suh GWAHR oh) cactus in the drawing stores much water. If you could squeeze out all the water this cactus holds, you could fill 25 bathtubs! Many desert plants, such as the creosote bush, have small, waxy leaves. How do you think this kind of leaf helps prevent the loss of water?

Desert animals also have adaptations that help prevent water loss. Snakes and lizards have dry, scaly skin. This kind of skin holds in moisture. Small desert mammals have other ways of staying cool. For example, the kangaroo rat shown survives on the water it gets from the seeds and roots it eats. The kangaroo rat burrows underground during the hot day and comes out at night to look for food. Animals that are active at night are called nocturnal animals.

Desert scene ▼

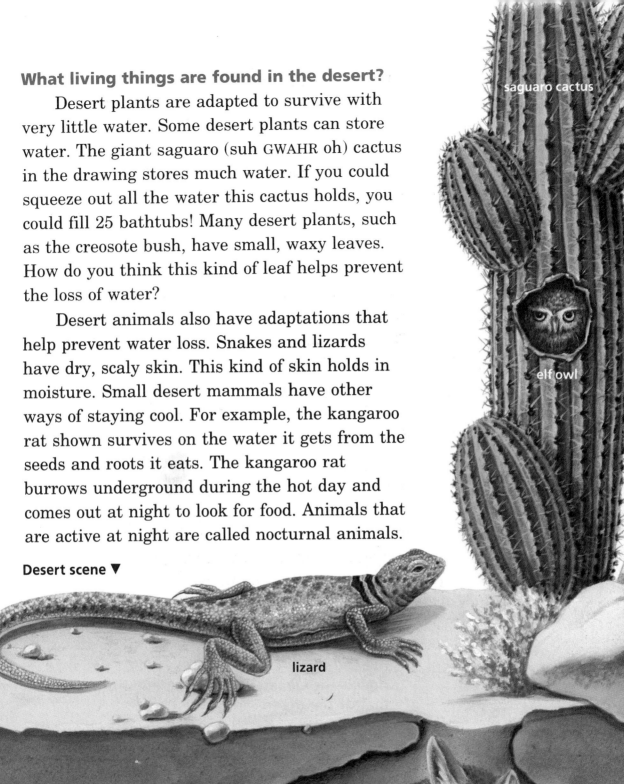

saguaro cactus

elf owl

lizard

fennec fox

kangaroo rat

149

Many of the small nocturnal animals are prey to carnivores like the sidewinder snake in the picture. This snake has an odd sideways means of moving. Notice the tracks it makes in the sand. Other desert carnivores include lizards, foxes, and owls. Why do they all hunt at night?

▼ Sidewinder snake

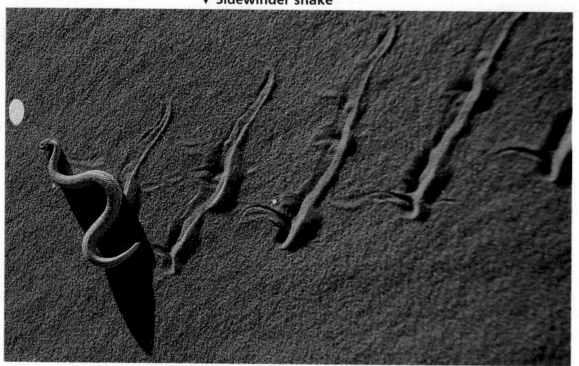

Lesson Review

1. How is the climate of the grassland different from that of the desert?

2. Choose one animal of the grassland and one animal of the desert. Describe the adaptations each has for surviving in their biome.

3. Choose one desert plant and describe how it is adapted for survival in the desert.

Think! What might happen to a grassland if the climate changed so that it received more rainfall? What if it received less rainfall?

*Read **One Day in the Desert**, page 156, to find out how some desert plants and animals survive the challenging climate.*

Chapter Connections

Draw a landscape of one of the boxes on the graphic organizer. Have a partner guess which biome you have drawn.

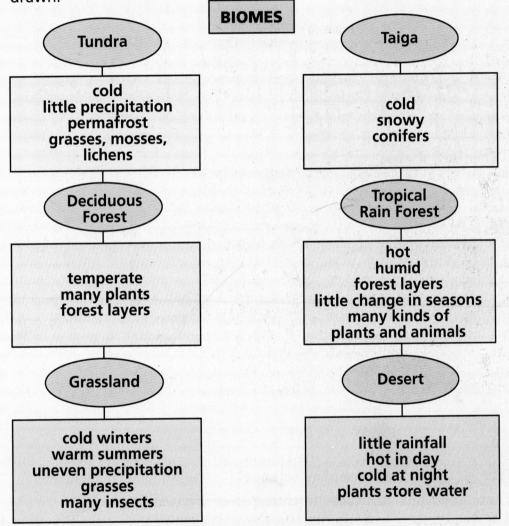

BIOMES

Tundra

cold
little precipitation
permafrost
grasses, mosses,
lichens

Taiga

cold
snowy
conifers

Deciduous Forest

temperate
many plants
forest layers

Tropical Rain Forest

hot
humid
forest layers
little change in seasons
many kinds of
plants and animals

Grassland

cold winters
warm summers
uneven precipitation
grasses
many insects

Desert

little rainfall
hot in day
cold at night
plants store water

Writing About Science • Describe

Choose one of the biomes you have studied. Design a home that would be comfortable and practical for the biome you chose. Draw a diagram of the home and write a paragraph describing it.

Science Terms

Matching

Write the letter of the biome that best matches the description.

1. Biome that is cold and has little precipitation
2. Biome that has cold winters, warm summers, and uneven precipitation
3. Biome in which many broad-leaf trees grow
4. Biome that receives less than 25 cm of rain each year
5. Biome in which main plant life is evergreen trees
6. Biome that has high temperatures and a large amount of rain

a. deciduous forest
b. desert
c. grassland
d. taiga
e. tropical rain forest
f. tundra

Fill in the Blanks

Copy the sentences below. Use the terms listed to complete the sentences.

biome   climate

1. The average weather conditions over a long time are a region's _____.
2. A _____ is a large region that has certain climate conditions and certain kinds of organisms adapted for survival in those conditions.

Science Ideas

Use complete sentences to answer the following.

1. What happens when you come to the edge of a biome?
2. Compare the winters and summers of the tundra and the taiga.
3. What is the difference between a carnivore and a herbivore?
4. Give two examples of how animals of the tundra survive the cold winters.
5. How does the precipitation in the deciduous forest compare to that of the tundra and taiga?

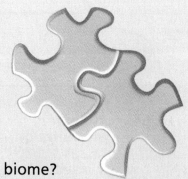

6. How are animals of the deciduous forest adapted to changes in the seasons?
7. Why do so few plants grow on the forest floor in a tropical rain forest?
8. Explain two ways animals in the grassland are protected from enemies.
9. Identify the biome that is home to each of these organisms. Letter your answers a-e.

a

b

c

d

e

Applying Science Ideas

1. What factor in the climate of a biome determines if the area will be deciduous forest, grassland, or desert?
2. Why are there great differences from season to season in the taiga and the grassland, but not in the tropical rain forests?
3. Describe how farmers clear the rain forest. How does this method of clearing trees affect the amount of carbon dioxide in the atmosphere?

Using Science Skills

Use the table on page 126 to find the temperature range of each biome. List the biomes in order by temperature range starting with the largest range.

Careers in Life Science

Forester

"As a child, I used to hike in the woods a lot with my dad," says Janet Gittlen. Janet loved the forest. She read nature magazines all the time. So when Janet went to college, she knew what she wanted to do. She wanted to be a forester.

Janet earned a college degree in forestry. Now she works in the state of Washington. She helps manage a forest for use by the public and lumber companies. A **forester** helps to balance the interests and needs of all the users of the forest.

Parts of the forest are used by visitors for recreation. Janet helps care for hiking trails that visitors use. She helps protect fishing streams from pollution. Janet has to take care of the trees, too. She removes trees with harmful diseases.

But foresters don't only think about the needs of hikers and trees. They also decide which trees are to be cut down. Private companies cut many trees in forests that belong to the government. These companies turn the wood into lumber, furniture, and paper. But if they cut all the trees, the forest would be gone. So foresters help decide how many trees can be cut. They also make sure that cut areas are replanted with young trees.

"Being a forester is never boring," Janet says. She gets to work with other foresters. She works with lumberjacks, who cut the trees. She also works with **wildlife scientists.**

Because of her job, Janet still gets to hike a lot in the forest. She hopes that her work will make it possible for others to hike there in the future.

"I would like to see forests cared for properly," Janet says. "Then they will remain a place of beauty and enjoyment for people."

Connecting Science Ideas

1. On pages 142–143 you read about the destruction of tropical rain forests. If you were a forester, what could you do to help protect the tropical rain forest?
   Chapter 4; Careers

2. Compare an ameba, a diatom, and a sponge. Describe how they are alike and different in body size and how they get food.   **Chapter 1; Chapter 2**

3. In what biome would you expect the trees to have wider annual rings — the tundra or the deciduous forest?
   Chapter 3; Chapter 4

4. In Chapter 3 you learned about the adaptations of plants. Describe some adaptations of worms.
   Chapter 3; Chapter 2

5. What are the five kingdoms of living things? Place each of the following organisms in one of the five kingdoms: jellyfish, ameba, mold, cactus, human, sponge, orchid, blue-green bacteria.   **Chapter 1; Chapter 2; Chapter 3**

6. Here is a riddle: What living thing is made of members of two different kingdoms but belongs to neither one? The answer is a lichen! Explain what two kingdoms are hinted at in the riddle.   **Chapter 4; Chapter 1**

7. Look at the picture of the sea anemone on page 67. What was the response of the sea anemone to the fish? What was the stimulus?   **Chapter 2; Chapter 3**

Computer Connections

Working in a group, use reference books to find out about a biome. Find out about the biome's climate, the types of plants and animals that live there, and the places on Earth in which the biome can be found. Be specific. Enter the information into a class database.

Have your group use the database to help them design a zoo that features plants and animals from each biome. Describe your zoo.

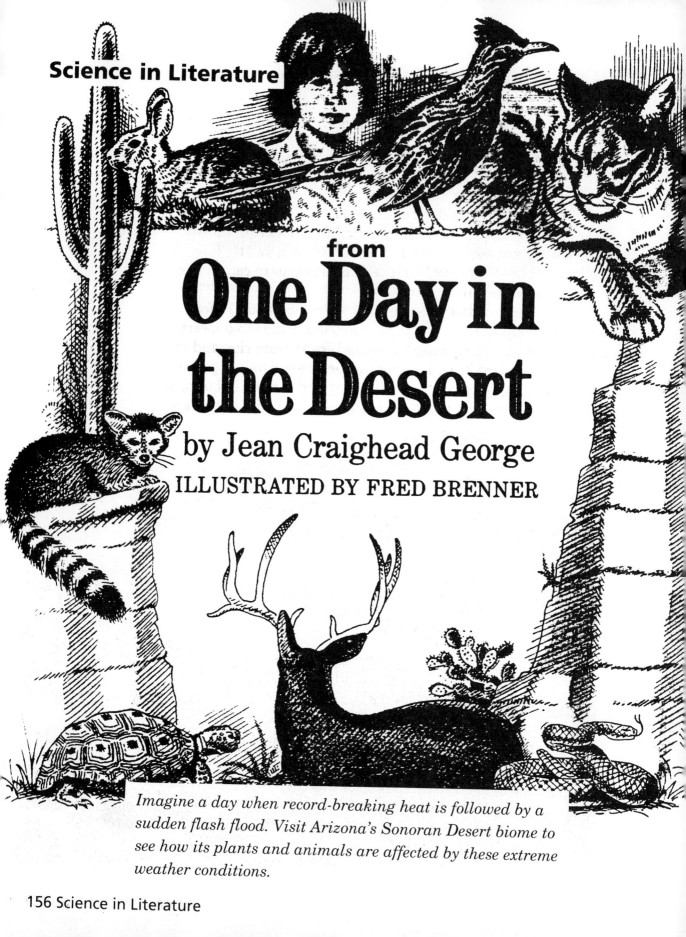

from

One Day in the Desert

by Jean Craighead George

ILLUSTRATED BY FRED BRENNER

Imagine a day when record-breaking heat is followed by a sudden flash flood. Visit Arizona's Sonoran Desert biome to see how its plants and animals are affected by these extreme weather conditions.

On July 10th the wounded mountain lion was forced to hunt in the heat of the day. He could not wait for darkness. He made his way slowly down the trail toward the Papago Indian hut.

By 9 A.M. he was above the dwelling on a mountain ledge. The temperature climbed another degree. He sought the shade of a giant saguaro cactus and lay down to rest.

The scent of lion reached the nose of a coyote who was cooling off under the dark embankment of the dry river not far from the Papago Indian hut. He lifted his head, flicked his ears nervously and got to his feet. He ran swiftly into his burrow beneath the roots of the ancient saguaro cactus that grew beside the hut.

The huge cactus was over 100 years old, stood 75 feet (22.5 meters) tall and weighed more than 6 tons (5.5 metric tons). The last of its watermelon-red fruits were ripe and on the ground. Bird Wing and her mother were going to gather them and boil them in the water they had carried in buckets from the village. The fruit makes a sweet, nourishing syrup.

At 11 A.M. they stretched out on their mats in the hut. It was much too hot to work. The temperature had reached 112°F. (44.4°C.).

The old cactus was drying up in the heat. It drew on the last of the water in the reservoir inside its trunk and shrank ever so slightly, for it could expand and contract like an accordion.

The mountain lion's tongue was swollen from lack of moisture. He got to his feet again.

A roadrunner, a ground-dwelling bird with a spiny crest and a long neck and legs, saw the lion pass his shady spot in the grass. He sped down the mountain, over the riverbank and into the dry riverbed. He stopped under the embankment where the coyote had been. There he lifted his feathers to keep cool. Bird feathers are perhaps the best protection from both heat and cold, for they form dead air space, and dead air is one of the best insulations.

The roadrunner passed a family of seven peccaries, piglike animals with coarse coats, tusks and almost no tails. They stay alive in the dry desert by eating the water-storing prickly pear cactus, spines and all. They were now lying in the cool of the paloverde trees that grow in thickets. Like the pencil-straight ocotillo and almost all the desert leafy plants, the paloverdes drop their leaves when the desert is extremely hot and dry. On July 10th they began falling faster and faster.

The scent of the lion reached the old boar. He lifted his head and watched the great beast. The lion turned away from the peccary family and limped toward the Indian hut. All the pigs, big and little, watched him.

As the lion limped across the embankment under which the roadrunner was hiding, the air around him began to fill with dust.

Near the coyote den dwelled a tarantula, a spider almost as big as a man's fist and covered with furlike hairs. She looked like a long-legged bear, and she was sitting near the top of her burrow, a shaft she had dug straight down into the ground. The hot desert air forced her to let go with all eight of her legs. She dropped to the bottom of her shaft, where the air was cooler. The spider survives the heat by digging underground and by hunting at night. The moist crickets and other insects she eats quench her thirst.

A headstand beetle felt the heat of the day and
became uncomfortable. He stopped hunting in the grass
and scurried into the entrance of the tarantula hole. He
was not afraid of the spider, with her poison fangs that kill
prey, but he was wary of her. Hearing the spider coming up
her shaft to see who was there, the headstand beetle got
ready to fend her off. He stood on his head, aimed his rear
end and mixed chemicals in his abdomen. The tarantula
rushed at him and lifted her fangs. The headstand beetle
shot a blistering-hot stream of quinonoid chemical at the
spider. She writhed and dropped to the bottom of her den.
The headstand beetle hid under a grass plant by the
tarantula's door.

The temperature rose several more degrees.

At 12:30 P.M. a desert tortoise, who was protected from the heat by two unusually thick shells of bone, went on eating the fruit of a prickly pear cactus. He was never thirsty. The moisture from the plants he ate was stored in his enormous bladder, a reservoir of pure water that desert tortoises have devised over the ages to adapt themselves to the dry heat. The water cools the reptiles on the hottest days and refreshes them on the driest.

At 1:20 P.M. the temperature reached 121°F. (49.4°C.).

This hour on July 10th was the hottest hour on record at the bottom of Mount Scorpion.

The clouds covered the sun.

Instantly, the temperature dropped four degrees.

The thunder boomed like Indian drums.

The temperature dropped five more degrees. A rattlesnake came out of the pack rat's nest and slid back to his hunting spot at the rear of the hut. The cicadas sang again. The cactus wren looked out of the entrance of her ball nest in the teddy-bear cactus.

A thunderclap exploded sharply. Bird Wing awoke. She saw the lion stretched in the doorway. She took her mother's arm and shook her gently until she awoke. Signaling her to be quiet, she pointed to the mountain lion. Bird Wing's mother parted the grass at the rear of the hut and, after pushing Bird Wing out, backed out herself

The rattlesnake buzzed a warning.

The sky darkened. Lightning danced from saguaro cactus to saguaro cactus. Bird Wing's mother looked at the clouds and the dry arroyo.

"We must get out of here," she said. "Follow me up the mountain." They scrambled over the rocks on hands and feet without looking back.

Huge raindrops splattered onto the dust. Bird Wing and her mother reached an overhanging rock on the mountain. Lightning flashed around them like white horsewhips.

The thunder cracked and boomed. Then water gushed out of the sky. The rain fell in such torrents that Bird Wing and her mother could not see the dry river, the hut or the old saguaro. They sat quietly, waiting and listening.

The rain became torrents, the torrents became waterfalls and the waterfalls cascaded out of the sky until all the moisture was wrung from the clouds. They drizzled and stopped giving rain. The storm clouds rumbled up the canyon above the dry riverbed.

The sun came out. Bird Wing and her mother did not move. They listened. The desert rocks dripped and the cacti crackled softly as they swelled with water. Cactus roots lie close to the surface, spreading out from the plants in all directions to absorb every possible drop of water. The roots send the water up into the trunks and barrels and pads to be stored.

Water came bubbling and singing down the arroyo. It filled the riverbed from bank to bank, then rose like a great cement wall, a flash flood that filled the canyon. It swept over the embankment, over the hut, over the old saguaro cactus. It rose higher, thundered into the paloverdes and roared over the rocks at the foot of the mountain. It boomed into the valley, spread out and disappeared into the dry earth.

Reader's Response

How do you think Bird Wing feels about the day's events?
How would you feel?

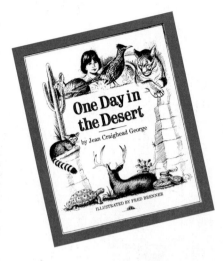

One Day in the Desert

 ## Responding to Literature

1. Choose one plant and one animal from the story and tell how each is able to adapt to the harsh desert climate.

2. Some of the plants and animals in the story have names that tell something about them. Choose a few good examples and explain what each of the names suggests.

3. Reread passages in the selection that describe the weather conditions. Tell what words and phrases help you to feel the heat of the day and the fury of the storm.

4. Pretend you are the author of this story. Add to the story by writing a brief description telling what happens to the wounded lion.

 ## Books to Enjoy

One Day in the Desert by Jean Craighead George
You might enjoy reading the rest of the book to find out what happens to Bird Wing and the lion.

Deserts by Keith Brandt
Learn more about the characteristics of deserts and the types of plants and animals that live in them by reading this book.

Storms by Seymour Simon
Find out more about storms by looking at the pictures in this book and reading about the conditions that cause different kinds of storms.

SCIENCE
HORIZONS

PHYSICAL SCIENCE

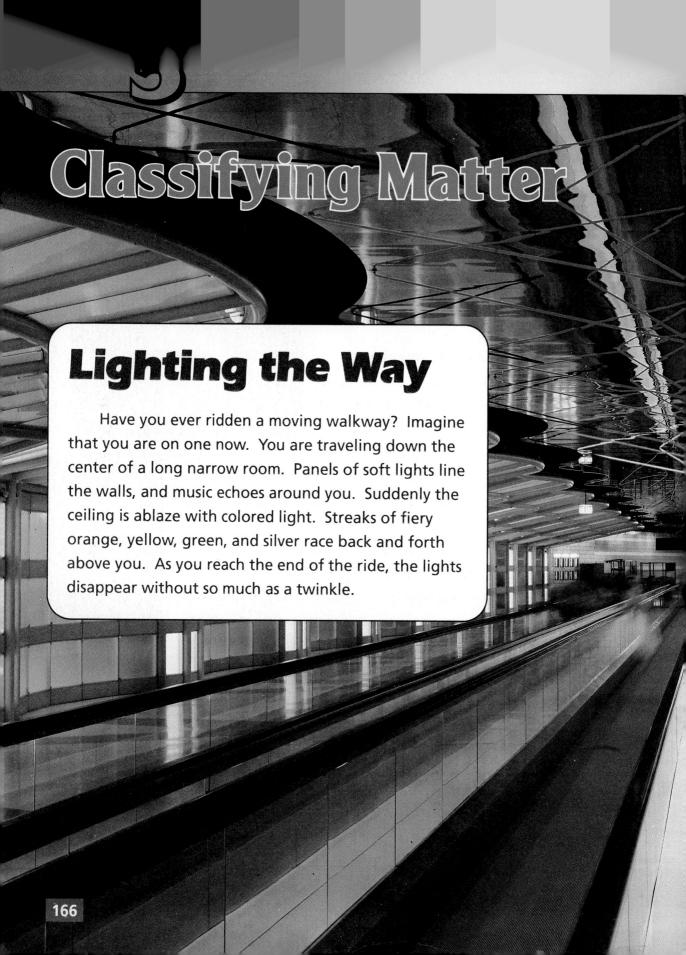

Classifying Matter

Lighting the Way

Have you ever ridden a moving walkway? Imagine that you are on one now. You are traveling down the center of a long narrow room. Panels of soft lights line the walls, and music echoes around you. Suddenly the ceiling is ablaze with colored light. Streaks of fiery orange, yellow, green, and silver race back and forth above you. As you reach the end of the ride, the lights disappear without so much as a twinkle.

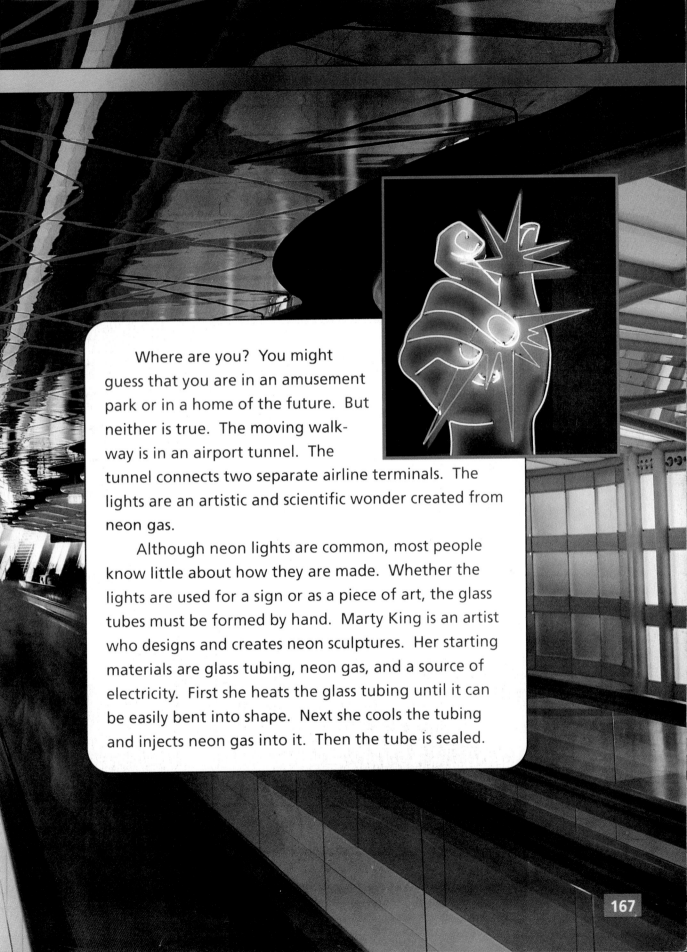

Where are you? You might guess that you are in an amusement park or in a home of the future. But neither is true. The moving walk-way is in an airport tunnel. The tunnel connects two separate airline terminals. The lights are an artistic and scientific wonder created from neon gas.

Although neon lights are common, most people know little about how they are made. Whether the lights are used for a sign or as a piece of art, the glass tubes must be formed by hand. Marty King is an artist who designs and creates neon sculptures. Her starting materials are glass tubing, neon gas, and a source of electricity. First she heats the glass tubing until it can be easily bent into shape. Next she cools the tubing and injects neon gas into it. Then the tube is sealed.

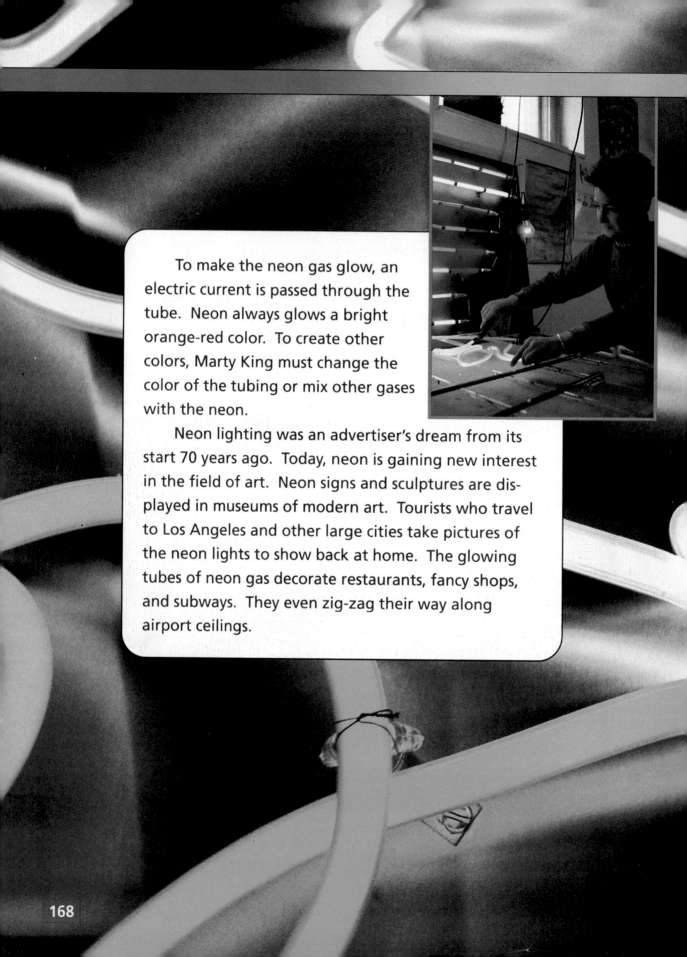

To make the neon gas glow, an electric current is passed through the tube. Neon always glows a bright orange-red color. To create other colors, Marty King must change the color of the tubing or mix other gases with the neon.

Neon lighting was an advertiser's dream from its start 70 years ago. Today, neon is gaining new interest in the field of art. Neon signs and sculptures are displayed in museums of modern art. Tourists who travel to Los Angeles and other large cities take pictures of the neon lights to show back at home. The glowing tubes of neon gas decorate restaurants, fancy shops, and subways. They even zig-zag their way along airport ceilings.

Discover

How can neon light be used to advertise a product?

Materials white construction paper · fluorescent paper · highlighter markers

Procedure

Choose a product you would like to sell, such as a video game. Devise a plan using neon signs to advertise your product. The plan should include how to advertise at the airport. Use the fluorescent paper and markers to construct one of your neon signs.

In this chapter you will learn that neon is one kind of matter. You will also learn what makes one kind of matter different from another. You will read how the different kinds of matter can be classified and grouped.

1. Many Kinds of Matter

Words to Know
matter
substance
mixture
element
compound

Getting Started Pretend that you and your desk are inside a clear plastic box. Make a list of all the different things in the box. How many things did you name? How could you classify, or group, the things on your list?

What is matter?

Have you ever heard the poem that begins, "Water, water, everywhere . . ."? A scientist might change it to read, "Matter, matter, everywhere . . ." **Matter** is anything that has mass and takes up space. It is found everywhere in the universe (YOON uh vurs).

Matter may be classified in many different ways. Some ways are more useful than other ways. Look at the picture of the garage sale. How might you classify the items in this sale? Why is it useful to classify them at all?

Garage Sale

How do scientists classify matter?

Scientists classify matter in different ways for many different reasons. Matter may be classified by its state. The common states of matter are solid, liquid, and gas.

Another way to classify matter is as a substance (SUB stuns) or as a mixture (MIHKS-chur). To a scientist, a **substance** is something made of only one kind of matter. Iron is a substance. Sugar is another substance. A **mixture** is matter that contains two or more different substances. The substances do not change their identities by being mixed.

Think of a pencil. The part that you call lead is made of graphite (GRA fyt). The "lead" of many pencils is surrounded by wood. The pencil may have a metal ring that holds a rubber eraser. Thus the pencil is a mixture.

Sometimes the materials that make up a mixture cannot be seen. That is the case with air—a mixture of gases. You cannot see the gases, but they can be separated.

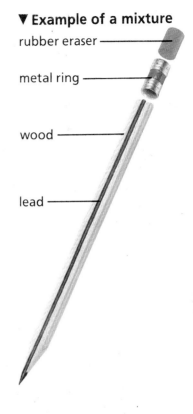

▼ Example of a mixture

rubber eraser ——————

metal ring ——————

wood ——————

lead ——————

171

▼ Some elements

zinc

copper

cadmium

How can substances be classified?

Some substances are called elements (EL uh-munts). An **element** is a substance that cannot be broken down by simple means into any other substance. Elements are the building blocks of matter. There are 109 known elements.

All other substances are called compounds (KAHM poundz). A **compound** is made when two or more elements combine to form a new substance. A compound is much different from the elements of which it is made. The baking soda in the picture is a compound. It is made of the elements sodium, hydrogen, carbon, and oxygen. Sodium is a soft, gray-white metal. One form of carbon is graphite. Hydrogen and oxygen are colorless, invisible gases. These four elements make up baking soda, a white powder.

sodium + hydrogen + carbon + oxygen → baking soda

▲ Baking soda—a compound formed from four elements

Lesson Review

1. What is matter?
2. Identify ways in which matter can be classified.
3. Describe how an element differs from a compound.

Think! Why may elements be thought of as the building blocks of matter?

Skills

Measuring and estimating volume

You can use a graduate to measure the volume of a liquid in milliliters (mL). The surface of the liquid forms a curve. Read the number at the bottom of the curve. Estimating can help you when you cannot measure. You can estimate by looking at the liquid and imagining how much of the graduate it would fill.

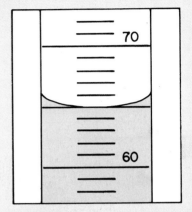

Practicing the skill

1. Put different amounts of water into each of three paper cups.

2. Estimate the volume of water in one cup by comparing with the graduate.

3. Pour the water from that cup into the graduate. Measure its volume. When you read the graduate, keep your eye level with the surface of the water. Read the mark at the bottom of the curve. Compare the measurement with your estimate.

4. Estimate and then measure the volumes of water in the other cups.

Thinking about the skill

Suppose a person's estimate is very different from the actual volume of the liquid. What could make this happen?

Applying the skill

Put some water in a paper cup. Estimate and measure the volume of the water. Without measuring, try to double the amount of water. Measure to check.

2. Properties of Elements

Words to Know
physical property
chemical property

Getting Started Choose one of the objects shown on this page. Tell as much as you can about the object by just looking at it. What can you not tell about the object by just looking at it? What do you think the object is?

A

B

C

D

E

How can properties be classified?

When you describe an object, you may state its color, size, shape, and other facts. These traits are called properties of the object. Elements and compounds have properties, too.

Properties can be classified as physical or chemical properties. A **physical property** is a trait that can be observed or measured without changing the identity of the substance. Color is a physical property. You can tell the color of a substance by just looking at it. Chemical properties are sometimes harder to describe than are physical properties. A **chemical property** describes how one substance reacts with another substance.

What are some physical properties?

Most physical properties can be measured, but many may simply be observed with your senses. You can tell much about a substance by just looking at it. First, you can tell if you can see it. Some substances, like oxygen, are invisible. Most gases are invisible.

Usually you can observe the color of a substance. You can also tell something about its size and shape. Based only on what you see, describe each substance in the picture. How are your two descriptions alike? How are they different? Without knowing what the substances are, can you tell the difference between them?

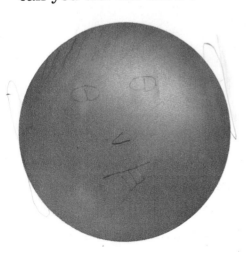 

▲ Metal objects with luster

Luster is another physical property. Luster is the shiny appearance of some substances. Most metals have luster. You can see the luster of the metal objects in the picture. What other physical properties can you see?

Many physical properties can be measured with instruments. Mass is one of those properties. Mass is a measure of the amount of matter in an object. You can tell that a golf ball has more mass than a table-tennis ball by holding them. But to find the exact mass of each ball, it must be measured with a balance.

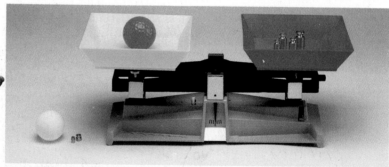

▲ Estimating mass; measuring mass (right)

Density is a property that is related to mass. Density is the measure of the mass of a certain volume of a substance. Suppose that two substances have the same mass but that one takes up more space. The one that takes up more space has the lower density.

Explore

How can you measure the density of an irregularly shaped object?

"**G**old! I've found gold!" cried the prospector as he picked up a large nugget. But is it really gold? Or is it another metal that only looks like gold? To find out, he measured the density of the nugget. He knew that the density of gold is 19.3 g/mL.

Materials
balance · metric masses · metal bolt · graduate · water · string

Procedure
A. Using the balance and metric masses, measure and record the mass of the metal bolt.
   1. In what unit did you measure mass?

B. Fill the graduate with water to the 30-mL mark.

C. Lower the bolt into the graduate. Be careful not to splash out any water.
   2. What is the volume of the water and the bolt together?
   3. By how many mL did the bolt increase the volume?
   4. What is the volume of the bolt alone?

D. Find the density of the bolt by dividing its mass by its volume.

E. Plan a way to measure the density of a wooden clothespin. Use any additional materials you need. Then try your plan.

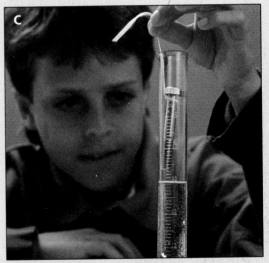

Writing and Sharing Results and Conclusions
1. In what units should you state the density you measured?

2. What is the bolt's density?

3. Is the bolt's density greater than or less than the density of water? How do you know?

4. In step E, what did you have to do differently than before?

The ability of a substance to transfer heat or electricity is a property called conductivity (kahn duk TIHV uh tee). Not all substances conduct heat or electricity equally well. Conductivity can also be measured.

Some elements and a few of their physical properties are shown in the table. Which properties can be observed with the senses? Which must be measured?

Properties of Some Elements					
Substance	State	Density (g/cm³)	Color	Melting Point (°C)	Boiling Point (°C)
aluminum	solid	2.7	silver-white	660.2	2,467.0
calcium	solid	1.5	silver-white	842.8	1,487.0
bromine	liquid	2.9	reddish-brown	−7.2	58.8
iodine	solid	4.9	black-violet	113.5	184.4
mercury	liquid	13.6	silver-white	−38.9	356.6
sulfur	solid	2.1	yellow	112.8	444.6
lead	solid	11.3	gray	327.4	1,755.0

What are some chemical properties?

Often there are basic changes in matter. For example, a cake is made from sugar, flour, and other materials. You can tell the physical properties of these materials. But once the cake is baked, there is no way to change it back to the materials of which it is made. The same is true of an egg. Once it is cooked, there is no way to change it back to a raw egg.

When matter changes in this way, it changes chemically. Its properties change, and a new kind of matter is formed. Remember, chemical properties tell how a substance reacts with

*When Lee helps Mrs. Crimmons plant a garden, he learns about more than vegetables. You can find out, too, when you read **Digging in the Dirt** in Horizons Plus.*

▲ Aerial rocket (inset) exploding

another substance. The changes are caused by a chemical reaction. A chemical reaction is a process by which two or more substances combine to form one or more new substances. Some substances react quickly; others react slowly. The rate at which a substance reacts is a property called reactivity (ree ak TIVH uh tee). How would you describe the reactivity of the chemical changes shown in the pictures?

▲ Another kind of chemical change

Lesson Review

1. Define the term *property*.
2. How do physical properties differ from chemical properties?
3. Why are some physical properties measured?

Think! Predict which properties of water will change when the water becomes ice. Identify each property as physical or chemical.

3. Organizing Elements

Getting Started Think about how a calendar is organized. In some ways it is organized in the same way scientists organize matter. A calendar shows the order of the days and dates in a month. Why is Monday always between Sunday and Tuesday? How is one Monday like every other Monday? How is each Monday different?

Words to Know
metals
nonmetals
semimetals
noble gases

How have people tried to group elements?

Some early scientists thought there were four basic kinds of matter—fire, earth, air, and water. When elements were discovered, scientists gave up this idea. By the mid-1700s, about 23 of the elements known today had been identified.

Aristotle and symbols for matter ▼

water earth fire air

arsenic tin gold platinum

mercury sulfur iron lead

180

As scientists began to study elements, they found that some elements were much like others. Elements with similar properties were grouped together. Mendeleev (men duh LAY uf), a Russian scientist, searched for a way to arrange the elements in an orderly manner. He gathered all that was known about the properties of each element. Then he arranged the elements in order of the weights of their atoms. He saw a pattern developing. The properties of the elements began to repeat.

			Ti = 50	Zr = 90	? = 180.
			V = 51	Nb = 94	Ta = 182.
			Cr = 52	Mo = 96	W = 186.
			Mu = 55	Rh = 104,4	Pt = 197,4
			Fe = 56	Ru = 104,4	Ir = 198.
			Ni = Co = 59	Pl = 1066,	Os = 199.
H = 1			Cu = 63,4	Ag = 108	Hg = 200.
	Be = 9,4	Mg = 24	Zn = 65,2	Cd = 112	
	B = 11	Al = 27,4	? = 68	Ur = 116	Au = 197?
	C = 12	Si = 28	? = 70	Sn = 118	
	N = 14	P = 31	As = 75	Sb = 122	Bi = 210
	O = 16	S = 32	Se = 79,4	Te = 128?	
	F = 19	Cl = 35,5	Br = 80	I = 127	
Li = 7	Na = 23	K = 39	Rb = 85,4	Cs = 138	Tl = 204
		Ca = 40	Sr = 87,6	Ba = 137	Pb = 207.
		? = 45	Ce = 92		
		?Er = 56	La = 94		
		?Yt = 60	Di = 95		
		?In = 75,6	Th = 118?		

▲ Mendeleev and early Periodic Table

Using the pattern of repeating properties, Mendeleev placed the elements in a table of rows and columns similar to how a calendar is organized. This resulted in some blank spaces in the table. By noting where the spaces were, Mendeleev predicted the properties of elements not yet discovered. After his death the table was completed. Today it is called the Periodic Table of Elements.

Periodic Table of Elements

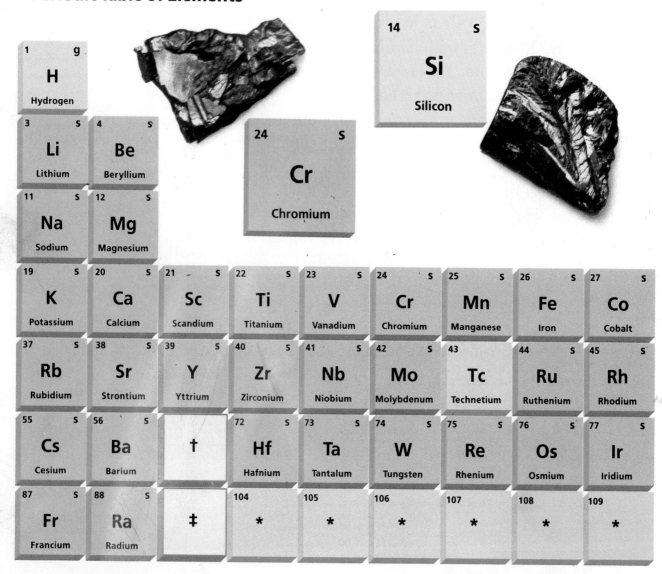

1 g **H** Hydrogen									
3 s **Li** Lithium	**4** s **Be** Beryllium								
11 s **Na** Sodium	**12** s **Mg** Magnesium								
19 s **K** Potassium	**20** s **Ca** Calcium	**21** s **Sc** Scandium	**22** s **Ti** Titanium	**23** s **V** Vanadium	**24** s **Cr** Chromium	**25** s **Mn** Manganese	**26** s **Fe** Iron	**27** s **Co** Cobalt
37 s **Rb** Rubidium	**38** s **Sr** Strontium	**39** s **Y** Yttrium	**40** s **Zr** Zirconium	**41** s **Nb** Niobium	**42** s **Mo** Molybdenum	**43** **Tc** Technetium	**44** s **Ru** Ruthenium	**45** s **Rh** Rhodium
55 s **Cs** Cesium	**56** s **Ba** Barium	†	**72** s **Hf** Hafnium	**73** s **Ta** Tantalum	**74** s **W** Tungsten	**75** s **Re** Rhenium	**76** s **Os** Osmium	**77** s **Ir** Iridium
87 s **Fr** Francium	**88** s **Ra** Radium	‡	**104** *	**105** *	**106** *	**107** *	**108** *	**109** *

These elements are metals.

These elements are semimetals.

These elements are noble gases.

These elements are nonmetals.

These elements do not occur in nature, and have been produced in laboratories.

†Elements 57 through 71 are not shown.
‡Elements 89 through 103 are not shown.
*No names have been given to these elements.

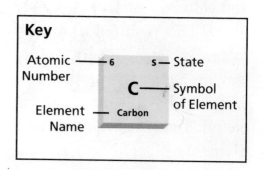

Key

Atomic Number — 6   s — State

C — Symbol of Element

Element Name — Carbon

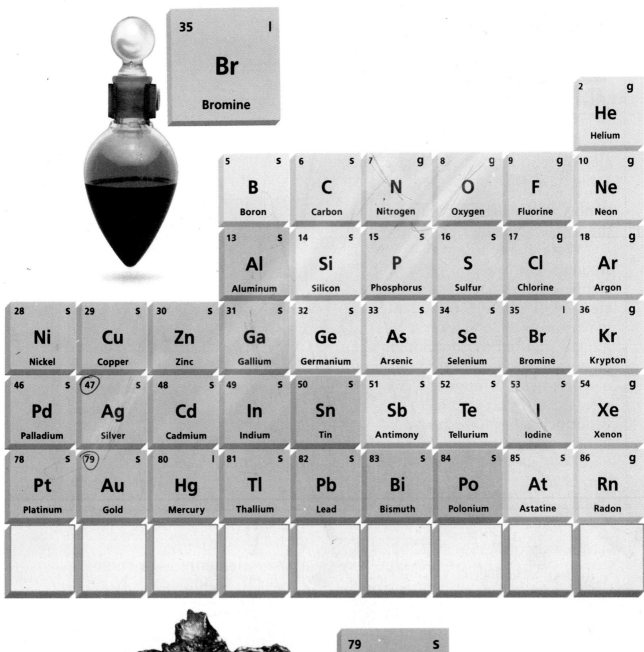

35	I
Br	
Bromine	

2	g
He	
Helium	

5	S
B	
Boron	

6	S
C	
Carbon	

7	g
N	
Nitrogen	

8	g
O	
Oxygen	

9	g
F	
Fluorine	

10	g
Ne	
Neon	

13	S
Al	
Aluminum	

14	S
Si	
Silicon	

15	S
P	
Phosphorus	

16	S
S	
Sulfur	

17	g
Cl	
Chlorine	

18	g
Ar	
Argon	

28	S
Ni	
Nickel	

29	S
Cu	
Copper	

30	S
Zn	
Zinc	

31	S
Ga	
Gallium	

32	S
Ge	
Germanium	

33	S
As	
Arsenic	

34	S
Se	
Selenium	

35	I
Br	
Bromine	

36	g
Kr	
Krypton	

46	S
Pd	
Palladium	

47	S
Ag	
Silver	

48	S
Cd	
Cadmium	

49	S
In	
Indium	

50	S
Sn	
Tin	

51	S
Sb	
Antimony	

52	S
Te	
Tellurium	

53	S
I	
Iodine	

54	g
Xe	
Xenon	

78	S
Pt	
Platinum	

79	S
Au	
Gold	

80	I
Hg	
Mercury	

81	S
Tl	
Thallium	

82	S
Pb	
Lead	

83	S
Bi	
Bismuth	

84	S
Po	
Polonium	

85	S
At	
Astatine	

86	g
Rn	
Radon	

50	S
Sn	
Tin	

79	S
Au	
Gold	

Problem Solving

Lay Your Cards on the Table

Imagine that you are Mendeleev, trying to classify elements. So far only the first 25 elements in the Periodic Table have been discovered.

In how many different ways can the 25 elements be classified?

Work in a group of five students. Each student picks five elements to research. For each element, find out its color, state, symbol, density, and atomic number. Write this information on a card, using one card for each element. Arrange the 25 element cards according to various classification schemes.

In how many ways can you classify these elements? Why is it harder to classify the elements if a classification scheme uses two or more traits?

▲ Silver—a metal

How can elements be classified?

One way to classify elements is by their state. Look at the Periodic Table, on pages 182–183. The state of each element is shown by a small letter *s, l,* or *g.* This letter is located in the upper right corner of each box. Most of the elements are solids at room temperature. Only two elements, mercury and bromine, are liquids.

Each element can also be classified as a metal, a nonmetal, a semimetal, or a noble (NOH-bul) gas. Metals are the largest group. About three fourths of the elements are metals. **Metals** are elements that are shiny and can be rolled or pounded into various shapes. Metals have high densities and are good conductors of heat and electricity. Iron, silver, and copper are metals.

Nonmetals are elements that have no shine and cannot be shaped. They are poor conductors of heat and electricity. Some nonmetals are sulfur, chlorine (KLOR een), carbon, and oxygen.

▲ Sulfur—a nonmetal

The **semimetals** are elements that have some properties of both metals and nonmetals. Arsenic, boron, and silicon are semimetals.

A fourth group of elements is the noble gases. **Noble gases** are gases that do not react readily with other elements. Noble gases used to be called inert gases. The term *inert* means "not active." Some noble gases are helium, neon, krypton (KRIHP tahn), and xenon (ZEE nahn). As you read in the beginning of the chapter, neon is used in signs like this one.

▲ Arsenic—a semimetal

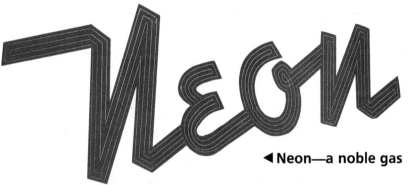

◄ Neon—a noble gas

Lesson Review

1. In what ways are elements arranged in the Periodic Table?
2. How are metals, nonmetals, and semimetals different from each other?
3. What is a property of noble gases?

Think! Find the element *radon* (Rn) in the Periodic Table. From its location in the Periodic Table, predict radon's properties.

Earth Science
CONNECTION

What is a mineral? Use a reference book to find examples of minerals. Look at the periodic table. What minerals can you find in the table?

4. How Elements Differ

Getting Started The car in the picture is being built from a kit. If the pieces are put together correctly, this car will look like the real car. How will this car be different from the real car? What can you tell about the real car from a copy of it?

How are atoms studied?

Elements may be thought of as the building blocks of matter. But what are elements made of? All matter is made of tiny particles called atoms (AT umz). An **atom** is the smallest particle of an element that has the chemical properties of the element.

No one has ever seen an atom. What scientists think an atom is like has come from indirect evidence. Indirect evidence cannot be observed or measured directly. But it can be used to build models. A **model** is a way to describe how something looks or acts. It is also a way to think about something. When the car in the picture is finished, it will be a model of the real car.

Scientists use models to make predictions. If the predictions are found to be true always, the model is probably correct. The model may become part of a theory (THEE uh ree). A theory is an explanation of a natural process or event. Over time, a theory may change or be replaced by a new theory.

What is an atom like?

According to atomic theory, an atom has a dense central core, called a **nucleus** (NOO klee-us). Two kinds of particles—protons (PROH tahnz) and neutrons (NOO trahnz) may be found in the nucleus. A **proton** is a particle with a positive electric charge. A **neutron** is a particle that has no electric charge. Traveling around the nucleus are one or more electrons (ee LEK trahnz). An **electron** is a particle with a negative electric charge.

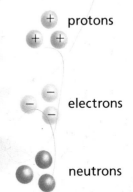

▲ Organization of particles in an element

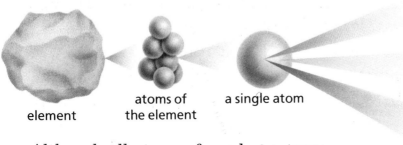

element   atoms of   a single atom
             the element

Although all atoms of an element are similar, the atoms of each element differ from those of every other element. They differ mainly in the number of protons they have. Turn to the Periodic Table, on pages 182–183. Notice that the elements are numbered from 1 to 109. These numbers are the atomic numbers of the elements. The **atomic number** is the number of protons in one atom of an element. The number

Explore Together

How can you build a model from indirect evidence?

Organizer

Materials

numbered lump of modeling clay · 15 toothpicks

Procedure

Recorder

A. Write down the number of your lump of clay.

Manager

B. Explain that a small object is hidden in the clay. Follow the procedure in steps **C** and **D** to discover as much as you can about the object. Do not break the clay open or squeeze it out of shape.

Investigator

C. Observe what happens as you carefully push a toothpick into the clay. If you wish, you may leave the toothpick in the clay. This may be helpful in making further observations.

Group, Recorder

1. What did you observe?

2. From this observation, what can you say about the object hidden in the clay?

Investigator, Group, Recorder

D. Repeat step **C** as often as you like. Each time, use a new toothpick. Stop when you think that you can describe a model of what is hidden in the clay.

Writing and Sharing Results and Conclusions

Group, Recorder

1. Describe your model of the object hidden in the clay.

2. Explain how your observations led to this description of the object.

3. How did you use indirect evidence to build this model?

Reporter

4. How successful were your classmates in building a model from indirect evidence?

of electrons in an atom equals the number of protons. Since the atomic number is the number of protons, it also tells the number of electrons.

Think of the element oxygen. The atomic number of oxygen is 8. This means there are 8 protons in the nucleus of an oxygen atom. It also means there are 8 electrons orbiting the nucleus. How many electrons does a carbon atom have? How many does a sulfur atom have?

Two models of atoms are shown here. In the past, atomic models pictured electrons as small particles moving in orbits around the nucleus. Today, however, the model that most scientists use is the electron cloud model. In this model, electrons have no definite locations at any instant in time. Electrons are pictured as existing in clouds, or energy levels, around the nucleus.

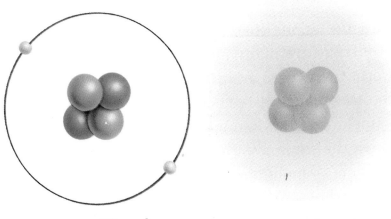

◀ Orbital model of an atom (left); electron cloud model of an atom (right)

Lesson Review

1. Define the term *atom*.
2. Describe the structure of an atom.
3. What is the main difference between an atom of one element and an atom of another element?

Think! Explain why a theory may change or be replaced by a new theory.

A

B

5. Combining Atoms

Words to Know
chemical bond
molecule
chemical symbol
formula

Getting Started Write the letters *a, e, o, r,* and *t* in a row. Use only these letters to make as many words as you can in 2 minutes. You may use a letter more than once in a word. How many words did you make? Suppose the letters represented elements. What would the words represent?

C

How do atoms form new substances?

There are many more kinds of matter in the world than there are different elements. How can this be? Think of how you combined letters to make words when you started this section. In much the same way, atoms of elements can combine to make many different compounds.

Earlier you learned that a compound is made when two or more elements combine to form a new substance. Compounds that exist in nature include minerals such as those in the pictures, water, carbon dioxide, and methane (METH ayn). Other compounds have been made by scientists. Such compounds include plastics and fibers like nylon, shown on the next page.

▲ Minerals:
(A) sapphire
(B) turquoise
(C) emerald

When elements combine, their atoms are held together by chemical bonds. A **chemical bond** is a force that holds two atoms together. There are different types of chemical bonds. Each type of bond holds atoms together in a certain way. A group of atoms held together by one type of chemical bond is called a **molecule** (MAHL ih kyool). A molecule is made up of two or more atoms.

Nylon objects (left); plastic objects (right) ▼

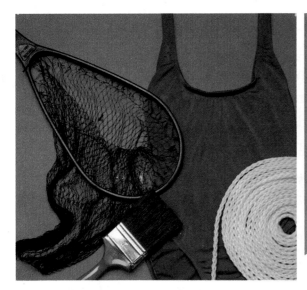

Look at the drawings of molecules. Some of the molecules are compounds. Water, for example, is formed from atoms of hydrogen and oxygen. How many kinds of atoms are in a molecule of methane? Not all molecules are

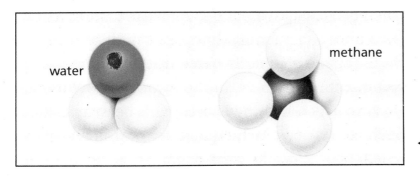

water

methane

◄ Molecules of compounds

191

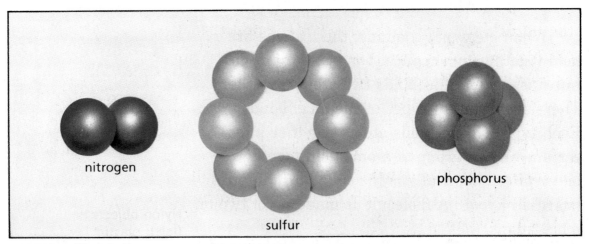

nitrogen

sulfur

phosphorus

▲ **Molecules of elements**

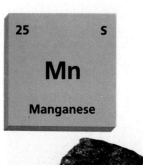

25   S

Mn

Manganese

74   S

W

Tungsten

made up of atoms of different elements. Some molecules are made up of two or more atoms of the same element. Look at the nitrogen molecule. It is formed by two atoms of nitrogen. What kinds of atoms are in the sulfur molecule? How many atoms make up the phosphorus molecule?

What are chemical symbols?

It takes much time and space to write the full names of elements and compounds. To make the job easier, scientists use a kind of shorthand. In it, each element has its own symbol. A **chemical symbol** is one or two letters that stand for the name of an element. Using a symbol to stand for an element is something like using initials to stand for your name.

Look at the pictures of elements and their symbols. Each symbol begins with a capital letter. In some cases, that letter is the first letter of the element's name. For example, the symbol for carbon is C. The symbol for hydrogen is H. Oxygen has the symbol O. The symbol for calcium has two letters. The letter a is added to the letter C to make the symbol Ca. For helium, the letter *e* is added to the letter *H* to make the symbol He. Why could the letter *H* not be used as the symbol for both hydrogen and helium?

What is a formula?

Chemical symbols are also used to write formulas (FOR myoo luhz). A **formula** is a group of symbols that shows how many atoms of each element are in a molecule of a compound.

You know that baking soda is a compound. Its chemical name is sodium bicarbonate (bye-KAHR bun ayt). Its formula is $NaHCO_3$. Compare its name with its formula. How many letters does each have? Which is quicker and easier to write, the name or the formula? Which tells you the kinds of atoms in baking soda?

The compound in the picture is used to make the products shown. What elements combine to form the compound?

▼ **Potassium dichromate**

$K_2Cr_2O_7$

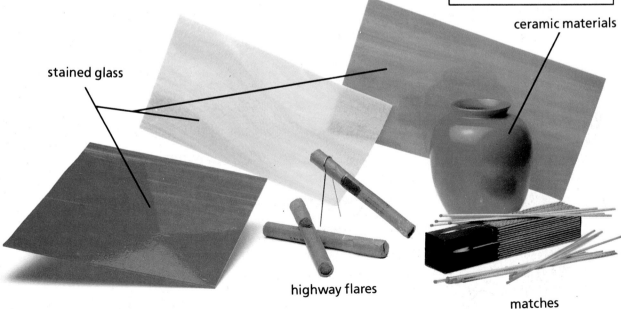

ceramic materials

stained glass

highway flares

matches

In many formulas there is a number after certain symbols. For example, the number 3 appears after the symbol O in $NaHCO_3$. A certain cleaning agent has the formula CCl_4. There is a 2 in H_2O, the formula for water. These numbers are always written a little below the line. They tell the number of atoms of a particular element in a molecule of the compound. If there is no number after a symbol, there is only one atom of that element in the molecule. The table lists some compounds and their formulas. How many kinds of atoms are in each compound? Use a calculator to find the total number of atoms in each molecule of the compound.

Common Compounds and Their Formulas			
Name of Compound	Formula	Number of Different Kinds of Atoms	Total Number of Atoms in Molecule
baking soda	$NaHCO_3$	4	6
water	H_2O	2	3
limestone	$CaCO_3$		
sugar	$C_{12}H_{22}O_{11}$		
sulfuric acid	H_2SO_4		
carbon dioxide	CO_2		
acetic acid	CH_3COOH		

Life Science
CONNECTION

One important group of compounds are called organic compounds. What are organic compounds? How are they important to all living things?

Lesson Review

1. What is a molecule?

2. Explain why each of the following is *not* a chemical symbol: (1) b, (2) cN, (3) Ref.

3. What can you learn about a substance from its formula?

Think! Imagine that Q, X, Y, and Z are elements. Show how you would write the formula for the compound XQZY. The molecule contains 14 atoms of X, 3 atoms of Q, 1 atom of Z, and 6 atoms of Y.

Chapter Connections

Add more information to the graphic organizer. Redraw it if you need to.

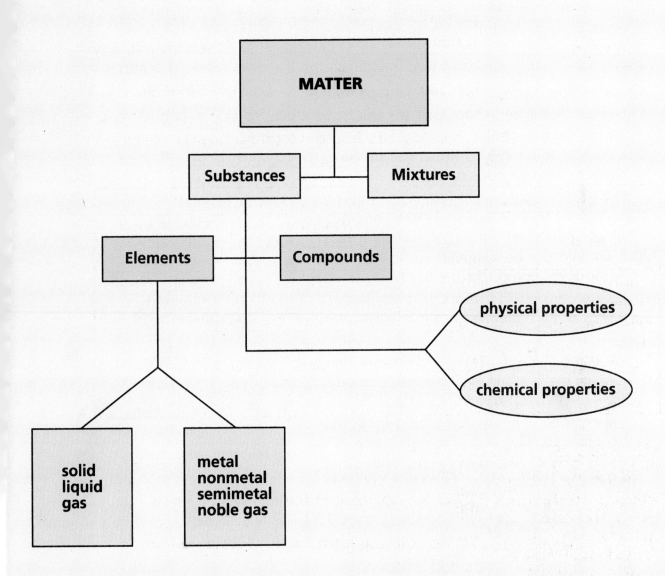

Writing About Science • Inform

Find out all you can about alchemy. Write a paragraph about it and share your paragraph with the class.

Science Terms

A. Write the letter of the term that best matches the definition.

1. Two or more elements combined chemically
2. Have properties of both metals and nonmetals
3. Number of protons in one atom of an element
4. Something made of only one kind of matter
5. One or two letters that stand for the name of an element
6. Elements that have no shine, cannot be shaped, and are poor conductors of heat and electricity
7. Substance that cannot be broken down by simple means into any other substance
8. Trait that can be observed and measured without changing the identity of a material
9. Group of symbols that shows how many atoms of each element are in a molecule of a compound
10. Anything that has mass and takes up space
11. Two or more atoms held together by one type of chemical bond
12. Way to describe how something looks or acts or a way to think about something
13. Gases that do not react readily with other elements
14. Describes how one substance reacts with another substance
15. Elements that are shiny, have high densities, and are good conductors of heat and electricity
16. Matter that contains two or more substances that do not change their identities
17. A force that holds two atoms together

a. atomic number
b. chemical bond
c. chemical property
d. chemical symbol
e. compound
f. element
g. formula
h. matter
i. metals
j. mixture
k. model
l. molecule
m. noble gases
n. nonmetals
o. physical property
p. semimetals
q. substance

B. Write a paragraph that uses each of the science terms listed below. The sentences must show that you understand the meaning of the science terms.

atom   electron   neutron   nucleus   proton

Science Ideas

Use complete sentences to answer the following.

1. How does a mixture differ from a substance?
2. Why are both an element and a compound classified as substances?
3. Name the three states of matter. Identify each state as being a physical property or a chemical property.
4. Why do the chemical properties of a substance change when the substance reacts chemically with another substance?
5. Into what groups are the elements classified in the Periodic Table?
6. What are elements made of?
7. Name the particles that make up an atom, and describe the charge each one has.
8. What does its atomic number tell you about an atom?
9. How many atoms are needed to form a molecule?
10. What does a chemical symbol stand for?

Applying Science Ideas

Design a classification scheme for the objects shown. Use only the traits *color* and *notched*. Into how many groups can the objects be classified?

Using Science Skills

Put some water in a small paper cup. Measure the volume. Pour that water into a larger cup. Estimate how much more water the larger cup could hold.

Chapter 6

Changes in Matter

The "Write" Paper

Have you ever cut a picture out of a newspaper? You probably cut one out to show to friends and then to save. You may even have pinned it up on a bulletin board. After a few months you may have noticed that your picture had turned yellow and the paper was cracked. What happened to the picture?

Nothing happened to the picture. But something did happen to the paper it was printed on. Most paper is made from a wood-fiber mash called pulp. Most paper also contains acid. Over time the acid in the paper begins to break down the pulp. The paper turns yellow and cracks. Harmful rays from the sun, moisture in the air, and temperature changes also cause paper to break down.

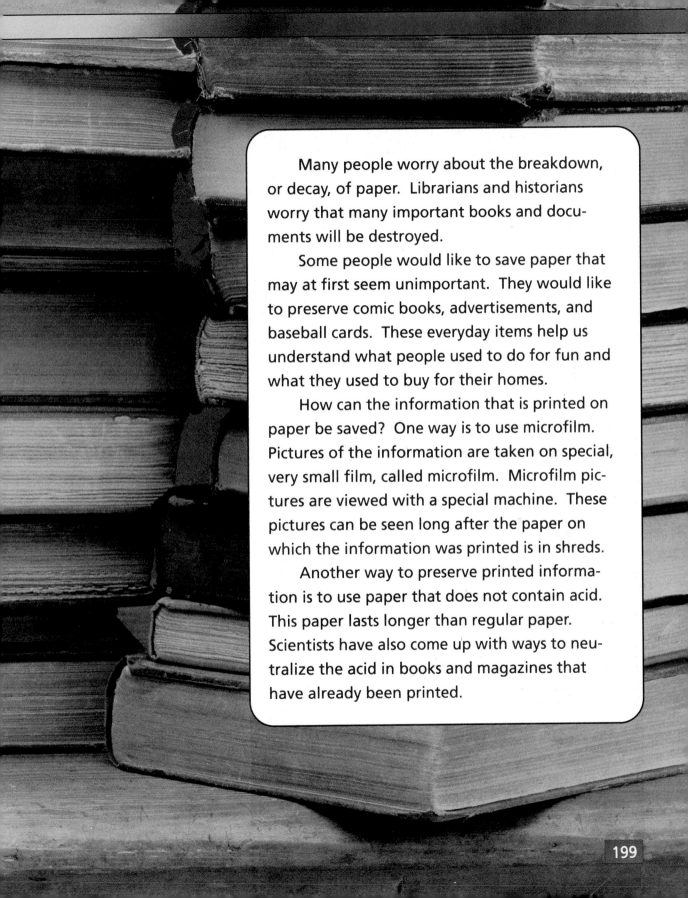

Many people worry about the breakdown, or decay, of paper. Librarians and historians worry that many important books and documents will be destroyed.

Some people would like to save paper that may at first seem unimportant. They would like to preserve comic books, advertisements, and baseball cards. These everyday items help us understand what people used to do for fun and what they used to buy for their homes.

How can the information that is printed on paper be saved? One way is to use microfilm. Pictures of the information are taken on special, very small film, called microfilm. Microfilm pictures are viewed with a special machine. These pictures can be seen long after the paper on which the information was printed is in shreds.

Another way to preserve printed information is to use paper that does not contain acid. This paper lasts longer than regular paper. Scientists have also come up with ways to neutralize the acid in books and magazines that have already been printed.

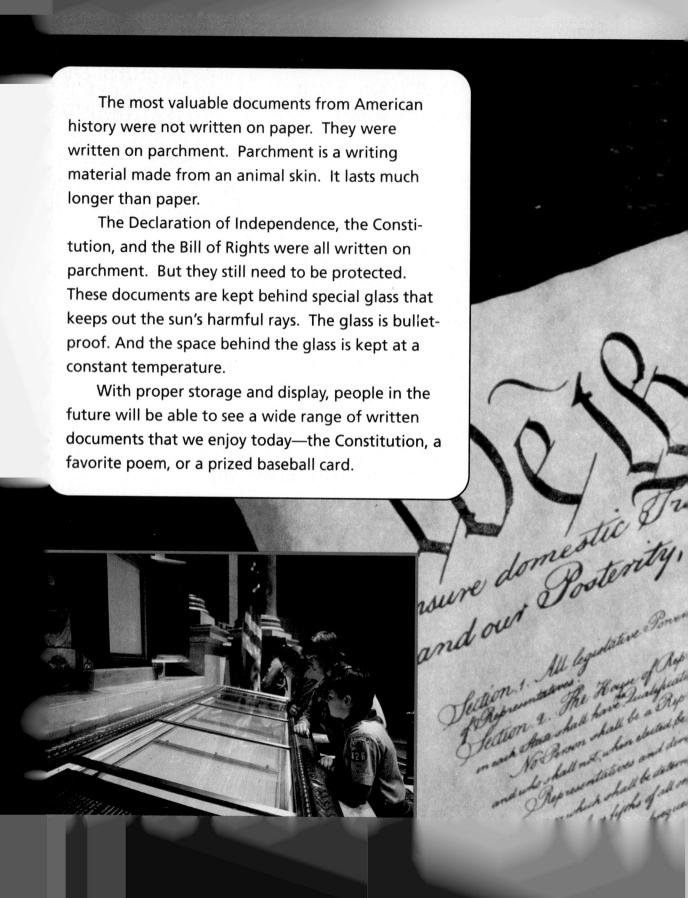

The most valuable documents from American history were not written on paper. They were written on parchment. Parchment is a writing material made from an animal skin. It lasts much longer than paper.

The Declaration of Independence, the Constitution, and the Bill of Rights were all written on parchment. But they still need to be protected. These documents are kept behind special glass that keeps out the sun's harmful rays. The glass is bullet-proof. And the space behind the glass is kept at a constant temperature.

With proper storage and display, people in the future will be able to see a wide range of written documents that we enjoy today—the Constitution, a favorite poem, or a prized baseball card.

Discover

How do different kinds of paper compare?

ACTIVITY

Materials hand lens or microviewer · paper samples

Procedure

Different kinds of paper are made up of different kinds of fibers. To find out more about the structure of paper, you will need a hand lens or microviewer and several different kinds of paper. Look at samples such as tissue paper, newsprint, construction paper, and writing paper.

With the magnifier, study the surface of each piece of paper. Some may be smooth. Others may be rough. Note the different thicknesses and colors. Notice if some papers are stronger than others. Tear some of the papers. Study how the fibers show up along the torn edge. What observations did you make about the structure of paper? Why are different types of paper used for different things?

In this chapter you will learn more about the elements that make up the things around you. You will also read about the properties that make things act and change the way they do.

201

1. Physical Changes

Getting Started   Look what happens when you rub chalk on a sheet of paper. How did the chalk change? How did the paper change?

What is a physical change?

Matter can change in different ways. For example, when you pour cold syrup, the syrup flows more slowly than when it is warm. A bar of soap gets smaller each time you use it. How does a rubber band change when you stretch it? What happens when you no longer stretch the rubber band? Which of these changes is similar to the way the chalk changed?

All of these changes are physical changes. A **physical change** is a change in the size, shape, or state of matter. After a physical change the matter is still the same kind of matter. For this reason, some physical changes can easily be reversed. Which of the physical changes mentioned above could easily be reversed?

How is heat related to physical change?

In the last chapter you learned about the particles that make up matter. Particles of matter are always in motion. They vibrate (VYE brayt), or move back and forth.

Heat affects the way particles of matter move. Heat is a form of energy. When matter gains heat, the particles of matter move faster. What do you think happens when matter loses heat? If heat is gained or lost by matter, the state of the matter may change. For example, when enough heat is lost by a liquid, the liquid becomes a solid. The liquid freezes. The temperature at which this happens is called the freezing point of the liquid.

Similarly, when a liquid gains enough heat, the liquid changes to a gas. The temperature at which this happens is called the boiling point of the liquid. The freezing point and the boiling point for some common liquids are shown in the table. For which two liquids are those temperatures the farthest apart?

Particle motion ▼

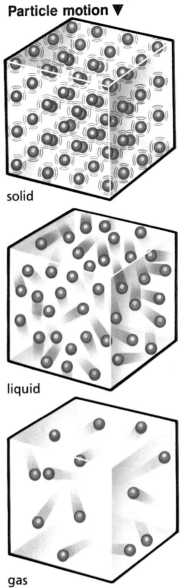

solid

liquid

gas

Freezing and Boiling Points of Some Common Liquids		
Liquid	Freezing Point (°C)	Boiling Point (°C)
Acetic acid	16.6	117.9
Acetone	−95.4	56.2
Benzene	5.6	80.1
Ethyl alcohol	−117.3	78.5
Mercury	−38.9	356.6
Water	0.0	100.0

**Expansion joint
(A) summer;
(B) winter** ▼

A

B

How do heat and cold change matter?

Most common materials expand (ek SPAND) when heated. To expand means to get larger. These materials also contract (kun TRAKT), or get smaller, when cooled. Expansion and contraction are physical changes that take place in the same state of matter.

What happens when matter expands or contracts? As matter gains heat, the particles of matter move more rapidly. They also move farther apart, so the matter takes up more space. Just the opposite happens when matter contracts. As heat is lost, the particles of matter move more slowly. They also move closer together, so the matter takes up less space.

Some structures, like the bridge in the picture, have expansion joints. The expansion joint is the fingerlike parts between two sections of the bridge. Look at the drawings. What purpose does the expansion joint serve? What

▼ **Bridge expansion joint**

might happen if the bridge did not have an expansion joint?

Although most common materials expand when heated and contract when cooled, some do not. Water, for example, expands when heated. It also contracts when cooled, but only to a certain point. At about 4°C (39°F), water begins to expand again as it cools further. You can see in the picture the effect this has when liquid water changes to ice. Where else have you observed the same effect?

◀ Water (left); ice (right)

Rubber also behaves in an unexpected way when heated or cooled. When rubber is heated, it contracts. When cooled, rubber expands.

Lesson Review

1. What is a physical change?
2. How is heat related to changes in the state of matter?
3. How does expansion and contraction of matter differ from a change in state of matter?

Think! Explain why there is a space, often filled with tar or another material, between sections of a concrete sidewalk.

Earth Science
CONNECTION

Many changes in the earth happen as a result of physical changes in matter. Find out what physical weathering *is.*

2. Mixtures

Getting Started   Many people put out bird-seed to feed wild birds. Birdseed can be compared to a tossed salad. In what ways is birdseed like a tossed salad? What word could you use to describe both of these foods?

What is a mixture?

As you know, matter may be classified as a mixture or as a substance. Recall that a substance is something made of only one kind of matter. A mixture, however, is made of two or more different substances. The substances do not change by being mixed. In most mixtures the kinds of matter may be present in any amount and need not be spread evenly. How does the birdseed in the picture fit this description?

Each kind of matter in a mixture keeps its properties. Look at the pictures. Salt and sugar

▼ Salt crystals

▼ Sugar crystals

206

look much alike. They both are small white solid crystals (KRIHS tulz). Suppose that salt is mixed with sugar. With the aid of a microscope, you could probably separate the crystals. If you tasted the mixture, you would taste both the salt and the sugar.

However, if salt is mixed with water, the salt seems to disappear. You cannot see the salt, but you can still taste it.

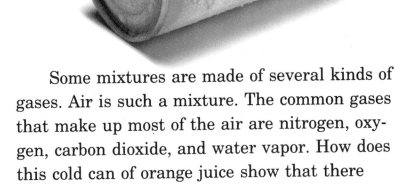

Some mixtures are made of several kinds of gases. Air is such a mixture. The common gases that make up most of the air are nitrogen, oxygen, carbon dioxide, and water vapor. How does this cold can of orange juice show that there is water vapor in air?

As you can see, there are different types of mixtures: solid-solid, solid-liquid, gas-gas, and so on. What type of mixture is the beverage in the picture? How do you know?

How can mixtures be separated?

The substances in a mixture can be separated by physical means. This is possible because the kinds of matter in a mixture keep their own properties.

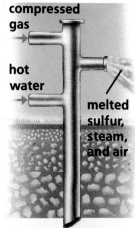

compressed
gas

hot
water

melted
sulfur,
steam,
and air

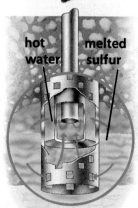

hot
water

melted
sulfur

Many mixtures found in the natural environment (en VYE run munt) contain useful materials. Before these materials can be used, they must be separated from the mixture.

Sulfur, for example, is found deep in the earth. Often it is under layers of rock, clay, and quicksand. Sulfur cannot simply be dug from the earth. Instead, very hot water is pumped into the earth to melt the sulfur. Sulfur melts at 112.8°C (235°F). Water usually boils at 100°C (212°F), but under pressure its temperature is much higher than the melting point of sulfur.

Look at the sulfur mine. Find the pool of melted sulfur. This sulfur-water mixture is pumped to the earth's surface. There the water evaporates (ee VAP uh rayts). When water evaporates, it changes from a liquid to a gas and enters the air. As the sulfur cools, it changes from a liquid to a solid. Sulfur that is mined this way is almost 100 percent pure.

▼ Liquid and solid mined sulfur.

Problem Solving
Divide and Conquer

UNMIXING MIXED-UP MATTER

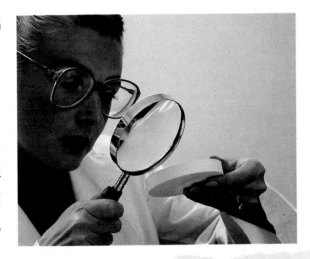

Today, Dr. Ima Brane once again demonstrated her science skills. Dr. Brane was asked to separate each kind of matter in the famous Martian Mixture. The Martian Mixture, scooped from the surface of Mars, seemed to be particles of various colors and sizes. Dr. Brane carefully examined the mixture with a hand lens. Then she announced, "This will be no problem at all for Ima Brane."

How can the kinds of matter in the Martian Mixture be separated?

Get a sample of the Martian Mixture from your teacher. Develop a plan for separating the mixture. Discuss the plan with your teacher. Then try it. Into how many kinds of matter did you separate the mixture? How can you be sure that all of each kind of matter is the same? How might Dr. Brane solve this problem?

Iron also is not found in a pure form in the earth. It exists as iron ore—a mixture of iron compounds and other materials. Some types of iron ore are magnetic. Rocks that contain this kind of iron ore are taken out of the earth in huge pieces. These are ground into smaller pieces until they are powder. The powder is then passed between magnets that act as separators. Since the iron compound in the ore is magnetic, it sticks to the separators. The rock and other materials that are not magnetic fall away.

▲ Taconite iron ore

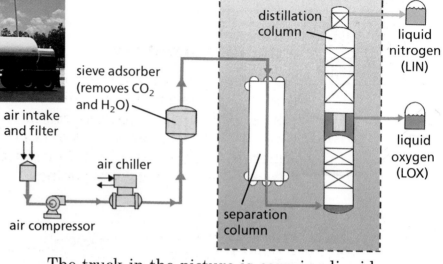

Separating the gases in air ▶

Gas	Boiling Point (°C)
Oxygen	− 183.0
Nitrogen	− 195.8
Argon	− 185.7
Neon	− 245.9
Helium	− 268.9
Xenon	− 109.1

The truck in the picture is carrying liquid oxygen. Oxygen is separated from the other gases in air as shown in the drawing. To separate the gases, the air must first be changed into a liquid. To do that, the air is cooled to a very low temperature while kept under high pressure.

Because air is a mixture, each gas in air has its own properties. One of these properties is the boiling point of the gas. When the liquid air is warmed again, each gas boils, or changes back to a gas, at a different temperature. As each gas boils, that gas is collected.

The boiling points of some of the gases in air are shown in the table. Which gas will boil first? Which will boil last?

Lesson Review

1. Define the term *mixture.*

2. Why can mixtures be separated?

Think! Liquids boil at different temperatures. Some boil at high temperatures; others boil at low temperatures. Explain the meaning of the term *boil* in relation to temperature.

Skills

THINKING

Testing a hypothesis

After you have observed how things happen, you may explain them with a hypothesis. A hypothesis is an explanation that you can test. To test a hypothesis, you collect more data. You may find that your hypothesis seems correct. Or you may learn that you must change your hypothesis.

Practicing the skill

1. When seltzer tablets are placed in water, they change. You can observe them dissolve.

2. Think about this hypothesis: Seltzer tablets in water form a solid-liquid mixture.

3. To test the hypothesis, put water into a container. Place a seltzer tablet in the water and make observations. The bubbles are a gas.

4. Does the hypothesis match your observations?

Thinking about the skill

Why might observations lead you to change the hypothesis?

Applying the skill

Test this hypothesis: When seltzer tablets are placed in water, they form a solid-liquid mixture. Place a seltzer tablet into water and let it dissolve. Put the water in a warm place. Allow the water to evaporate and observe what is left. Do your observations match the hypothesis?

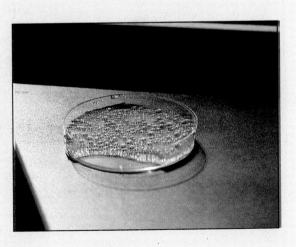

3. Solutions

Words to Know
solution
solvent
solute

Getting Started   Suppose you have a bad cough. Which would last longer in your mouth, one large cough drop or two cough drops each half that size? Why do you think so?

What are the characteristics of a solution?

All solutions (su LOO shunz) are mixtures, but not all mixtures are solutions. A **solution** is a mixture in which the different particles of matter are spread evenly throughout. Also, the particles are so small that they cannot be seen.

Think about a salt-and-sugar mixture. There might be more salt crystals in one place than in another. The mixture may not always be uniform, or even. Look at the drawing below. It represents a sugar-and-water mixture. When sugar is mixed with water, a solution is formed. The sugar spreads evenly throughout the water and seems to disappear.

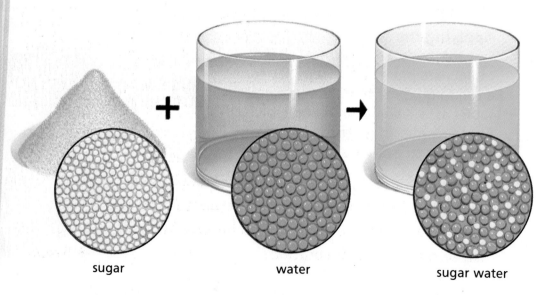

sugar   water   sugar water

A solution has two main parts. These are the solvent (SAHL vunt) and the solute (SAHL-yoot). The **solvent** is the material that is present in the greater amount in a solution. The **solute** is the material that is present in the smaller amount. It is dissolved in the solvent.

▲ Dissolving salt in water

Different amounts of solute can dissolve in a certain amount of solvent. For example, a few crystals of salt will dissolve in a cup of water. A spoonful of salt, or even several spoonfuls, will also dissolve in a cup of water (jar *A*). But finally a point is reached at which no more salt will dissolve (jar *B*). There is a limit to the amount of solute and solvent that can form a solution.

Liquid solutions are always transparent, or clear. They may be colored or colorless. Which of these mixtures is a solution?

▲ Two mixtures

Explore Together

How can you separate the substances in black ink?

Organizer

Materials

filter paper · metric ruler · scissors · black felt-tip pen · 250-mL beaker · water · paper clip

Procedure

Investigator

A. Cut a strip of filter paper about 2 cm wide by 10 cm long. Cut one end of the strip to form a point.

Investigator

B. Draw a heavy line across the strip of paper with a black felt-tip pen. Draw the line about 0.5 cm above the slanted sides of the point.

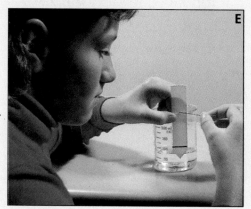

Manager

C. Fill a beaker with water to the 75-mL mark. Also bend a paper clip to make a straight wire.

Manager

D. Hold the strip of paper against the outside of the beaker. The tip of the point should be just below the water level.

Investigator

E. Push the straightened paper clip through the strip of paper at the rim of the beaker.

Investigator, Group

F. Hang the strip of paper inside the beaker by laying the straightened paper clip across the rim of the beaker. Do not let the paper touch the beaker. Observe closely what happens.

Writing and Sharing Results and Conclusions

Group, Recorder

1. Describe what happened to the ink line on the strip of paper.

2. What does each color represent?

3. Why did the separation move up the paper instead of down?

Reporter

4. How are your results the same as or different from those of your classmates?

What affects how a solute dissolves?

Several factors affect the rate at which a solute dissolves. One factor is the particle size of the solute. Consider the most common type of solution—a solid solute dissolved in a liquid solvent. Suppose that the solute is represented by the large block in the drawing. How many surfaces does it have? Its surface area is marked off in small squares. How many squares equal the total area of the outside surfaces?

Now suppose that a corner is removed from the block, as shown. How many *new* surfaces are exposed? What is the total area of the outside surfaces of the solute now?

How surface area changes ▼

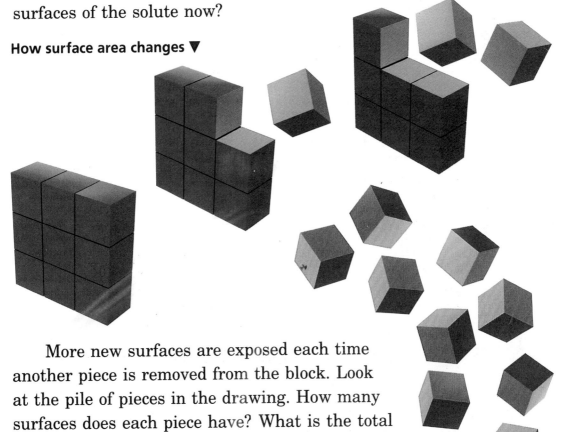

More new surfaces are exposed each time another piece is removed from the block. Look at the pile of pieces in the drawing. How many surfaces does each piece have? What is the total area of all the surfaces of the solute now? How does this surface area compare with the surface area of the large block of solute?

Think of the cough drops at the beginning of this section. When the solute has a large surface area, more solute comes into contact with the solvent. This speeds the rate at which the solute dissolves. Which do you think will dissolve faster, a sugar cube or an equal volume of loose sugar crystals?

Heating the solvent may also speed dissolving. When matter is heated, the motion of its particles increases. The particles vibrate more rapidly and move farther apart than do the particles in a cold substance. Why does this speed the rate at which the solute dissolves?

Cold solvent (left); warm solvent (right) ▶

Another factor that affects the rate at which a solute dissolves is stirring. It speeds dissolving. Stirring causes the particles of solute to mix more quickly with the particles of solvent.

Stirring to mix particles quickly ▼

What are some types of solutions?

You know that a solution has two parts. But is the solute always a solid? Is the solvent always a liquid? Did you know there are other types of solutions? For example, did you know there are solutions of solids dissolved in solids?

Different types of solutions are shown in the table. How many types of solutions are possible?

Type of Solution	Solute	Solvent	Name of Solution
solid-solid	tin (solid)	copper (solid)	bronze
solid-liquid	salt (solid)	water (liquid)	salt water
solid-gas	iodine (solid)	air (gas)	iodine fumes
liquid-solid	mercury (liquid)	silver (solid)	amalgam (tooth filling)
liquid-liquid	acetic acid (liquid)	water (liquid)	vinegar
liquid-gas	water (liquid)	air (gas)	fog
gas-solid	hydrogen (gas)	palladium (solid)	gas stove lighter
gas-liquid	carbon dioxide (gas)	water (liquid)	carbonated water
gas-gas	helium (gas)	oxygen (gas)	diver's gas

Lesson Review

1. How does a solution differ from other mixtures?
2. Name and describe the parts of a solution.
3. What factors affect the speed at which a material will dissolve?

Think! Look at the drawing. What is the difference between a gas-liquid solution and a liquid-gas solution?

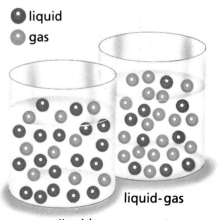

● liquid
● gas

liquid-gas

gas-liquid

217

How can corrosion be prevented?

Many bridges and planes built years ago are falling apart. Some bridges have had to be closed. Planes have lost parts in midair. The metal and other materials in these aging structures have been weakened by physical and chemical changes.

In some cases a physical change called metal fatigue is at fault. Great pressure can force a metal to change shape. Every time a plane takes off and lands, there is pressure on the landing gear and wings. During a flight, the pressure inside a plane is greater than that on the outside. This causes the metal skin of the plane to stretch. Back on the ground, the metal skin returns to its former shape. Cracks can form. Tiny at first, the cracks can spread and grow, weakening the metal. Scientists are searching for ways to detect fatigue cracks.

Metal in planes and other structures is also affected by corrosion. Corrosion is a chemical change that takes place when metals react with certain liquids, especially water. Scientists have discovered that many chemicals in the environment can increase corrosion. In some cases, even fungi, algae, and bacteria can cause corrosion.

STS

Rusting is a form of corrosion which occurs on steel. Rusting is a major cause of many bridge closings. Salt is spread to melt snow and used on roads and bridges in order to make them less slippery. The concrete used for bridge roadways and supports contains steel rods to strengthen it. These rods corrode when water and salt seep down through the concrete. As the rust forms, it expands and cracks the concrete. This allows more water to enter, causing further corrosion.

Paint, special coatings, and different metals are some ways to prevent corrosion of most structures. Scientists have found another way to stop this type of corrosion. First a network of wire is laid over the bridge surfaces. The wire is then covered with a new layer of concrete. Then an electric current is sent through the network of wire. The electric current stops the corrosion.

Critical thinking

Salt should not be used to make roads less slippery. Do you agree with this statement? Research in the library and then write a paragraph giving evidence to support your opinion.

Using what you learned

Make a list of metal structures where you live. Check with local officials to find out if any of these structures have been damaged by corrosion or metal fatigue. Then find out what things are being done to stop the corrosion.

4. Chemical Changes

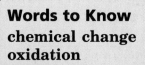

Words to Know
chemical change
oxidation

Getting Started The pictures of the burning match were taken a fraction of a second apart. Describe what is happening. Could the match ever be whole and unburned again? Why?

What is a chemical change?

What, do you think, produced the images on this film? Why do bright, shiny objects like those in the pictures become dull and blackened? Copper may even turn green.

These changes in matter are all chemical changes. A **chemical change** is a change in which one or more new substances are formed. The new matter forms due to a chemical reaction. For example, when vinegar is added to baking soda, much bubbling and fizzing take place. A gas is formed and given off. When the bubbling and fizzing stop, all that is left is water and another substance. Because of a chemical reaction, the vinegar and baking soda no longer exist.

How fast do chemical changes take place?

Some chemical changes take place slowly, others occur rapidly. For example, consider oxidation (ahks ih DAY shun). **Oxidation** is the process by which oxygen combines with another substance. Some examples of oxidation are shown in the pictures.

Sometimes oxidation takes place slowly, as when iron rusts. Burning is rapid oxidation. Another form of rapid oxidation is shown in the drawing. Here oxygen combines so rapidly with gasoline that it almost explodes. This happens in a car's engine. The force produced moves the pistons in the engine.

*How can knowing about chemical changes bring you fame and fortune? Find out as you try **Investigating Chemical Reactions**.*

Rusting iron ▼

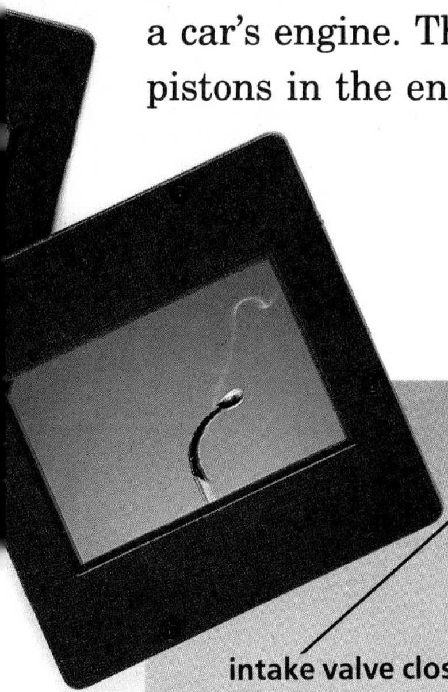

▼ Oxidation of gasoline in an engine

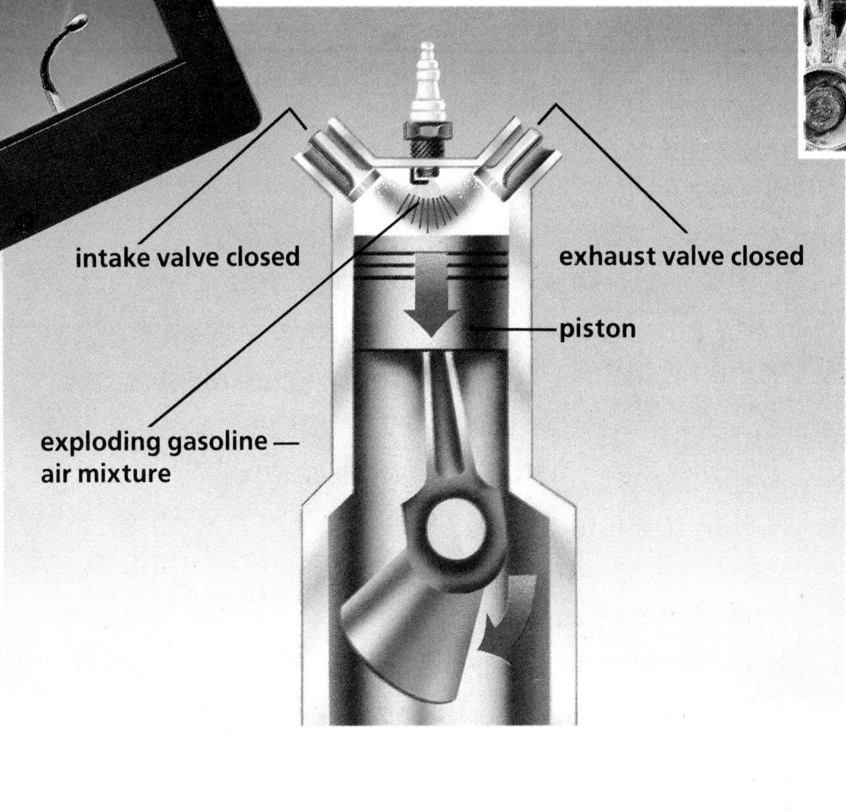

intake valve closed

exhaust valve closed

piston

exploding gasoline — air mixture

Explore

How can you show that oxidation is a chemical reaction that uses oxygen?

" . . .and now, the 10 o-clock news. A fire on Main St. today was blamed on oily rags kept in a closet. Firefighters said that slow oxidation of the oil caused heat to build up in the rags. Because of poor ventilation, the heat could not escape. Suddenly slow oxidation became rapid oxidation."

Materials

grease pencil · metric ruler · 2 test tubes · steel wool · water · 250-mL beaker · graph paper

Procedure

A. With a grease pencil, make a mark every 0.5 cm along the length of each test tube.

B. Put some steel wool in one test tube. Use a piece large enough so that it will not fall out. Push the steel wool all the way to the bottom with the pencil.
   1. Describe the steel wool.

C. Pour about 100 mL of water into a beaker. Also, half-fill the test tubes with water; then empty them.

D. Stand the test tubes upside down in the beaker of water. Record the water level in each tube.

E. Observe the test tubes for a week. Record the water level in the tubes each day.
   2. In what direction do the water levels move?
   3. Make a bar graph to show what happens to the water level in each tube?

Writing and Sharing Results and Conclusions

1. How did the steel wool change?
2. Why did the steel wool change?
3. Why did the water level in the one test tube change?
4. How do these results show that oxidation uses oxygen?

What are some ways compounds break apart?

Oxidation is one example of a chemical reaction in which substances combine. But in some chemical reactions, substances are separated, or broken apart. Hydrogen peroxide, for example, can be used to clean a cut. Hydrogen peroxide is a liquid with the formula H_2O_2. When put on a cut, hydrogen peroxide bubbles. It breaks apart into water and oxygen gas. Oxygen destroys germs which might cause an infection.

Do you think it is possible to break apart water? One way is to use a device like the one shown here. Recall that the formula for water is H_2O. As an electric current is run through the water, hydrogen gas collects in one tube. Oxygen gas collects in the other tube. Which tube contains the hydrogen? How can you tell?

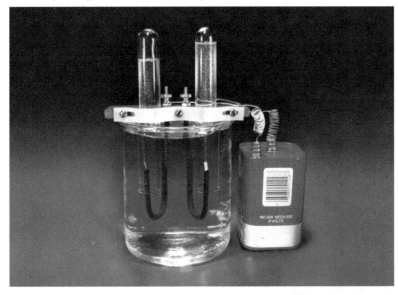

◀ Breaking apart the compound water

How can you write a chemical reaction?

Earlier you learned that scientists use chemical symbols as a kind of shorthand. Symbols are also used to show what happens during a chemical reaction. For example, this is the way a scientist would show how salt forms.

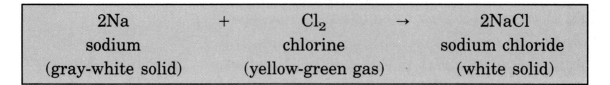

2Na	+	Cl$_2$	→	2NaCl
sodium		chlorine		sodium chloride
(gray-white solid)		(yellow-green gas)		(white solid)

This reaction might be read as follows: When the gray-white solid *sodium* combines chemically with the yellow-green gas *chlorine,* the white, solid compound *sodium chloride,* or salt, is formed. You can see how much shorter and simpler it is to use symbols.

Another simple reaction is shown below. Make up a sentence to describe the reaction. Tell how the new substance is different from those that reacted to form it.

2Cu	+	Cl$_2$	→	2CuCl
copper		chlorine		cuprous chloride
(red-brown solid)		(yellow-green gas)		(white solid)

Lesson Review

1. What is a chemical change?
2. Describe oxidation in terms of a chemical change.
3. Why is the breaking apart of a compound a chemical change?

Think! Use the letters on the puzzle pieces to show the right half of this chemical reaction.

Life Science
CONNECTION

Photosynthesis is the process by which plants make food. Find out what chemicals are involved in photosynthesis.

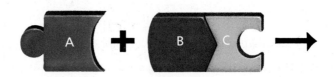

Chapter Connections

Choose four words from the graphic organizer. Illustrate them with drawings or pictures from magazines.

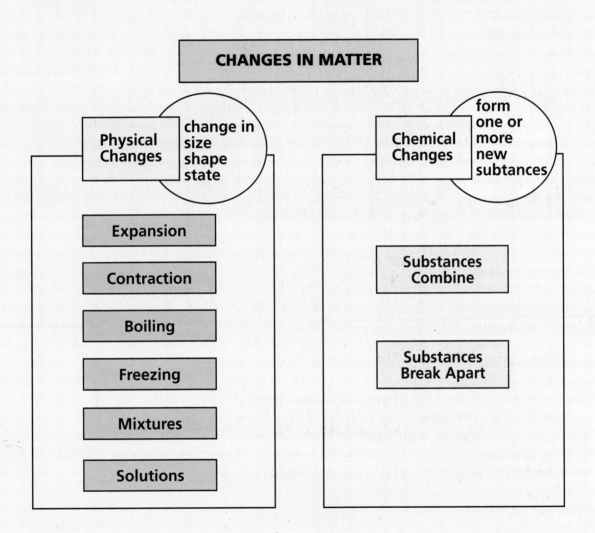

Writing About Science • Research

With a partner think of careers that need an understanding of physical and chemical changes. Find out more about one of these careers and write a report to share with the class.

Science Terms

Copy the sentences below. Use the terms listed to complete the sentences.

chemical change   oxidation   physical change
solute   solution   solvent

1. The _____ is the part of a solution that is present in the greatest amount.
2. A change in matter that does not change the makeup of matter is a _____.
3. _____ is the process by which oxygen combines with another substance.
4. In a solution, the _____ is the material that is dissolved.
5. A _____ is a change in which one or more new kinds of matter form.
6. In a _____, the different particles of matter are spread evenly throughout.

Science Ideas

Use complete sentences to answer the following.

1. Why is matter still the same kind of matter after a physical change?
2. Name two physical changes that take place in the same state of matter.
3. What is the temperature called at which a liquid changes to a gas?
4. How many kinds of matter are needed to make a mixture?
5. How may a mixture of gases be separated?
6. Why is a solution called a mixture?
7. In a solution, how does the solute differ from the solvent?
8. How is surface area related to the rate at which a solid dissolves?
9. Why does a chemical reaction result in the formation of new kinds of matter?

10. Why does a chemical change change the chemical makeup of matter?

Applying Science Ideas

1. The temperature at which a solid becomes a liquid is called the melting point of the solid. Are the melting point of the solid and the freezing point of the liquid the same temperature? Explain your answer.

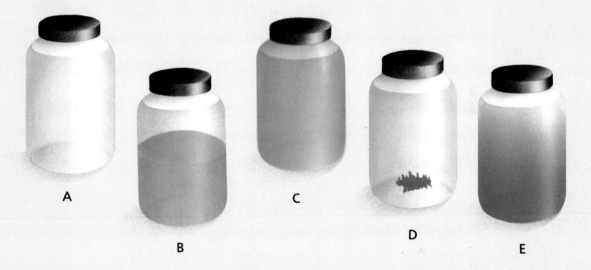

A   B   C   D   E

2. A blue solid is dissolved in a jar of water. A lid is placed on the jar, and the jar is left undisturbed for a week. Which drawing shows how the matter in the jar would look after one week?

3. Why does a painted metal surface resist corrosion better than an unpainted metal surface?

Using Science Skills

Test this hypothesis: Ice always melts at 0°C. Put ice cubes made from distilled water in a beaker. Put ice cubes made from salt water in another beaker. Place a thermometer in each beaker. Record the temperatures every 5 minutes. Write why you chose to keep or change the hypothesis.

Motion and Forces

Rolling Along

The bar slams closed in front of you. You do not have to be told to hang on tightly. Slowly your car climbs to the top of the hill. You can hear the creaking of the chain that lifts you higher. As you near the top, you look down. Your friends on the ground are so far away! Suddenly your attention comes back to your car. You are heading down the track and gaining speed fast!

It may sound funny, but people enjoy being scared, as long as they know they are safe. That is why roller coasters are such popular rides. As you swoop up and down along the track, you feel as though you may fly off into the air at any minute. But this does not happen. Seat belts and a safety bar hold you in your seat. And the three sets of wheels on the cars are designed for safety. One set of wheels runs on top of the track. The other sets of wheels run beneath the track and in the car. So the car will stay safely attached, even when it is upside down!

The first modern roller coaster was built in Coney Island in 1884. It raced along the track at 10 km (6 mi) per hour. The ride was a line of hills, with no curves or loops. The first hill was the highest, and after that, each hill was a little lower than the one before it. This roller coaster had no machine to pull the car to the top. Workers had to do that. Riders climbed to the top of the ride and got in the car up there.

Today there are over 250 roller coasters in the United States. Modern roller coasters are longer, higher, and faster than the early ones were. On some roller coasters you move as fast as 100 km (60 mi) per hour. You go up and down hills, around curves, through spirals, and even loop upside down! Although there are new machines to pull the car to the top of the ride, one thing has not changed. Gravity still makes the car move down the track, just as it did 100 years ago.

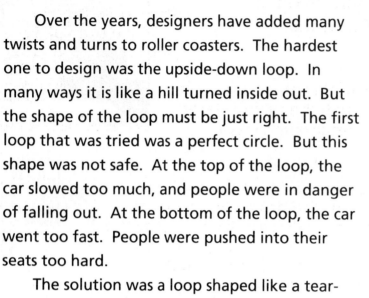

Over the years, designers have added many twists and turns to roller coasters. The hardest one to design was the upside-down loop. In many ways it is like a hill turned inside out. But the shape of the loop must be just right. The first loop that was tried was a perfect circle. But this shape was not safe. At the top of the loop, the car slowed too much, and people were in danger of falling out. At the bottom of the loop, the car went too fast. People were pushed into their seats too hard.

The solution was a loop shaped like a tear-drop, where the top of the loop is wider than the bottom. Here the car moves slower at the top and not too quickly at the bottom.

Building roller coasters has become a kind of contest. Designers keep trying to make new curves and loops. They try to make tracks that run sideways and upside down. Who knows what they will think of next? Whatever it is, riders will surely love it!

Discover

How can you make a model of a roller coaster?

Materials 1-m piece of flexible plastic tubing · marble that will fit through the tubing · large piece of cardboard or poster board · tape

Procedure

A roller coaster is designed so that the cars will gain speed as they move down the first drop. The amount of speed they gain depends on the shape of the drop. Use some tubing and a marble to create a model of the first drop of a roller coaster. Design your drop so that the marble travels the greatest possible distance after it leaves the tube. When you have found your best design, tape the tubing in that shape on the poster board. Compare your design with those of your classmates. Which design works best? What variables affect the distance the marble travels?

In this chapter you will learn how gravity makes things move. You will also learn about other forces and how they affect objects.

1. How and Why Objects Move

Getting Started Imagine that you are an artist. Think of different ways to show that an object is moving. Draw or describe in words each of those ways.

Words to Know
motion
speed
force
inertia

What is motion?

Look outside. You will see some objects that are moving and some that are not moving. An object that is not moving is at rest. Objects that are at rest remain in the same place or position.

But what about objects that are not at rest? The positions of those objects change. They are at one place at one moment and somewhere else at the next moment. They are in motion. **Motion** is any change in the position of an object. The same duck is shown here several times. When is it at rest? When is it in motion?

How can motion be described?

Look at the map. Find the corner of Main Street and Center Avenue. Suppose that you walk from there to the drugstore on Main Street. The drugstore is 500 m (550 yd) from the corner. How far will you be from your starting point?

Suppose that you had walked 500 m along Main Street in the opposite direction. How far from the drugstore would you be? The distance that you moved was the same, but your end point was quite different. Motion cannot be described by distance alone. You must state the direction of motion, too.

Speed is also used to describe motion. It might take you 5 minutes to walk the 500 m to the drugstore. On a bicycle it might take you 2 minutes. What is your speed? **Speed** is the distance an object moves in a certain period of time. If you walk 500 m in 5 minutes, your speed is 100 m per minute. What is your speed on the bicycle if it takes 2 minutes to travel 500 m?

233

Explore Together

How can you measure the speed of a moving object?

Organizer

Materials

hammer · carpet tack · large wooden spool · rubber band · flat washer · wooden dowel, 10 cm long · meterstick · chalk · timer

Procedure

Investigator, Manager

A. Hammer the tack into one end of the spool near the hole. Push the rubber band through the hole and loop it over the tack. Arrange the washer and the dowel at the other end, as shown.

Manager

B. Make two chalk marks 1 m apart on a smooth, hard floor.

Investigator, Manager

C. Wind the rubber band by turning the dowel 5–10 times. Then place the spool on one of the chalk marks. Let go of the spool. Measure the time it takes for the spool to reach the second chalk mark.

Recorder

1. How long did it take for the spool to travel 1 m?

2. What was the spool's speed?

Writing and Sharing Results and Conclusions

Group, Recorder

1. Where did the energy to move the spool come from?

2. Why was it important to mark off a 1-m track and to use a timer?

Reporter

3. How does the speed of your spool compare with the speeds of your classmates' spools?

What are some kinds of motion?

An object that moves in a straight line in one direction travels farther and farther from its starting point. But motion in a straight line is only one kind of motion.

Think about the motion of the swing in the picture. The swing moves first in one direction, and then in the opposite direction. It moves back and forth through the same positions over and over. This kind of back-and-forth motion is called periodic motion. What are some other examples of periodic motion?

▼ **Periodic motion**

▲ Merry-go-round

How would you describe the motion of a merry-go-round? Its motion is circular. The motion of a spinning top and the motion of Earth around the sun are circular.

Look at the drawing. You can see that in circular motion the direction of motion keeps changing. At point A the object is moving to the left. In which direction is it moving at points *B, C,* and *D*?

In some ways, circular motion is like periodic motion. In both kinds of motion, the moving object passes through the same positions again and again. How are these two kinds of motion different?

▼ Circular motion

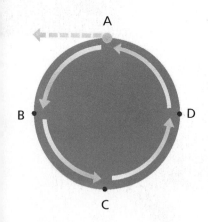

How can motion be changed?

If you watch or play baseball, these scenes may be familiar to you. The pitcher winds up and sends the ball speeding toward the plate. The batter swings and misses, and the ball is stopped by the catcher's glove. On the next pitch the batter does not miss. The bat hits the ball and sends it down the left-field line.

Each change in the motion of the ball was caused by a force. A **force** is a push or a pull on an object, caused by another object. The push of the pitcher's hand against the ball started the ball moving. The push of the catcher's glove stopped the ball's motion. What force changed the direction of the ball's motion?

A force can start a motion, stop a motion, or change the direction of a motion. It can also change the speed of motion. If a force pushes an object in the same direction as the object's motion, the speed will increase. If it pushes in the opposite direction, the speed will decrease.

An object at rest remains at rest unless a force acts on it. Also, an object in motion continues to move in a straight line at the same speed unless a force acts on it. All matter resists a change in its motion. A force is needed to overcome this resistance and change the motion.

▼ **How inertia can affect motion**

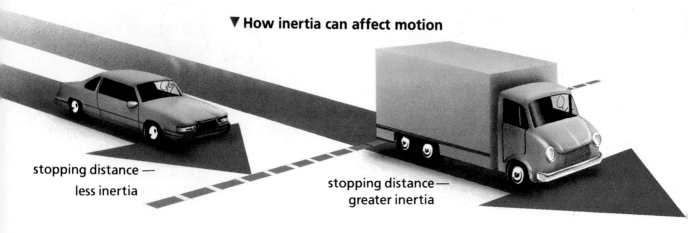

stopping distance —
less inertia

stopping distance—
greater inertia

The resistance of matter to a change in its motion is called **inertia** (ihn UR shuh). The inertia of an object depends on the object's mass. For example, it takes more force to stop a tractor-trailer than a car traveling at the same speed. Why? The tractor-trailer has more mass than the car. Because it has more mass, it has more inertia than the car and takes longer to stop.

Lesson Review
1. What is motion, and how can it be described?
2. Name three kinds of motion.
3. What is inertia, and how is it overcome?
Think! A car and a bus are both stopped at a stop sign. Which one needs the least force to start moving again, and why?

Earth Science
CONNECTION

What kind of motion describes how the planet Earth moves?

Skills

Constructing a table

How fast? How far? Sometimes you want to answer these questions when you are studying how things move. Finding the answers is easy if you organize the information in a data table.

Practicing the skill

Three teams competed in a swimming relay race. Each team had four swimmers. Each swimmer swam 100 m. The times for the four American swimmers were 63 sec, 70 sec, 60 sec, and 55 sec. The times for the four Canadian swimmers were 64 sec, 68 sec, 62 sec, and 56 sec. The times for the four West German swimmers were 61 sec, 68 sec, 60 sec, and 55 sec. You can organize the data by making a data table. Then you can compare the swimmers.

Women's Swimming Relay

Team	Swimmer 1	Swimmer 2	Swimmer 3	Swimmer 4
American	63	70	60	55
Canadian				
West German				

1. Make a data table like the one above. First draw the column for the team names. Then draw four more columns for the times. Enter the times for the swimmers on each team. The American team is completed.

2. Which team was ahead when the second swimmers had finished?

Thinking about the skill
For what other sports might you make a data table?

Applying the skill

Look at the data table you made. Using a calculator, total the times for the swimmers on each team. Add another column. Write the team totals in the new column. Which team was the fastest?

Should the height of a skyscraper be limited?

There is one problem at the top of superskyscrapers: wind. Winds get stronger the higher you go. Suppose you were standing on the roof of a 50-story building. You would feel winds blowing at speeds of 30 km (18 miles) per hour. At the top of a building with 100 floors, winds could blow at 125 km (75 miles) per hour. You would feel as if you were in a hurricane. Wind makes the tops of tall buildings vibrate, or sway back and forth.

The swaying causes problems. Furniture can slide, and doors can swing open. People can feel sick from the motion. Boston's Hancock Tower used to sway. But now two huge, heavy weights have been placed on a top floor. When the tower sways one way, the weights slide the other way. As a result, the tower sways less.

◄Hancock Tower   ▲ Sliding weights

Today, architects design skyscrapers that will not sway as much. They test a small model of a skyscraper in a wind tunnel, which is like a huge room where they can create strong winds. They can see how the model stands up to the wind. If it sways too much, they can change the design. In some buildings, computers detect high winds. The computers send signals that make the building stiffen up by using motors to pull on the building's metal structures.

Superskyscrapers will let more and more people live and work together in cities. But some cities want to limit the height of new buildings. Some people do not want new buildings to change the beautiful views and historic skylines in their cities. They also worry that as people crowd higher and higher, the problems of traffic and pollution will get worse and worse.

Critical thinking

Suppose a superskyscraper was being built near your home. How would you feel if you owned a shop in the new building? How would you feel if the building would block all the sun on your street? Who else might object to the building?

Using what you learned

Ask your family, friends, and neighbors what they think about superskyscrapers that might be over 440 floors high. Write down their answers. Then discuss their answers with your classmates.

241

2. A Force Between Objects in Contact

Words to Know
friction

Getting Started Snap a coin across the top of your desk with your finger. How do you know that a force is acting on the coin?

What is friction?

When you snapped the coin, it slid across your desk. But as the coin slid, it gradually slowed and stopped because of friction (FRIHK-shun). **Friction** is the force that resists the movement of one object against another when the objects touch.

Sprinters, like this one, use starting blocks to get a faster start. When you walk or run, there is friction between your feet and the ground. Friction enables you to push against the ground and move your body forward. Friction is involved in most of the ordinary actions of your daily life. Have you ever tried to turn a doorknob when your hands were soapy?

242

Although friction is often needed to produce motion, it also is needed to reduce motion. Brakes on a car or a bicycle use friction to slow or stop the vehicle. Friction between the nail and the wood it is in will hold the pieces of wood together.

Holding things together ▼

Bicycle brake
▼

There are times when friction is not useful. In machines extra energy is needed to overcome friction between moving parts. This energy is wasted. It does no useful work.

Friction also causes what is called wear and tear. Where objects rub together, friction wears material away. In machines, parts worn by friction may break or fail to work properly. Sneakers and jeans wear out because of friction. Compare these coins. Why do they look so different?

Problem Solving

Rolling Along

How is the Space Shuttle moved to the launch pad? The shuttle and the vehicle to carry it weigh about 5 million kg (11 million lb). The vehicle and the road to the pad are specially designed to move that great weight.

How can a heavy load be moved by using a system of ball bearings?

Use a 1-kg can of juice to represent the Shuttle. Think of how you can move the can, using the least amount of force. Design a system of ball bearings, using marbles and plastic or metal can lids. Measure the force with a spring scale. What was the least amount of force needed? How does the number of marbles used affect the amount of force needed?

How can the amount of friction be changed?

Suppose you want to move a piece of furniture. On a rug, there would be more friction than on a bare wood floor. A rough surface, like a rug, causes more friction than a smooth surface, like bare wood.

Friction can often be reduced. One way is by changing the shape of the surfaces that rub. Chairs often have legs with rounded metal glides. Because of their shape, the glides reduce friction and make the chair easier to move.

Rolling motion instead of sliding motion also reduces friction. Push a heavy book across your desk. Do it again with the book on some round pencils. In which case is there less friction? The wheels of roller skates have ball bearings. When the wheels turn, the small balls roll around the axle. How do ball bearings reduce friction?

▲ Ball bearings in a roller skate wheel

Have you ever had a wet bar of soap slip out of your hands? A wet surface, especially an oily or a greasy one, has much less friction than a dry surface. The use of a slippery liquid to reduce friction is called lubrication (loo brih KAY-shun). Oil makes wheels and hinges turn more easily and quietly. Friction can damage a car's engine if the engine is not lubricated with oil.

Lesson Review

1. What is friction?
2. How is friction useful, and when is it not useful?
3. How may friction be reduced?

Think! The tires on race cars are much wider than those on ordinary cars. Often they also have a smooth rather than a grooved surface. Why?

Earth Science
CONNECTION

In what ways does friction cause changes to the surface of the earth?

3. Forces Between Objects Not in Contact

Getting Started   Where you live, an object falls down, not up. Tell what the term *down* means. In which direction would an object fall in Australia?

Words to Know

gravity
weight
magnetic force
magnet
magnetic field
poles
repel

What is gravity?

Many forces are the result of contact between two objects. But can a force act between objects that are not in contact? Is there a force acting between these skydivers and the earth?

Yes, the force called **gravity** (GRAV ih tee) pulls, or attracts, all objects toward one another. Gravity decreases with distance between objects.

Gravity acts between all objects, even when they are far apart. It pulls the earth and the sun toward one another. Stars that are millions of kilometers apart are attracted to one another by gravity. The earth also weakly attracts these objects, and is weakly attracted by them.

▼ How tides are produced

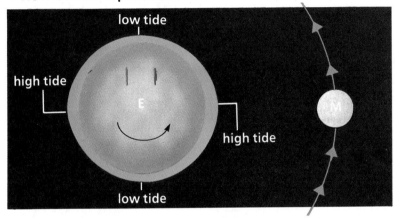

The moon's gravity causes tides. The moon attracts the ocean water on the near side of Earth more strongly than the moon attracts the solid earth, because that ocean is closer to the moon. The moon attracts the ocean water on the far side of Earth less strongly then it attracts the solid earth, because that ocean is farther away. Two high tides result. Between the high tides are two low tides. As the earth turns, the tides rise and fall.

You cannot feel the attraction due to gravity between small objects, such as two baseballs. The earth, however, is so large that you are aware of its gravity all the time. What effect of gravity can be seen in this picture?

◄ How a spring scale measures weight

When you lift or carry something, you feel the pull of the earth's gravity on the object. This force of gravity between the earth and the object is called **weight**. Weight can be measured with a spring scale. A force on the spring stretches it. The greater the force, the more the spring stretches. The amount the spring stretches is a measure of the weight of the object.

Can the weight of an object change?

The pull of gravity between objects depends on two things. It depends on the mass of each object. It also depends on the distance between the objects' centers. Suppose that an object is far from the earth. It would be attracted less to the earth than if it were near. Its weight would also be less than if the object were near the earth.

Would you weigh more or less at the top of a mountain than at sea level? You would weigh less, because you would be farther from the center of the earth.

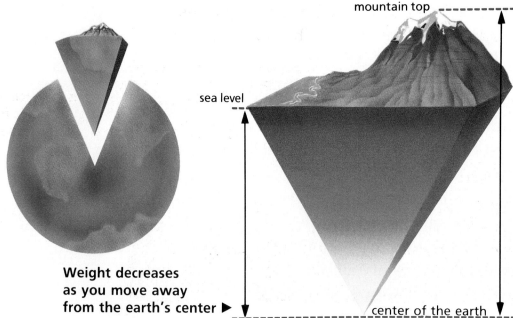

Weight decreases as you move away from the earth's center ►

mountain top

sea level

center of the earth

What is magnetic force?

Another, but quite different, force may also act between objects that are not in contact. **Magnetic** (mag NET ihk) **force**, or magnetism is a force that acts between magnets. Like gravity, the magnetic force between objects becomes less as the distance between the objects increases. Magnetic force acts only on magnetic materials, such as iron, steel, nickel, and cobalt. Nonmagnetic materials, such as silver and glass, are not affected by magnetic force.

Lodestone is a type of rock that is a natural magnet. Other magnets are artificial magnets made from magnetic materials. A **magnet** is any object surrounded by magnetic lines of force. You cannot see the magnetic lines of force. But you can see how they affect magnetic objects. Often you can also feel how they affect these objects.

Magnetic lines of force form a **magnetic field** around a magnet. Iron filings were used to show the magnetic field of the magnet in the picture. The iron filings lined up along the magnetic lines of force in the magnetic field.

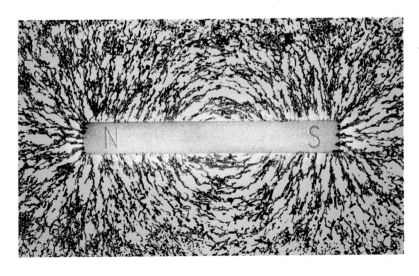

◀ Lines of force in the magnetic field of a bar magnet

Explore

What kind of materials can change the effects of magnets?

You probably have attached notes and other objects to your refrigerator with a magnet. But sometimes the magnet didn't hold an object. Why does a magnet seem to work sometimes but not all the time?

Materials

tape · strong magnet · metric ruler · books · thin string or thread · paper clip · paper and other assorted materials to test

Procedure

A. Tape a strong magnet to the end of a 30-cm ruler. Place the ruler on a stack of books. The end with the magnet should extend about 10 cm from the books. Hold the ruler in place with one or more heavy books.

B. Tie a string to a paper clip. Hold the paper clip about 3 cm below the magnet. Then tape the free end of the string to your desk. The paper clip should be attracted to the magnet, but not touch it.

C. Now test the materials. Slip a thin piece of each material between the magnet and the paper clip. Start with paper.

Writing and Sharing Results and Conclusions

1. Why is the paper clip attracted to the magnet?

2. How could you tell which materials cut, or blocked, the magnetic lines of force?

3. What kind of materials block magnetic lines of force, and what kind do not?

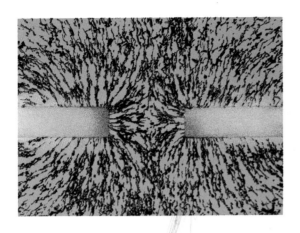 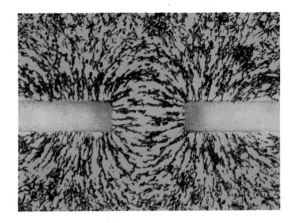

You can see that the lines of force are closest together at the poles, or ends, of the magnet. The **poles** of a magnet are where the magnetic force is strongest. There is little magnetic force near the middle of a magnet. Every magnet has a north and a south pole.

A magnetic material is attracted to either pole of a magnet. However, the like poles of two magnets always repel (rih PEL) each other. To **repel** means to push away. The unlike poles of two magnets always attract each other. Compare the lines of force in the magnetic fields of the magnets shown above. Which picture shows that like poles repel each other? Which shows that unlike poles attract each other?

Lesson Review

1. What are two forces that act between objects that are not in contact?
2. Define the term *weight*. Explain how the weight of an object may vary with its location.
3. What is a magnet?
4. How does magnetic force differ from gravity?

Think! When salt is poured on a table, it makes a mound. Why does gravity not cause the salt to spread out in a flat layer?

> **Earth Science**
> **CONNECTION**
>
> *How is the force of gravity on the moon different from the force on the earth? Where would you weigh more — on the earth or on the moon?*

4. A Force on an Object in a Fluid

Getting Started   Have you ever seen a hot-air balloon in the sky? It is filled with air, but it floats in the air. Why does a balloon that you fill with air behave differently?

Words to Know
fluid
buoyant force

What is a fluid?

The water in a stream flows and changes shape easily. Matter that flows is called a **fluid** (FLOO ihd). There are two kinds of fluids—liquids and gases.

Water is a fluid that is a liquid. A liquid at rest in a container takes the shape of the container. The liquid also has a level surface. Notice the level of the liquid in this container. It is the same in every part of the container. Gravity always causes a liquid to flow until its surface is at the same level everywhere.

▼ Constant-level tubes

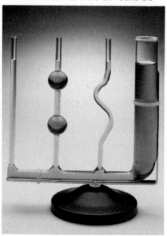

A bottle may look empty, but it is filled with air. If you blow into a balloon, it becomes filled with air. Air is a mixture of gases. Like a liquid, a gas is a fluid. A gas takes the shape of its container. But a gas has no definite volume. It always completely fills any container it is in.

Why do some objects float?

Look at the block of wood floating in water. If you pushed down on the block, you would feel the water push back. This upward force the water exerts on the block is called **bouyant** (BOI unt) **force**, or buoyancy. Every fluid exerts buoyant force on any object in the fluid.

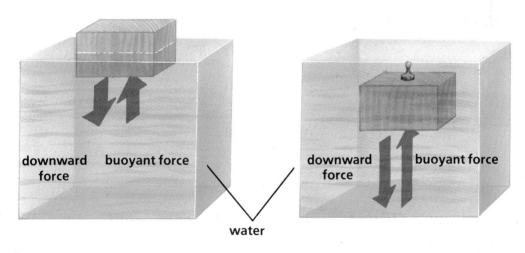

downward force   buoyant force

downward force   buoyant force

water

▲ Forces acting on floating (left) and submerged (right) blocks of wood

The buoyant force on an object is equal to the weight of the water the object pushes aside, or displaces. The buoyant force on the block of wood is greatest when the entire block is submerged. When the block is floating, only part of it is submerged, and the buoyant force is less. On the floating block, the buoyant force is equal to the weight of the block.

Earlier in this unit you learned about density. You learned that density is the measure of the mass of a certain volume of an object. In a fluid, objects that are more dense than the fluid will sink. Objects that are less dense than the fluid will float.

Suppose that the volume of a solid block of steel is 1 cm³. When dropped into water, the steel sinks. Why? Two things cannot occupy the same space at the same time. Upon entering the water, the block of steel pushes aside, or displaces, 1 cm³ of water. The density of steel is much greater than the density of water. The block of steel sinks because its weight is greater than the weight of the water it displaces.

Displacement of water by a solid ▼

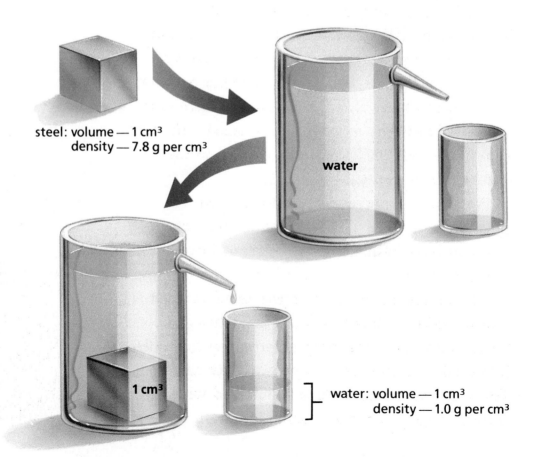

steel: volume — 1 cm³
density — 7.8 g per cm³

water

1 cm³

water: volume — 1 cm³
density — 1.0 g per cm³

◄ Hollow construction of a steel ship

If steel sinks in water, why does a steel ship float? Suppose that the steel block in the previous example was rolled into a very thin sheet. Then the edges were bent up to form a hollow, steel "ship." Because the ship is hollow, its volume is many times greater than that of the solid steel block. It will displace more water than did the steel block. The buoyant force is increased because more water is displaced. The steel ship floats because its weight is equal to the weight of the water it displaces.

As you learned earlier, air is a mixture of gases. It is a fluid. The balloons in the picture rise and float because of the buoyant force air exerts on them.

The buoyant force of air is much less than that of water. A block of wood is too heavy to be lifted by the buoyant force of air. Even a balloon filled with air weighs too much to float in air. The balloons in the picture were filled with helium, a gas that is less dense than air.

The beads in these pictures are the same size. The wooden beads float in water, but the glass beads do not. The wooden beads float because the density of wood is less than the density of water. The glass beads sink because the density of glass is greater than that of water.

▲ The effect of buoyancy on wooden and glass beads in water

Buoyant force pushes on any object in a fluid. But sometimes the force is not enough to lift the object. Because of buoyant force, objects in a fluid feel lighter than they really are. For example, have you ever tried to lift a rock under water? In the water the rock feels much lighter than it does out of the water.

Lesson Review

1. Define the term *fluid* and name two kinds of fluids.
2. What is the force called that a fluid exerts on an object in the fluid?
3. Why do some objects float in a fluid, and other objects sink?

Think! Imagine that you step into a boat from a dock. Why does the boat move lower into the water?

Chapter Connections

Design a new graphic organizer. Use the same information but organize it in a different way.

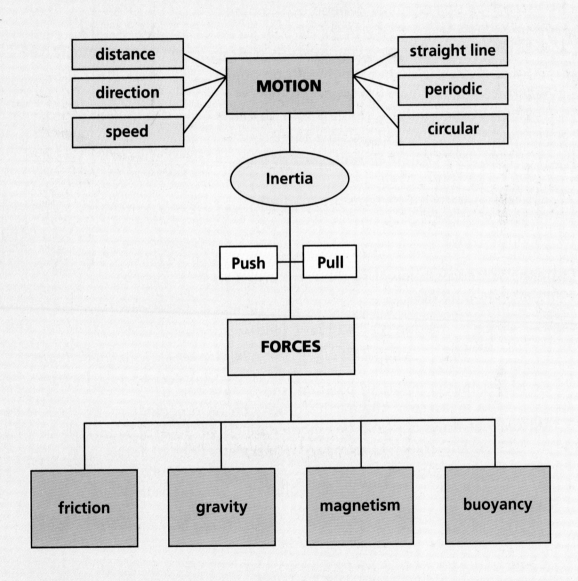

Writing About Science • Narrate

What if the earth's gravity were only half of what it really is? Write a story about how your life would be different.

Chapter 7 Review

Science Terms

A. Write the letter of the term that best matches the definition.

a. buoyant force
b. friction
c. gravity
d. inertia
e. magnetic force
f. poles
g. repel
h. speed

1. Distance an object moves divided by the time it takes to move
2. Resistance of matter to a change in its motion
3. Force that resists the movement of one object against another when the objects touch
4. Force of attraction between any two objects
5. Upward force on any object in a fluid
6. Acts only on certain materials, such as iron, steel, nickel, and cobalt
7. Regions of a magnet where the magnetic force is strongest
8. To push away

B. Copy the sentences below. Use the terms listed to complete the sentences.

fluid   force   magnet   magnetic field
motion   weight

1. An object that is changing position is in a state of _____.
2. _____ is a measure of the earth's gravity on an object.
3. Matter that flows and changes shape easily is called a _____.
4. A _____ is any object surrounded by magnetic lines of force.
5. Magnetic lines of force form a _____ around a magnet.
6. A _____ is a push or a pull on an object, caused by another object.

Science Ideas

Copy the chart on a sheet of paper. At the top of the chart are the names of four kinds of forces. The statements at the left may be true or false for each force. In each box write *true* or *false* for each force.

	Friction	Earth's Gravity	Buoyancy	Magnetism
Acts only between bodies in contact				
Can act between bodies not in contact				
Always attracts a body it acts on				
May repel a body it acts on				
Acts on all substances				
Acts only on certain substances				
Always acts upward				
Always acts downward				
May act in any direction				

Applying Science Ideas

1. Suppose you were standing still on a rotating platform. Would you be in motion? Explain your answer.
2. Would building tunnels through a skyscraper make it sway less? Explain your answer.

Using Science Skills

 Carol Osborn competes in a sport called a triathlon. In one competition, she had to swim 1.5 km, ride a bike 40 km, and run 10 km. It took her 50 minutes to swim, 94 minutes to ride, and 74 minutes to run. Organize these data in a table. Then use a calculator to calculate Carol's total time in the triathlon.

Chapter 8

Electricity and Magnetism

Magical Light

Is this a magic trick? You know that it takes electricity to make a lamp glow. But these fluorescent (floo uh RES unt) tubes do not have any source of electricity. Or do they?

Notice the wires in the picture. They carry electricity to homes, factories, stores, and schools. There the electricity is used to make some light, sound, heat, and motion. But electricity also makes something you cannot see, hear, or feel. Moving electricity produces invisible fields of electricity and magnetism. Such fields give off energy in the form of electromagnetic (ee lek troh mag NET ihk) radiation (ray dee AY shun) (EMR).

These wires carry a large amount of electricity, so they produce a field with a large amount of EMR. If you hold a fluorescent tube beneath the wires, the EMR makes the tube glow. The EMR cannot make you glow like the tube. But some people wonder if the EMR might harm you in some way.

Scientists are trying to answer this question. Some studies have shown that people who live near high-power wires have a number of health problems. One study of children with cancer showed that many of the children live near high-power wires. But not every child who lives near these wires becomes ill. So it is hard to tell if the EMR caused by the wires is really dangerous.

Think of all the electric appliances you have in your home. Each of these things produces some EMR when it is turned on. But some appliances give off more EMR than others. A toaster gives off little EMR because it does not have a motor. It makes heat but not motion. A hair dryer, however, makes both heat and motion. It has a motor, so it gives off more EMR than a toaster does.

What about appliances that are near you for long periods of time? For example, if you use an electric blanket, you sleep surrounded by EMR. One scientist says you should use the electric blanket only to warm the bed. You should then turn the blanket off when you get into bed.

Many scientists say that people should not be afraid of EMR. Most of the electric appliances you use are not running all the time. Also, many are left alone while they are working. If you do not stand near a clothes dryer while it is running, you will not be near any EMR.

Scientists all over the world are checking to see if EMR affects health. But it may be several years before they find the answer.

Discover

How can you locate the lines of force of a magnetic field?

Materials   small plastic jar with lid · cooking oil · iron filings · spoon · bar magnet

Procedure

Scientists use meters to measure electric and magnetic fields. You cannot measure how strong a magnetic field is, but you can show where it is.

Fill a jar three-fourths full with cooking oil. Stir in some iron filings. Put the lid on the jar. Shake the jar to mix the iron filings with the oil. Touch the magnet to the side of the jar as shown. Look at the iron filings. How do they move? Do they form a pattern? Describe what you see.

In this chapter you will learn more about electricity. You will discover how an electric current can produce magnetism, and how magnetism can produce an electric current.

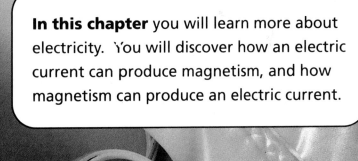

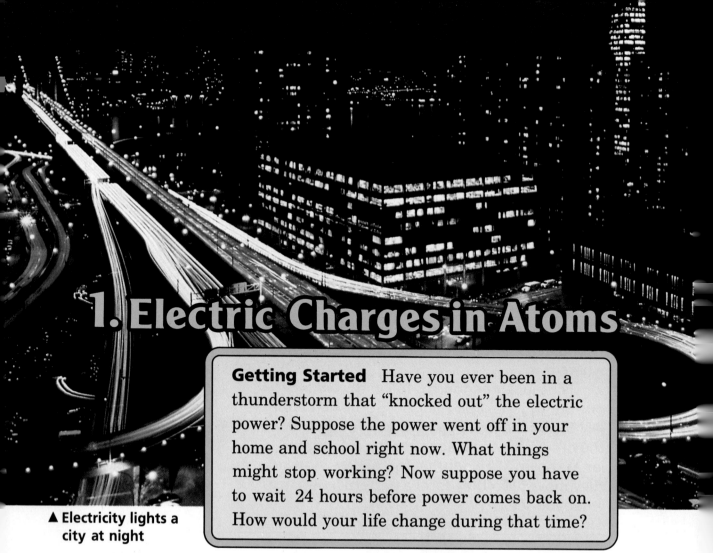

1. Electric Charges in Atoms

Getting Started Have you ever been in a thunderstorm that "knocked out" the electric power? Suppose the power went off in your home and school right now. What things might stop working? Now suppose you have to wait 24 hours before power comes back on. How would your life change during that time?

▲ **Electricity lights a city at night**

What are the kinds of electric charges in an atom?

Electricity is needed to light a lamp, play a record, and run a refrigerator. But what *is* electricity? Electricity is a form of energy called electrical energy. How is electrical energy being used in the picture?

Electrical energy comes from electric charges found in matter. Where are the charges found? You know that matter is made up of atoms. Every atom has a nucleus that contains protons and neutrons. The space around the nucleus contains rapidly moving electrons.

Look at the models of atoms in the drawings. Each proton has one positive electric charge, written +. Each electron has one negative electric charge, written −. The neutrons have no charge. You can see that the number of protons and the number of electrons in an atom are the same. Because there are the same number of positive and negative charges in the atom, the atom is neutral. The charges balance one another.

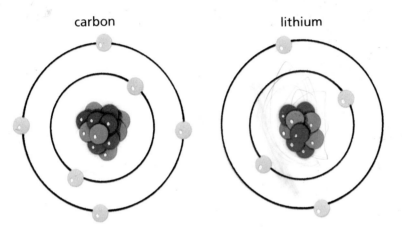

carbon   lithium   helium

How can atoms become charged?

There are two ways that neutral atoms become charged. One way they become charged is to lose electrons. The other way is to gain electrons.

Why are only electrons lost or gained? The protons and neutrons in the nucleus of an atom are held tightly together. It takes much energy to cause a nuclear change. So protons do not usually leave an atom. Electrons are held less strongly than protons are. It takes little force to remove outer electrons. In fact, atoms often lose outer electrons. These electrons often move to other atoms.

 neutron

 proton

 electron

Study the drawings of an atom of lithium (LIHTH ee um). Notice that this atom loses an electron. Then it has more positive charges than negative charges. So the lithium atom is positively charged. Why do the neutrons have no effect on the charge of the atom?

Now study the drawings of an atom of fluorine (FLAWR een). Notice that this atom gains an electron. Why is the fluorine atom then negatively charged?

How atoms become charged ▼

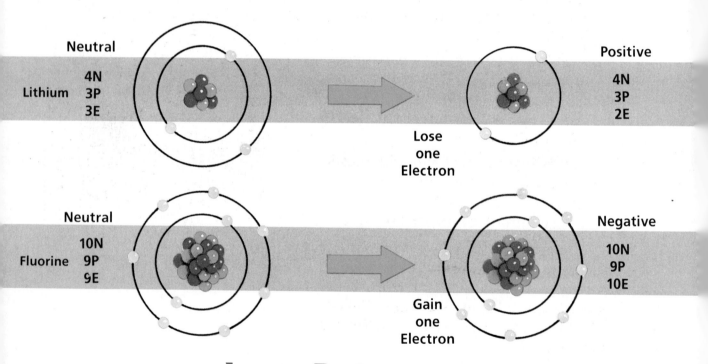

Neutral

Lithium 4N 3P 3E

Lose one Electron

Positive 4N 3P 2E

Neutral

Fluorine 10N 9P 9E

Gain one Electron

Negative 10N 9P 10E

Lesson Review ⎯⎯⎯⎯⎯

1. What two kinds of charged particles are found in atoms, and what are their charges?

2. How can an atom be electrically neutral?

3. In what ways can neutral atoms become charged?

Think! Suppose an atom has 10 protons and 8 electrons. What is its charge? If this atom gains 1 electron, what is its charge? Explain.

THINKING

Skills

Checking an inference

Imagine that when you turn on a lamp switch, you observe that the bulb does not light. You might decide that the bulb is burned out. Your idea is an inference—an explanation for a set of observations. More observations can help you decide if the inference is a good explanation.

Practicing the skill

A student observes the picture and makes the inference that yarn always picks up small pieces of paper.

1. Place tiny pieces of tissue paper on your desk. Check the inference by passing yarn over the pieces of paper. Do your observations support the inference?

2. Rub the yarn many times with plastic wrap. Now pass the yarn over the pieces of paper. What do you observe? Use this observation to make a new inference.

Thinking about the skill

The student made the inference that yarn *always* picks up tissue paper. What might make you think that something is always true?

Applying the skill

A girl at a picnic observes tiny pieces of a foam cup clinging to the back of a plastic spoon. She makes the inference that the foam is stuck to the spoon because the spoon is wet. How could she check her inference? What other inference could she make?

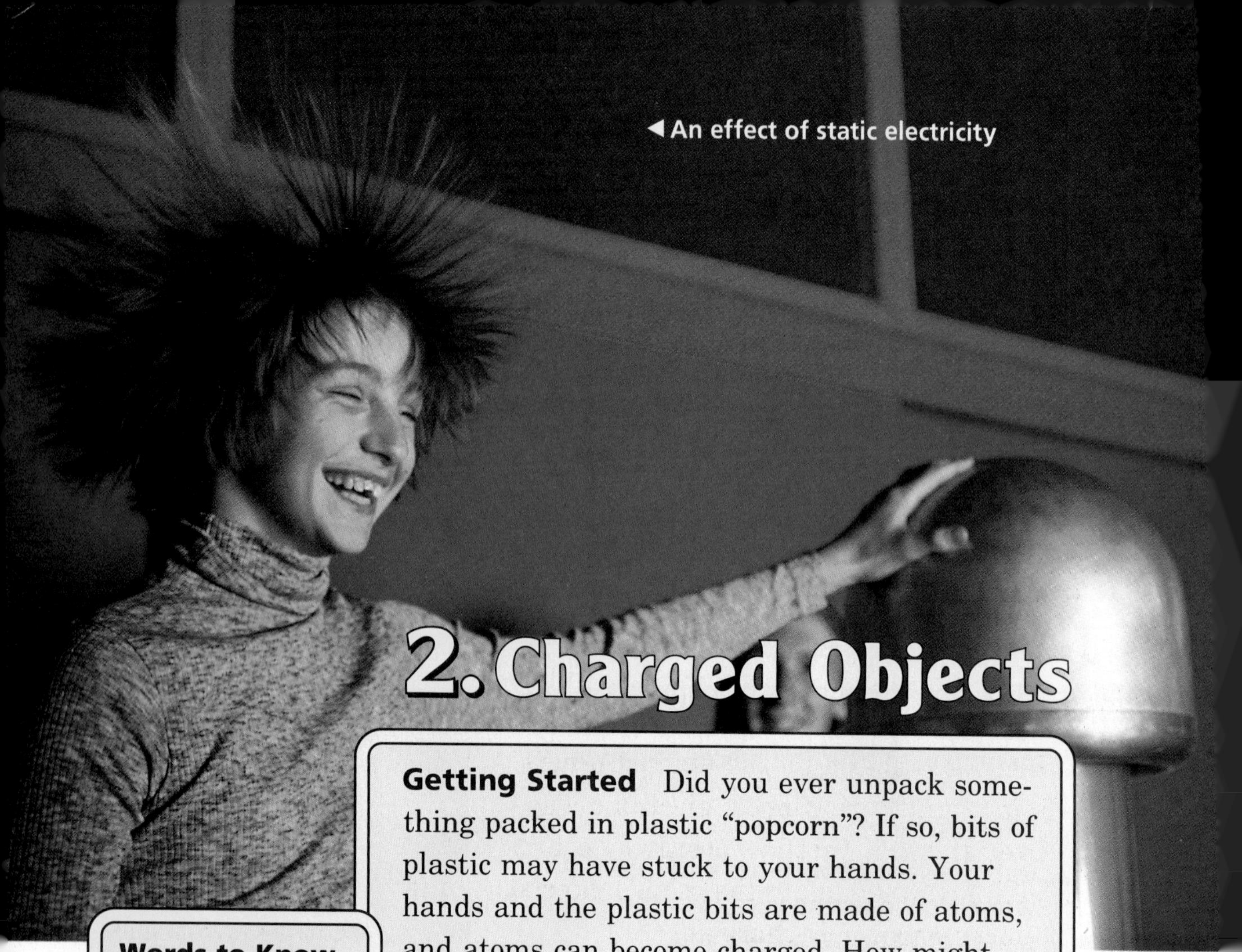

◀ An effect of static electricity

2. Charged Objects

Getting Started Did you ever unpack something packed in plastic "popcorn"? If so, bits of plastic may have stuck to your hands. Your hands and the plastic bits are made of atoms, and atoms can become charged. How might charges on the plastic help explain the way it behaves?

Words to Know
static electricity
electric discharge

How do charged objects affect each other?

This boy is touching a machine that causes his hair to become charged with static (STAT-ihk) electricity. **Static electricity** is an electric charge that collects on the surface of an object. Many materials become charged with static electricity when they are rubbed or touched by another material. The charge can be either positive or negative, depending on whether electrons are lost or gained.

When you comb your hair, you may notice that your hair is attracted to the comb. Look at the picture of a girl combing her hair. The + and − signs indicate the charges on the comb and hairs where they touch. Electrons leave the atoms of the hair and become attached to atoms of the comb. How does the number of protons in the hair now compare with the number of electrons in the hair? What kind of charge does the girl's hair have?

How does the number of protons in the comb compare with the number of electrons in the comb? What kind of charge does the comb have? Objects often become charged because they lose or gain electrons. This may happen when some materials rub against others. When the materials are rubbed, electrons leave one material and it becomes positively charged. The electrons are added to the other material, and it becomes negatively charged.

▼ Charges on hair and comb

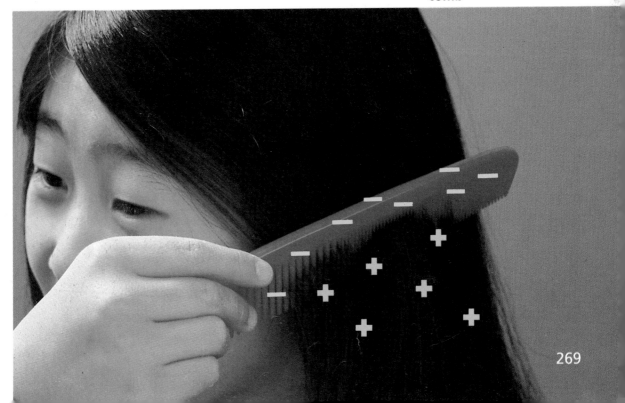

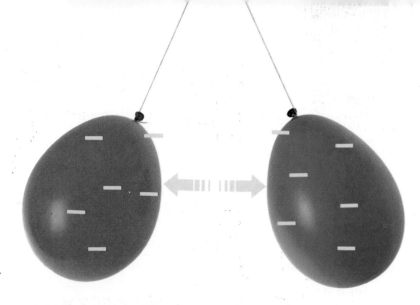

Balloons charged alike ▶

The two balloons in the picture have been rubbed with wool cloth. Notice how the two balloons repel each other. *Repel* means to "push apart." Why do the balloons push apart? When you rub a balloon with a wool cloth, electrons leave the atoms of the wool and move to the balloon. Because electrons are added to the balloon, it becomes negatively charged. Two negatively charged balloons repel one another because they have like charges. Any two objects with the same kind of charge repel each other.

Charged cat's hair and balloon ▼

You know what happens when you comb your hair. Electrons leave your hair and enter the comb. The hair becomes positively charged and the comb becomes negatively charged. Suppose you comb your hair and hold the comb near your hair after combing it. Some of the hairs are attracted to the comb. You can see the same effect on the hair of this cat soon after it was rubbed with a balloon. Two objects with opposite, or unlike, charges attract each other.

Objects with opposite charges attract. A charged object can also attract matter that is neutral. Did you ever use a charged plastic pen

Problem Solving

You Will Get a Charge Out of This

You know that wool may give a balloon a negative charge. The charge given to a balloon by other materials may be negative or it may be positive.

How can you identify the kind of charge given to a balloon?

Rub a balloon with materials such as these: plastic wrap, plastic bags, nylon, newspaper, and tissue paper. How can you find out whether the rubbed balloon becomes charged? How can you tell if the charge is positive or negative?

to pick up neutral bits of paper? The drawings show how this happens. (1) The negative charge of the pen repels the negative electrons in the paper. (2) The electrons move toward the opposite end of the paper. The end of the paper near the pen now has a positive charge. How do you explain why the pen attracts the paper?

Paper attracted by charged pen ▼

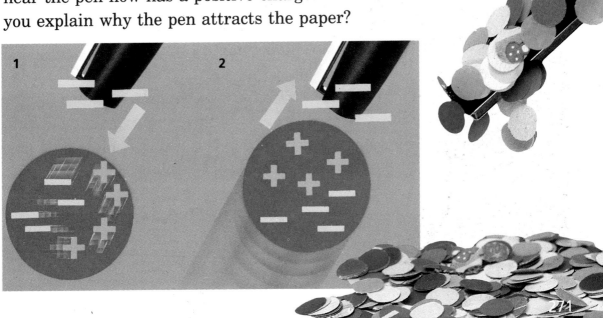

How can a charged object lose its charge?

When you walk across a carpet, your shoes rub electrons off the carpet. The electrons may then collect on your body. That is, your body becomes negatively charged. If you then touch a metal doorknob, you may feel an electric shock. You may even see a spark jump between your finger and the metal.

What caused the shock and the spark? Electrons move rapidly from a place that is negatively charged to a place that is positively charged or neutral. Your body had gained extra electrons. Then, when you touched the metal doorknob, electrons moved rapidly from your body to the doorknob. This movement of the extra electrons is called an **electric discharge** (DIHS chahrj). The drawing shows this movement of electrons. After the electric discharge, your body became less negative.

Small electric discharge ▼

Lightning is an electric discharge between the earth and a cloud, or between clouds. Look at the drawing of how lightning may occur. What do you notice about the charge on the bottom of the cloud? What is the charge on the water's surface? How is lightning similar to the spark you may see if you touch a metal object after walking on a carpet?

▲ **Large electric discharge**

Lesson Review

1. Define the term *static electricity.*
2. How do objects become negatively charged or positively charged?
3. How do objects with like charges and objects with unlike charges affect one another?
4. How can a charged object lose its charge, and what is this process called?

Think! Static electricity can be a nuisance. For example, it makes clothes stick together in a clothes dryer. How does this happen?

In *What's The Big Idea, Ben Franklin?*, page 292, you will find out whether he really did fly a kite in a storm and a lot more about his experiments with electricity.

3. Moving Electrons

Getting Started Think about a bolt of lightning and a flashlight. How are they alike? How are they different? Check your ideas as you read about the effects of moving electrons.

Words to Know
electric current
conductor
filament
insulator
electric circuit

What materials carry electric currents?

You know that lightning is an electric discharge. In lightning, electrons move quickly and then stop. A lightning flash lasts only a split second. Electrons also move through parts of a flashlight, but they keep moving as long as the flashlight is turned on. The continuous movement of electrons is an **electric current.**

How does electric current move through a lamp cord to a lamp? Look at the picture of the inside of a lamp cord. Find the two wires. These wires are conductors (kun DUK turz). An electrical **conductor** is a material through which

▼ Conducting wires in a lamp cord

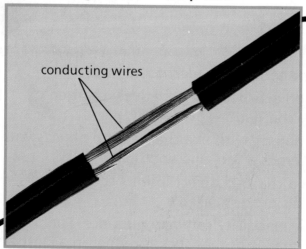

conducting wires

electrons move easily. The wires in a lamp cord are made of copper, a metal that is one of the best conductors.

Another metal helps produce light in a light bulb. Find the filament (FIHL uh munt) in the picture. The **filament** is a thin wire inside the glass bulb. This filament is made of the metal tungsten (TUNG stun). Tungsten is not as good a conductor as copper. Because the electrons do not move easily through tungsten, much of the electrical energy changes to heat. The filament gets so hot that it gives off light.

In the lamp cord shown, find the rubbery material that covers the copper wires. This material is an insulator (IHN suh layt ur). An **insulator** is a material through which electrons do not move easily. Rubber and many plastics are examples of insulators.

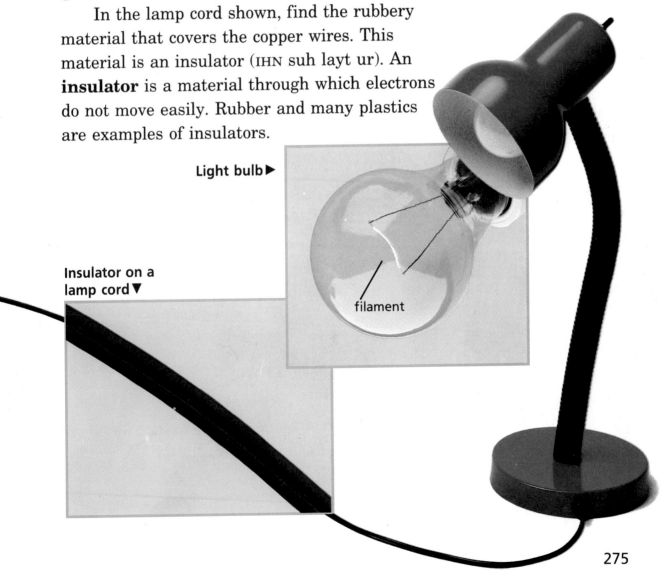

Light bulb ▶

Insulator on a
lamp cord ▼

filament

What is an electric circuit?

A path on which electrons move continuously is called an **electric circuit** (SUR kiht). Trace the path of electrons in this circuit. Begin at the battery that produces energy that moves the electrons. The electrons come from the atoms that make up the conductor, or wire. From the battery the electrons move along the conductor to the bulb. The bulb lights. Then the electrons move on the path back to the battery.

An electric circuit ▶

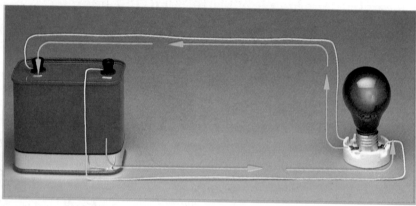

Now look at the circuit that contains a switch. A switch has two metal parts that touch when the switch is on. The two metal parts do not touch when the switch is off. Find these metal parts in the picture.

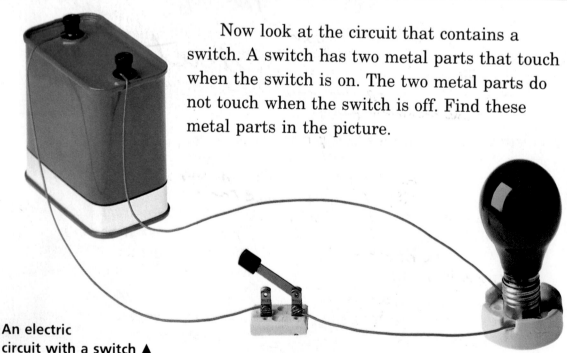

An electric circuit with a switch ▲

Explore

How can you find out if a material is a conductor or an insulator?

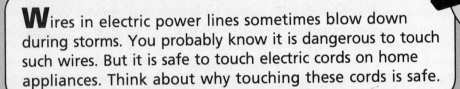

Wires in electric power lines sometimes blow down during storms. You probably know it is dangerous to touch such wires. But it is safe to touch electric cords on home appliances. Think about why touching these cords is safe.

Materials

safety goggles · size D battery in holder · light bulb in a bulb holder · 3 test leads · 8-cm copper wire · straw · penny · toothpick · paper clip · rubber band · cardboard strip · aluminum foil strip

Procedure

Caution: *Wear safety goggles for this activity.*

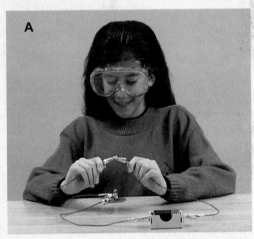

A

A. Connect a size D battery, a copper wire, and two test leads to form a circuit as shown.

  1. Does the bulb light? What does this show about this circuit?

B. Unclip the two test leads. Clip one test lead to one end of a straw.

  2. Predict whether or not the bulb will light if you clip the other test lead to the other end of the straw.

  3. What happens? Record your answer in a table.

C. Repeat steps **A** and **B** for a penny and for each of the other materials listed above.

Writing and Sharing Results and Conclusions

1. Which of the materials you tested are conductors? Which are insulators? How do you know? Write your answers in the table.

2. How do your results and conclusions compare with those of your classmates?

How does a switch work? A switch opens or closes a circuit. When a circuit is open, there is a break in the circuit. A circuit in which there is a break does not provide a path on which the electrons can move. Why is there no current in an open circuit?

When there is no break in a circuit, the circuit is closed and electrons can move. Which circuit shown is closed? Which circuit is open?

▼ **Switch closed**

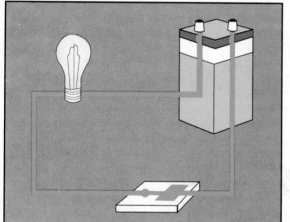

▼ **Switch open**

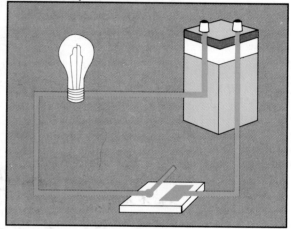

How can you use electricity safely?

You use batteries in such things as flash-lights and small radios. You handle these batteries without receiving an electric shock. But if you touch bare wires connected to an electrical outlet, you will feel a painful shock. If your skin happens to be wet, the current through you will be greater and more dangerous. Water makes your skin a better conductor.

Electricity from batteries that you use is harmless. But electricity from other sources can harm or kill living things. You can help prevent electrical accidents by following the rules on the next page.

Can you imagine living without electricity? Read **Connected!** *in Horizons Plus. Find out how the life of a family is changed by having electricity.*

278

	Never touch an electric appliance or a light switch when you are wet.
	Do not use a lamp or appliance that has a worn out or torn cord.
	Do not plug many electric devices into one outlet. The current may "overload" your house wiring. The wires may get hot and start a fire.
	Never put anything except an electrical plug in good condition into an electrical outlet.
	Stay away from electric power lines. Do not fly a kite near a power line or touch a fallen line.
	Do not swim, play in an open field, or stand under a tree during a lightning storm.

Lesson Review

1. What is an electric current?
2. Compare a conductor with an insulator.
3. What is an electric circuit?
4. List six rules for using electricity safely.

Think! Why are the rules related to safety in a lightning storm included among the rules for preventing electrical accidents?

Life Science
CONNECTION

Lightning is an important source of ammonia, which is used in the nitrogen cycle. Find out what the nitrogen cycle is and why it is important.

4. Magnetism and Electricity

Getting Started You know a magnet attracts certain objects. So does a charged balloon. Think about a magnet and a charged balloon. How are they alike? How are they different? If you have a magnet today, will it still be a magnet tomorrow? How long does a charged balloon stay charged?

When do electric charges produce magnetism?

For a long time, scientists believed that electricity and magnetic forces were not related in any way. Then, in 1820, Hans Oersted (hanz UR sted) found that an electric current produces a magnetic field.

Oersted did an experiment in which he used a battery, a coil of wire, and a compass. A compass needle usually points north. But if a compass is placed near a magnet, its needle may point in another direction.

Look at the picture of a wire placed in a north-south direction. There is no electric current in the wire. The needle of a compass held over the wire points north. Use the numbered drawings to follow an experiment with this wire.

1. The wire is made part of an electric circuit. There is now an electric current in the wire. In which direction is the compass needle pointing now?

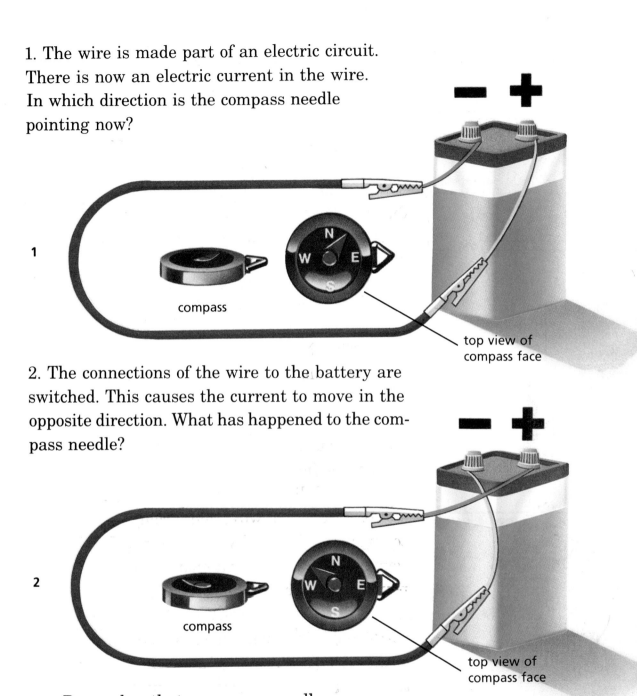

compass

top view of compass face

2. The connections of the wire to the battery are switched. This causes the current to move in the opposite direction. What has happened to the compass needle?

compass

top view of compass face

Remember that a compass needle may change direction when it is near a magnet. The space around a magnet is called a magnetic field. The experiment shows that there is a magnetic field around a wire in which there is an electric current. In other words, electric current can be used to produce magnetism.

What is an electromagnet?

An electric current can be used to make a useful magnet. Suppose a coil of wire is connected to a battery and a switch. If the coil is wrapped around an iron core, the magnet becomes stronger. When the switch is closed, the coil becomes a magnet. A magnet made when electrons move through a coil of wire wrapped around an iron core is called an **electromagnet** (ee LEK troh mag niht). What will happen to the objects clinging to this electromagnet if the circuit is opened?

You know that a magnet has poles. One end of the coil becomes a north pole and the other end becomes a south pole. But when the direction of the current in the coil is changed, the poles change places. Look at the needle of the compass in the picture. How will the needle change if the direction of the current is changed?

Simple electromagnet ▼

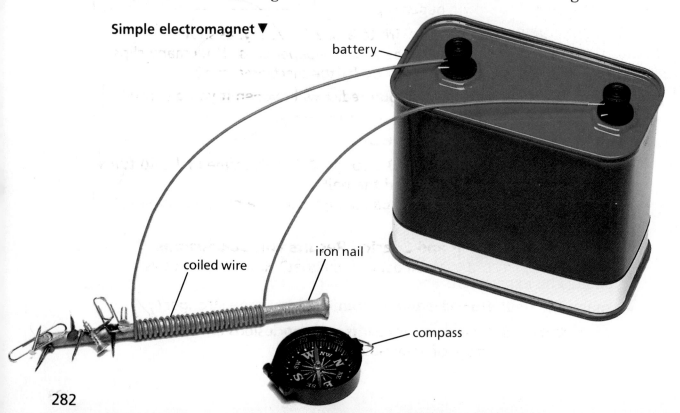

battery

coiled wire

iron nail

compass

ACTIVITY

Explore Together

How can you build an electromagnet?

Materials

Organizer

safety goggles · wire strippers · metric ruler · size D battery in battery holder · 1.5-m length of insulated bell wire · large nail · paper clips

Caution: *Wear safety goggles for this activity.*

Procedure

Manager

A. Use wire strippers to strip 5 cm of insulation from each end of a 1.5 m length of bell wire.

Investigator

B. Starting about 20 cm from the end of the wire, make 20 turns around the nail.

Investigator

C. Make a pile of paper clips. Bring the point of the nail near the pile.

Group, Recorder

1. What happens to the paper clips?

Investigator
Group, Recorder

D. Attach the wire to a size D battery, as shown.

2. What happens to the paper clips? How many clips were picked up by the electromagnet?

3. What do you predict will happen if you disconnect one end of the wire? Try it.

4. What happens?

E. Repeat steps **B** through **D**, but this time make 40 turns of wire around the nail.

5. How many paper clips does the nail pick up now?

Writing and Sharing Results and Conclusions

Group, Recorder

1. Did the nail act as a magnet? How do you know?

2. How can an electromagnet be made stronger?

Reporter

3. How do your results and conclusions compare with those of your classmates?

Like an ordinary magnet, an electromagnet can pick up paper clips, iron nails, and other magnetic objects. Unlike an ordinary magnet, an electromagnet can be turned on and off just by closing and opening its electric circuit. How does this feature make an electromagnet useful for moving steel in a junk yard?

How can a magnet produce an electric current?

If electric currents produce magnetic fields, do magnetic fields produce electric currents? Look at the numbered drawings of an experiment in which an electric current is produced.

1. A magnet is placed inside a coil of wire. The ends of the wire are connected to an electric meter. Look at the numbers on the meter. Notice that the pointer is on zero. This shows that no current is in the wire. As long as the magnet is not moved, the pointer stays on zero.

▲ **Electromagnet used in junkyard**

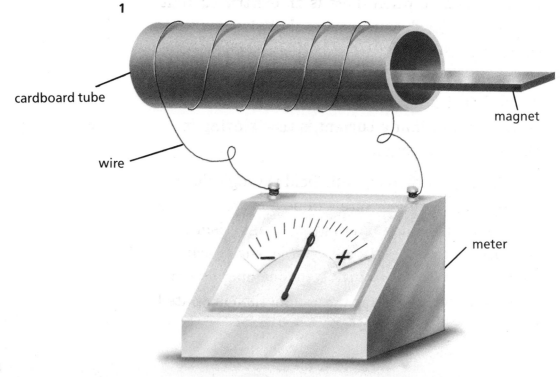

1

cardboard tube

magnet

wire

meter

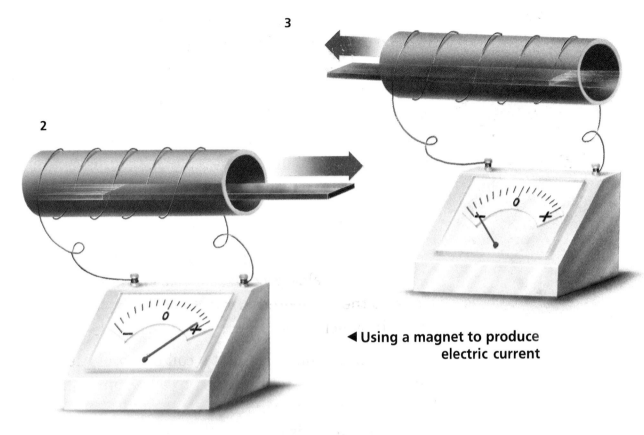

◄ **Using a magnet to produce electric current**

2. The magnet is being moved through the coil to the right. The pointer of the meter moves away from zero when there is an electric current in the wire. Look at the meter. Is there a current in the wire now? How do you know?

3. The magnet is being moved through the coil to the left. Look at the meter. The position of the pointer shows that a current is now moving in the opposite direction.

As long as the magnetic field through the coil is changing in time, there will be a current in the coil. This experiment shows that magnetism can produce an electric current. You learned earlier that an electric current can produce magnetism. These are two ways in which magnetism is related to electricity.

What energy changes occur in generators?

Look at the picture of a generator (JEN ur-ayt ur) in a power plant. A **generator** is a machine that changes mechanical energy into electrical energy. Inside the generator there are large magnets and coils of wire. As the coils of wire turn, they move through the magnetic fields. Electric current is produced in the coils. Generators are the source of electrical energy carried by power lines into homes, schools, factories, and office buildings. You will learn more about generators in Chapter 11.

Generator ▶

Lesson Review

1. When may electric charges produce a magnetic field?
2. What is an electromagnet?
3. When may a magnet produce an electric current?
4. What energy change takes place in a generator?

Think! Many electric companies are working to produce solar-powered electric plants. How might a solar-powered electric plant work?

Chapter Connections

Write a paragraph about the main ideas in this chapter.
Use the graphic organizer to help you.

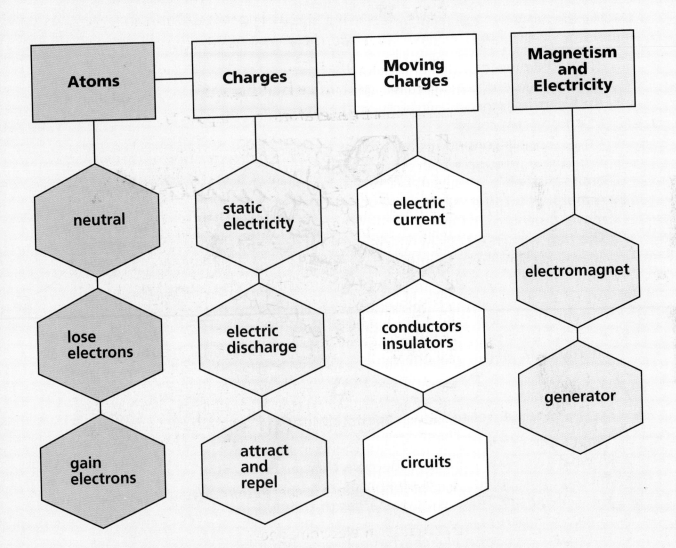

Writing About Science • Create

Make a poster about electrical safety rules. Design the
poster to teach young children how to use electricity safely.
Write a paragraph explaining your poster.

Science Terms

Copy the sentences below. Use the terms listed to complete the sentences.

conductor   electric circuit   electric current
electric discharge   electromagnet   filament
generator   insulator   static electricity

1. The rapid movement of extra electrons away from a charged object is called an _____.
2. An electric charge that collects on the surface of an object is called _____.
3. An _____ is a continuous movement of electrons.
4. A material through which electrons move easily is called a _____.
5. A material through which electrons do *not* move easily is called an _____.
6. The thin wire in a bulb in which electrical energy is changed to heat and light is called a _____.
7. An _____ is a path through which electrons can move.
8. An _____ is a magnet produced by an electric current in a coil of wire wrapped around an iron core.
9. A _____ is a device that produces electrical energy from mechanical energy.

Science Ideas

Use complete sentences to answer the following.

1. What kinds of electric charges are found in all atoms?
2. In what two ways can atoms become charged?
3. Suppose two objects are rubbed together to produce static electricity. How will the charges of the two objects compare?
4. How do objects with like charges behave if brought near each other?
5. How do objects with unlike charges behave if brought near each other?
6. What happens during an electric discharge?

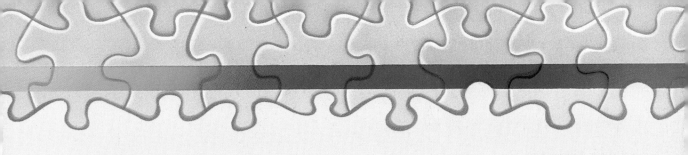

7. Name two conductors and two insulators.
8. Which drawing, *A* or *B*, shows a closed electric circuit? Which shows an open circuit? Explain your answers.
9. Why is it wise not to use a hair dryer in or near a shower or bathtub?
10. Why does a compass needle change direction when it is brought near a wire carrying a current?
11. How are an electromagnet and a bar magnet different?
12. How can a magnet and a coil of wire be used to produce electric current?
13. In what device is mechanical energy changed into electrical energy?

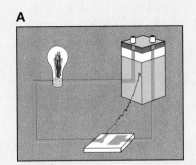

A

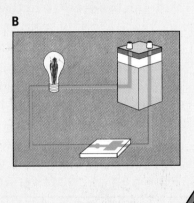

B

Applying Science Ideas

Use complete sentences to answer the following.
1. Why is it safe inside a house during a lightning storm? What things in the house should you avoid using until the lightning has stopped, and why?
2. Many people are trying to produce an electric car that will run as well as a gasoline-powered car. What problems do you think an electric car would have? What advantages would it have?

Using Science Skills

Look at the drawings of two compasses.
Notice that one is near a wire. What do you observe?
What inference can you make based on your observations?
How could you check your inference?

Careers in Physical Science

Bridge Painter

Many people drive over the Oakland Bay Bridge in California each day. They look up and see **bridge painters**. The painters work high up on the bridge. Most of the painters are men, but some are women. Deborah Torres is one of them.

Bridges aren't painted just to make them look pretty. The paint protects the steel structure from the air. Oxygen, pollutants, and salt in the air cause the steel to corrode. This could weaken the bridge.

Deborah cleans, scrapes, and paints the steel towers of the bridge. She climbs one of the towers each day. She carries five gallons of paint and a spider basket. She also carries rigging equipment. Her equipment includes cables, ropes, and a safety belt. Deborah uses the cables to attach the basket and her safety belt to the bridge. Then she climbs into the basket to paint.

Deborah had to train for two years for her job. She took classes at night. She learned about the properties of paints. She also learned to use rigging equipment. Rigging must be done just right. If not, Deborah could fall from the bridge.

Deborah did not always want to paint bridges. She finished high school. Then she was a bookkeeper. But she did not like to work in an office. "I like being outdoors," Deborah says.

So Deborah decided to get a new job. Deborah has worked on the bridge for four years. "When I started, I was the only woman," she says. Some people thought this would be a strange job for a woman. They said Deborah would not be big or strong enough. But Deborah proved these people were wrong.

"Now there are six women painting on the bridge," Deborah says. "I am very happy about that!"

Connecting Science Ideas

1. You have learned about physical and chemical changes. Which kind of change does Deborah Torres prevent by painting steel?   **Careers; Chapter 6**

2. Suppose you traveled to a planet with less gravity than Earth. Would your mass change? Would your weight change? Explain your answers.   **Chapter 5; Chapter 7**

3. Is the property that allows a steel ship to float in water a physical property or a chemical property? Explain your answer.   **Chapter 5; Chapter 7**

4. On page 168 you read about how a neon light works. Compare this with how a tungsten light bulb works. Use the term *current* and describe how electrical energy is changed.   **Chapter 5; Chapter 8**

5. How could you use electromagnets to replace the friction brakes on a bicycle?   **Chapter 7; Chapter 8**

Unit Project
Make some models of molecules, using modeling clay to represent atoms and toothpicks to represent chemical bonds. Use the same size and color of clay balls to represent a single kind of atom. Label each molecule with its formula.

from

What's the Big Idea, Ben Franklin?

Written by JEAN FRITZ
Illustrated by Margot Tomes

Ben Franklin, statesman, scientist, and inventor, was born in Boston. He moved to Philadelphia in 1723. It was there that he turned his scientific mind to the task of solving practical problems. His ideas led to many inventions, most of which are still used today. Find out about those inventions and what Ben called his "Big Idea!"

Philadelphia suited young Benjamin perfectly. He lived on High Street, the busiest and noisiest street in town. On one end of the street was the Delaware River to jump into when he felt like a goat leap. On the other end of the street was Debbie Read, whom he courted and married.

Benjamin and Debbie were married in 1730. Benjamin was 24 years old now and getting ahead in the world. He had his own printshop, owned his own newspaper, and because he was such a good printer, he did the printing for the government of Pennsylvania. (He always used the blackest ink and the whitest paper he could find.) In addition, Debbie and Benjamin ran a store in the front of their house. They sold books, sealing wax, pencils, maps, pictures of birds and animals, fishnets, chocolate, compasses, codfish, and cloth. And they always had a good supply of Mr. Franklin's soap for sale.

Yet no matter how busy he was, Benjamin found time to try out new ideas. Sometimes he had ideas on why things happen the way they do. He wrote about comets. He formed a theory about hurricanes; they moved, he said, from the southwest to the northeast, contrary to the way winds usually move. Once he made an experiment with a pot of molasses and an ant. He hung the pot on a string and watched for the ant to crawl down. Soon there was a swarm of ants crawling up the string, so Benjamin concluded that ants have a way of telling each other news.

Sometimes Benjamin's ideas were for the improvement of
Philadelphia. He formed the first circulating library in
America. He helped organize Philadelphia's fire department.
He suggested ways to light the streets, deepen the rivers,
dispose of garbage, and keep people from slipping on ice in
winter.

Sometimes his ideas turned into inventions. At the head
of his bed he hung a cord which was connected to an iron bolt
on his door. When he wanted to lock his door at night, he
didn't have to get out of bed. He just pulled the cord, rolled
over, and shut his eyes.

He invented a stepladder stool with a seat that turned up.
And a rocking chair with a fan over it. When he rocked, the
fan would turn and keep the flies off his head. He fixed up a
pole with movable fingers to use when he wanted to take
books down from high shelves. He cut a hole in his kitchen
wall and put in a windmill to turn his meat roaster. And he

invented an iron stove with a pipe leading outside. The stove produced more heat than an ordinary fireplace, cost less to operate, was less smoky, and became very popular.

In 1732, when he was 26 years old, Benjamin Franklin had one of his best ideas. He decided to publish an almanac. Every family bought an almanac each year. People read it to find out the holidays, the weather forecasts, the schedule of tides, the time the sun came up and went down, when the moon would be full, when to plant what. It was just the kind of book that Benjamin loved—full of odd pieces of information and bits of advice on this and that. It was, in addition to being a calendar, a grand how-to book and Benjamin figured he knew as many how-to's as anyone else. Besides, he knew a lot of jokes.

He put them all in his almanac, called it *Poor Richard's Almanack,* and published the first edition in 1733. His specialty was short one-line sayings.

Sometimes these one-liners were quick how-to hints for everyday living: "Eat to live, not live to eat"; "A penny saved is a penny earned"; "Half Wits talk much but say little."

In a few years Franklin was selling 10,000 copies of his almanac every year. (He kept it up for 25 years.)

This was certainly a good idea, but it was not Benjamin Franklin's Big Idea. He was 40 years old when he first became interested in the idea that would become the Big one.

The idea had to do with electricity, which had become a new fad. For some time it had been known that electricity could be generated by rubbing glass tubes with silk. Now a Dutch scientist had found that this electricity could be stored in specially equipped bottles, then drawn from them by applying wires (or conductors) to the 2 sides of the bottle. All over Europe people were meeting in darkened rooms to see these sparks and the tricks that could be performed. Wires

twisted into the shape of giant spiders were electrified. Sparks were drawn from a cake of ice and even from the head of a boy suspended from the ceiling by a silk rope. Electrical performers traveled from town to town selling shocks to curious people. Once, before a large audience in Spain, 180 grenadiers were linked together by wire, then given a shock to make them jump into the air at the same time.

His Big Idea was that electricity and lightning were the same. Up to that time most people had thought lightning was (and always would be) as mysterious as heaven itself. And here was Franklin saying it was the same stuff that you saw in parlor tricks—only on a grander scale. What was more, Franklin believed he could prove it. Let a sentry box be built on the top of a high tower, he wrote a scientist in Europe. Put a pointed rod in the tower and let a man stand in the box during a storm. Franklin knew that electricity was attracted to pointed iron rods; if the man in the sentry box could find that lightning was also attracted to a rod, that would prove they were the same. The only reason Franklin didn't make the experiment himself was that Philadelphia didn't have a high enough tower or even a high hill.

In the spring of 1752 three scientists in Europe tried the experiment and all three proved that Franklin's Big Idea was right. (One scientist was killed, but that was because he was careless.) Meanwhile Benjamin thought of a way to prove the Idea himself. One stormy day he raised a kite with a long pointed wire at the tip and felt the electric shock come through a key he had tied to the kite string near his hand. So he already had his own proof when the news reached him about the experiments in Europe. Still, he was surprised to hear how excited people were about his Idea. He was suddenly famous. Indeed, he was becoming the most celebrated man in America. The King of France sent him congratulations; the Royal Society of England presented him with a medal; universities gave him honors and called him Dr. Franklin; newspapers praised him. Benjamin was pleased. He felt secretly as proud, he said, as a girl wearing a new pair of garters.

A Big Idea, however, meant little to Benjamin Franklin unless he could put it to everyday use. So he invented the lightning rod, a pointed iron rod that could be raised from the roof of a house or barn to attract lightning and lead it harmlessly through a wire and into the ground. For his own lightning rod, he also fixed up a contraption that would ring a bell in the house whenever lightning hit. (Debbie hated that bell.)

Reader's Response
What did you learn about Benjamin Franklin that you didn't know before?

What's the Big Idea, Ben Franklin?

 Responding to Literature

1. What was Ben Franklin's Big Idea? Do you agree it was a big idea? Tell why or why not.

2. Ben Franklin was full of ideas about many things. Which of his ideas impressed you the most? Explain why. Talk about your choice with classmates.

3. Using information from the story, explain this statement: Benjamin Franklin was a scientific thinker.

4. How does Franklin's lightning rod demonstrate that he was concerned with the well-being of his neighbors?

5. You are a reporter working for a colonial newspaper that has chosen Ben Franklin "Philadelphia's Man of the Year." Write an article explaining why you think he deserves the award.

 Books to Enjoy

What's the Big Idea, Ben Franklin? by Jean Fritz
Electricity and almanacs were only a few of Ben Franklin's many inventions. Read the book to find out about his other inventions and to learn more about this interesting man.

Thomas Alva Edison by Christopher Lampton
Follow the advances made by Thomas Edison, another scientist who experimented with electricity. Read about his invention of the light bulb.

Power Up: Experiments, Puzzles, and Games Exploring Electricity by Sandra Markle
Unlike some of the early experiments with electricity, these experiments are safe! **Power Up** also contains information about the development of electricity.

SCIENCE HORIZONS

EARTH SCIENCE

Chapter 9

Predicting the Weather

Weathering the Storm

Are there many storms where you live? There probably are. The United States has tornadoes, hurricanes, blizzards, thunderstorms, and dust storms. Scientists are working on better ways to predict these severe storms. Better predictions will mean earlier warnings about tornadoes and floods. These warnings could save lives.

Since 1959, radar has been used to predict weather. You may have seen radar weather maps on television. Radar sends out radio waves that bounce off raindrops. The radar shows how much rain is falling. Some types of radar also show the speed and direction of storms.

Radar cannot detect tornadoes. It can spot storms that might produce tornadoes. But nobody is sure that a tornado has formed until someone sees the funnel cloud. By the time the funnel cloud has been spotted, there may be only 5 minutes before it reaches the ground. That does not give people much time to get out of the way.

NEXRAD is an important new tool for predicting weather. NEXRAD stands for Next Generation Weather Radar. This radar does not just bounce waves off the outside of clouds. NEXRAD waves go inside clouds. The waves bounce off drops of water in the clouds. Now scientists can find out how the drops of water in a cloud are moving. Movement inside the clouds tells how strong the storm is. It can also show that a tornado is starting to form. Now people will get earlier tornado warnings.

Another new tool is the Wind Profiler. It uses radar to track winds high in the atmosphere. The profiler measures the speed and direction of winds. It can measure winds at 72 different heights up to 16 km (10 miles) above the ground. The data from each profiler go to a computer. The computer makes a model that shows the wind patterns.

Knowing wind patterns helps the people who predict weather. Weather systems are moved from place to place by these winds. If scientists know how the winds are blowing, they can tell where a storm system is headed.

Discover

Can wind direction predict the weather?

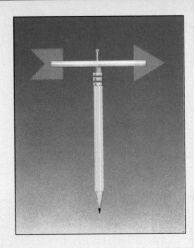

Materials ruler · index card, 10 cm x 15 cm · scissors · plastic straw · tape · straight pin · new pencil with an eraser

Procedure

Does wind from a certain direction bring a certain kind of weather? Make a simple wind vane to find out. On an index card, draw the shapes of the ends of the wind vane. Cut out these shapes. Cut a slot in each end of a straw. Insert the head of the vane in one slot and the tail in the other. Tape the pieces together. Push a straight pin through the center of the straw and push the pin into the eraser of a pencil. Make sure your wind vane can turn easily.

Hold the wind vane outside in the breeze. The vane will point toward the direction from which the wind blows. Record the wind direction each day at the same time for a month. Keep track of the weather, too. What patterns can you find? What weather can you predict when the wind blows from the north? What if it blows from the south?

In this chapter you will learn more about storms and how they form. You will see other ways that scientists study weather and predict changes.

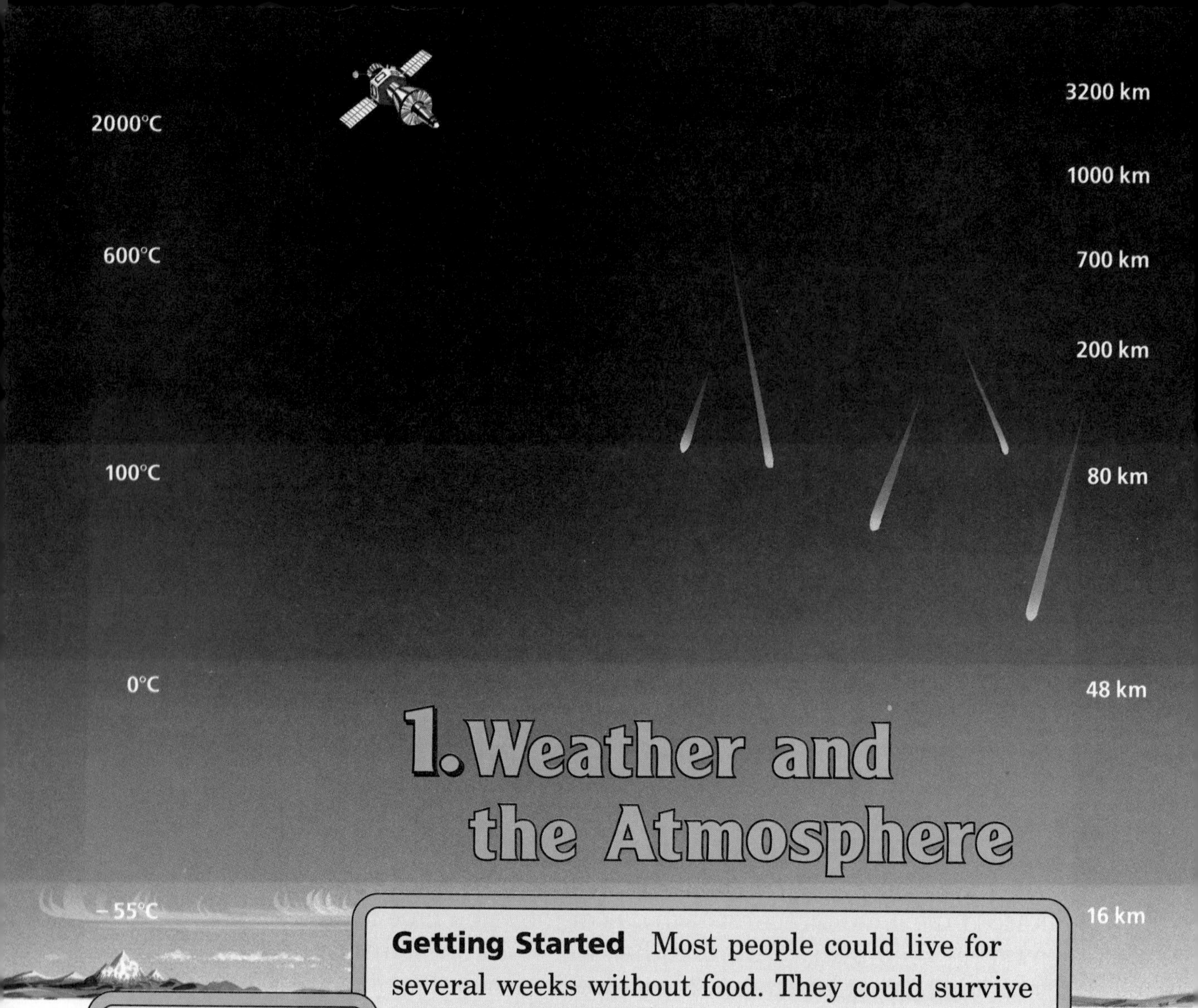
2000°C
3200 km
1000 km
600°C
700 km
200 km
100°C
80 km
0°C
48 km
-55°C
16 km

1. Weather and the Atmosphere

Words to Know
troposphere
relative humidity

Getting Started Most people could live for several weeks without food. They could survive several days without water. But they could only live for a few minutes without breathing air. List some other uses of air.

What is the troposphere?

The earth is surrounded by an invisible blanket of air called the atmosphere. The atmosphere can be divided into layers. The layers are divided by the large changes in temperature from layer to layer. You can see where each layer begins in the drawing of the atmosphere.

The layer of the atmosphere closest to the earth's surface is called the **troposphere** (TROH poh sfihr). Most of the air in the atmosphere is found in the troposphere. This is because air has mass. Gravity pulls the air toward the earth's surface. How thick is the troposphere? How thick are the other layers?

The atmosphere is mostly a mixture of gases. The pie chart shows the gases that make up this mixture. What two gases make up most of the air? The air also contains tiny particles of different kinds of solids. Particles such as dust and salt enter the air naturally. But human activities add particles of soot and smoke, as well as extra dust. How do you think humans add some of these particles?

▼ Gases in the atmosphere

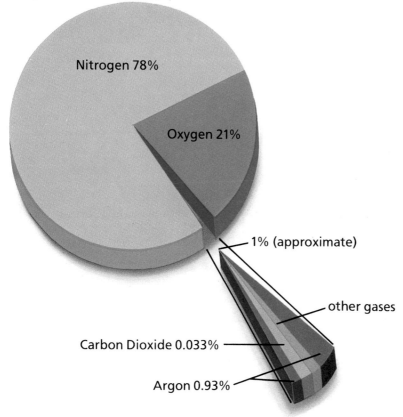

Nitrogen 78%

Oxygen 21%

1% (approximate)

other gases

Carbon Dioxide 0.033%

Argon 0.93%

307

The amounts of nitrogen and oxygen in the air are always about the same. But the amounts of water vapor and carbon dioxide change from time to time and place to place. Air near large bodies of water contains more water vapor than air in dry regions. Warm air often contains more water vapor than cool air.

The drawing shows how nitrogen leaves and returns to the air. Bacteria remove nitrogen from the air and add it to the soil. Plants use this nitrogen. Animals take in nitrogen when they eat the plants. When plants and animals die, nitrogen is released and returns to the air.

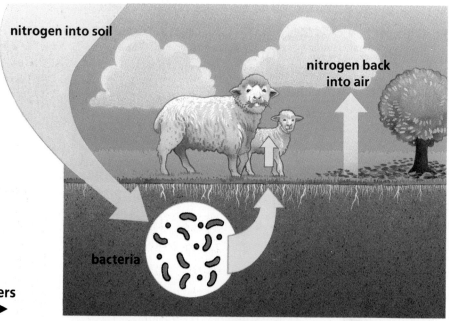

nitrogen into soil

nitrogen back into air

bacteria

How nitrogen enters and leaves the air ▶

The drawing on the next page shows how carbon dioxide enters and leaves the air. Most carbon dioxide enters the air when it is given off by animals and plants. Most carbon dioxide that leaves the air is removed by green plants.

The burning of fuels such as coal and gasoline adds carbon dioxide to the air. This extra carbon dioxide may be causing the atmosphere to become warmer by trapping heat in it.

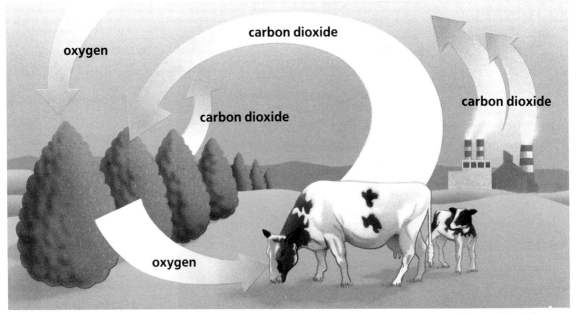

▲ How carbon dioxide enters and leaves the air

What is weather?

Weather is the condition of the atmosphere at a given time and place. The conditions that make up weather include air temperature, air pressure, wind, and water in the form of ice, water droplets, and water vapor. The water vapor in the air is called humidity. Humidity varies from time to time and from place to place.

Relative humidity is the amount of water vapor in the air compared with the total amount that the air can hold at that temperature. Relative humidity is measured with a psychrometer (sye KRAHM ut ur) such as the one shown. Relative humidity is expressed as a percent.

Air temperature depends on energy from the sun. Some of this energy is absorbed by and warms the earth's surface. The warmed surface gives off heat that warms the troposphere.

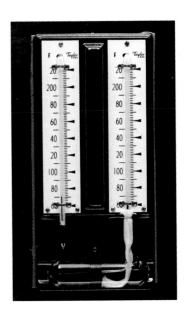

▲ A psychrometer

Explore

How does a psychrometer work?

During the summer, many people try to stay cool by going swimming. When you sit in the sun after swimming, you feel cool as long as you stay wet. You are kept cool because the water on your skin evaporates, or changes to water vapor. As the water evaporates into the air, it takes heat away from your body.

Materials
2 thermometers · hollow shoelace · water

Procedure

A. Cut a 6 cm piece of shoelace. Dip the shoelace in the water.

B. Slip the bulb of one thermometer inside the end of the shoelace. This will be the wet-bulb thermometer. The other is the dry-bulb thermometer.

C. Fan both thermometers for about 10 minutes.

  1. What temperatures are show on both thermometers?

  2. What is the difference between the temperatures shown on the two thermometers?

D. Use the table to find the relative humidity.

Writing and Sharing Results and Conclusions

1. What caused the differences in temperatures shown on the two thermometers?

2. Suppose that both thermometers showed the same temperature. What would be the relative humidity?

Relative Humidity %									
Dry-bulb temp. (°C)	Difference between wet-bulb and dry-bulb temp. (°C)								
	1	2	3	4	5	6	7	8	9
15	90	81	71	61	53	44	36	27	20
16	90	81	71	63	54	46	38	30	23
17	90	81	72	64	55	47	40	32	25
18	91	82	73	65	57	49	41	34	27
19	91	82	74	65	58	50	43	36	29
20	91	83	74	66	59	51	44	37	31
21	91	83	75	67	60	53	46	39	32
22	92	83	76	68	61	54	47	40	34
23	92	84	76	69	62	55	48	42	36
24	92	84	77	69	62	56	49	43	37
25	92	84	77	70	63	57	50	44	39
26	92	85	78	71	64	58	51	46	40
27	92	85	78	71	65	58	52	47	41

Relative humidity

The earth's surface is not heated evenly. So the troposphere is also not heated evenly. Air over a warm surface will be warm. Air over a cool surface will be cool. Particles of warm air are spread out more than those of cool air. So warm air is less dense than cool air.

Another condition that makes up weather is air pressure. Because the air has weight, it presses with a force. The force exerted by the air is called air pressure. Air pressure is not the same all over the earth's surface. The drawing shows why.

▲ **Rising and sinking air**

Cool air is denser than warm air, so cool air tends to sink. As cool air sinks, it exerts more pressure on the earth's surface. On the other hand, warm air tends to rise. As it rises, it exerts less pressure on the surface. Look at the drawing. Is air pressure greater at point A or at point B?

Because the atmosphere is not heated evenly, regions of different air pressures form.

Air tends to move from regions of high pressure to regions of low pressure. This moving air is called wind. Local winds are caused by differences in pressure between air over small areas of the earth. These local winds are part of larger circular patterns of moving air. The drawing shows the larger circular wind patterns of the earth. Do the large winds blowing along the earth's surface move toward or away from regions of low pressure?

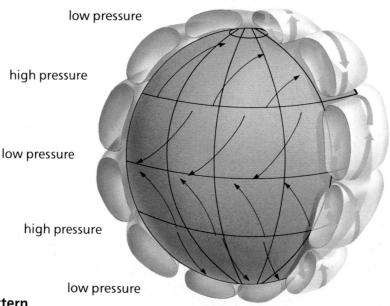

low pressure

high pressure

low pressure

high pressure

low pressure

Circular wind pattern of the earth ▶

Life Science
CONNECTION

Find out how photosynthesis affects the amount of oxygen and carbon dioxide in the atmosphere.

Lesson Review

1. What two gases make up most of the air? What percentage of the air does each make up?

2. What are four conditions that make up weather?

3. What causes air pressure?

4. What causes winds?

Think! Suppose you are rising through the atmosphere in a hot air balloon. What happens to air pressure as you rise? What causes this change?

312

Skills

Using data to make predictions

Sometimes, as you watch teams play a sport, you can predict who will win. To make this prediction, you can see how well each team is playing in the game. You can also think about the record of each team. Data such as the number of games that a team has won are useful in making a prediction.

Practicing the skill

1. Air near the ground sometimes moves upward to higher levels. When air rises, it becomes cooler. The graph shows what the temperature of rising air would be if it were at 35°C on the ground. The graph shows that the air would be 34°C at 100 m above the ground. What is the temperature of the air at 200 m? At 500 m?

2. For every 100 m the air rises, how many degrees does its temperature decrease?

3. Suppose the temperature of the air on the ground is 43°C. Use your answer to Step 2 to predict what the temperature of this air would be if it rose to 300 m. What would its temperature be at 500 m and 800 m?

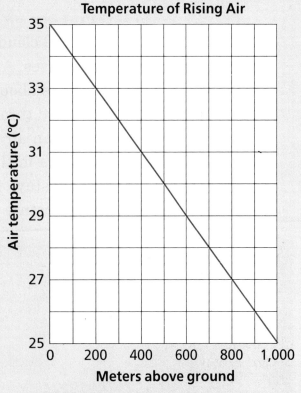

Thinking about the skill

What information would you need to be able to check your prediction?

Applying the skill

Suppose air that is 200 m above the ground has a temperature of 27°C. What will its temperature be if it rises to 700 m above the ground? What will its temperature be at 1,000 m above the ground?

2. Air Masses and Fronts

Words to Know
air mass
front

Getting Started Look at the clouds in the picture. On one side of these clouds is warm air. On the other side of them is cold air. Why do you think the clouds formed between the cold air and the warm air?

What are air masses?

The clouds in the picture are between two air masses. An **air mass** is a large body of air that has about the same temperature and moisture throughout. Air masses cover large areas. An air mass forms when a large body of air stays in the same place for several days. As the air stays there, it takes on the temperature and moisture conditions of the surface under it.

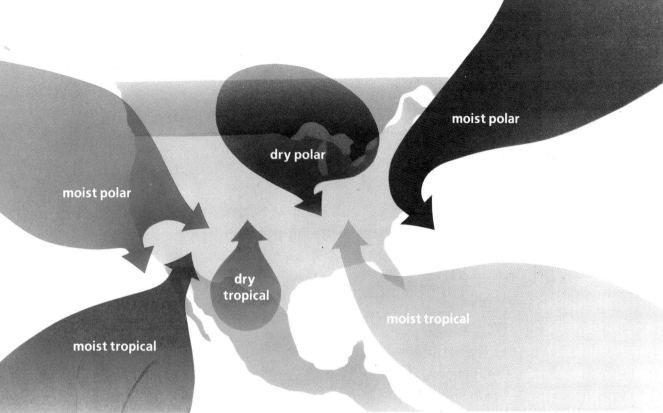

▲ Air masses that affect the United States

Most air masses that affect weather in the United States form in the regions shown on the map. You can learn a lot about air masses from the regions over which they form. Air masses that form near the North or South Pole are polar air masses. Polar air masses are cold. Air masses that form near the equator are tropical air masses. Tropical air masses are warm. Air masses that form over land are often dry. Those that form over water are often moist. A polar air mass that forms over water often is cool and moist. What would a tropical air mass that forms over water be like?

As an air mass moves, it takes on some conditions of the surface under it. Suppose a cool, moist air mass moves over warm, dry land. The air mass will become warmer and drier. What will happen to a cool, dry air mass that moves over a warm ocean?

Explore Together

What happens when air is warmed and cooled?

Organizer

Materials
lamp · two 20 cm x 25 cm pieces of poster board · tape · incense stick · 14-16 oz tin can · ice

Procedure

Investigator

A. Form a tube with the poster board to fit around the lamp bulb. Tape the tube so that it holds its shape. Form another tube that fits around the can. Tape this tube also.

Investigator, Manager

B. Cover most of the lamp bulb with the tube. Fill the can with ice. Cover most of the can with the second tube.

C. Turn on the lamp. Have your teacher light the incense stick. *Caution: Handle the incense carefully.*

Investigator, Group, Recorder

D. Hold the incense over the top of the tube on the lamp.
1. Predict where the smoke will go.
2. Where does the smoke go?

E. Hold the incense over the top of the tube on the can.
3. Predict where the smoke will go.
4. Where does the smoke go?

Writing and Sharing Results and Conclusions

Recorder, Reporter

1. How did the warm air move? How did the cold air move?

2. Are your results like others in the class?

3. Why do you think cold air pushes up warm air at a cold front?

What happens when air masses move?

Once they are formed, air masses often move in the directions shown on the air mass map. As an air mass moves, it may come in contact with another air mass. The boundary (BOWN-duh ree), or area of contact, between two air masses is called a **front.** Most weather changes take place along fronts.

Fronts often form when one air mass overtakes a slower air mass. A cold front forms when a cold air mass overtakes a warm air mass. Along a cold front, moving cold air is

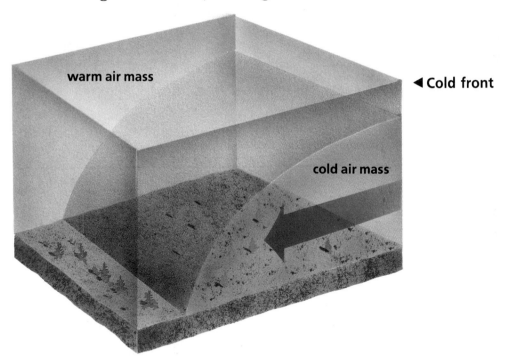

warm air mass

cold air mass

◀ Cold front

forced under the less dense warm air ahead of it. As the warm air is forced to rise, it cools. Cool air cannot hold as much water vapor as warm air. So the water vapor condenses to form clouds in this rising air. Often storms form along cold fronts. These storms can produce heavy rains or hail.

After a cold front passes, the weather behind it is often fair and cool. The sky is usually clear. Some white, puffy cumulus clouds may form.

A warm front forms when a warm air mass overtakes a cold air mass. The drawing shows that the slope of a warm front is not as steep as that of a cold front. Along a warm front, warm air "slides" over the denser cold air ahead of it. If enough moisture is present, clouds form all along the front.

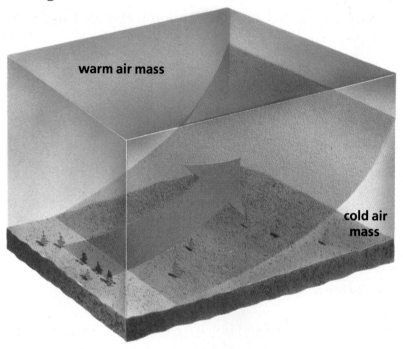

warm air mass

cold air mass

Warm front ▲

At the leading edge of the front, thin cirrus clouds form high in the atmosphere. Cirrus clouds are often the first sign that a warm front is coming. You would see these clouds several days before a warm front arrives.

As a warm front moves closer, the sky may be covered by low, gray stratus clouds. These

clouds often bring steady rains that last for
several days. The passing of a warm front often
brings warm, cloudy weather.

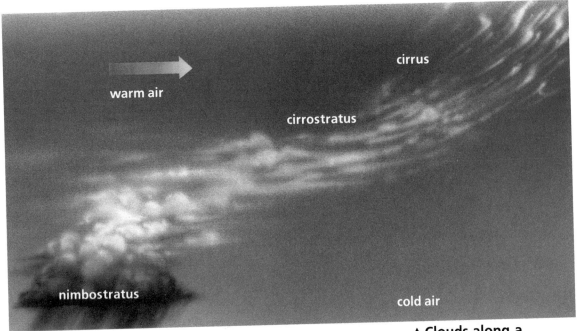

▲ Clouds along a
warm front

Sometimes two air masses next to each
other stop moving. The boundary between two
unmoving air masses is called a stationary front.
The weather along a stationary front is like that
along a warm front. This weather may continue
for many days until the front moves on.

Lesson Review

1. What kind of air mass would form over the ocean
   near the equator?
2. How might a cold, moist air mass change as it
   moved over a warm, dry land region?
3. What kind of weather occurs along a cold front?

Think! Suppose that in the morning the weather is
hot and humid, and the sky is very hazy. You hear
that a cold front will pass by late in the afternoon.
What weather changes would you expect to see
during the day?

3. Storms

Words to Know
storm
thunderstorm
hurricane
tornado

Getting Started Lightning flashes and thunder rumbles. Rain pounds and wind roars. These are some sights and sounds of a storm. How might you create storm sights and sounds for a school play?

What do different kinds of storms have in common?

A **storm** is a weather disturbance caused by unusual weather conditions. There are many kinds of storms. But all storms have some conditions in common. For example, all storms start when warm, moist air rises. This rising air results in low air pressure at the earth's surface.

Other common weather conditions include clouds and either rain, sleet, hail, or snow. All storms also have strong winds because the pressure near the center of the storm is lower than the pressure outside the storm. The greater the difference in air pressure, the stronger the winds.

What are some different types of storms?

The most common type of storm is a thunderstorm. A **thunderstorm** is a small, local storm with tall clouds, heavy rain, and thunder and lightning. The chart lists safety measures to take during thunderstorms.

Most thunderstorms form along cold fronts. Warm, moist air is forced up over colder air. Cumulonimbus (cyoo myoo loh NIHM buhs) clouds form in the rising air. When enough water vapor condenses, rain or snow begins to fall. The falling rain or snow produces strong downward-moving air currents. In time, the downward currents stop the air from rising. These currents form strong winds that sweep ahead of the rains at the earth's surface.

Thunderstorms Precautions
DO:
1. stay indoors or inside a car.
2. crouch down low to the ground if outdoors.
3. stay off hilltops and open fields.
DO NOT:
1. stand under trees or other tall objects.
2. go in or near any body of water.
3. stay on open metal vehicles such as bicycles or farm equipment.

How a thunderstorm forms ▼

Thunderstorms often last less than an hour. But some last longer. These storms can be severe. A strong thunderstorm may release 50 times as much energy as a small nuclear bomb.

The storm that is largest in size is a hurricane (HUR ih kayn). A **hurricane** is a large tropical storm that has very high winds and heavy rainfall. A hurricane may cover an area almost as large as the state of Texas.

The picture of a hurricane taken from a satellite on the next page shows spiral bands of clouds. The clouds surround the circular center called the eye of the hurricane. Warm air rises in the hurricane's eye. Air pressure in the eye is very low.

Winds in a hurricane ▼

Hurricanes form over warm tropical oceans. A hurricane starts when warm, moist air rises over the ocean. This produces low air pressure below the rising air. As the rising air cools, water vapor condenses and clouds form. At this point, the system is called a tropical storm.

When water vapor condenses, heat is released into the air. This heat causes the air in the storm's center to rise faster. Air pressure at the surface becomes even lower. Winds around the center of the storm become stronger.

The storm continues to grow bigger and stronger until it becomes a hurricane. Hurricanes move across the ocean surface at speeds of about 10-20 kilometers per hour. Winds may reach speeds of up to 300 kilometers per hour.

*Alicia's visit was one that Josie would never forget. Read about it in **Josie and Hurricane Pie** in Horizons Plus.*

▼ A hurricane

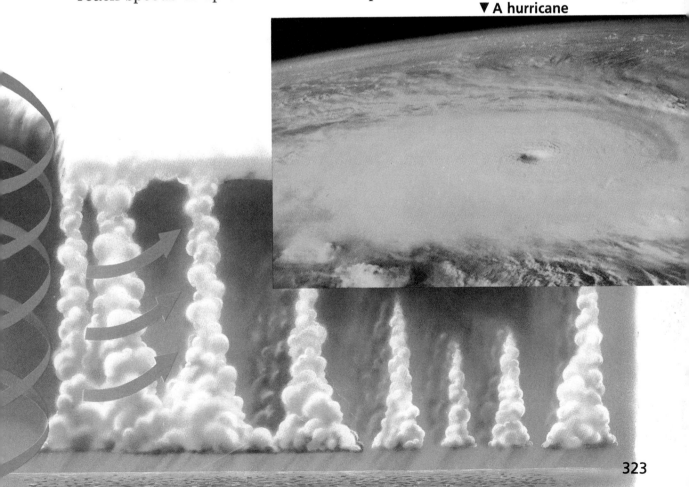

323

Problem Solving

Better to Be Safe Than Sorry

Suppose you were expecting a thunderstorm, hurricane, or tornado. These storms can be dangerous. So you want to be prepared when one occurs. You want to prevent injury to your family and damage to your home.

How can you prepare for a violent storm that is predicted for your region?

Plan a storm safety drill for a thunderstorm, hurricane, or tornado. Will you have to leave your home? If you do not leave, where is the safest place to be inside? What should you do to your home?

Damage caused by a hurricane ▼

Hurricanes cause much damage when they move over land. The heavy rains and strong winds cause much destruction. But most often, the greatest damage is caused by flooding. The high winds combine with high tides causing much flooding.

If a hurricane moves over land, it soon loses much of its energy. In time, it becomes nothing more than a heavy rainstorm. The chart on page 322 lists some things to do when you are in a region where a hurricane may strike.

It may seem strange, but the most damaging type of storm is also the smallest in size. A **tornado** is a small funnel of quickly spinning air. Tornadoes often form during violent thunderstorms. The picture shows a tornado that seems to be hanging from a cloud.

The air pressure in the center of the funnel of a tornado is very low. So winds move very quickly toward the center of the funnel. The

winds in a tornado may reach speeds as high as 800 kilometers per hour. Such winds can pick up an automobile and toss it aside like a toy. Wherever a funnel touches the surface, it behaves much like a vacuum cleaner. Objects are pushed into the low pressure center by the high pressure winds of the tornado.

More tornadoes occur in the United States than in any other part of the world. Most of them occur in the Midwest and along the coasts of the Gulf of Mexico and the Atlantic Ocean. The chart lists some safety rules to follow if a tornado is expected.

A tornado ▲

Lesson Review

1. What do most storms have in common?
2. How is a thunderstorm different than a hurricane?
3. What type of storm has the strongest winds?

Think! The midwestern part of the United States has many tornadoes but no hurricanes. Why do you think this is so?

Tornado Precautions
DO:
1. go to a storm cellar, basement, or first floor room with no windows.
2. lie flat under a heavy piece of furniture if in a first floor room.
3. lie face-down in a low place and cover your head if outdoors.
DO NOT:
1. stand near a window.
2. go to an attic.

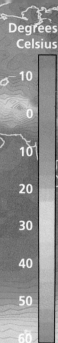

Degrees
Celsius

- 10
- 0
- 10
- 20
- 30
- 40
- 50
- 60

4. Predicting Weather Changes

Getting Started Some people pretend to predict the future by looking into a crystal ball. What do you think scientists use to predict future weather conditions?

▲ A meteorologist

What is a weather forecast?

Suppose that you are planning to spend most of your weekend outdoors. You might turn on the television or look in the paper for the weather forecast. A **weather forecast** (FOR-kast) is a prediction of what future weather conditions will be.

Weather forecasts are made by meteorologists (meet ee ur AHL uh jihsts). A **meteorologist** is a scientist who studies weather. Meteorologists study present weather conditions to help them predict what the weather will be in the future. They may use maps such as this to study the weather.

Meteorologists measure all of the present weather conditions. For example, air temperature is measured in degrees Celsius (°C). Relative humidity is expressed as a percent. Air pressure is measured in units called millibars (MIHL ih bahrz). At sea level, air pressure is about 1,013 millibars (mb).

What do weather maps show?

Meteorologists all around the world measure the weather conditions in their local regions. In the United States, the National Weather Service (NWS) collects and organizes these measurements. Using these measurements, weather maps are made. This map shows the air pressure in the eastern United States on the date shown.

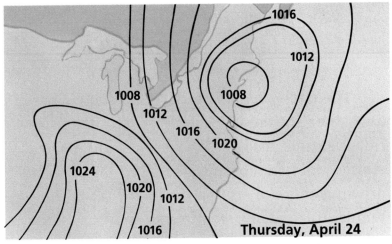

◀ Isobars on a weather map

The curved lines running through the map are called isobars (EYE soh bahrz). **Isobars** are lines on a weather map that connect places that have the same air pressure. Some of the isobars form closed circles. These circles show either a center of high pressure or a center of low pressure.

Symbols (SIHM buhlz) are used on a weather map to show certain weather conditions. Meteorologists all over the world use the same weather symbols. The chart shows some of these weather symbols.

Weather Map Symbols							
Weather	Symbol	Wind Speed (mph)	Symbol	Cloud Cover (%)	Symbol	Fronts and Pressure Systems	Symbol
Hail	△△△△ △△△△	1–4		0	○	Cold Front	▼▼
		5–8		10	◑		
Rain		9–14		20–30	◕	Warm Front	●●
		15–20		40	◑		
Showers		21–25		50	◑	Stationary Front	●▼
		26–31		60	◑		
Snow	✳✳✳✳ ✳✳✳✳	32–37		70–80	◕	High Pressure	Ⓗ
		38–43		90	◉		
Hurricane	⚡	44–49		100	●	Low Pressure	Ⓛ

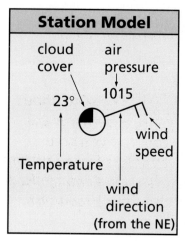

Station Model

cloud cover   air pressure

23°   1015

Temperature   wind speed

wind direction (from the NE)

The circles on a weather map show where a weather station is located. These circles are called station models. Weather conditions at a station are listed beside its station model. The drawing shows a station model. What is the temperature at the weather station? What is the wind direction? What is the wind speed?

How are weather maps used to predict weather changes?

A weather map of the United States shows the weather conditions that exist across the country at a given time and day. This information may be interesting. But, by itself, it is not very useful. Today's weather map can't tell you much about tomorrow's weather. Or can it?

Suppose yesterday's weather map was placed next to today's map. Look at the two maps together. What happened to the cold front between yesterday and today? What happened to the areas of rain?

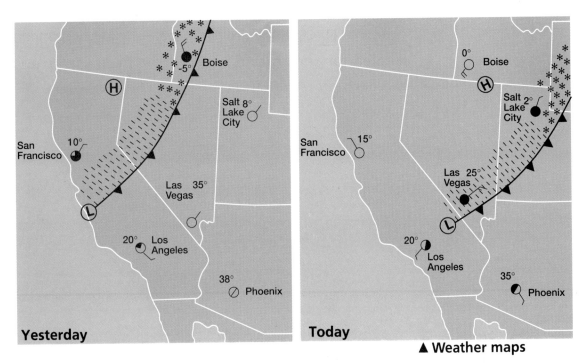

▲ **Weather maps**

By comparing the two maps, you can see how the weather systems moved over a 24-hour period. You can see how weather conditions at the different weather stations changed. How would studying these weather changes help you predict what tomorrow's map might look like?

Meteorologists use weather maps in much the same way that you used the two maps. But, meteorologists use many more maps. In fact, the NWS collects weather information from its stations eight times a day. Every three hours, updated weather maps are produced.

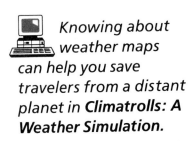

Knowing about weather maps can help you save travelers from a distant planet in **Climatrolls: A Weather Simulation.**

By studying these maps, meteorologists can see how weather systems are moving. Tracing the past movements of the systems helps the meteorologists predict where the systems will go next. Meteorologists use this information to make their weather forecasts. The forecast for each day can be shown on a map like this one. What parts of the country will have rain or snow? Describe the weather conditions predicted for the station nearest to where you live.

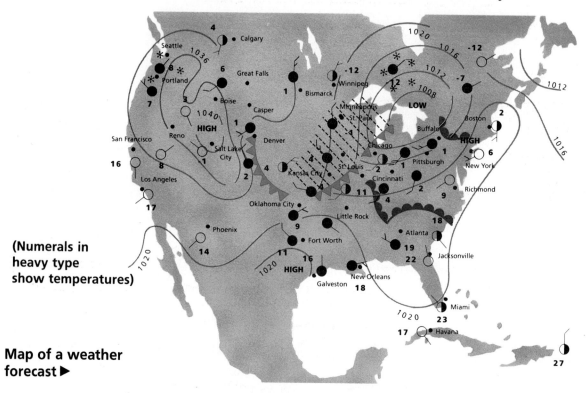

(Numerals in heavy type show temperatures)

Map of a weather forecast ▶

Lesson Review

1. What is a weather forecast?
2. What is a station model?
3. How many weather maps do you need to make a weather forecast? Explain your answer.

Think! How do you think predicting weather in Los Angeles, California is different from predicting weather in St. Louis, Missouri?

330

Chapter Connections

Pretend you are a meteorologist giving a weather report. Make up a symbol for each word in the graphic organizer that you would use in your forecast.

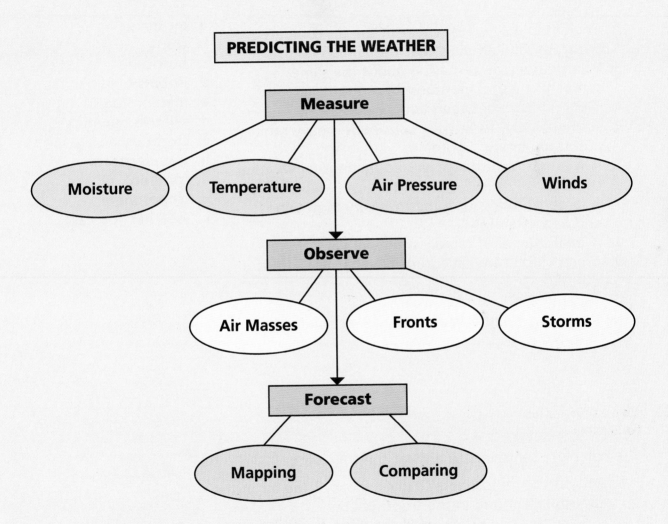

Writing About Science • Narrate

Imagine living in a climate that is the exact opposite of the one you live in now. Tell a story about what the weather is like and how your life has changed because of it.

Science Terms

Write the letter of the word that best matches the definition.

1. The layer of the atmosphere closest to the earth's surface.
2. The amount of water vapor in the air compared with the total amount that the air can hold.
3. A large body of air having about the same temperature and moisture throughout.
4. The boundary between two air masses.
5. A small, local storm with tall clouds, heavy rain, and thunder and lightning.
6. A weather disturbance caused by unusual weather conditions.
7. A large tropical storm that has very high winds and heavy rainfall.
8. A small funnel of rapidly spinning air.
9. A prediction of what future weather conditions will be.
10. A scientist who studies weather.
11. Lines on a weather map that connect places that have the same air pressure.

a. air mass
b. front
c. hurricane
d. isobars
e. meteorologist
f. relative humidity
g. storm
h. thunderstorm
i. tornado
j. troposphere
k. weather forecast

Science Ideas

Use complete sentences to answer the following.

1. What is the atmosphere? Why is most of the air in the atmosphere found in the troposphere?
2. Explain how the direction of the wind depends on air pressure.
3. What general temperature and moisture conditions would you expect to have in Seattle, Washington? **Hint:** Use what you know about the air masses that affect the weather in the United States.

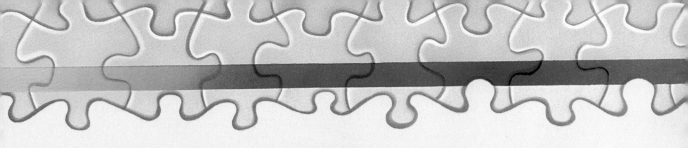

4. How are thunderstorms, hurricanes, and tornadoes the same? How are they different?
5. Describe the weather conditions for the city shown by the station model.

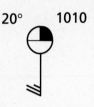

6. Suppose you are given yesterday's and today's weather map. What would you compare on the two maps to predict tomorrow's weather?

Applying Science Ideas

Use complete sentences to answer the following.

1. Draw the station model of a place that has 25% cloud cover, 15 miles per hour winds blowing from the northwest, and air temperature of 20°C.
2. Suppose you lived in Kansas and were having warm, dry weather. Do you think the air mass passing over Kansas is tropical or polar? Do you think it formed over land or water?

Using Science Skills

Each year, hurricanes form in the North Atlantic Ocean. The graph shows the number of hurricanes that occurred each year for nine years. Use the graph to predict how many hurricanes might occur next year.

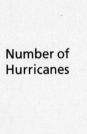

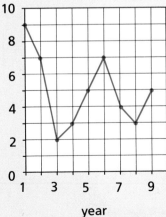

Number of Hurricanes

year

Weathering

An Underground World

You are crawling through a low, narrow tunnel. A hard hat with a light on it is perched on your head. Knee pads, elbow pads, and work gloves help to protect you as you inch yourself along. Water drips on your face and back.

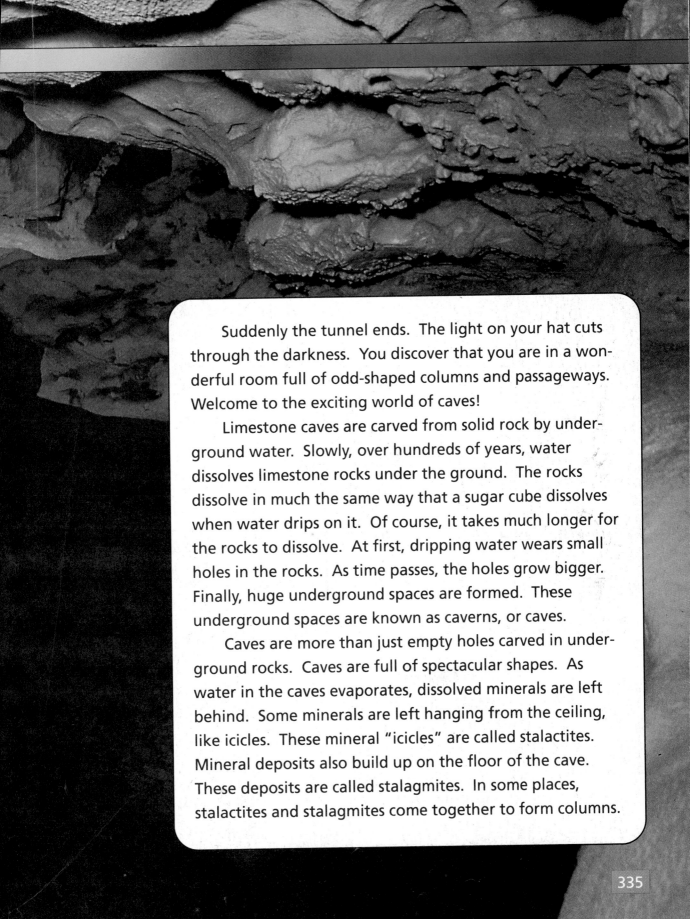

Suddenly the tunnel ends. The light on your hat cuts through the darkness. You discover that you are in a wonderful room full of odd-shaped columns and passageways. Welcome to the exciting world of caves!

Limestone caves are carved from solid rock by underground water. Slowly, over hundreds of years, water dissolves limestone rocks under the ground. The rocks dissolve in much the same way that a sugar cube dissolves when water drips on it. Of course, it takes much longer for the rocks to dissolve. At first, dripping water wears small holes in the rocks. As time passes, the holes grow bigger. Finally, huge underground spaces are formed. These underground spaces are known as caverns, or caves.

Caves are more than just empty holes carved in underground rocks. Caves are full of spectacular shapes. As water in the caves evaporates, dissolved minerals are left behind. Some minerals are left hanging from the ceiling, like icicles. These mineral "icicles" are called stalactites. Mineral deposits also build up on the floor of the cave. These deposits are called stalagmites. In some places, stalactites and stalagmites come together to form columns.

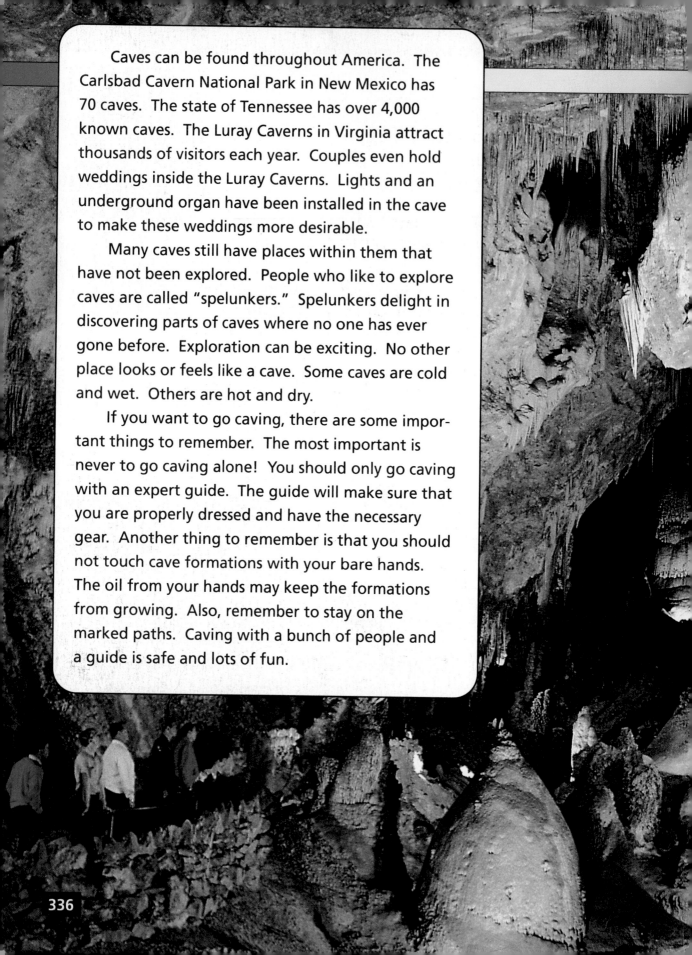

Caves can be found throughout America. The Carlsbad Cavern National Park in New Mexico has 70 caves. The state of Tennessee has over 4,000 known caves. The Luray Caverns in Virginia attract thousands of visitors each year. Couples even hold weddings inside the Luray Caverns. Lights and an underground organ have been installed in the cave to make these weddings more desirable.

Many caves still have places within them that have not been explored. People who like to explore caves are called "spelunkers." Spelunkers delight in discovering parts of caves where no one has ever gone before. Exploration can be exciting. No other place looks or feels like a cave. Some caves are cold and wet. Others are hot and dry.

If you want to go caving, there are some important things to remember. The most important is never to go caving alone! You should only go caving with an expert guide. The guide will make sure that you are properly dressed and have the necessary gear. Another thing to remember is that you should not touch cave formations with your bare hands. The oil from your hands may keep the formations from growing. Also, remember to stay on the marked paths. Caving with a bunch of people and a guide is safe and lots of fun.

Discover

How can you grow your own stalactites and stalagmites?

Materials   yarn · two plastic jars · baking soda · spoon · water · paper towel

Procedure

You can watch your own stalactites and stalagmites form. Twist several 30-cm lengths of yarn together. Fill each of the jars with warm water. Dissolve as much baking soda in each jar as you can. When no more will dissolve, suspend one end of the string in each jar. Make sure that the yarn hangs down between the jars. Place the jars on a paper towel in a warm place. Observe the jars each day for 5 days. Make careful notes about what you observe. Draw pictures of what you have observed.

In this chapter you will learn about Earth's crust. You will also learn about forces that can change Earth's crust.

1. Changes in the Earth's Surface

Words to Know
weathering

Getting Started The Grand Canyon, in Arizona, is a very deep opening in the earth's surface. What do the walls of the canyon look like to you, in the picture above?

What is the earth's surface made of?

crust

mantle

core

▲ Parts of the earth

Perhaps you thought the walls of the Grand Canyon look like they are made of rock. Most of the earth is indeed made up of solid rock. Much of this rock is covered with water or by a thin layer of smaller loose rocks and soil. The rocks near the surface are part of the earth's crust. The crust is the outer layer of the solid earth. The other layers of the earth—the mantle and the core—lie deep beneath the crust as shown in the drawing.

The crust is made of many kinds of rocks. Rocks can be classified into three groups, based on how the rocks were formed. Igneous (IHG nee-us) rocks are formed from melted material that cools and hardens. Most igneous rocks form deep under the surface. As shown in the drawing, other igneous rocks form from lava that hardens at the earth's surface. Sedimentary (sed uh MEN-tur ee) rocks are formed from small pieces of rock and other material called sediment. Most of the rocks you can see at the earth's surface are sedimentary rocks. Metamorphic (met uh MOR-fihk) rocks are formed when existing rocks are changed by heat or pressure.

The earth's surface is always changing. New rocks are being added to the surface, and old rocks are being worn away. These changes tend to be in balance. So the amount of rock at the earth's surface stays about the same.

How some rocks form ▼

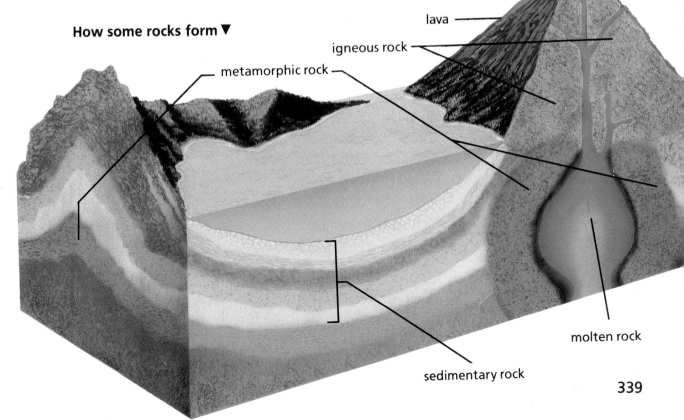

lava

igneous rock

metamorphic rock

molten rock

sedimentary rock

What forces build up the earth's surface?

Inside the crust, there are forces that raise and build up the earth's surface. Scientists believe that the crust is not one solid layer of rock. It is made of several huge blocks called plates. The drawing shows where the edges of two plates meet. These plates are moving very slowly past each other. The picture shows the land at the edges of the two plates. Other plates are moving away from each other. Many of the actions that change the earth's surface take place at the edges of these plates.

Edges of two plates ▼

California

Sacramento

San Francisco

Pacific plate

North American plate

Los Angeles

Palm Springs

San Diego

▼ Surface of land where plates meet

You cannot see the plates of the earth moving. But, you can see the results of the forces that move the plates. Mountains are formed by these forces. Volcanoes also result from these forces. Earthquakes—sudden movements of the crust—are caused by these forces. All these changes help to build up the earth's surface and to bring buried rock to the surface.

▲ Physical change

What forces break rocks?

Materials on the earth's surface are constantly being changed. Some changes are physical. The bucket loader in the picture above is moving rocks. This helps to break larger rocks into smaller pieces. Breaking rocks into smaller pieces is a physical change. The smaller pieces of rock have the same chemical makeup as that of the larger piece.

Other changes are chemical. Look closely at the picture of the broken rock. You can see that the color of the inside of the rock is different from that of the outside. This color difference shows that the chemical makeup of the outside part of the rock is different from that of the inside. Any change that affects the chemical makeup of a rock is a chemical change. When a chemical change takes place, new substances are formed. The processes that break apart and change the chemical makeup of rocks are called **weathering.**

▲ Chemical change

Weathering takes place slowly. But, the speed at which weathering occurs can be affected by climate. More than 3,000 years ago, stone structures were carved in Egypt. This stone structure is called an obelisk (AHB uh lihsk). The picture on the left shows what an obelisk looks like in Egypt today. In 1880 an obelisk was moved to New York City. Here the climate is much wetter than in Egypt. The pictures to the right show what the obelisk in New York looks like today. What changes caused by climate can you see?

▼ **Obelisk in New York today with closeup**

▲ **Obelisk in Egypt**

Lesson Review

1. Name some of the changes that build up the earth's surface.
2. What is weathering?
3. What are two ways to tell that a rock has been weathered?
4. How does climate affect weathering?

Think! If there are forces that are always building up the earth's surface, why doesn't the earth's crust continue to get thicker?

Skills

Identifying what changes in an experiment

A variable is anything that can be changed in an experiment. Imagine that you wanted to test the effect of falling water on rocks. You would find two rocks of the same type and size. Then you would put one rock beneath a waterfall and the other on dry ground. After 6 months, you would compare the two rocks. The location of the rocks is a variable you changed.

Practicing the skill

The following experiment is similar to what can happen to parts of the earth's crust when rocks are worn away.

1. Fill a large plastic bag halfway with water and seal it. Put it in a pan.

2. Place two petri dishes next to each other on the bag. These will act like sections of the earth's crust. Put 15 marbles in each dish. Do the dishes float at the same level?

3. Remove all the marbles from one dish. What happens to the level of that dish? What variable did you change? What variables stayed the same?

Thinking about the skill

Think of a different variable that could have been changed. What would the experiment have been testing then?

Applying the skill

Prepare two stacks of bread, each with ten slices. The slices of bread represent layers of sediment. Place a heavy book on one stack and nothing on the other. After 10 minutes, remove the book. What do you observe? What variable did you change? What variables were not changed?

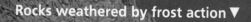

Rocks weathered by frost action ▼

2. Weathering Processes

Getting Started You have learned that weathering can change rock by breaking it or by changing its chemical makeup. Suppose you had a large rock that you wanted to change physically. In what ways might you do it? What might you do to change the rock chemically?

What causes physical weathering?

As you know, physical weathering is any process in which rocks are broken into smaller pieces. Frost action and pressure changes are two agents of physical weathering. Other agents include the actions of wind and water.

◯ **Frost action** is the weathering of rock by repeated freezing and melting of water. To understand how frost action works, think about what happens to water as it freezes. As water freezes, it changes from a liquid to a solid. When water freezes, it increases in size. In other words, the same amount of water takes up more space as solid ice.

When it rains, water seeps into the cracks and small spaces of a rock. Then the water may freeze. As it does, the expanding ice acts like a wedge. The cracks and spaces get a little bigger. The rocks, in the picture on page 344, were weathered by frost action.

Rocks under the earth's surface are under a lot of pressure. Sometimes rocks that have been buried for a long time will become uncovered. Then they will be under less pressure. When this happens, the outer layers of the rocks will expand and peel off. The picture shows what these rocks look like. How do they compare with the rocks weathered by frost action on page 344?

Rocks weathered by pressure changes ▼

Moving water and wind also help to weather rocks. Ocean waves have much force. When they pound on rocks along the shore, waves may crack the rocks. Also, they may push rocks against one another. In this way, rocks along the shore are broken into smaller and smaller pieces. The picture shows how ocean waves weather rocks.

Rivers and streams can carry sand and small pebbles. These materials can help to break up larger rocks along the bottoms and banks of the rivers and streams.

Winds often carry dust and sand. When these particles are blown against larger rocks, they act like sandpaper. The particles scrape and scratch the rocks and wear them away. The rocks shown in the picture were shaped in this way. How do these rocks differ from those that were weathered by ocean waves?

▲ Rocks weathered by water

▲ Rocks weathered by wind-blown sand

Plants and animals can also help break up rocks. You may have seen sections of cracked and tilted sidewalk. Such changes are caused by tree roots growing beneath the pavement. Roots can also break rocks.

Animals that dig in the soil help weather rocks. Animals such as ants, earthworms, and rodents make tunnels through the soil. The ants in the picture bring buried rock and soil material to the surface. On the surface agents of weathering act on these materials.

▼ Animals help weather rocks

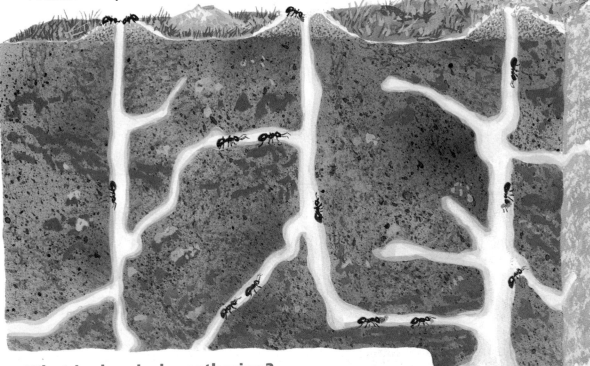

What is chemical weathering?

Chemical weathering is any process that breaks up rock by changing its chemical make-up. Rocks are made of substances called minerals (MIHN ur ulz). New minerals are formed by chemical weathering. Acids, oxygen, and some kinds of plants cause much chemical weathering.

347

Explore Together

What types of rocks are weathered most easily by acids?

Organizer

Materials

calcite or chalk · 5 small paper cups · plastic cup half-filled with vinegar · limestone · sandstone · marble · obsidian

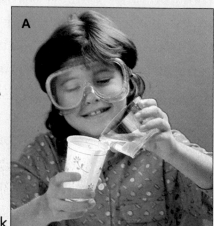

A

Procedure

Investigator

A. **Caution:** *Wear safety goggles during this investigation.* Place a piece of chalk or calcite into a small paper cup. Pour enough vinegar, an acid, over the piece to cover it.

Group

B. Observe what happens.

Recorder

C. After 10 minutes, describe and record observations of the chalk or calcite on a chart like the one below.

Rock type	Calcite or Chalk	Limestone	Sandstone	Marble	Obsidian
Observations					

Investigator, Manager

D. Repeat step **A** using the limestone, sandstone, marble, and obsidian.

Recorder

E. Describe and record what happens to each rock.

Writing and Sharing Results and Conclusions

Group, Recorder

1. With which rocks did bubbling occur?

2. Which rocks probably contain calcite?

3. What mineral found in rocks is most affected by acids?

An acid is a substance that can dissolve, or break apart, other substances. Some kinds of plants make acids. Acids are also made by mosses and lichens (LYE kunz). Mosses and lichens are often found living on rocks. The acids they make change the minerals in the rock.

Acids form when water combines with certain gases. The gases that water combines with include carbon dioxide (dye AHK syd) and sulfur oxides. These gases enter the air when fossil fuels are burned. Fossil fuels include coal, gas, and oil. Carbon dioxide is also given off in natural processes. For example, when animals breathe, they take in oxygen and give off carbon dioxide. How do gases that produce acids enter the air in the pictures below?[5]

▼ Burning charcoal

▲ Cars burn fossil fuels.

▲ Factories burn fossil fuels.

▲ Limestone cave

One common acid formed in nature is carbonic (kahr BAHN ihk) acid. This acid forms when water combines with carbon dioxide. Earlier you read about caves. The picture above also shows a cave. Both caves were formed when carbonic acid dissolved limestone.

Another type of acid is sulfuric (sul FYOOR-ihk) acid. This acid forms when sulfur oxides combine with water. Sulfur oxides enter the air when fossil fuels are burned.

Carbonic acid or sulfuric acid often mix with rainwater. A mixture of acid and rainwater is called **acid rain.** Acid rain damages statues and buildings, and is harmful to living things.

How does air cause chemical weathering?

Another reaction that causes chemical weathering is oxidation (ahks ih DAY shun). Oxidation is a chemical reaction that takes place when oxygen combines with other substances. The pictures show iron oxide formed from the oxidation of iron. What is the common name for the iron oxide formed by this reaction?

Iron is an element found in many rocks. When iron combines with oxygen, iron oxide forms. Iron oxide weakens rocks.

◄ Cars weathered by oxidation

Lesson Review

1. What change takes place in chemical weathering that does not take place in physical weathering?

2. What is frost action?

3. How do burrowing animals aid in the weathering of rock?

4. Why is oxidation a type of chemical weathering?

Think! Chemical weathering takes place faster in some places than in other places. Why do you think is this so?

▲ Rocks weathered by oxidation

3. Soil

Words to Know
soil
topsoil
humus
subsoil

Getting Started Have you ever worked in a garden? Gardeners pay close attention to the soil in which their plants grow. Much of this soil is weathered rock material. What else might you expect to find in garden soil?

How does soil form?

You have learned that most of the earth's crust is made up of solid rock. But at the surface much of this rock is covered by a thin layer of soil. **Soil** is the loose material on the earth's surface in which plants can grow.

Weathering of rock is the first stage in the formation of soil. Physical weathering breaks large rocks into smaller rocks. Chemical weathering changes the makeup of certain minerals in rocks. For example, after a long time, physical weathering can change a large solid rock into small grains of sand. Chemical weathering can also produce soft, powdery materials such as clay. Both sand and clay are found in many soils. But sand and clay alone do not make up soil.

The picture shows soil taken from a garden. What materials can you recognize in this soil? As the picture shows, soil is more than weathered rock materials. Soil also contains water, air, and decayed remains of plant and animal matter. All these materials are needed for plants to grow.

◀ Parts of soil

The formation of soil takes a long time. Keep in mind that soil-forming processes include the weathering of large rocks. In some places it can take several hundred years for a single centimeter of soil to form.

What are the layers of soil formation?

Soil changes as you go deeper into the ground. The picture shows a side view of a well developed soil. Such a side view is known as a soil profile. Different soils have different soil profiles.

The soil profile below shows that a well developed soil has four layers. The upper layer of soil is called **topsoil**. Topsoil has the smallest particles because it is the most weathered. Topsoil also contains organic material.

Soil profile ▼

Organic material is the decayed remains of plant and animal matter. This decayed material is called **humus** (HYOO mus). Humus gives topsoil its dark color. Humus is an important part of topsoil. It provides many minerals that plants need to grow. Gardeners sometimes collect piles of decaying leaves and other plant parts to add to the topsoil in their gardens. This partly decayed material, called compost, loosens and adds humus to the topsoil.

Topsoil also contains burrowing animals such as earthworms and insects. These animals make tunnels in the soil that allow water and air to flow easily into the soil. The water carries dissolved minerals deeper into the ground.

The soil just below the topsoil is called **subsoil.** Subsoil has less humus than does topsoil. Also the weathered particles in subsoil are larger than those in topsoil. Clay and minerals carried down through the topsoil are found in the subsoil.

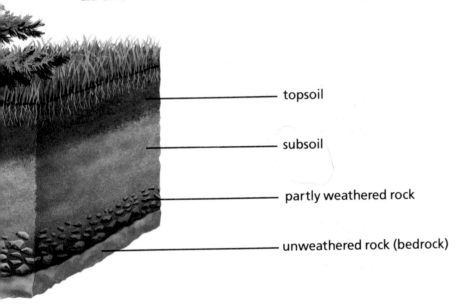

topsoil

subsoil

partly weathered rock

unweathered rock (bedrock)

The layer just beneath the subsoil is made of partly weathered rock. The minerals found in this layer show that some chemical weathering has taken place. Water and acids formed by plants move down to this layer and weather the original rock. The material in this layer cannot support plant life.

The bottom layer of the soil profile is made up of unweathered rock. Unweathered rock is also called bedrock.

Explore

What are the layers of a soil profile?

It takes thousands of years for a thick layer of topsoil to form. During this time much weathering of rock occurs. A soil profile shows changes in rock as it weathers. You can make a model of a soil profile.

Materials

tall, plastic jar · small rock · spoon · pebbles · unsharpened pencil · clay · sand · humus · 4" x 6" index card · clear tape

Procedure

A. Tilt the plastic jar as shown, and gently slide a small rock to the bottom. **Caution:** *Be careful not to break the jar.*

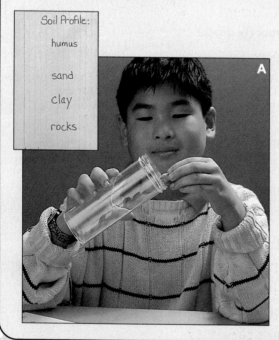

Soil Profile:

humus

sand

clay

rocks

A

B. Using the spoon, add a layer of pebbles to the jar. Use the unsharpened pencil to gently pack down the layer of rock.

C. Repeat step **B** with the other kinds of rock material, in the following order: clay, sand, and humus. Pack each layer gently before adding the next layer. Add the cover to the jar.

D. Tape the index card to the jar. Label the four layers as shown.

Writing and Sharing Results and Conclusions

1. Which of the layers contain weathered rock?

2. How is your model of a soil profile like a real soil profile? How is it different?

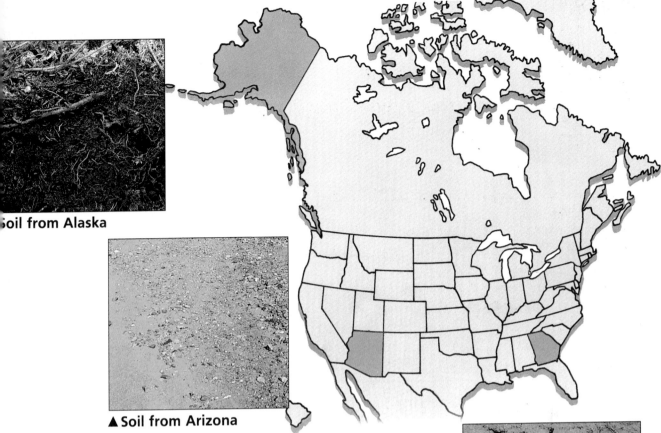

Soil from Alaska

▲ Soil from Arizona

How do soils differ?

There are many different kinds of soil. Soils differ in the amounts and kinds of materials they contain. Different soils support different kinds of plant life. This, in turn, affects the kinds of humus that will be found in the topsoil. Scientists have found that climate is the most important factor in determining what the soil is like in any one place. Which soil above appears to have the least amount of humus?

▲ Soil from Georgia

Lesson Review

1. What is soil?
2. Describe the four layers of a soil profile.
3. What is in topsoil that is not is subsoil?
4. What is humus and why is it important?

Think! Why are soils in places with dry, cool climates different from soils in places with wet, hot climates?

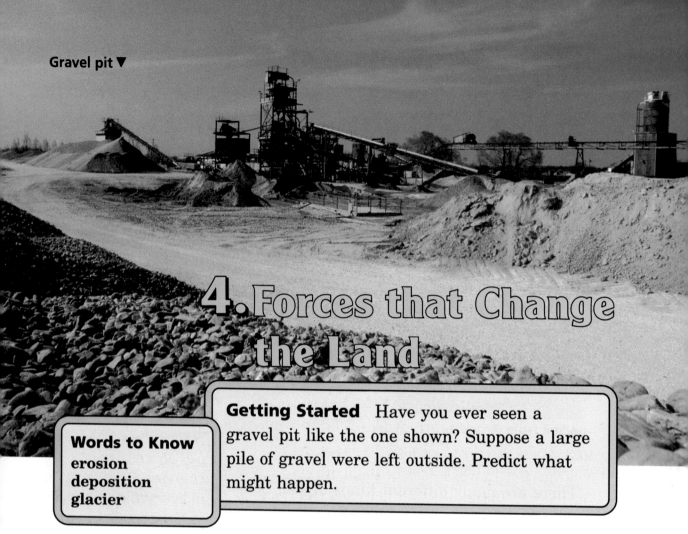

Gravel pit ▼

4. Forces that Change the Land

Words to Know
erosion
deposition
glacier

Getting Started Have you ever seen a gravel pit like the one shown? Suppose a large pile of gravel were left outside. Predict what might happen.

What is erosion?

Recall that weathering changes solid rock into small pieces of rock and soil. Much of the rocks and soil are carried away by moving water, wind, and ice. Rocks and soil that are carried away are called sediment.

Erosion (ee ROH zhun) is the picking up and moving away of weathered rock and soil. Water, wind, and ice that carry away weathered material are called agents of erosion. When an agent of erosion slows down, it drops, or deposits, its load of sediment. The dropping of sediment by agents of erosion is called **deposition** (dep uh ZIHSH un).

How is water an agent of erosion?

Moving water is the most important agent of erosion. Moving water has a great deal of energy. Because moving water has energy, it picks up and moves sediment. In a stream, sand and smaller sediment are carried in the water. During a flood, water overflows the banks of the stream. It covers the land on both sides of the stream. As the flood waters decrease, they leave behind deposits of sediments.

Stream erosion can change the shape of the land. It can cut down into the land forming canyons. As a canyon deepens, weathering and erosion work to make it wider.

Stream deposits also change the shape of the land. When a stream enters a large body of water, such as a lake or sea, the stream slows down. So, as shown below, it deposits its load of sediment. As sediment builds up on the floor of the lake or sea, a delta is formed.

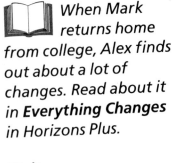 *When Mark returns home from college, Alex finds out about a lot of changes. Read about it in **Everything Changes** in Horizons Plus.*

◀ **Delta**

359

Problem Solving

That's the Way the World Crumbles

Agents of weathering are constantly wearing down rocks in the earth's crust. Most weathering changes take place slowly, but some produce changes faster than others.

How can you wear down a sugar cube "rock"?

Using only natural forms of weathering, how fast can you wear down a sugar cube "rock"? You may not touch the cube directly during the weathering process.

Which actions were not effective in wearing down the cube? Is the sugar cube a good model for illustrating weathering processes on earth? Why or why not?

How does wind cause erosion?

Wind is moving air. Like moving water, wind has energy. It can move sediment. The faster the wind blows, the more energy it has and the more sediment it can move. A strong wind can move dust particles through the air. As shown in the picture, strong winds can also roll or bounce sand grains along the ground.

Wind blowing sand▶

When the wind slows down the particles are deposited. Deposits of sand left by wind are called sand dunes. In some parts of the world, windblown dust and clay can form large deposits called loess (lus). The picture shows a deposit of loess.

Wind moves sediment that is not held in place by plant roots or protected by windbreaks. A windbreak is a fence or row of trees that provides protection from the wind. Why do you think it is called a windbreak? Without wind breaks, dust storms can result.

How is ice an agent of erosion?

Parts of the earth's surface are covered by glaciers (GLAY shurz). A **glacier** is a large body of moving ice. Glaciers are found in those parts of the world where all the snow from the winter does not melt in the summer. Some glaciers are found in valleys high up in mountains as shown in the picture. The drawing shows how gravity causes these glaciers to move slowly, like rivers of ice, down the sides of the mountains.

▼ How a glacier moves

glacier

water

land

◄ Glacier found between two mountains

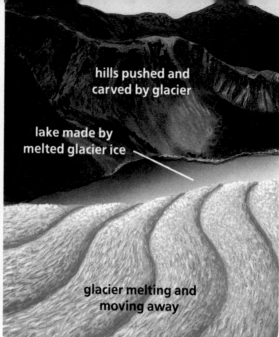

hills pushed and carved by glacier

lake made by melted glacier ice

glacier melting and moving away

▲ **Lake left after glacier melted**

Other glaciers are huge sheets of ice. These ice sheets are thick enough to bury mountains. Today, these glaciers are covering much of Greenland and Antarctica.

As you can imagine, glaciers have energy. As a glacier moves, it picks up soil, rocks, and boulders. These materials are carried along in the ice of the glacier. They act like scraping tools, scratching and gouging the surface as the ice moves.

Glaciers change the shape of the land over which they move. But they also change the shape of the land as they melt. Sediment is deposited, and sometimes streams or lakes, as shown above, are formed.

Life Science
CONNECTION

During the ice ages large areas of the earth were covered by ice. Find out what living things could be found during the ice ages.

Lesson Review

1. What is erosion?
2. How do the agents of erosion cause change?
3. What happens when an agent of erosion slows down?

Think! Why are windbreaks important?

Chapter Connections

Copy the shapes of this graphic organizer on a piece of paper. Try to fill them in without looking at your book.

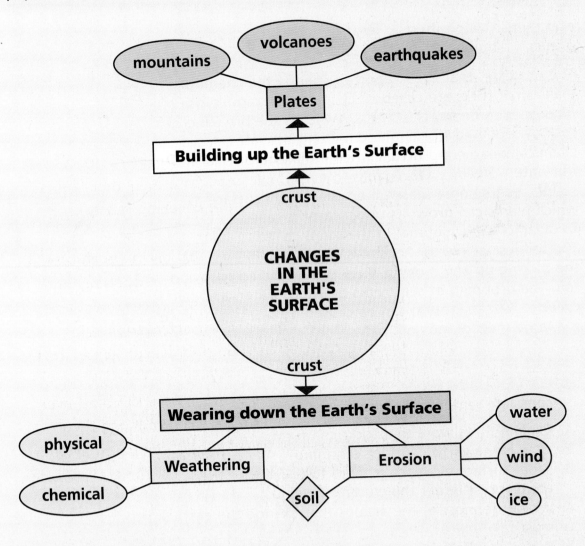

Writing About Science • Describe

Find a place around your house that shows signs of weathering. Write a paragraph describing what the weathered areas look like. Explain what you think caused the weathering that you see.

Science Terms

Number your paper from **1** to **10**. Use the terms below to complete the sentences. Write the correct term next to each number.

acid rain   deposition   erosion   frost action
glacier   humus   soil   subsoil   topsoil   weathering

The processes that break apart or change the chemical makeup of rocks are called ___(1)___. One example of physical weathering is ___(2)___, which is the breaking of rock by repeated freezing and melting of water. A type of chemical weathering occurs when a mixture of acid and rainwater, called ___(3)___, falls to earth.
___(4)___ is the loose material on the earth's surface in which plants can grow. Its upper layer is called ___(5)___. Decayed organic material in the soil is called ___(6)___. The soil just below the topsoil is called ___(7)___. ___(8)___ is the picking up and moving away of weathered rock and soil. The dropping of sediments by wind, water, and rain is called ___(9)___. Erosion can be caused by a ___(10)___ which is a large mass of moving ice.

Science Ideas

Use complete sentences to answer the following.

1. Explain three ways that rocks can form.
2. How is the earth's surface changing?
3. What surface evidence is there to prove that there are great forces under the crust?
4. Where do most of the actions that change the earth's crust take place?
5. Why does the amount of rock at the earth's surface stay about the same?
6. What forces build up the earth's surface?
7. What forces wear down the earth's surface?
8. List examples of physical weathering.
9. List examples of chemical weathering.

Label the layers of a well-developed soil profile below.

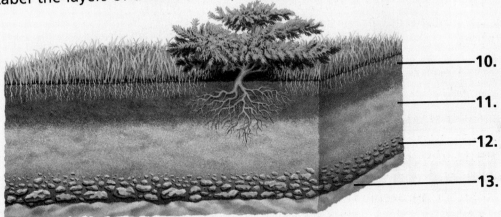

— 10.

— 11.

— 12.

— 13.

14. What is soil made of?
15. What gives topsoil its dark color and the minerals needed for plants to grow?
16. What is the most important factor in determining what the soil in a place will look like?
17. How is erosion different from weathering?
18. What kinds of changes may be caused by water erosion?
19. What kinds of changes may be caused by wind erosion?
20. What kinds of changes may be caused by ice erosion?

Applying Science Ideas
Use complete sentences to answer the following.

1. How do humans cause physical and chemical weathering?
2. Rock materials are used for buildings, statues, and roads as well as other things. What can be done to prevent this rock material from weathering?

Using Science Skills
Look at the obelisks on page 342. What conditions other than a climate change may have affected the obelisk in New York City?

Chapter 11

Energy Resources

Riding the Waves

Imagine an airplane that can fly for months without landing and without refueling. This new airplane will not use fuel. Instead, it will be powered by microwaves (MYE kroh wayvz).

Microwaves are one form of energy. You may know of other types of energy, such as light, radio waves, or X rays. All these forms of energy travel in a straight line. Like radio waves and X rays, microwaves can pass through clouds, fog, and rain. What makes microwaves useful is that they are absorbed, or taken up, by some types of matter. Usually when matter absorbs microwaves, it becomes hot. That is the way a microwave oven works. Food is cooked when it absorbs microwaves.

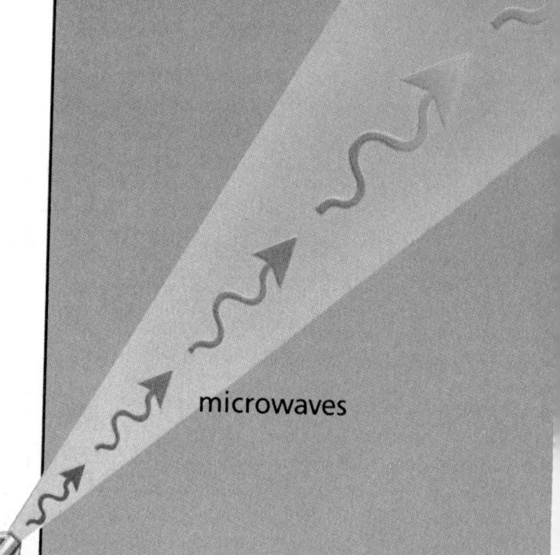

microwaves

antenna

generator

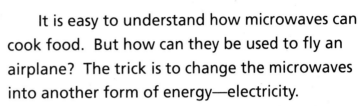

It is easy to understand how microwaves can cook food. But how can they be used to fly an airplane? The trick is to change the microwaves into another form of energy—electricity.

Look at the drawing to see how the microwave airplane works. Electricity is sent to an antenna (an TEN uh). The antenna changes the electricity to microwaves, much the same way as it does in a microwave oven. The antenna sends the microwaves up to the airplane. The airplane has special panels that absorb the microwaves. The panels then change the microwaves back to electricity, which moves the airplane!

The inventors of this new airplane have built a model to test their idea. Their model is 4 m (13 ft) wide, from wing tip to wing tip. It has been tested several times and can fly at an altitude of 100 m (330 ft). Microwaves move the airplane while it is in flight. Batteries are used for takeoffs and landings.

The airplane will be eight times as large as the model. It will have a wingspan of over 30 m (99 ft). The plane will be able to fly at altitudes of over 20 km (12 mi). Like the model, the airplane will be controlled from the ground. No pilot will be aboard.

How will this new plane be used? It will not be used to carry passengers or cargo. Instead, it will carry information. The new plane may replace costly satellites now in use. The plane could be used to transmit radio, television, and telephone signals. In addition, it could be used to track the movement of weather, traffic, or even icebergs. It could be used to watch for forest fires. Photographs of large areas could be taken from the plane as it circles above the earth.

Questions still remain about the safety of the microwave airplane. Large amounts of microwaves would be needed for the full-sized airplanes. How would all these microwaves affect people and other living things near the antennas? The inventors of the airplane say that it can be made safe. They are convinced that microwave planes will someday be cleared for takeoff!

Discover

How can microwave airplanes be used?

Materials pencil · paper

Procedure

The inventors of the microwave airplane believe that it will serve people in many ways. Farmers, police officers, weather forecasters, and forest rangers may use the airplanes.

List ways in which these workers might use the information collected by microwave airplanes. How might you be helped by the information when you go on a vacation or ride a bike? How might your life be made easier by using information gathered by microwave airplanes? Brainstorm ways that you might use this information.

In this chapter you will learn about other energy sources that are being used. You will also learn how the sun, the atom, the wind, water, and even garbage may be used to run cities, cars, and homes.

1. Energy from Fossil Fuels

Getting Started Imagine it is a very cold day. You turn up the heat in your house. But the house stays cold. You try to warm up soup on the stove. But the burners do not light. You have run out of fuel! What would your life be like if there were no fuel?

What are some common fuels?

Life without fuel would be hard, if not impossible. What is fuel (FYOO ul)? **Fuel** is a substance that is burned to release its stored energy. Coal, oil, and natural gas are some of the most important fuels. These fuels are also called fossil fuels (FAHS ul FYOO ulz).

▼ How coal is formed

1. About 250 million years ago, huge plants grew in swamps. These plants contained energy.

2. When the plants died, they were buried under water and mud. The plants' energy was trapped.

Fossil fuels are fuels formed from decayed plants and animals that lived long ago. Fossil fuels contain much stored energy. When these fuels are burned, their energy can be changed to other forms of energy. Follow the drawings on the previous page and below to see how coal forms.

Is all coal alike?

Coal differs in age and in the amount of energy stored. It also differs in the length of time the layers of plant matter were under pressure and in the temperature of the layers.

Coals may be broadly grouped as either hard coals or soft coals. The soft coals were formed most recently. They were under low pressures and temperatures. Hard coals are the oldest coals and were formed under high pressures and temperatures.

3. As other plants died, more layers were formed over the first. The pressure on the plants and temperature of the decaying plants increased.

4. After millions of years, pressure changed the layers of decayed plants into coal. Coal contains the energy trapped in plants.

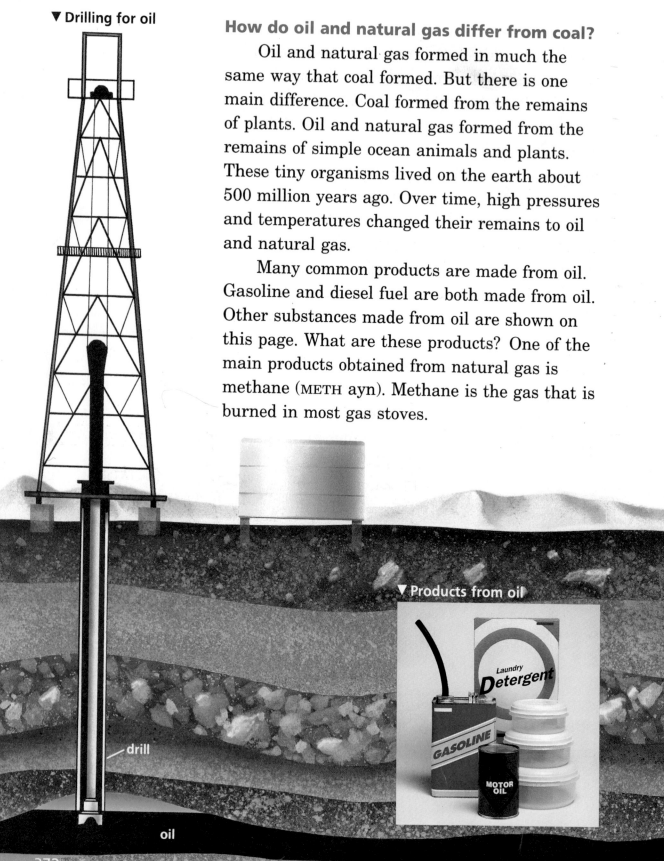

▼ Drilling for oil

How do oil and natural gas differ from coal?

Oil and natural gas formed in much the same way that coal formed. But there is one main difference. Coal formed from the remains of plants. Oil and natural gas formed from the remains of simple ocean animals and plants. These tiny organisms lived on the earth about 500 million years ago. Over time, high pressures and temperatures changed their remains to oil and natural gas.

Many common products are made from oil. Gasoline and diesel fuel are both made from oil. Other substances made from oil are shown on this page. What are these products? One of the main products obtained from natural gas is methane (METH ayn). Methane is the gas that is burned in most gas stoves.

▼ Products from oil

Laundry Detergent

GASOLINE

MOTOR OIL

drill

oil

How are fossil fuels used?

Coal, oil, and natural gas are all natural resources. A **natural resource** is a useful material taken from the environment. Air, land, and water are other natural resources. Substances that cannot easily be replaced once they are used are called **nonrenewable resources.** Since fossil fuels take millions of years to form, they are nonrenewable resources. A **renewable resource** is a resource that is fairly easy to replace if it is used. Lumber is one example.

Fossil fuels are used to heat homes. They are also used to produce electrical energy. In power plants, the heat released from fossil fuels changes water into steam. Moving steam turns the blades

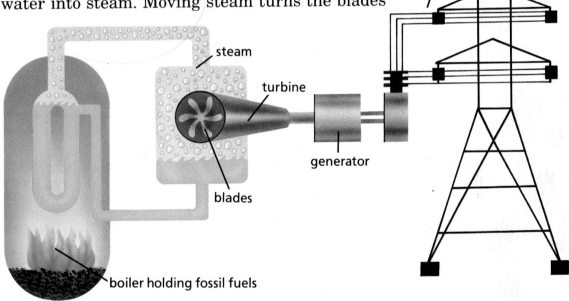

electric power lines

steam

turbine

generator

blades

boiler holding fossil fuels

of a turbine (TUR bihn). A **turbine** is a machine with a wheel and blades that changes the energy in steam to mechanical energy. The blades are attached to a shaft connected to a generator. A **generator** is a machine that changes the mechanical energy of a turbine to electrical energy.

▲ Generating electrical energy

ACTIVITY

Explore Together

Can density help to distinguish among coal samples?

Organizer

Materials
marking pencil · masking tape · 3 coal samples · balance 100-mL graduate · water

Procedure

Recorder   A. With a marking pencil, write *1, 2,* and *3* on pieces of tape. Stick one piece of tape on each coal sample.

Investigator, Recorder   B. Copy the table on a piece of paper. Use a balance to find the mass of sample *1.* Record the mass in column A.

Investigator, Recorder   C. Half fill a graduate with water. Record the exact volume in column B.

Investigator, Recorder   D. Tilt the graduate and slide in sample *1.* In column C, record the water level with the coal in the water.

Recorder   E. Subtract the level of the water without the coal from the level of water with the coal (C − B). The answer is the volume of the coal. Record this volume in column D.

Recorder   F. Divide the mass of sample 1 by its volume to find its density. Record the density in column E.

Manager, Recorder   G. Repeat steps **A** to **F** for samples *2* and *3.*

Writing and Sharing Results and Conclusions

Group, Recorder   1. What is the density of each sample of coal?

2. Do the densities help to distinguish among the samples?

Reporter   3. Compare your findings with those of other groups.

Coal sample	A Mass (g)	B Volume of water (mL)	C Level of water with coal (mL)	D Volume of coal C−B	E Density of coal (g/mL)
1					
2					
3					

burning of fossil fuels

gases from fossil fuels + water vapor

acid rain

What are some problems in using fossil fuels?

▲ **How acid rain forms and cycles**

When fossil fuels burn, many of them give off harmful substances into the environment. For example, when soft coal is burned, certain gases are given off. The gases combine with water vapor in the air, forming acids. These acids can fall as acid rain. Acid rain can harm living things in lakes and ponds. Another problem with fossil fuels is that they can be used up. They are nonrenewable resources. It takes millions of years for fossil fuels to form.

Lesson Review

1. Define *fossil fuel*. List three fossil fuels.
2. List four steps in the formation of coal.
3. What is a nonrenewable resource? Explain why fossil fuels are nonrenewable resources.
4. Describe how fossil fuels are related to the production of electrical energy.

Think! Describe some ways to reduce the kind and amount of harmful substances fossil fuels add to the air. What can *you* do to help?

> **Physical Science**
> **CONNECTION**
>
> *Energy is obtained from fossil fuels through oxidation. What is oxidation? Is the burning of fossil fuels fast oxidation or slow oxidation?*

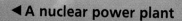
◄ A nuclear power plant

2. Energy from Atoms

Getting Started Pretend that you are small enough to fit inside a helium atom. What would you see in the center of the atom? Then, imagine that you are inside a carbon atom. How would it differ from the inside of a helium atom?

Words to Know
nuclear energy
nuclear fission
nuclear fusion

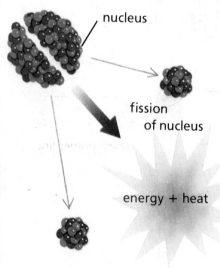

nucleus

fission of nucleus

energy + heat

▲ Nuclear fission of an atom

How do atoms provide energy?

Atoms contain a vast amount of energy. The energy locked in the nucleus of the atom is called **nuclear** (NOO klee ur) **energy.** Remember that the nucleus of nearly all atoms contains two kinds of particles—protons and neutrons. Energy holds these particles together.

The nucleus of an atom can be split. When the nucleus splits, the energy holding the particles together is released. Splitting the nucleus of an atom to release energy is called **nuclear fission** (FIHSH un). Most of the energy from splitting an atom is released as heat. The drawing at the left shows nuclear fission of an atom.

376

How is nuclear energy used?

You learned in Chapter 5 that there are 109 elements. Of these 109 elements, uranium (yoo-RAY nee um) is the one most often used in a nuclear fission reaction. Uranium is often used because its atoms are easiest to split.

The great energy released during nuclear fission can be used to produce electrical energy. The drawing below shows the main parts of a nuclear power plant. A nuclear power plant has a nuclear reactor, a boiler, a turbine, and a generator. Nuclear fission occurs inside the reactor. Locate each part in the drawing.

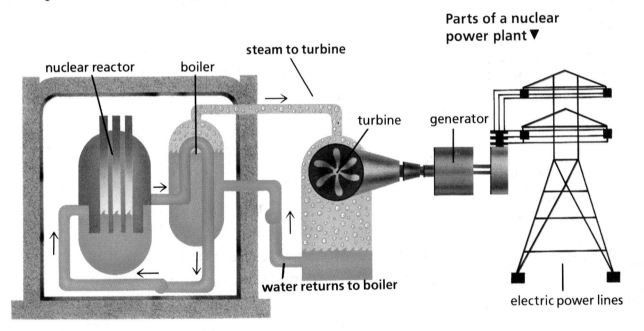

Parts of a nuclear power plant ▼

nuclear reactor   boiler   steam to turbine   turbine   generator

water returns to boiler

electric power lines

The heat released during nuclear fission heats a liquid that is carried through pipes into the boiler. In the boiler, water is changed to steam. This steam travels from the boiler to the turbine, causing the turbine blades to turn. Electrical energy is then produced in the generator.

How does nuclear energy compare with other kinds of energy?

In some ways, nuclear energy is better than fossil fuels. For example, nuclear energy does not pollute the air. By using nuclear energy, people can conserve fossil fuels.

There are also problems in using nuclear energy. Nuclear power plants are very costly to build. During fission reactions, radioactive substances are produced. These substances give off particles with high energy levels. Such particles can harm or kill cells of living things. The picture below shows that workers at a nuclear power plant must be very careful.

People concerned about nuclear energy worry about what could happen if radioactive wastes get into the air, water, and soil. They are concerned that an accident could occur at a

Workers in a nuclear power plant must follow strict safety regulations. ▼

▼ Underwater storage of used fuel in a nuclear power plant

nuclear power plant. Harmful radiation could be released into the environment. Scientists are working on safe ways to move, store, and dispose of radioactive wastes.

What is another form of nuclear energy?

Energy can be released from atoms in another way—during nuclear fusion (FYOO-zhun). **Nuclear fusion** is a nuclear reaction in which the nuclei of atoms fuse, or join together. Fusion reactions take place only at very high temperatures. Unlike fission reactions, fusion reactions use light atoms, such as hydrogen. A light atom is one that has only a few particles in its nucleus.

Fusion of hydrogen atoms ▼

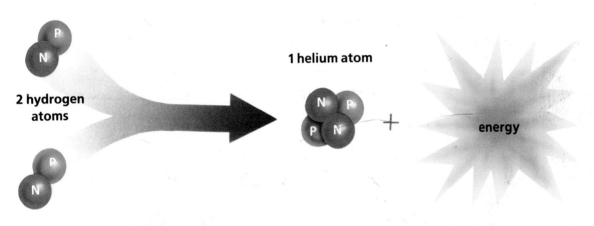

2 hydrogen atoms

1 helium atom

+ energy

Hydrogen is the lightest of all atoms. It exists in several forms. The most common form has only one proton and no neutrons in its nucleus. Another form has one proton and one neutron in its nucleus. When two atoms of this form of hydrogen fuse, one helium atom forms. The drawing above shows this reaction. This nuclear fusion reaction releases a great deal of energy.

Nuclear fusion takes place in the device shown below. The device is called a tokamak (TOH kuh mak). The name comes from a group of Russian words meaning "doughnut-shaped." Scientists have not yet been able to harness fusion reactions to produce energy on a large scale. They have only been able to use it in the hydrogen bomb. But they are working on ways to use the energy released by nuclear fusion. Many scientists think that fusion will be controlled before the year 2050.

Tokamak, a device in which fusion reactions occur ▶

Lesson Review

1. Define *nuclear energy* and *nuclear fission*.
2. Which atom is most often used in nuclear fission reactions? Why is it used?
3. What form of energy is the end result of the reactions in a nuclear power plant?
4. List some advantages and some disadvantages of nuclear energy.

Think! Unlike fission reactions, fusion reactions do not give off radioactive wastes. If scientists can control fusion reactions, what would be some of the advantages to this form of energy?

Skills

Constructing a bar graph

A bar graph uses thick bars to display information. Electricity use is measured in kilowatt hours. The graph shows the amount of electricity used in one home for 6 months. The vertical axis shows the amount of electricity used. The horizontal axis lists the months.

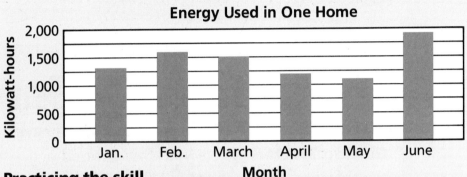

Energy Used in One Home

Practicing the skill

1. Geothermal power plants produce electricity by using underground sources of heat. Nevada and California each have eight geothermal plants. Hawaii has one. Utah has two geothermal plants.

2. Construct a bar graph showing the number of power plants in the states listed in Step 1. Begin by copying the empty graph shown on the right. Put the numbers of plants on the vertical axis. List state names on the horizontal axis.

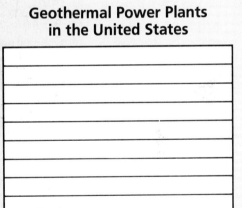

Geothermal Power Plants in the United States

Thinking about the skill

Compare your bar graph to the written information. What information is easier to see on the graph?

Applying the skill

The Colorado River runs through four states. Each state has dams on the river to produce electricity. Arizona has three dams; Colorado has two; California has one; and Nevada has one. Construct a bar graph showing this information.

Fusion reactions take place in the sun's core.▶

nuclear fusion reactions

core

3. Energy from the Sun

Getting Started Have you ever entered a car that had been parked in the hot summer sun with the windows closed? How did the inside of the car feel?

Words to Know
solar energy
solar collector
solar cell

How does the sun supply energy and heat?

The sun is the greatest single source of energy for Earth. Energy from the sun is called **solar energy** (SOH lur EN ur jee). Solar energy is produced by the reactions taking place in the sun's core. These reactions, which occur at very high temperatures, are nuclear fusion reactions. During nuclear fusion in the sun's core, hydrogen atoms combine to form helium atoms. Huge amounts of energy are released.

Solar energy supplies heat in two ways. First, it supplies heat by passive solar heating. Remember how hot a closed car felt in summer. Solar energy passed through the windows. Then the solar energy was absorbed. Once absorbed, the solar energy changed to heat that was trapped inside the car. What occurred in the car is an example of passive solar heating.

Second, solar energy supplies heat by means of active solar heating. Active solar heating uses machines such as pumps and fans to move water heated by solar energy. The picture below shows an active solar heating system. A **solar collector**

A solar house with passive and active solar heating ▼

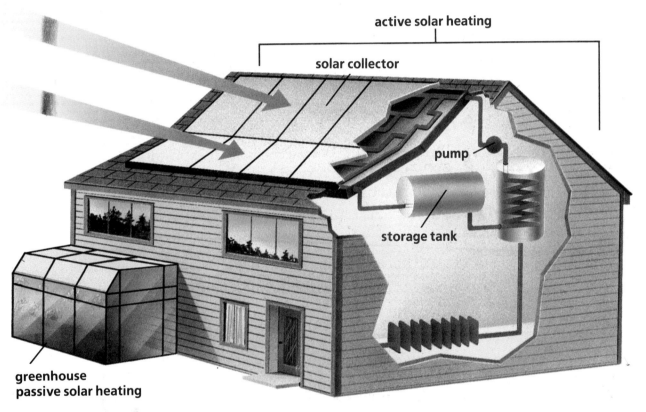

active solar heating

solar collector

pump

storage tank

greenhouse
passive solar heating

is a device used to collect solar energy. Look for the solar collector in the drawing.

There are many benefits to using solar energy. Sunlight is available nearly everywhere on Earth. Solar energy is free, and it does not pollute. Finally, there is a continuous supply of solar energy. Scientists believe that the sun will give off energy for another 5 billion years!

Problem Solving

Getting to the Heat of the Matter

Imagine walking in a rocky canyon on a hot day. A lizard is sunning itself on a rock. Now picture this same animal after sunset. In the evening the air in the canyon cools. How can the lizard stay warm? It can crawl into cracks between and under rocks. The rocks feel warm for several hours after sunset. Heat from the sun is stored in the rocks. Many other substances can store heat from the sun.

How do substances differ in the amount of heat they can store?

Select several substances to test. Design a way to heat the substances in the sun. Measure the temperature of each material before and after it has been heated by the sun. Which substances become the warmest? Which substances stay warm longest?

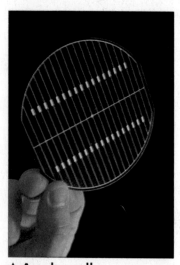

▲ A solar cell

There are also some problems in using solar energy. Energy can be collected only during the day. The energy must be collected and stored. Only small amounts of energy are available on cloudy days. In the winter, many places have few hours of sunlight. The farther a region is from the equator, the less solar energy it receives. When and where on the earth would a solar collector work best?

How can solar energy be changed to electricity?

Solar energy can also be used to produce electricity. A **solar cell** is a device that changes solar energy directly to electrical energy. When sunlight strikes a solar cell, a small amount of

384

electric current is produced. The picture at the right shows a car that uses solar cells. When can this device *not* be used?

With the use of many mirrors, solar energy can be changed to electrical energy. The picture below shows a solar power plant. A computer controls the 1,800 mirrors. The sun's rays are reflected off the mirrors onto a central tower. Inside the tower, the solar energy is used to produce steam. Electrical energy is then produced by means of a turbine and a generator.

▲ A car that runs on solar energy

▲ Solar One, a solar power plant

Lesson Review

1. What is the source of solar energy?
2. Compare passive with active solar heating. Give an example of passive solar heating.
3. Describe a device that can be used to produce electrical energy directly from solar energy.
4. What are two benefits of using solar energy? What are two problems in using solar energy?

Think! You want to design a home using solar energy. Where would be the best region on Earth to build your house? Explain your answer.

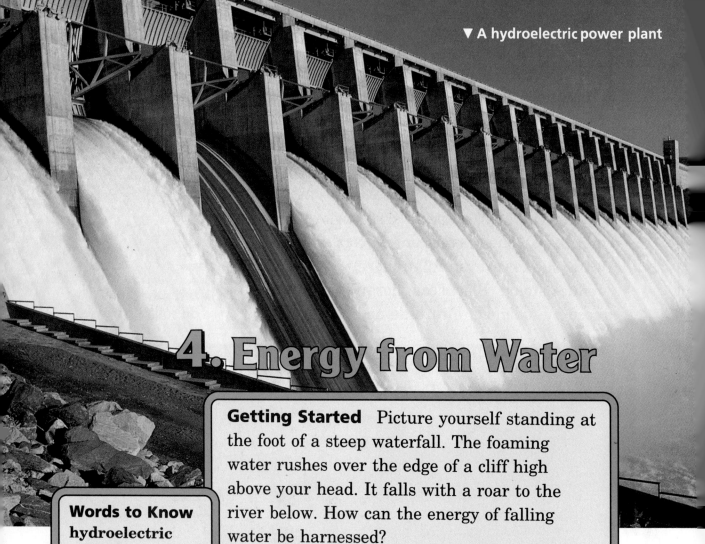

4. Energy from Water

Getting Started Picture yourself standing at the foot of a steep waterfall. The foaming water rushes over the edge of a cliff high above your head. It falls with a roar to the river below. How can the energy of falling water be harnessed?

Words to Know
hydroelectric
  energy
tidal energy

How can water be used as an energy source?

Water flowing downhill has energy of motion. Such moving water can be used to produce electrical energy. **Hydroelectric** (hye droh ee-LEK trihk) **energy** is electrical energy produced from moving water. The word part *hydro-* means "water."

A hydroelectric power plant uses the energy of moving water to produce electrical energy. Most hydroelectric plants use water that is stored behind a dam, such as the one shown here. The water is stored in a large lake, or reservoir

386

(REZ ur vwahr). The water is released from the reservoir and falls into the river below. As it falls, the water gains energy of motion.

The water passes through huge pipes to the river below the dam. Then the water flows through a turbine, turning its blades. The blades are attached to a spinning shaft connected to a generator. The generator changes the mechanical energy of the turbine to electrical energy.

▼ **Inside a hydroelectric power plant**

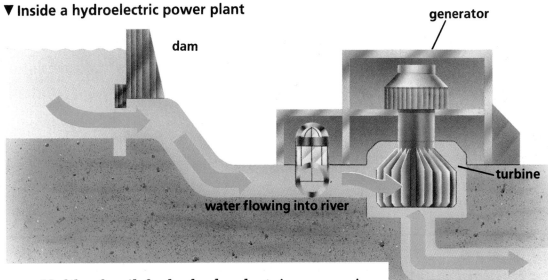

dam

generator

turbine

water flowing into river

Unlike fossil fuels, hydroelectric energy is a renewable resource. Water is always above and on the earth. Like nuclear and solar energy, hydroelectric energy does not pollute.

There are some problems in using water energy. During times of drought, the flow of water is low. Hydroelectric power plants are very expensive to build. They require a great deal of space. Sometimes the reservoir floods the land behind the dam. The power plants must be built where there is a large supply of flowing water. For all these reasons, such plants are not built in many regions.

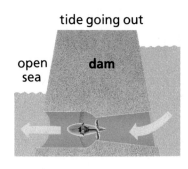

tide going out

open sea   **dam**

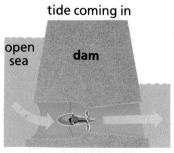

tide coming in

open sea   **dam**

▲ **Moving tidal water turns the turbine blades.**

How can the tides be used for energy?

Tides are the rise and fall of ocean water. Twice a day the water level rises and falls along the seacoast. **Tidal energy** is the energy of the moving water of tides. Tides are another source of energy.

Tidal energy can be used in only a few places on the earth. There must be a large difference between the heights of the high tide and the low tide. The amount of energy in the moving water varies. It depends on the difference between the levels of high tides and low tides.

The drawing shows that a tidal power plant is part of the dam. Openings in the dam let the tide water move past the turbine blades. The tide water spins the turbine blades to help produce electricity in the generator.

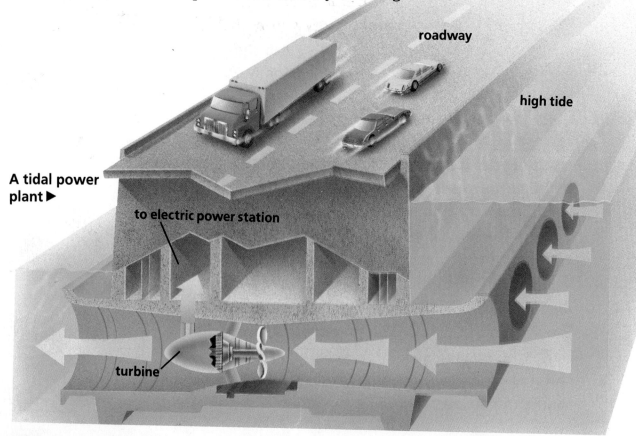

roadway

high tide

A tidal power plant ▶

to electric power station

turbine

▲ A tidal power plant in the Bay of Fundy

One of the best known tidal power plants in the world is in the Bay of Fundy. In the picture above you can see a view of this plant taken from an airplane. But tidal energy will probably not be an important source of energy in the future. Why? Tidal power plants can be built only where there is a great difference between high tide and low tide. This great difference is not found in many places. So, there are only a few suitable places to build tidal power plants.

Lesson Review

1. Describe how one form of energy is changed to another form of energy in a hydroelectric plant.
2. What are three problems in the use of hydroelectric energy?
3. What is a tidal power plant?

Think! You are on a committee to decide whether to build a hydroelectric plant or a nuclear power plant. Which kind of plant would you favor? Give reasons for your answer.

Life Science
CONNECTION

Tidal energy is just one resource obtained from the oceans. What living resources are found in the ocean?

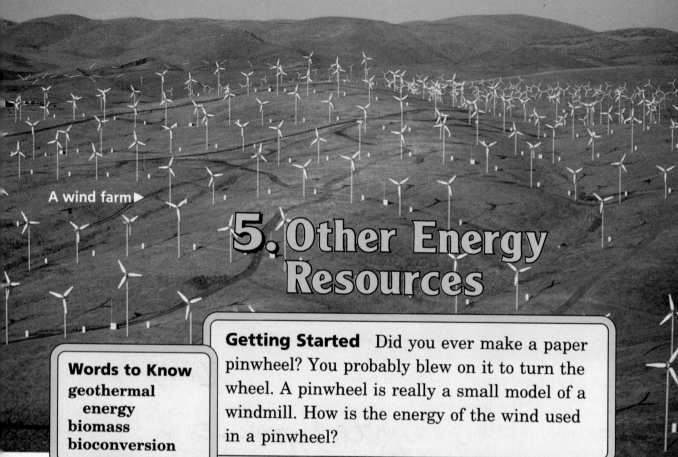

A wind farm ▶

5. Other Energy Resources

Getting Started Did you ever make a paper pinwheel? You probably blew on it to turn the wheel. A pinwheel is really a small model of a windmill. How is the energy of the wind used in a pinwheel?

▲ A windmill

How is the wind a source of energy?

Wind is moving air. Differences in the temperature and pressure of air around the earth cause air to move. Wind energy is the energy of moving air. Wind energy can be used to turn the blades of a pinwheel. In the same way, wind energy can be used to turn the blades of windmills. Windmills are devices that change the kinetic energy of wind to mechanical energy. How do the windmills shown on this page differ?

Windmills were probably first used in Persia in the seventh century A.D. Those early windmills were used to pump water and to grind grain. Today windmills are often used to produce electrical energy. Large wind farms can produce electrical energy for many people.

How is the earth a source of energy?

Geothermal (jee oh THUR mul) **energy** is energy from the natural heat within the earth's crust. Deep inside the earth, the temperature is high enough to melt rock. The melted rock often moves up into the crust and forms a hot spot.

Hot springs and geysers (GYE zurz) form in places where underground water is heated by pockets of magma. In a hot spring, heated water flows onto the earth's surface. In a geyser, it spurts, or erupts, onto the surface.

▼ A geothermal power plant in Hawaii

"Old Faithful," a geyser in Wyoming ▼

The temperature near magma may be high enough to change water to steam. So, geothermal energy can be used to produce electricity. Electricity is produced in much the same way as with other sources of energy. The main difference is that the energy source is heat from the earth. You can see a geothermal energy plant located in Hawaii in the picture above.

Explore

How can wind be used as a source of energy?

Picture a warm summer day with the wind blowing gently. You are holding a brightly colored pinwheel. You hold the pinwheel up so that the wind turns the blades. Did you know that this pinwheel could do work?

Materials
scissors · paper · straw · pins · tape · cup · paper punch · thread · paper clips

Procedure

A. Use scissors to cut an 11-12 cm paper square. Fold it into fourths (drawing *A*).

B. Use scissors to make a cut about 5 cm long on each fold, as shown in drawing *B*.

C. Use a pencil to poke a small hole in the corner of each section and at the square's center.

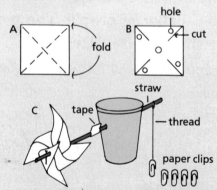

D. Put a straw through the holes to make a fan blade (drawing *C*).

E. Poke pins through the straw in front of and behind the blade.

F. Wrap tape behind the blade.

G. Use a paper punch to make two holes in the cup. Push the straw through the holes in the cup.

H. At the end of the straw, tape a piece of thread 1 m long with a paper clip attached.

I. Blow on the blade so it turns.

J. Use several methods to make a breeze to turn the blade. Add paper clips (drawing *C*).

Writing and Sharing Results and Conclusions

1. Describe each method you used to make a breeze.

2. Which method lifted the most paper clips?

How can garbage be used for energy?

Have you ever wondered whether something useful could be done with garbage? Well, garbage can be a good source of energy. Garbage, wood, and animal wastes are called biomass (BYE oh mas). **Biomass** is any kind of organic matter that can be used as a fuel. Organic matter is any substance that was once alive or was produced by a living thing.

Biomass can be used directly for heating. For example, wood can be burned in a fireplace. In some countries, animal wastes are burned like wood to give off heat for cooking. The picture below shows a biomass unit that changes cow wastes into cooking fuel.

Biomass can also be used to produce fuel for a large number of people. The picture shows a factory that changes corn to fuel. The process by which biomass is changed to a liquid or gaseous fuel is **bioconversion** (bye oh kin VUR zhun).

Conversion of corn to synthetic fuel ▼

◄ A small biomass unit in India

393

How do the three forms of energy compare?

The table below compares the benefits and problems of three forms of energy.

Comparison of Three Kinds of Energy		
Type of Energy	Benefits	Problems
Wind	Free; renewable resource	Not dependable; many regions have little wind. Large wind mills are expensive.
Geothermal	Renewable resource	Not widely available; may be far from where needed. Small amount of energy produced.
Biomass	Renewable resource; helps get rid of trash	Pollutes air; produces unpleasant odors. Much waste material may be left.

In spite of the problems, wind energy, geothermal energy, and biomass may become more important forms of energy. Which do you think will become important where you live?

Lesson Review

1. Define *wind energy.* Name a device that changes wind energy to another form of energy.
2. What is geothermal energy? How is it obtained?
3. What is biomass? Describe how one kind of biomass can be a source of energy.
4. Compare the advantages and disadvantages of wind energy and geothermal energy.

Think! On pages 366–369 you read about a microwave airplane. Predict whether this form of energy will be more or less important in the future. Why?

Chapter Connections

Look at all the sources of energy in this graphic organizer. Which of these might become more important in the future? Discuss your ideas with a partner. Then share your ideas with the class.

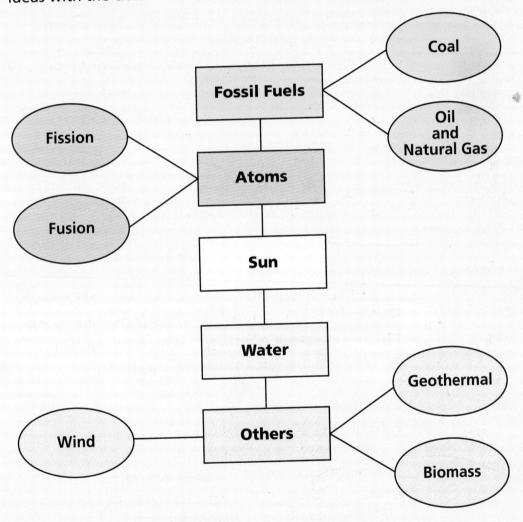

Writing About Science • Classify

Find five things in your house that use energy. What is the source of energy for each? Write a paragraph about these sources of energy.

Science Terms

A. Write the letter of the term that best matches the definition.

1. The splitting of the nucleus of an atom, releasing energy
2. A device used to collect solar energy
3. The energy of the moving water of tides
4. Fuel formed from decayed plants and animals
5. A useful material that is taken from the environment
6. A device that changes solar energy to electrical energy
7. The energy contained in the nucleus of the atom
8. Organic matter that can be used as fuel
9. A device with a wheel and blades that changes the energy of steam to mechanical energy
10. Nuclear reaction in which atomic nuclei fuse
11. Electrical energy produced from moving water
12. A machine that changes the mechanical energy of a turbine to electrical energy

a. biomass
b. fossil fuel
c. generator
d. hydroelectric energy
e. natural resource
f. nuclear energy
g. nuclear fission
h. nuclear fusion
i. solar cell
j. solar collector
k. tidal energy
l. turbine

B. Write a paragraph that uses all of the science terms listed below. The sentences must show that you understand the meaning of the science terms.

bioconversion   fuel   geothermal energy
nonrenewable resource   renewable resource   solar energy

Science Ideas

1. Describe how a commonly used kind of fossil fuel formed.

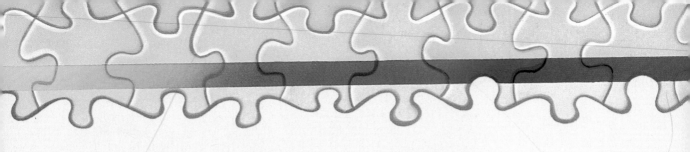

2. Explain why oil is considered to be a nonrenewable resource.

3. In general terms, describe what happens to uranium during a nuclear fission reaction.

4. Describe two advantages and two disadvantages to the use of nuclear energy in producing electrical energy.

5. What takes place in the sun to produce solar energy?

6. Give an example of a device that uses electrical energy produced from solar energy.

7. List two problems in using solar energy.

8. Describe a region where it would be useful to build a hydroelectric plant.

9. How can tides be used to produce electrical energy?

10. How might the use of biomass help both the trash problem and an energy shortage?

Applying Science Ideas

1. Some scientists say that "almost all the earth's energy can be traced back to the sun." You can see how solar energy comes from the sun. But explain how the energy of burning coal can also be traced back to the sun.

2. Your community has a smelly, ugly dump. Suggest a way that this dump could be cleaned up and also provide energy and other resources.

Using Science Skills

Each week a car is filled with gasoline. The first week it uses 40 liters of gas. The second week it uses 50 liters. It uses only 25 liters the third week and 35 liters the fourth week. Make a bar graph to show the weekly usage of gasoline over the four-week period.

Resources and Pollution

Oil Overboard

The Aleutian (uh LOO shun) Indians named it *Alaska*, meaning "great land." Today it is the state with the largest amount of land, the fewest people, and the most oil. Alaskans boast that they have the biggest forests, the purest water, and the best fishing.

Alaskans have always been proud of the wildlife found in their state. Sea otters and sea lions dive for food in bays. Salmon and herring breed in rivers. Birds nest on islands near the coastline. The largest group of bald eagles in the world hunt there. Suddenly, on March 24, 1989, many of these animals were in great danger.

An accident happened in Prince William Sound near Valdez, Alaska. Just after midnight an oil tanker hit a reef. In the first dark minutes after the crash, the amount of damage was not clear. Then the report came—the tanker had three gaping holes in its hull. Forty million liters (10 million gallons) of oil began to pour into the bay.

By daybreak, oil covered the water in all directions. Sludge as thick as hot-fudge sauce stuck to rocks. Each high tide carried oil to new places along the shore.

Thousands of animals died almost immediately. Others died later after eating oil-soaked food. The oil even killed deer that ate plants near the shore.

People rushed to help at the Valdez Bird and Animal Rescue Center. Scientists at the scene directed the efforts. Bringing the animals in was the hardest part. Imagine trying to catch a frightened, oily bird. Once a bird was caught, it was washed in soap and water. After it was warm and rested, the bird was set free far from the oil spill.

After the oil spill, concerned people asked this question: How can people protect resources from such accidents?

Discover

How can you clean up oil spills?

ACTIVITY

Materials   paper cup · sand · cooking oil

Procedure

In Alaska, scientists worked with clean-up crews to remove the oil from sandy beaches. How would you do this? Put some sand in a paper cup. Pour 1/2 cup of cooking oil on the sand. Do not touch the cup for 1 hour.

Look at the oily sand and think of ways to remove the oil. Test one of the ways. How well did it work? How can you tell if all the oil is gone? Would your way work on a real oil spill? Explain why or why not.

In this chapter you will find out why resources such as water and wildlife need to be protected. You will also learn about kinds of pollution and how they can be avoided.

1. Substances from the Earth

Words to Know
pollution
conservation

Getting Started Open your notebook. Count the number of pages on which you have written on only *one* side of the paper. How many are there? Suppose that you never again write on a new page until you have filled up *both sides* of the previous page. How many trees would be saved if every student in your school did this?

▼ Timber, a renewable resource

Are our natural resources in danger?

The trees that are used to produce the paper in your notebook are a valuable natural resource. Remember that natural resources are useful substances taken from the environment. Air, land, and water are all natural resources.

Some natural resources, such as trees, can be replaced if they are used up. Such substances are called renewable resources. Remember that a renewable resource is one that can be replaced if it is used. Trees are a renewable resource.

▲ Paper produced in a paper mill

Suppose you have $100 in the bank. Every year you add $.01 to the account. But every month you take out $5. What will happen to your account after a year? How long will it take you to remove all the money in your account? The earth is like a bank account. Think of its natural resources as money in the bank. Suppose natural resources, such as coal, oil, and natural gas, are taken from the "bank." What would happen if these resources were never returned?

Some resources, such as fossil fuels, are called nonrenewable. They are nonrenewable because they cannot be easily replaced once they are used up. Using nonrenewable resources is like using the bank account. More resources are being used than are being replaced.

▼ Oil, a nonrenewable resource

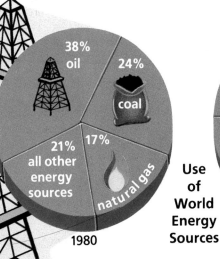

Use of World Energy Sources

The drawing above shows what the major energy sources were in 1980 and what they will probably be in the year 2000. How might the uses of coal and natural gas change? What two energy sources will probably change the most, and how will they change?

How does pollution affect natural resources?

Pollution (puh LOO shun) is the addition of unwanted substances to the environment. Usable supplies of natural resources are reduced by pollution. For example, oil spills can harm or kill living things in the oceans and along shorelines.

People can help control pollution by conserving natural resources. **Conservation** (kahn sur VAY shun) is the careful use of natural resources.

Think back to your notebook paper. You can practice conservation by using paper wisely. The chart below shows some simple ways you can conserve natural resources. What are some other ways you can conserve resources?

▲ Ways to conserve natural resources

Resource	Conservation Activity
Water	Turn off water when you brush your teeth.
Land	Recycle newspaper, glass, and aluminum.
Air	Carpool or take public transportation.

Lesson Review _____

1. Name three natural resources that are in danger.
2. Why is the wasteful use of resources a problem?
3. What is pollution?
4. What is conservation? List three ways that you can help to conserve natural resources.

Think! Plan what your class can do to reduce a pollution problem in your neighborhood.

Skills

Writing a definition from what you observe

Sometimes you can write your own definition of words based on what you observe. *Pollution* can be defined in many ways. You may know that pollution is happening when the air is made less healthy to breathe. Suppose you watch black smoke pouring from a smokestack into the air. You might define *pollution* as what happens to the air when smoke gets into it.

Practicing the skill

Water is a natural resource. Sometimes natural resources are wasted. Your observations in this activity will help you define *waste*.

1. Make a pinhole in the bottom of a milk carton. Hold the carton over a glass and fill the carton with water.

2. After 2 minutes, check the volume of water in the glass.

3. Imagine that the pinhole was a leak in a water pipe. Figure out how much water would be lost in 1 day.

4. Use what you observed to write a definition of *waste*.

Thinking about the skill

Describe a time in the last month when you learned what something is and how it works by making your own observations.

Applying the skill

Think of an item that you have thrown away. Then think of a way that you could have reused it instead of throwing it out. Use this idea to write a definition of *conservation*.

2. Air Pollution

Getting Started Have you ever been in a traffic jam? Perhaps you were leaving a parking lot after a big ball game. You might have smelled car exhaust. Perhaps you had some trouble breathing. What was happening to the air around you?

Words to Know
pollutant
greenhouse effect
smog
ozone layer
radon

What are some types of air pollution?

Air is a natural resource needed by almost all living things. All the air around the earth forms the earth's atmosphere. The table at the left shows the gases naturally found in the atmosphere. Which gas is found in the greatest amount?

Harmful matter added to the environment is called a **pollutant** (puh LOOT unt). Air pollutants can be produced by human actions or by a natural event, such as an erupting volcano.

One major cause of air pollution is the burning of fossil fuels. Carbon dioxide, carbon monoxide, and sulfur dioxide are gases given off into the air when fossil fuels are burned. All of these gases can be air pollutants. Burning fossil fuels also adds soot, or small particles, to the air.

Gases in the Atmosphere	
Gas	Percentage by Volume
Nitrogen	78.08
Oxygen	20.95
Argon	0.93
Carbon dioxide	0.03
Neon	trace
Helium	trace
Methane	trace
Krypton	trace
Hydrogen	trace
Xenon	trace
Ozone	trace

A second type of air pollution is acid rain. Burning fossil fuels causes an excess amount of carbon dioxide gas and sulfur dioxide gas in the air. Acid rain is the result of the mixing of these gases with water vapor in the air. The gases mix with water vapor, forming acids. Snow and ice can also contain acids.

Acid rain is harmful or deadly to living things in rivers, lakes, and streams. It also harms living things on land. The picture shows trees that have died from acid rain.

▲ Effects of acid rain on evergreen trees

What is the greenhouse effect?

Have you ever been inside a greenhouse? Energy from the sun passes through the glass, is absorbed and changed to heat. The heat is trapped inside the greenhouse. Heat can collect in the earth's atmosphere in much the same way. The trapping and building up of heat in the atmosphere is called the **greenhouse effect.** Certain gases, such as carbon dioxide, keep some of the heat that radiates from the earth from escaping into space.

▼ The greenhouse effect

▼ Heating the air inside a greenhouse

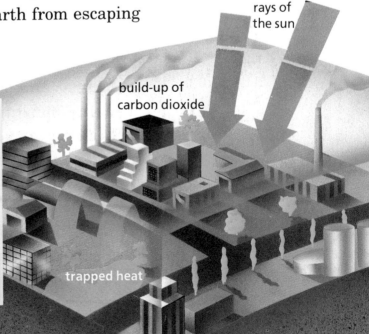

rays of the sun

build-up of carbon dioxide

trapped heat

407

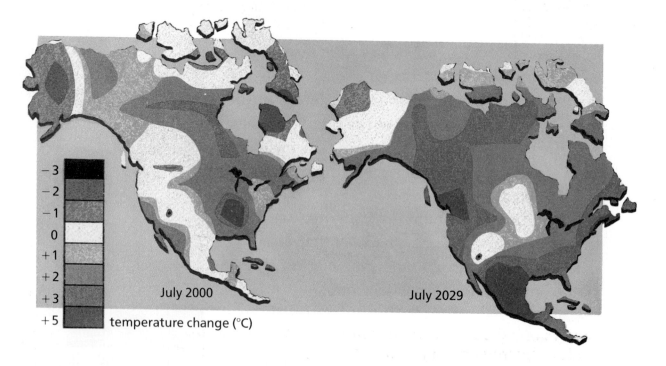

-3
-2
-1
0
+1
+2
+3
+5   temperature change (°C)

July 2000   July 2029

▲ Predicted warming of North America because of the greenhouse effect

Scientists feel that the greenhouse effect may be harmful. It may cause temperatures on the earth to rise. Such increased temperatures could cause droughts. Droughts, in turn, could lead to food shortages. The maps above show some predicted temperature changes in North America. By 2029, how might the temperature change where you live?

What is smog?

Another form of air pollution is smog. **Smog** (smahg) is a mixture of smoke and fog in the air. Sulfur dioxide and soot in the air produce smog. Smog may cause coughing and watery eyes.

Some progress has been made in controlling air pollution from acid rain and smog. "Scrubbers" have been put on smokestacks in factories. These scrubbers reduce the amount of gases released into the air. Pollution-control devices on cars have reduced pollution from car exhausts.

▼ Smog over a major city

Explore

ACTIVITY

How clean is the air you breathe?

Have you ever been on vacation for a few weeks? When you came home, you probably noticed a layer of dust on all your furniture. Where did the dust come from? How clean is the air in your home?

Materials

wax marking pencil · metric ruler · 5 glass microscope slides · petroleum jelly · map of your school · hand-held microscope

Procedure

A. Use a wax marking pencil to draw a square 2 cm on a side on one side of a microscope slide.

B. On the other side of the slide, smear a thin layer of petroleum jelly over the square.

C. Repeat steps **A** and **B** on four other slides.

D. On a map of your school, mark five locations where you will place the slides. Number the locations 1–5. Number the slides 1–5.

E. Place each of your slides at one of the chosen locations. Leave the slides in place 3 days. Record where each slide is placed.

F. After 3 days, collect the slides and observe them with a hand-held microscope. Count the number of particles in the square you marked.

G. Record your observations in a chart.

Writing and Sharing Results and Conclusions

1. Which slide had the most particles? Where was it located?

2. Which slide had the fewest particles? Where was it located?

3. Suggest some reasons for the differences in the number of particles on the slides.

What are other kinds of air pollutants?

CFCs are another form of air pollutant. *CFCs* stands for a group of chemicals called *chlorofluorocarbons*. These chemicals contain chlorine, fluorine, carbon, and sometimes hydrogen. CFCs cause the cooling effect in refrigerators and in air conditioners. The plastic foam of plates and cups is also made of CFCs. In the picture are products that contain CFCs.

CFCs have caused a hole in the ozone (OH-zohn) layer. The **ozone layer** is a very thin layer of ozone gas high above the earth. Ozone is a gas made up of three oxygen atoms.

The ozone layer acts like a giant filter. It screens out many of the harmful ultraviolet (UV) rays of the sun. Too many UV rays can damage crops and living things in the ocean. These extra UV rays might cause an increase in skin cancer.

The hole in the ozone layer, which is over Antarctica, is about the size of the United States. On this page is a picture showing the hole. What will happen as the hole gets bigger?

▲ Products containing CFCs

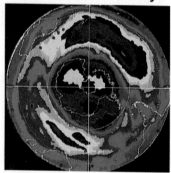

▼ Satellite view of the hole in the ozone layer

▼ Harmful UV rays pass through the hole in the ozone layer.

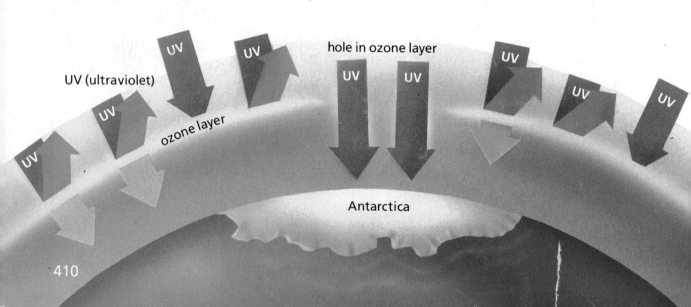

UV (ultraviolet)

UV

ozone layer

hole in ozone layer

Antarctica

How can radon pollute the air?

The release of radon (RAY dahn) gas is another natural form of air pollution. **Radon** is a gas produced by the decay of uranium in rocks and in soil. Radon may be released from rocks and pass without harm into the atmosphere. But when radon collects inside a house, it can be harmful. High levels of radon in homes have been linked with cancer in humans.

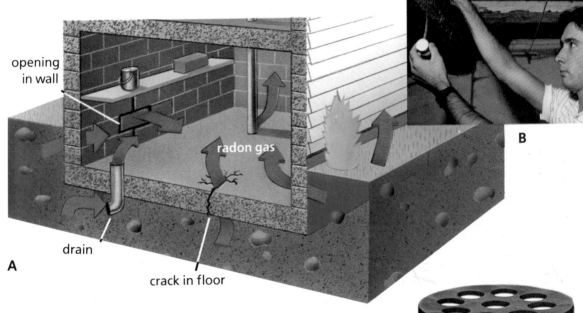

opening in wall

radon gas

drain

A

crack in floor

B

Lesson Review

1. List some pollutants produced by burning fossil fuels.
2. What is the greenhouse effect? List one possible danger resulting from the greenhouse effect.
3. Describe the cause and effects of acid rain.
4. What is smog? What causes it? Describe some ways that smog can be controlled.
5. Explain why a buildup of CFCs is dangerous.

Think! The hole in the ozone layer is now over Antarctica. Would the hole be more dangerous or less dangerous if it were over the United States? Explain.

C

Radtrak

034140

▲ (A) Collection of harmful radon gas inside a home; (B) Protecting a home from radon gas; (C) A home radon-detection device

3. Land Pollution

Words to Know
sanitary landfill
biodegradable
   substance
incinerator
pesticide

What are sources of land pollution?

Land pollution occurs when harmful substances are put in or on the land. Garbage is one source of land pollution. Garbage often includes waste paper, plastics, bottles and cans, and unusable food. In one year, each person in the United States produces about a metric ton of garbage! The table below compares the amount of garbage produced by people in five major cities. How does the amount produced in Rome compare with that produced in New York?

B One person's garbage (kg/day)

New York	
Tokyo	
Paris	
Hamburg	
Rome	

kilograms of garbage 0   1.0   2.0
kilograms of garbage

A

▲ (A) One person produces about a ton of garbage in a year. (B) The average number of kilograms of garbage produced by people in different cities

Garbage must be disposed of every few days. Microbes very quickly begin breaking down garbage, producing strong odors. The smell of garbage attracts flies and rats. The disposal of garbage is a very important health concern.

How is garbage disposed of?

In the United States, collected garbage is disposed of in one of two ways. Most garbage is dumped in a sanitary (SAN uh ter ee) landfill. A **sanitary landfill** is a place on land in which wastes are dumped. It is either a low place, such as a valley, or a hole that has been dug.

▲ Spreading layers of garbage in a sanitary landfill

Garbage is dumped into the landfill, spread out, and covered with soil every day. The layers are then pressed down by a tractor. Layers of garbage and soil build up until the low place or hole is filled. Completely filled landfills may later be used as parks or athletic fields.

There are problems with landfills. They require a lot of open space. They need daily care so that they do not produce foul odors. Buried garbage is broken down by bacteria and molds. This breakdown produces natural gas and other substances. Landfills must be patrolled so that illegal wastes are not dumped in them.

Problem Solving

ACTIVITY

Litter Things Mean a Lot!

Someone has computed that in one day, people in this country discard 150,000 tons of paper trash. Paper trash includes cardboard boxes, paper bags, and wrappers. To cart away all this junk would require a line of tractor-trailer trucks more than 190 km long.

Your teacher will give you a bag of junk. This bag contains the same kind of junk people throw away every day. Sanitation engineers call it solid waste. Imagine you are a solid-waste manager.

How can you separate and sort this collection of solid waste?

Discuss the best ways to separate and sort all the things in your bag. Then separate and sort the things. How would your methods work with a truckful of trash?

▲ Incinerator plant

The substances dumped in sanitary landfills should be biodegradable (bye oh dih GRAY duh-bul). A **biodegradable substance** is one that can be broken down by microbes. In time, this substance will become part of the soil. Waste foods, such as egg shells and corn husks, are biodegradable. What happens to substances such as plastic bags?

Some types of garbage may be disposed of by incinerators (ihn SIHN ur ayt urz). An **incinerator** is a huge furnace for burning garbage. One is shown in the picture at the left. An incinerator does not take up as much space as a landfill. But it does release gases and solid particles into the air. Each town or city must decide which kind of waste disposal is best for its needs.

How are chemical wastes disposed of?

Chemical wastes produced by industries also pollute the land. Industries must find ways to dispose of their wastes safely. Pesticides (PES-tuh sydz) used on farms are another main source of pollution. A **pesticide** is a chemical used to kill insect pests that harm crops. Other wastes from farms include chemicals used to kill weeds that grow among the crops. Pesticides and weed-killers can be harmful to humans and to wildlife.

Chemical wastes can pollute both the land and the water. ▼

industrial wastes

animal wastes

pesticides

Safe disposal of chemical wastes is a big problem. In general, these substances cannot be dumped into any landfill. Chemicals that have been emptied into landfills have seeped down through the soil. They pass through the soil into the groundwater supply, as shown in the drawing. Chemicals in the water are harmful to living things in the water. They are also harmful to humans who drink the water or swim in it.

How can land pollution be reduced?

To reduce land pollution, harmful chemicals can be dumped into specially designed landfills. Such landfills must be lined with plastic sheets. How would the plastic help reduce the pollution problem? Harmful chemicals can also be dumped into strong cans that do not leak. These cans must then be stored in a safe place, such as underground. Some chemical wastes can be safely burned in incinerators.

▲ Wastes can be "fed" to microorganisms.

▲ Safe storage of chemical wastes underground

Recycling is a good way to reduce land pollution. Today many cities and towns have recycling centers. At these centers, things that were discarded are changed in form and then used again. Newspapers, glass bottles and jars, and aluminum cans are often recycled. These substances are later turned into useful products. For example, you may have seen books or greeting cards from recycled paper. What other items are made of recycled paper? Recycling is a way that each person can help to reduce land pollution.

▲ Recycling of paper, a valuable product from timber

Lesson Review

1. Describe two ways to dispose of garbage.
2. Define *biodegradable*. Give an example of one biodegradable substance and one nonbiodegradable substance.
3. List two main sources of chemical wastes in soil.
4. What is recycling? What are some kinds of substances that can be recycled?

Think! Identify one main type of land pollution in your community. Design a way that you and your class can reduce land pollution.

Is there a place for toxic waste?

Each year factories make tons of toxic, or poisonous, wastes. Some are radioactive. They give off small amounts of energy that can be dangerous to living things. Many of these wastes could cause diseases, such as cancer. The wastes must be gotten rid of safely. Many of them have been put into barrels at dumps. But the wastes can leak out of the barrels into soil and water. Many dumps now have this problem. The government is trying to clean them up. But cleanup is dangerous. Workers must wear special suits, such as those in the picture.

One solution to getting rid of poisoned soil is to change the soil into blocks of glassy rock. How is this done? Workers dig trenches at the dump site. The workers fill the trenches with graphite. Graphite is the gray substance in pencils. Then special rods heat the ground to thousands of degrees with electric currents. The soil around and beneath the graphite melts. When it cools, it forms a solid block. The toxic wastes are either destroyed or permanently locked in the glass blocks.

CAUTION
PCBs

Scientists say that these blocks would lock in the wastes for more than a million years. The wastes could not harm nearby plants and animals. But the scientists still have some questions about the glass-block method. They wonder if the blocks could be made in all kinds of soils. Also they are not sure if this method would trap the wastes that are deep in the soil.

In Nevada, officials are studying a way to bury radioactive wastes. They are testing tunnels under the land ridge. The tunnels would be filled with wastes in containers. Then the tunnels would be sealed. Scientists think the wastes stay toxic for about 10,000 years. These tunnels would have to hold the wastes that long.

Some people worry about putting radioactive wastes in tunnels. They think it is not wise to store such dangerous wastes for so long. Changes could occur in the tunnels. And there is not yet a container that would last for 10,000 years.

Critical thinking

1. Suppose you had to decide whether glass blocks and tunnels are good ways to bury toxic wastes. What more would you need to know before you decide?

2. What are some other ways to keep toxic wastes from poisoning the earth?

Using what you learned

Take a survey. Ask your family and neighbors about toxic wastes. Ask if they would want to have toxic wastes stored in your neighborhood, town, or state. What are the reasons for their answers? Add your own answer to the survey results. Discuss your results in class.

◀ **Three fourths of the earth is covered by water.**

4. Water Pollution

Getting Started You have probably seen a cowboy movie on television. The movie might have shown what life was like about 100 years ago. Perhaps the cowboys were shown drinking from a river or stream. Would you do this today? Why or why not?

How are sources of water polluted?

About three fourths of the earth is covered with water. But most of this water is salty. Salt water cannot be used for drinking, industry, or farms. Only fresh water can be used. From the graph, you can see that most fresh water is locked up in icecaps and glaciers. Less than 1 percent of the water on the earth is usable fresh water, found in lakes and rivers.

Fresh water can be polluted by sewage, chemicals, and even heat. Sewage is the material that passes down drains in sinks and is flushed down toilets. Some of the microbes in sewage can cause disease in humans and other animals. Sewage that gets into water supplies can make the water unsafe to drink.

▼ **Most of the earth's water is salty.**

☐ salt water (97.41%)

◼ unavailable fresh water

◼ available fresh water

(2.59%)

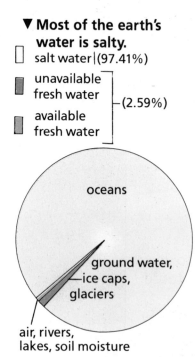

oceans

ground water,
ice caps,
glaciers

air, rivers,
lakes, soil moisture

The drawing below shows that chemicals such as pesticides can also pollute water supplies. A pesticide is a chemical used to kill insect pests. Fertilizers (FUR tuh lye zurz) can also pollute water. A **fertilizer** is a chemical that adds minerals to the soil. Fertilizers are often carried away by runoff. Runoff is water that flows off the land's surface. The runoff carries fertilizers to streams and lakes.

Laundry detergents can also pollute water. A detergent is a substance used for cleaning. Both fertilizers and detergents contain phosphorus. Phosphorus in water may cause some living things to grow and others to die.

Simple plants called algae (AL jee) may grow quickly in water with phosphorus. When the algae die, their remains are broken down by microbes, which use up oxygen needed by fish. What has happened to many of the fish shown in the pond?

▼ Algae have covered this pond.

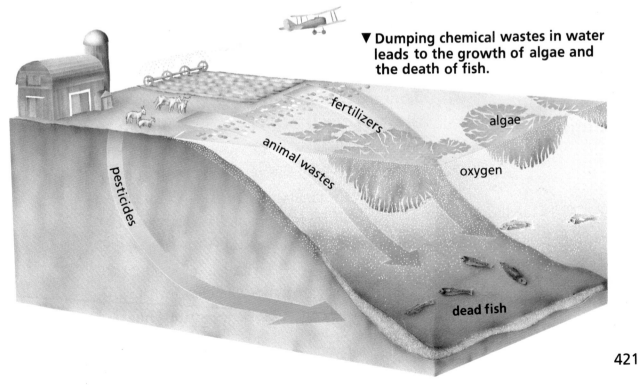

▼ Dumping chemical wastes in water leads to the growth of algae and the death of fish.

fertilizers

algae

animal wastes

pesticides

oxygen

dead fish

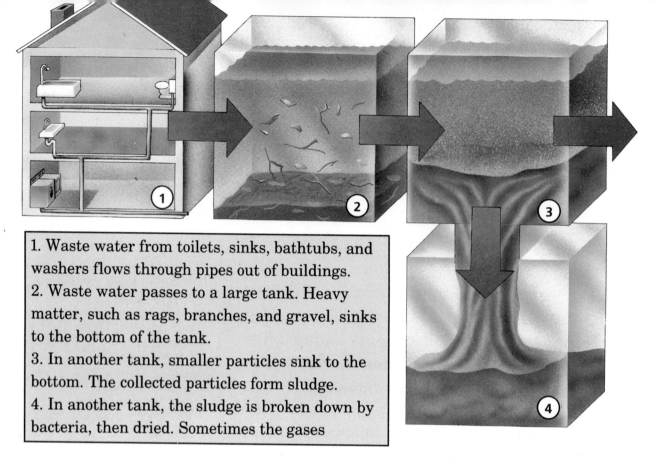

1. Waste water from toilets, sinks, bathtubs, and washers flows through pipes out of buildings.
2. Waste water passes to a large tank. Heavy matter, such as rags, branches, and gravel, sinks to the bottom of the tank.
3. In another tank, smaller particles sink to the bottom. The collected particles form sludge.
4. In another tank, the sludge is broken down by bacteria, then dried. Sometimes the gases

▲ **How water is purified**

▼ **Thermal pollution at a nuclear power plant**

How is waste water purified? Cities and towns have complex systems to purify used water from homes and industry. Follow the drawings above to see how this water is treated.

How can heat pollute water?

Thermal pollution (THUR mul puh LOO-shun), or heat added to water, is another type of water pollution. How does water become heated? One way is by means of nuclear power plants, which produce a great deal of heat. The excess heat is released into ponds or rivers near the plant. This heat raises the water temperature.

Warm water can hold less oxygen than the same amount of cool water. So adding heat

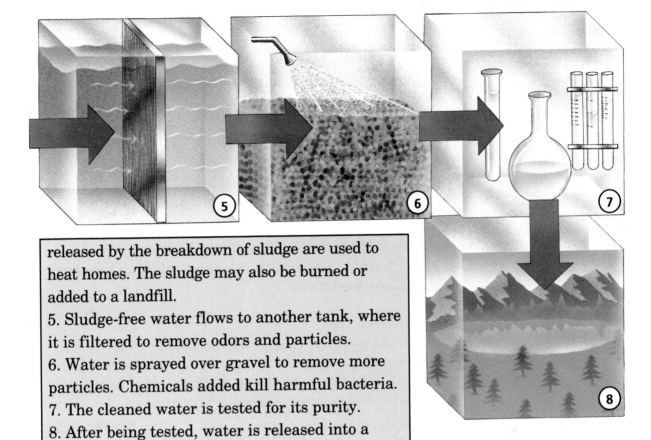

released by the breakdown of sludge are used to heat homes. The sludge may also be burned or added to a landfill.

5. Sludge-free water flows to another tank, where it is filtered to remove odors and particles.
6. Water is sprayed over gravel to remove more particles. Chemicals added kill harmful bacteria.
7. The cleaned water is tested for its purity.
8. After being tested, water is released into a large body of water such as a river or lake.

reduces the amount of oxygen available to the living things in water. Warm water makes certain fish more active. It also increases their need for oxgyen. Why might the warming of water be harmful to some fish?

What are sources of ocean pollution?

Oceans are polluted by natural means and by humans. Most pollution comes from things humans have done. People dump waste material into the ocean, and it later washes up onto the beach. Often the waste consists of non-biodegradable substances, such as plastics. Plastic waste can be harmful to various kinds of sea life, which often eat the plastics. The picture shows a sea bird strangling from plastic rings.

▼ Plastic can harm or kill sea animals.

Explore Together

How does a charcoal filter help to purify water?

Materials

Organizer

cotton ball · toothpick · 2 clear plastic straws · activated charcoal · water · 3 plastic cups · food coloring · stirrer · 2 droppers · metric ruler

Procedure

Investigator

A. Pull a small piece of cotton from a cotton ball. With a toothpick, stuff this piece into one end of each of two straws. In one straw pour a layer of charcoal I cm high. The charcoal should be above the cotton.

Manager

B. Fill a plastic cup, cup A, 1/3 full of water. Add 1 drop of food coloring. With a stirrer, mix the food coloring and water thoroughly.

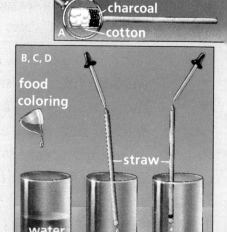

Investigator, Manager

C. Draw up the colored water into a dropper. Drop the colored water through the straw that has only cotton in one end. Catch the water dripping from the straw in cup B, as shown.

Investigator

D. Repeat step **C**, using the straw with charcoal and cotton. Collect the water in cup C.

Manager

E. Compare the water color in cup B with that in cup C.

Writing and Sharing Results and Conclusions

Group, Recorder

1. How does the color of the water in cup B compare with that in cup C?

2. What could account for any difference in color?

Reporter

3. How do your results compare with those of your classmates?

▲ Preventing the spread of an oil slick

Oil spills are another source of pollution. Some oil spills, such as the one described on pages 398 to 401, are from accidents that occur on ships carrying oil. Most spills result from oil drilling or from cleaning oil tankers.

Sometimes oil from underwater oil wells leaks out and floats onto the sea water. This floating oil is called an **oil slick.** Oil slicks can harm sea animals. The oil can coat birds' feathers and mammals' fur. Animals coated with oil can die because they cannot fly, swim, or keep warm. Oil often prevents the organisms from breathing normally.

▲ Oil from an oil spill can harm or kill sea animals.

With oil spills at sea, there is danger of the oils washing up on the shore. There are several ways to clean up the oil. It can be soaked up by substances that absorb oil. Another way is to spray it with detergents that break up the oil into droplets. Skimmers can be used to remove the oil from the water's surface. The oil can be burned by spraying it with laser beams from helicopters. Still another way is to add bacteria that digest oil to the water and to the beach.

Ocean pollution can be reduced in many ways. Water can be treated before it flows into the ocean. Industries can be more careful about how and where they discard wastes. Scientists are working to develop new kinds of plastics that are biodegradable. More substances can be recycled so that they can be reused and not dumped.

▼ **Nonbiodegradable plastics; Biodegradable plastics**

nonbiodegradable plastic bags

biodegradable plastic bags

Lesson Review

1. List the main sources of fresh water on the earth. What percentage of fresh water is usable?

2. List and describe three ways that fresh water is being polluted today. Explain how one of the pollutants affects the living things in water.

3. Describe what occurs in a water-treatment plant.

4. List two ways that the oceans are being polluted. How can this pollution be reduced?

Think! A whale that washed up on the beach was found to have died from plastic bags in its stomach. How could its death have been prevented?

Chapter 12 Putting It All Together

Chapter Connections

Is there any part of this graphic organizer that might have been different in the past? Which part? Discuss your ideas with a partner. Then share your ideas with the class.

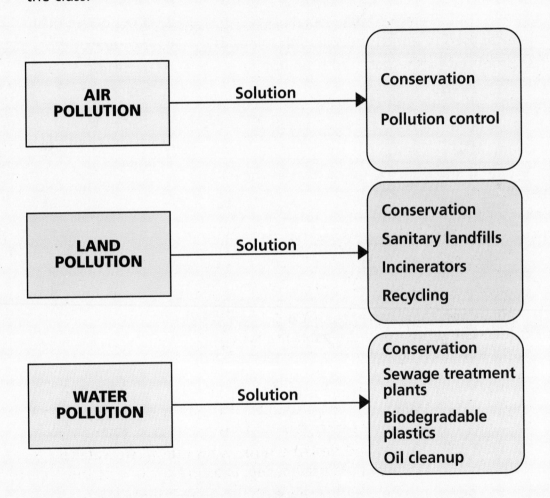

Writing About Science • Persuade

Plastic-foam containers, which are made of CFC's, add to air pollution. Imagine that some of your classmates own a business that uses or makes plastic-foam products. Convince them of the problem and suggest other types of packaging.

Science Terms

A. Write the letter of the term that best matches the definition.

1. A huge furnace for burning trash
2. The careful use of natural resources
3. The addition of heat to water
4. A chemical used to enrich the soil with minerals
5. A gas produced by the decay of uranium in rocks
6. A mixture of smoke and fog
7. The addition of unwanted substances to the environment
8. The trapping and building up of heat in the atmosphere
9. A low place where wastes are dumped
10. A chemical used to kill insect pests

a. conservation
b. fertilizer
c. greenhouse effect
d. incinerator
e. pesticide
f. pollution
g. radon
h. sanitary landfill
i. smog
j. thermal pollution

B. Write a paragraph that uses each of the science terms listed below. The sentences must show that you understand the meanings of the science terms.

biodegradable substance   incinerator   oil slick
ozone layer   pollutant

Science Ideas

Use complete sentences to answer the following.

1. What is the difference between renewable and nonrenewable resources? Give two examples of each kind of resource.
2. Give three examples of pollution that is caused by human activity.
3. Describe two ways that your community can conserve natural resources.

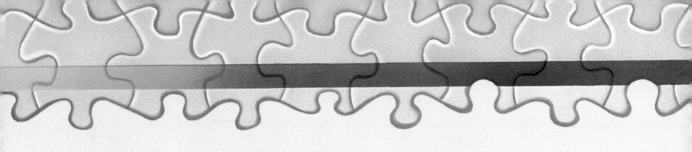

4. Identify one kind of pollutant that is not caused by humans. Explain its possible effect on human health.

5. Describe some of the possible end results of the greenhouse effect on the earth.

6. Describe why many people are concerned about a hole in the ozone layer.

7. Identify one nonbiodegradable substance. Explain why the disposal of this substance is a problem.

8. How can chemical wastes be disposed of safely?

9. What are the major ways in which water is changed as it passes through a water-treatment plant?

10. Identify one major source of ocean pollution. Describe a way that this pollution can be reduced.

Applying Science Ideas

1. Scientists already know the dangers of CFCs. Why might it be difficult for them to reduce the amount of CFCs in the environment?

2. Pollution of the environment is a problem that each person can help to control. Brainstorm with your class ways that each of you can reduce the problem of pollution in your community.

3. Prepare a booklet on the safe disposal of chemical wastes in classroom laboratories.

4. The discussion on pages 418 to 419 is about the disposal of toxic waste. Describe the two main ways suggested for the safe disposal of the waste.

Using Science Skills

Observe what students throw away at lunch. How can you save leftover food that can still be eaten? Write how saving this food would be an act of conservation.

15

The Solar System

A Walk on the Red Planet

Now it is only a matter of minutes. A pink haze surrounds the spacecraft as it slowly approaches the landing site. With a thud, the small spacecraft lands on the dusty red surface. Soon you will be the first person to walk on Mars!

So far, no one has really landed on Mars. But a trip to Mars is not just a dream. For several years, scientists have been planning such a trip.

The round trip to Mars will take 2 years. This trip will be the longest flight of a spacecraft with people on board. Because Mars is so far away and the flight will take so long, plans for the trip are complex. On other flights, astronauts have been able to come home if there was an emergency. Even on a trip to the moon, the spacecraft is only 3 days from Earth. But an emergency on the long flight to Mars could be fatal. With careful planning, most emergencies may be avoided.

One part of planning this trip is designing and testing equipment. All parts of the spacecraft will be tested again and again to make sure they are safe for the long trip. One possible model of the spacecraft is the design shown here. It is made up of two separate spacecrafts. One spacecraft will be built in the U.S.S.R. The other will be built in the United States. Astronauts from both countries will land on Mars. Information they gather will be shared by the two countries.

Plans will also be made for the needs of the astronauts. Providing enough food and water will be a challenge. Each person will need 2 metric tons of food and water during the 2-year trip. The 20 metric tons needed for an entire crew would be much too heavy for the spacecraft. So the astronauts will eat the usual dried foods. In addition, all water will be recycled. Even the moisture in the air inside the spacecraft will be purified and used again.

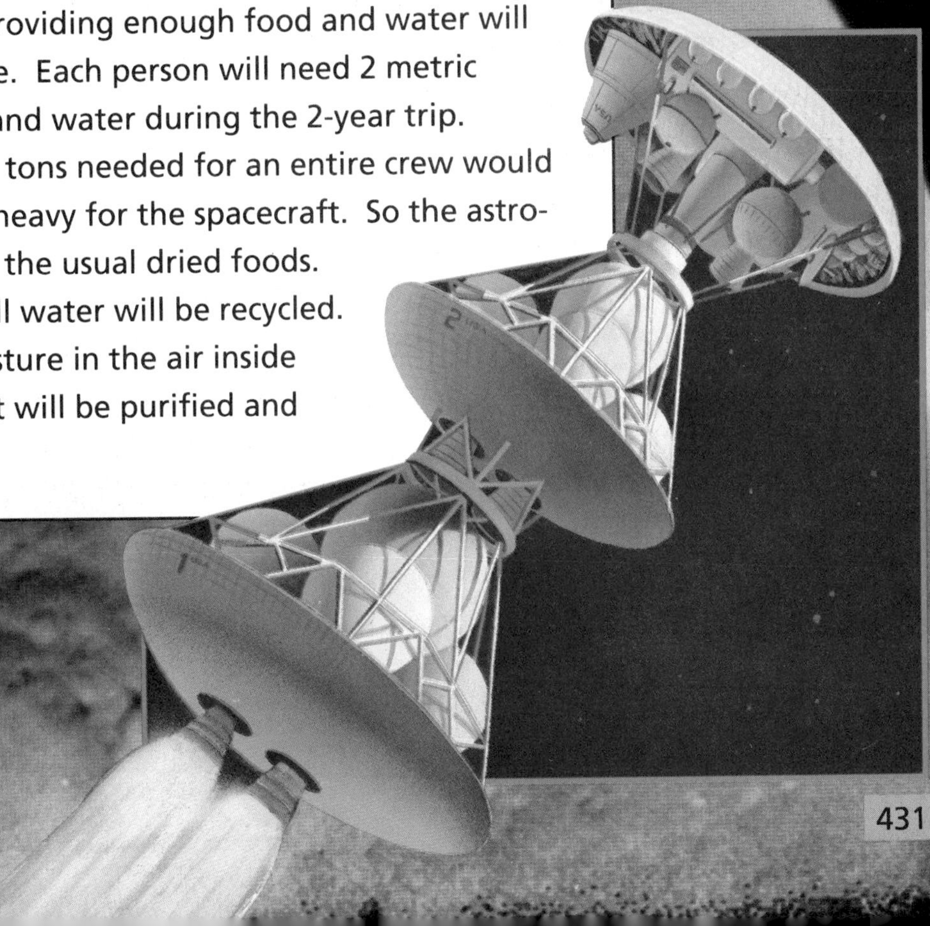

Plans must also be made for the health of the astronauts. A long space flight has added dangers. Weightlessness can cause problems. Weightlessness occurs when a spacecraft is so far from Earth that gravity has little effect on objects. The result is that people float within the spacecraft. Without gravity, bones and muscles do less work than on Earth. Over time, this lack of work causes bones to get thinner and muscles to shrink. Exercises to keep bones and muscles healthy are planned for the trip. However, the long-term effects of weightlessness are still unknown.

There is much to be learned on the long trip to Mars. But the most exciting part of the trip will be the end. Astronauts will land on and explore an alien planet.

Discover

How can you improve a flight to Mars?

Materials   pencil · paper

Procedure

The long period of weightlessness is one challenge for the crew on a flight to Mars. What other problems will they find? The crew will be away from their homes and families for 2 years. They must stay in a very small space with people they may not always like. They will have little or no privacy. Out of their small windows they will see only a night sky. Each day and night will look the same as all others.

Think of some problems that the crew might have on a flight to Mars. Suggest ways to solve these problems. Present your ideas to the class. Explain what problems you have solved.

In this chapter you will learn how space has been studied and which instruments have been used to study it. You will learn some facts about the many objects in space.

Pluto

Neptune

Mercury

Venus

Uranus

Earth

Saturn

Mars

Jupiter

1. The Solar System

Getting Started   Have you ever seen a solar panel on a building? What does the word *solar* mean? The word *sol* means "sun." *Solar* means "relating to the sun." What do you think the solar system is?

Words to Know

solar system
planet
orbit
revolution
rotation

*Home is a special place for everyone — even for "people" living on Mars. Find out how a Martian home might be different from your home in **A Martian Birthday** in Horizons Plus.*

How did the solar system form?

People in ancient times thought the sun was a god who rode across the sky. Today, scientists know that the sun is a star—a ball of extremely hot gases. The sun and the bodies that move around it form the **solar system**.

Planets and moons are part of our solar system. A **planet** is one of the nine large bodies that move around the sun. A moon is a body that moves around a planet. Besides planets and moons, the solar system contains many other smaller bodies. Look for each of the planets in the drawing of the solar system.

Most scientists think that the solar system formed from a huge spinning cloud of gas and dust. This cloud was not like the water clouds above Earth. It was much larger than the whole solar system. The cloud was made up mostly of the gases hydrogen and helium.

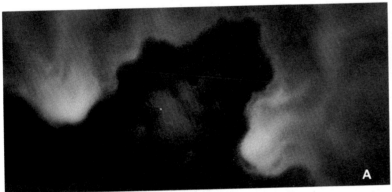

▲ How the solar system might have formed

Follow the drawings to see how the solar system might have formed. (A) About 4.6 billion years ago, the huge gas and dust cloud began to grow smaller. Most of the matter was drawn toward the center of the cloud. (B) A fiery ball, the sun, formed in the center. (C) Much of the rest of the matter collected in smaller, swirling clouds around this center. (D) Such smaller clouds formed the planets.

What kinds of motions do planets have?

Most objects in the solar system travel in orbits around the sun. An **orbit** is a path on which an object travels as it moves around another object. A planet's orbit is the oval-shaped path the planet travels around the sun.

All planets are in motion. First, they revolve, or move in orbits around the sun. The movement of a planet along its orbit around the sun is called **revolution** (rev uh LOO shun).

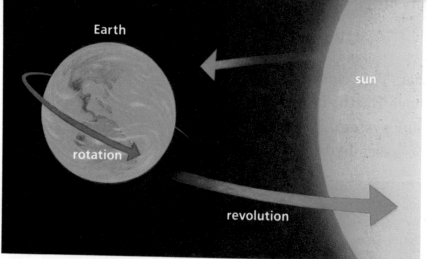

The difference between rotation and revolution ▶

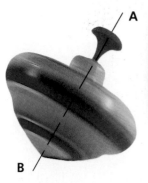

▲ Rotating top

A planet's year is the time it takes that planet to complete one orbit—or one revolution—around the sun. How many days is one revolution of Earth around the sun?[2]Second, planets rotate, or spin, much as a top spins. Look at the top. Picture an axis running from *A* to *B*. An axis is a straight line that runs through an object. When a top spins, it rotates. The turning of a body on its axis is **rotation** (roh TAY shun).

Picture the earth having an axis running from the North Pole to the South Pole. The time it takes the Earth to rotate once on its axis is an Earth day. The time of rotation differs for each planet. So the length of a day also differs.

Lesson Review

1. Name three types of bodies in the solar system.
2. Describe one idea scientists have about how our solar system might have formed.
3. What is the difference between the rotation and the revolution of a planet?
4. How are length of day and length of year related to the rotation and revolution of a planet?

Think! Suppose the length of time for rotation and revolution of a planet were the same. What would be the effect on the day and year?

THINKING

Skills

Making models

Have you ever built a model? Perhaps you have built a model car. A model of a car can help you imagine what a real car looks like. You can pick up the model and look closely at the parts. You can use a model to study something in ways that you cannot study the real thing. However, no model is exactly like the thing it represents.

Practicing the skill

You can use a model to study how planets move.

1. Hold a small ball between the thumb and index finger of one hand, as shown in the picture. Use the fingers of your other hand to turn the ball slowly. Observe how the ball moves. How is the model like a planet? How is it different from a planet?

1

2

2. Take the ball outside. Toss the ball into the air so that it spins as it travels. Observe the ball as it moves through the air. How is this model like a planet? How is it different?

Thinking about the skill

What did you think about to compare the movement of the model to the movement of a planet?

Applying the skill

Make a model of the sun and one planet. Use two balls of different sizes to construct this model. Move one ball around the other. How is moving one ball around another like the movement of a planet?

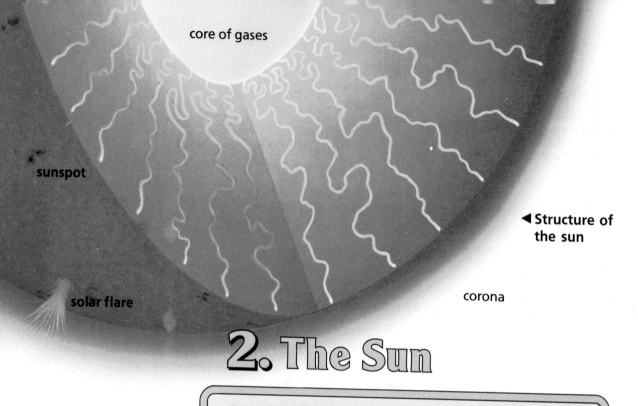

core of gases

sunspot

◀ Structure of
the sun

solar flare

corona

2. The Sun

Getting Started Think of the most beautiful sunset you can remember. Where were you? What time was it? What color was the sun? Perhaps you wondered what the sun is made of and how far away it is. Write down a few facts you already know about the sun.

Words to Know
corona
solar flare
sunspot

What are some features of the sun?

Nearly nine tenths of the sun is hydrogen gas. About one tenth of the sun is helium gas. There are small amounts of about 80 other substances in the sun.

Look at the drawing of the sun. Scientists believe that the sun has a dense core of gases. Almost half the mass of the sun is in this core. The energy of the sun comes from changes in the core. Hydrogen in the core is changed to helium. Tremendous amounts of heat and light are produced from these changes.

▲ The corona

▲ An eclipse of the sun

The hot, outer atmosphere of the sun is called the **corona** (kuh ROH nuh). The corona can be seen from Earth only during a total eclipse of the sun. During an eclipse, the corona appears to be a halo around the sun. Find the corona in the picture above. An eclipse of the sun occurs when Earth passes through the moon's shadow, as shown. During this eclipse, all of the sun, except the corona, is blocked from view at the *X*.

The surface of the sun is in constant motion. Violent motion on the sun's surface may take the form of a solar flare. A **solar flare** is an eruption on the surface of the sun. Locate a solar flare in the drawing of the sun.

A **sunspot** is a dark region in the atmosphere of the sun. Find a sunspot in the picture. Such a region is cooler than surrounding regions. The number of sunspots increases and decreases during 11-year cycles. Some scientists believe the number of sunspots and the earth's climate are linked. They think that when the number of sunspots increases, Earth is warmer.

▼ Sunspots

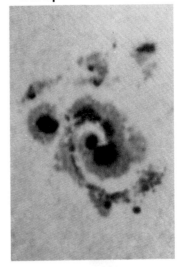

▲ Both searchlights are equally bright, but the nearer one *looks* brighter.

How does the sun compare with other stars?

Although the sun is a star, from Earth it does not look like other stars. The sun appears much larger and brighter. Why is this? Look at the picture of the searchlights. Notice that the two searchlights look different. One searchlight looks large and bright because it is close to the viewer. The other looks small and dim because it is farther away. In a similar way, from Earth the sun looks larger and brighter than other stars. It appears this way because it is much closer to Earth than are other stars.

Compared with other stars, the sun is a mid-size star. Compared with Earth, the sun is very large. The drawing shows that 109 Earths could fit across the sun's diameter.

The sun is 150 million km (93 million miles) from Earth. The next closest star is Proxima Centauri (PRAHK suh muh sen TOR eye). This star is 40 trillion km (24.8 trillion miles) away!

The sun compared with Earth ▼

109 Earths

Light moves at a speed of about 300,000 km (186,000 miles) per second. It takes 8 minutes for light from the sun to reach Earth. But it takes over four years for light from the next closest star to reach Earth!

Light takes 8 minutes to reach Earth from the sun. ▼

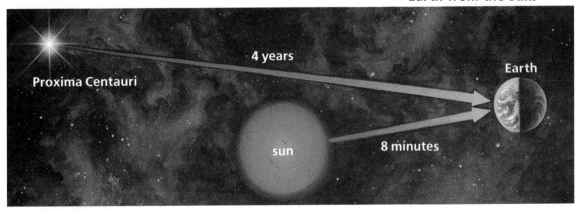

Proxima Centauri

4 years

sun

8 minutes

Earth

Like people, stars pass through a life cycle. Stars are born, grow older, and die. The life cycle of some stars takes billions of years. Some stars have a life cycle of a few hundred million years. The sun is a middle-aged star, at least 4.6 billion years old. Many scientists believe the sun will keep shining for another 5 billion years.

Lesson Review

1. What are the main materials in the sun?

2. What is the source of the sun's heat and light?

3. Describe the sun's corona and explain when it can be seen from Earth.

4. Define *solar flare* and *sunspot*. Describe any changes that occur in sunspots over time.

5. How far is the sun from Earth? From Earth, why does the sun appear much brighter and larger than other stars?

Suppose the temperature of the sun decreased by 1,000°C. Predict the effect that that decrease in temperature would have on Earth.

Physical Science
CONNECTION

The sun gives off many types of energy. Find out about infrared rays and ultraviolet rays. Which form of radiation heats the earth?

The moon as seen with the unaided eye ▼

3. Studying the Sky

Getting Started Look at the picture of the moon, above. Then look at the picture below of the moon. The top picture represents the moon as you see it with the unaided eye. The picture below shows the moon as seen through a telescope. How do the two pictures compare?

What devices are used to study the sky?

The science that deals with the study of objects in space is **astronomy** (un STRAHN uh-mee). A scientist who studies objects in space is called an astronomer (uh STRAHN uh mur). Astronomers use devices, including telescopes (TEL uh skohps), to study distant objects in space. A **telescope** is a device used to study objects in the solar system and beyond. Some telescopes do this by collecting more light than the unaided eye can see. Others collect invisible energy waves, such as radio waves and X rays.

A light telescope collects visible light and

The moon as seen through a telescope ▼

uses it to form images of distant objects. There are two main types of light telescopes. One type, called a refracting (rih FRAK ting) telescope, uses lenses to form images.

Another type of light telescope collects light with a saucer-shaped mirror. Such a telescope is called a reflecting (rih FLEK ting) telescope. A well-known reflecting telescope is shown here.

Scientists now have a reflecting telescope out in space. It is called the Hubble Space Telescope, or HST. Until the HST was in place, all observations of objects in space were made from the earth's surface. The HST is designed to be in orbit around Earth and to send images to Earth from space.

What is the advantage of the HST? This telescope is in orbit beyond the atmosphere. So the image it produces is not affected by the atmosphere. The image is clearer than any formed by telescopes on Earth. Using the HST, astronomers can study distant objects far beyond the view of any telescope on the earth's surface.

▲ A refracting telescope

▲ The Hale Telescope, a reflecting telescope

The Hubble Space Telescope ▶

Explore

How can you build a telescope?

Would you like to see the moon and stars more clearly? You can build your own telescope. This telescope works like one used by the famous astronomer Galileo in the 1600s!

Materials

scissors · cardboard tube · metric ruler · tape · lens *A* · lens *B* · modeling clay

Procedure

A. Use scissors to cut a cardboard tube into two pieces. One piece should be 12 cm long; the other should be 15 cm long.

B. Tape lens *A* into one end of the longer tube. Use modeling clay to hold lens *B* in place in one end of the shorter tube.

C. In the shorter tube make a lengthwise cut as shown. Turn the cut edges inward, forming a slightly tapered tube. Tape the cut edges as shown.

D. Place the open end of the shorter tube into the open end of the longer tube.

E. Hold the device up to your eye. Look through the lens that is in the shorter tube.

F. Move the shorter tube back and forth inside the longer tube until the image is clear.

G. Use the refracting telescope you have built to observe an object in your room. Look through a window at an object outdoors. **Caution:** *Do not look at the sun with your telescope. To do so can injure your eyes.*

Writing and Sharing Results and Conclusions

1. Describe how the objects you observed looked when viewed through your telescope.

2. How did the images compare with the real objects?

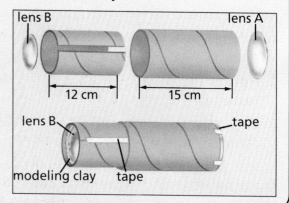

What are other methods of studying space?

A **space probe** is a spacecraft without humans aboard that gathers data about objects in space. A probe may fly by, orbit, or land on objects in space. It sends data back to Earth.

Probes have sent back data about the surface temperatures and atmospheres of some planets. Starting in 1962, 15 American space probes have flown by or landed on all the planets except Pluto. Probe cameras have sent back pictures of the planets and their moons. The pictures below show Jupiter as seen through a telescope on Earth and as seen by a space probe camera. How do the two pictures compare?

The space probe Voyager 2 ▼

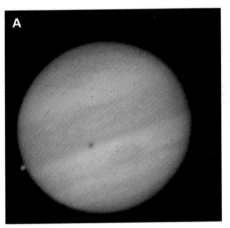

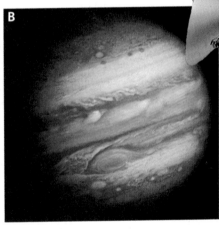

(A) Jupiter as seen through a telescope
(B) Jupiter as seen through a space probe camera

Lesson Review

1. What is the difference between the two main types of light telescopes used on Earth?
2. How is the space telescope better than light telescopes used on Earth?
3. Define *space probe*. What kinds of information can be gathered by space probes?

Think! Large telescopes are usually located on mountaintops and away from cities. Suggest reasons why these devices are located where they are.

Physical Science
CONNECTION

Use reference books to find out the types of lenses that are used in telescopes.

445

4. The Planets

Getting Started Have you ever seen a movie about visitors from outer space? Many stories have been written about invasions by creatures from Mars and other planets. Write down what you already know about Mars. Share this information with your class.

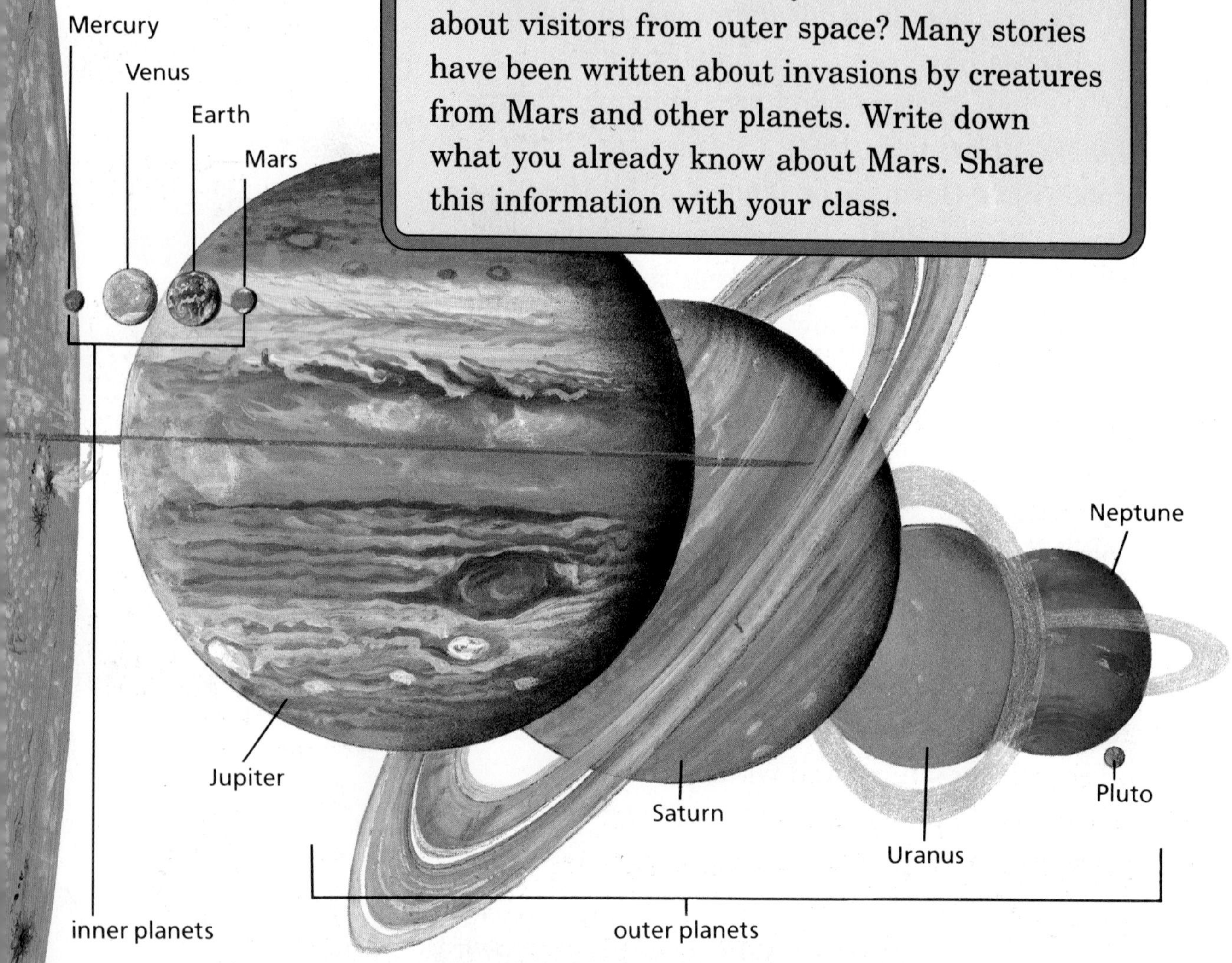

Mercury

Venus

Earth

Mars

Neptune

Jupiter

Saturn

Uranus

Pluto

inner planets

outer planets

What are the inner planets?

The nine planets of the solar system can be divided into two groups. The four planets closest to the sun are called the **inner planets.** They are Mercury, Venus, Earth, and Mars. The **outer planets** are the five planets farthest from the sun. They are Jupiter, Saturn, Uranus, Neptune, and Pluto.

446

MERCURY Look at the drawing of the planets and locate Mercury. It is the planet closest to the sun. Mercury is about the size of Earth's moon. It has hardly any atmosphere at all.

The table on the next two pages lists facts about the planets. For example, it lists the length of a day and a year on each planet. How long is a year on Mercury? How long is a day?

Pictures from a space probe show that the surface of Mercury is somewhat like the surface of Earth's moon. Compare the pictures of Mercury and Earth's moon. How are they alike?

▲ The surface of Mercury

VENUS Venus is the second planet from the sun. In the night sky, Venus is the second brightest object that can be seen from Earth. What is the brightest object in the night sky? Sometimes called Earth's twin, Venus is about the same size as Earth.

Scientists think that Venus has a rocky core and surface. Pictures of its surface show mountains, rolling plains, and what may be active volcanoes. There is no liquid water on Venus.

▲ The surface of the moon

◄ The surface of Venus

Planet Facts

Planet	Average Distance to Sun (in millions of km)	Diameter (in km)	Length of Year (in Earth time)
Mercury	58	4,878	88.0 days
Venus	108	12,100	224.7 days
Earth	150	12,756	365.3 days
Mars	228	6,787	687.0 days
Jupiter	778	142,800	11.9 years
Saturn	1,427	120,000	29.5 years
Uranus	2,870	51,200	84.0 years
Neptune	4,497	48,600	164.8 years
Pluto	5,900	2,300	248.5 years

Space probes have shown that Venus is covered by a thick atmosphere, mainly of carbon dioxide gas. This thick atmosphere acts like a blanket, trapping heat near the surface of the planet.

EARTH Earth is the third planet from the sun. As an Earth dweller, you know many facts about this planet. Suppose you have to describe Earth in an article you are writing. Here are some facts you might want to use.

Temperatures on Earth range from 58°C to −90°C (136°F to −130°F). About four fifths of Earth's atmosphere is nitrogen gas. The remaining one fifth is mostly oxygen gas. Earth is the only planet with such a large amount of oxygen.

Oceans of liquid water cover nearly three quarters of the surface. Clouds of tiny droplets of water or ice crystals hang above Earth's surface. Ice covers the poles.

Mountains, valleys, and deep canyons are found on Earth. Active volcanoes are often found

▲ Earth as seen from space

Length of Day (in Earth time)	Number of Known Moons	Main Gases in Atmosphere
58.7 days	0	helium, hydrogen, oxygen
243.0 days	0	carbon dioxide, nitrogen
23.9 hours	1	nitrogen, oxygen, water
24.6 hours	2	carbon dioxide, nitrogen
9.9 hours	16	hydrogen, helium
10.7 hours	20	hydrogen, helium, methane
17.2 hours	15	hydrogen, helium, methane
17–18 hours	8	hydrogen, helium, methane
6.4 days	1	methane

near the edges of some land masses. Earth seems to be the only planet that has living things on it.

Earth is orbited by one moon, made of rock. The moon orbits Earth every 28 days. The moon's surface has large and small craters, or holes. It is covered with a rocklike dust.

Mars Mars, sometimes called the Red Planet, is the fourth planet from the sun. It is somewhat smaller than Earth. Refer to the table of planet facts. What is the length of a day and a year on Mars? How many moons orbit Mars?

On page 430 you read about Mars' red color. This color is from the rust-colored dust on the surface of Mars. Notice the rocks and rust-color in the space-probe picture on this page.

The atmosphere of Mars is thin and consists mainly of carbon dioxide gas. This gas freezes, forming polar ice caps in winter. Mars has volcanoes, canyons, craters, and sand dunes. So far, there is no evidence of life on Mars.

▲ The surface of Mars

What are some features of the outer planets?

JUPITER Jupiter, one of the outer planets, is the fifth planet from the sun. It is also the largest planet in the solar system.

One well known feature of Jupiter's atmosphere is the Great Red Spot. This region is believed to be a swirling storm in the atmosphere. It is about twice the size of Earth. Find the Great Red Spot in the drawing.

▼ **The Great Red Spot of Jupiter**

Like the sun, Jupiter is made mainly of hydrogen and helium. Voyager 1 showed that Jupiter is surrounded by a system of thin, dark rings. The rings are thought to be made of dust and rock particles.

SATURN Saturn is the sixth planet from the sun. It is the second largest planet in the solar system. The diameter of Saturn is about 9 times that of Earth. What are the main gases in Saturn's atmosphere?

The many bright rings that surround the planet are Saturn's most famous feature. These rings are made up of many small, roundish objects. They are thought to be made of ice.

▲ The rings of Saturn

It is hard to imagine the great size of Saturn's ring system. Suppose you could walk around the outer edge of the rings. If you walked 25 km (16 miles) each day, it would take you 95 years to walk around the outer edge of the rings!

URANUS Uranus (YOOR uh nus) is the seventh planet from the sun. It is the third largest planet in the solar system. Uranus has a mass greater than the mass of 14 Earths. Its diameter is about 4 times that of Earth.

From the drawing shown below, you can see that Uranus has one strange feature. It rotates

▼ Uranus as seen from one of its moons

on its side! How long does it take Uranus to rotate once? Like Jupiter and Saturn, Uranus has an atmosphere that is mostly hydrogen with some helium and methane. The Voyager 2 space probe showed that it has 11 rings.

NEPTUNE The eighth planet from the sun is Neptune. It is the fourth largest planet. In August 1989, the space probe Voyager 2 came within 4,840 km (3,000 miles) of Neptune. Pictures from the probe showed that Neptune is a pale blue planet with an atmosphere of methane.

Neptune's atmosphere has a Great Dark Spot. This "spot" is believed to be a huge storm system the size of Earth. Neptune is orbited by eight moons, including Triton, a large pink moon. Five rings circle Neptune.

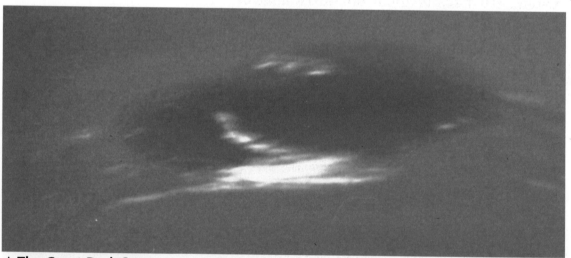

▲ **The Great Dark Spot of Neptune**

PLUTO Pluto is usually the ninth planet from the sun. But since 1979, Pluto has been the eighth planet from the sun. In 1979, Pluto moved into a part of its orbit that is closer to the sun. The

▲ A view of its moon from Pluto

▲ The orbits of Neptune and Pluto between 1979 and 1999

orbits of Pluto and Neptune overlap. In 1999, Pluto will move into the part of its orbit that is beyond Neptune. Then Pluto will again become the ninth planet from the sun.

Pluto is the smallest planet in the solar system. Its mass is about one-sixth that of Earth's moon. Most of Pluto is made of frozen gases. Pluto is the coldest of all the planets. Scientists believe Pluto has a thin atmosphere of methane.

Lesson Review

1. Name in order the four inner planets and the five outer planets.
2. How are the atmospheres and surface features of Venus and Mars alike? How are they different?
3. What major feature is shared by Jupiter, Saturn, and Uranus?
4. Why is Pluto now the eighth, rather than the ninth, planet from the sun?

Think! On Venus a year is 225 Earth days long and a day is 243 Earth days long. How can a day be longer than a year?

Will people be able to live on other planets?

Will humans ever live on other planets? One day there may be a space colony on Mars. But the Martian environment is harsh. It is very cold and there is no oxygen or liquid water.

One way that people could survive on Mars would be to stay inside a sealed, protective structure. It would contain all the air, water, food, and heat needed for life. A group of researchers has already built such a structure. But it will not be sent to Mars. It will stay right here on Earth, in the Arizona desert.

The structure is called Biosphere (BYE oh sfihr) II. *Biosphere* means "a system of living things and their environment." Biosphere II is a huge glass and metal structure. It contains different Earth habitats. For example, it contains a desert, a rain forest, and a grassland, as well as bodies of fresh water and salt water.

STS

But Biosphere II holds more than habitats. Eight researchers live and work inside Biosphere II. They will remain in the structure for 2 years. During that time nothing will enter or leave Biosphere II. The researchers grow their own food and recycle their wastes. They use computers to keep track of the temperature and the quality of the air and water inside the structure.

Biosphere II is designed to be a mini-Earth. It may help people learn more ways to protect Earth's environment and to recycle natural resources. And although Biosphere II will not go into space, it may be helpful to space travelers. Biosphere II may provide answers to important questions. What food and other goods will people need in space? Can living things survive and stay healthy in a closed environment over a long period of time?

Critical thinking

1. Biosphere II is the first such sealed structure to be built. What do you think Biosphere I is?

2. The knowledge gained from Biosphere II may be helpful in designing space stations and space ships. List all your reasons for thinking that human space travel might be a good idea. Then list all your reasons for thinking it might not be a good idea.

Using what you learned

Biosphere II can be thought of as a mini-Earth. Sometimes a glass or plastic bowl is set up with plants and animals and is then sealed shut. It is a small Biosphere II called a terrarium (tuh RER ee um), and it is also a mini-Earth. How do plants help the terrarium? What do animals provide? Set up your own classroom terrarium.

Meteor

Meteoroid

5. Meteoroids, Asteroids, and Comets

Getting Started Look carefully at the picture below. In the sky, you can see a white streak. Such a streak is called a "shooting star." But it is not really a star. What do you think the white streak is?

How do meteoroids and meteors differ?

A mass of metal or stone moving through space is called a **meteoroid** (MEET ee ur oid). Meteoroids vary in size. They can range in size from pebbles to tiny moons. Some meteoroids come near Earth and enter its atmosphere. The streak of light caused by a meteoroid passing through Earth's atmosphere is called a **meteor** (MEET ee ur). The streak of light in the picture at the left is a meteor. Sometimes, meteors are called "shooting stars." Most often, meteoroids burn up when they enter Earth's atmosphere. From Earth, burning meteoroids look like streaks of light in the sky.

▼ A meteor in the sky

A meteor shower occurs when a large number of meteoroids enter Earth's atmosphere. During some meteor showers, you might see as many as 40 streaks of light in an hour. With other meteor showers, you might see as few as 10 streaks in an hour. Certain meteor showers occur every year at about the same time. For example, the Perseid (PER see ihd) showers, seen in August, last for five nights.

▲ A meteorite

Most meteoroids burn up before they reach the ground. But sometimes a piece of a meteoroid may reach the earth's surface. A meteoroid that lands on the earth is called a **meteorite** (MEET ee uh ryt). Scientists have found many types of meteorites. Some meteorites are stones made of different minerals. Others have different amounts of stone, iron, and nickel. Large meteorites produce craters, or holes, in the earth's surface. Barringer Crater, shown in the picture, is a large meteorite crater in Arizona.

▼ Barringer Crater, formed when a meteorite struck Earth

Problem Solving
Rocky Rover

Someday astronauts may land on Mars. Traveling on the surface of this rocky planet will not be easy. Astronauts will need a special vehicle to travel over the surface. What kind of a vehicle could be used?

How can you build a model of a vehicle that could be used on Mars?

Design your vehicle to go through deep craters and climb up and down rocky slopes. Your teacher will give you various kinds of materials for building your model.

Draw your design on a sheet of paper. Then build your model. Next, test it on some rocky slopes. Compare your model with those made by other members of your class. Then improve upon your design. Test your model again.

What is an asteroid?

Chunks of rock found mainly in the region of space between Mars and Jupiter are called **asteroids** (AS tur oidz). The region of the asteroids divides the solar system into the inner planets and the outer planets.

Most asteroids have irregular shapes and are the size of boulders or smaller. But some are as large as tiny moons. Asteroids are made of rock, metal, or ice. The largest of the known asteroids is Ceres (SIHR eez). It is about 1,000 km (620 miles) across. Sometimes asteroids come very close to Earth. In fact, in 1989 an asteroid came within 805,000 km (about 500,000 miles) of Earth! How does the size of the asteroid compare with the size of the state?

Like a tiny planet, each asteroid has its own orbit around the sun. Some scientists think that asteroids are small pieces of a planet that began to form early in the history of the solar system.

▲ Asteroid compared with Texas

What are some features of a comet?

A **comet** is a body in space that is formed of rocks, frozen water, frozen gases, and dust. Some of the gases are carbon dioxide, carbon monoxide, nitrogen, hydrogen, and methane.

Comets orbit the sun. At one end of its orbit, a comet comes close to the sun. At the other end of its orbit, a comet is very far from the sun. Some comets have orbits that reach only as far as the outer planets. The orbits of other comets take them to more distant parts of our solar system. Below, follow the path of the comet.

▼ The orbit of a comet

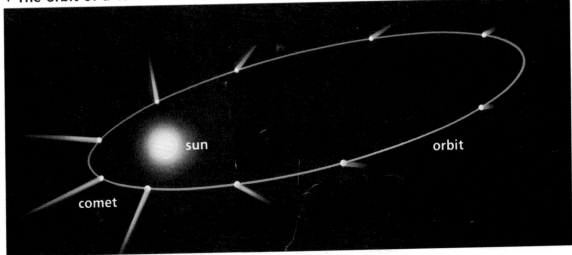

tail

·coma

▲ The structure of a comet

Comets cannot be seen from the earth until they come close to the sun. As it nears the sun, a comet warms up. Then the gases in the frozen center ball begin to glow. These glowing gases form a coma (KOH muh), or halo, around the ball. The coma forms a tail of dust and gas. The tail of a comet usually points away from the sun.

The tail of a comet may stretch out into space for millions of kilometers. In the picture, you can see a comet's tail. The tail streams out, away from the ball and away from the sun. Each time a comet goes around the sun, it loses dust and gas. Some scientists think that when comets break up, they form meteoroids. Many small meteoroids may come from the tails of comets.

In 1986, scientists studied Halley's (HAL eez) Comet, a comet that passes close to Earth every 76 years. A space probe from Europe came to within 600 km (373 miles) of the comet! Probes showed that the comet has a central core shaped like a peanut. Its surface is covered with a crust of black dust. When will Halley's Comet again be seen from Earth?

Lesson Review

1. What are the differences between a meteoroid, a meteor, and a meteorite?
2. Define *asteroid* and identify one that has been named.
3. What is the composition of a comet? How do comets differ from one another?
4. Name a famous comet.

Think! Barringer Crater looks a lot like craters on the moon. Suggest one way that moon craters might have formed.

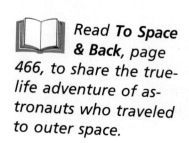

Read **To Space & Back**, page 466, to share the true-life adventure of astronauts who traveled to outer space.

Chapter Connections

Use the graphic organizer to make up a memory device that will help another person remember the names and order of the planets. Work with a partner. Test each other to see if the memory device works.

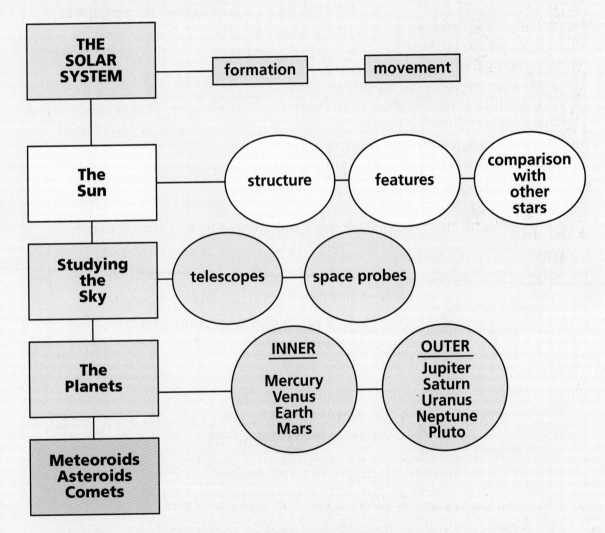

Writing About Science • Imagine

Imagine that you have just stepped out of your spacecraft onto the surface of one of the planets. Describe what you see as you look around for the first time.

Science Terms

A. Write the letter of the term that best matches the definition.

1. The motion of a body as it turns on its axis
2. A chunk of rock in space between Mars and Jupiter
3. A dark region on the surface of the sun
4. A device that makes distant objects look clearer
5. A mass of metal or stone moving through space
6. A body in space formed of rocks, frozen water, and having a long tail of gas and dust
7. The path of a planet around the sun
8. A spacecraft without humans aboard
9. The hot, outer atmosphere of the sun
10. The movement of a planet along its orbit around the sun

a. asteroid
b. comet
c. corona
d. meteoroid
e. orbit
f. revolution
g. rotation
h. space probe
i. sunspot
j. telescope

B. Write a paragraph that uses each of the science terms listed below. The sentences must show that you understand the meaning of the science terms.

astronomy   inner planets   meteor   meteorite
outer planets   planet   solar flare   solar system

Science Ideas

A. Use complete sentences to answer the following.

1. Describe one idea on how the solar system formed.
2. Explain how the motion of a planet is related to the length of a day and a year on that planet. Use the terms *rotation* and *revolution* in your answer.
3. Describe the composition of the sun and explain what produces the heat and light from the sun.
4. Give one reason why from Earth the sun appears much brighter than other stars. Use an example from your own experience to explain your answer.
5. How far is the sun from Earth? How long does it take light from the sun to reach Earth?

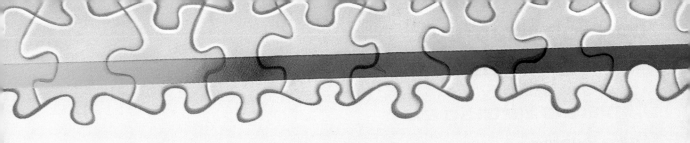

6. How does the reflecting telescope differ from the refracting telescope?

7. List some kinds of information that can be gathered by a space probe.

8. In what ways is the space telescope better than a light telescope on Earth?

9. What is the difference between an asteroid and a comet? Where in space might each be found?

B. Copy the chart below on a separate sheet of paper. On your paper write the correct answer in each box.

	What is its usual position from the sun?	Is it an inner or outer planet?	Does it have moons?
Earth			
Jupiter		outer	ye
Mars		inner	no
Mercury			
Neptune			
Pluto			
Saturn			
Uranus			
Venus			

Applying Science Ideas
How can information that is gathered from Biosphere II help people on Earth?

Using Science Skills
Build a model that compares the sizes of the nine planets. Use the information in the table on pages 448–449 to help you plan your model.

Careers in Earth Science

Lease Pumper

Robby Huggins lives in oil country — eastern Texas. There are 36,000 oil wells there. They are in cemeteries, schoolyards, and backyards. So Robby's job won't surprise you. He is a **lease pumper.** He works in the oil fields.

Robby supervises the people who handle oil drilling equipment. He sees that the oil is pumped properly. He checks the quality of the oil. He makes sure that the oil flows into pipes that take it out of the oil fields.

Natural gas comes out of the ground with the oil. Sometimes there are dangerous oil or gas leaks. "I go around in a truck looking for leaks," Robby says. "That's a job no machine can do." Robby relies on his senses of smell and sight. If he finds a leak, he reports it. Then a crew comes to shut off the leak and clean up.

When Robby was growing up, he knew he wanted to work in the oil fields. "My father and uncle worked there," he says. "I loved to listen to the stories they told." So, after he graduated from high school, Robby got a job in the oil fields, too. But his education did not stop then.

Oil companies develop new equipment. The equipment includes computers. So Robby and his workers are learning all the time.

Robby thinks that drilling for oil is important. Oil is a source of energy for heating our homes and generating electricity. But he thinks part of his job is to take care of the land he drills.

"My job takes me along the river," Robby says. "I love to see the animals that live there. Part of our job is to make sure the land stays the way we found it."

Connecting Science Ideas

1. Suppose you were the person to decide whether or not to hire a lease pumper like Robby Huggins for your oil company. Explain how you would make your decision.
   Careers; Chapter 12

2. How might an increase in the burning of fossil fuels affect the chemical weathering of rocks? **Chapter 10; Chapter 11**

3. How is the formation of coal like the operation of a sanitary landfill? **Chapter 11; Chapter 12**

4. You read about the color of the dust on the surface of Mars. What chemical weathering process do you think caused this coloring? What other kinds of weather are hinted at by the surface features of Mars?
   Chapter 10; Chapter 13

5. Suppose a colony is to be built on Mars. It is your job to choose the source of energy that would provide the colony with power. What form or forms of energy would you choose? Describe the advantages and problems of the energy source chosen. **Chapter 11; Chapter 13**

6. You have read about the advantages of the Space Telescope. What characteristics of the atmosphere might affect a planet's image as seen through a telescope on Earth? **Chapter 13; Chapter 9**

Calculator Connections

How much would you weigh on other planets? Find your weight on Earth. Then choose a planet from the table below. Using a calculator, multiply your weight on Earth by the surface gravity of the planet you choose. The product will be your weight on that planet.

PLANET	SURFACE GRAVITY	PLANET	SURFACE GRAVITY
Mercury	0.38	Saturn	1.07
Venus	0.91	Uranus	0.90
Mars	0.38	Neptune	1.15
Jupiter	2.54	Pluto	0.05

from

TO SPACE & BACK

Sally Ride with Susan Okie

After circling Earth for seven days, the spaceplane Challenger *is scheduled for re-entry. Join astronaut Sally Ride and the rest of the crew as they prepare themselves and their spacecraft to re-enter Earth's atmosphere.*

"What's it like to be in space?" "Is it scary?" "Is it cold?" "Do you have trouble sleeping?" These are questions that everyone asks astronauts who have been in space.

My first space flight was in June 1983, with four other astronauts: Bob Crippen, Rick Hauck, John Fabian, and Norm Thagard. We went up in the space shuttle, the world's first spaceplane, which carries all of today's astronauts into space. We blasted off from a launch pad in Florida; then we circled the Earth for seven days. As we went around and around the planet, we launched two satellites, studied the Earth, and learned about weightlessness. After a week in orbit we returned to Earth. Our adventure ended as the space shuttle glided back through the atmosphere to a smooth landing in California.

◆

Crew members of the spaceplane *Challenger,* (left to right) Bob Crippen, Sally Ride, Norm Thagard, Rick Hauck, and John Fabian.

Before re-entry, Sally Ride will put away her food tray and all other loose equipment.

The day before the shuttle returns to Earth, astronauts have to put away all loose equipment. Cameras, food trays, and books will stay attached to the ceiling or walls with Velcro as long as they are weightless, but they would come crashing to the floor if we left them out during re-entry. We drift around collecting things and stowing them in drawers. An amazing number of lost pencils and books turn up floating behind wall and ceiling panels.

Immediately after launch we folded and put away all but two of our seats to give us more room inside. Now we have to reattach them to the floor so we can sit in them during re-entry. We must also find the suits, boots, helmets, and life vests that we haven't worn since launch and put them on again for landing. It is often hard to remember where we stored everything. Once I almost had to come back to Earth barefoot because I had forgotten where I had put my boots!

Four or five hours before landing, we begin to drink liquid—four or more big glasses each—and take salt pills to keep the liquid in our bodies. We have to do this because our bodies have gotten rid of some water during the flight to adjust to weightlessness. Now we are about to feel Earth's gravity again, and if we do not replace the lost fluid ahead of time, we will feel very thirsty and lightheaded—and maybe even pass out—as gravity pulls the fluid in our bodies toward our legs.

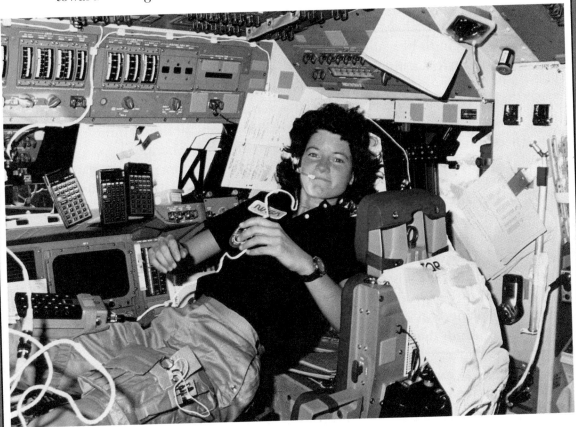

The astronauts must reattach their seats to the floor of the flight deck before re-entry begins.

We also put on "g-suits," pants that can be inflated to keep the blood from pooling in our legs. If we begin to feel lightheaded as we re-enter the atmosphere, a sign that not enough blood is reaching the brain, we can inflate our g-suits.

Finally we strap ourselves into our seats, connect our helmets to the oxygen supply, and fire the shuttle's small space engines. This "de-orbit burn" slows the shuttle down and brings us back into Earth's atmosphere. Once the engines are fired to start re-entry, there is no turning back.

The space shuttle re-enters the atmosphere about thirty minutes later. It is moving very fast, and as it collides with molecules of gas in the air it becomes very hot—in places, over twenty-five hundred degrees Fahrenheit. Only the special heat tiles glued on the outside of the spaceplane keep it from melting. The tiles protect the shuttle so well that inside we do not even feel the heat. But we can tell that it is very hot outside, because all we can see through the windows is a bright, flickering orange glow from the hot air around us.

After we have traveled a short distance down into the atmosphere, we begin to hear the rushing of wind as we shoot through the thin air. We feel a little vibration, like what passengers might feel on a slightly bumpy airplane ride. Gravity slowly begins pulling us into our seats, and we start to feel heavier and heavier. Since we are used to weightless books, pencils, arms, and heads, all these things now seem very heavy to us. It's an effort even to lift a hand.

As the shuttle falls farther down into the atmosphere, it flies less and less like a spacecraft and more and more like an airplane. It gradually stops using its small space jets to maneuver and starts using the control surfaces on its tail and wings instead. These surfaces were useless in the vacuum of space, but they become more effective as the air thickens. When the shuttle is about as low as most airplanes fly, it is only a few miles from the runway and is traveling below the speed of sound. At this point it is flying like a glider—an airplane with no engines.

Until this stage of re-entry the computers have been flying the spaceplane, but now the commander takes control. We approach the runway much more steeply than we would in an ordinary airplane, and we feel almost as if we're flying straight down. We slide forward in our seats, held back only by our shoulder harnesses, as the shuttle

▶ The spaceplane, with its landing gear lowered, is ready to land on the runway.

dives toward the ground. The pilot lowers the landing gear when the spaceplane is only a few hundred feet above the ground. The landing gear slows us down, but we still land at about two hundred miles per hour—quite a bit faster than most airplanes. The rear wheels touch the runway first, so gently that inside we can't even be sure we've landed. Then the nose wheel comes down with a hard thump, and we know we're back on Earth.

The space shuttle rolls to a stop. As I unstrap myself from my seat and try to stand up, I am amazed at how heavy my whole body feels. My arms, my head, my neck—each part of me seems to be made of lead. It is hard to stand straight, it is hard to lift my legs to walk, and it is hard to carry my helmet and books. I start down the ladder from the flight deck to the mid-deck—the same ladder that was unnecessary just an hour ago—and I have to concentrate just to place my feet on the rungs. My muscles are nearly as strong as they were before the one-week space flight, but my brain expects everything to be light and easy to lift.

My heart, too, has gotten used to weightlessness. For several days, it has not had to pump blood up from my legs against gravity. Now it is working harder again, and for several minutes after we land it beats much faster than normal.

My sense of balance also needs to adjust to gravity. For a few minutes I feel dizzy every time I move my head. I have trouble keeping my balance or walking in a straight line for about fifteen minutes after landing.

We stay inside the spaceplane for a little while to give ourselves a chance to get over these strange sensations. We do knee bends and practice walking while the ground crew moves a boarding platform over to the shuttle and opens the hatch. Then a doctor comes on board to make sure everyone is in shape to get off. We are all still a little wobbly, but about thirty minutes after landing we are ready to climb out of the space shuttle and walk down the stairs to the runway.

Once my feet are on the ground, I look back and admire the space shuttle. I take a few moments to get used to being back on Earth and to say goodbye to the plane that took us to space and back.

▶ The crew of the *Challenger* leaves the spaceplane and take their first steps back on Earth.

Reader's Response

Before landing, astronauts must prepare themselves to enter Earth's atmosphere. What did they do that surprised you? Explain why.

TO SPACE & BACK

 Responding to Literature

1. Describe the effect weightlessness has on objects in the spacecraft. Then tell what the astronauts must do to the objects before re-entry into the earth's atmosphere.

2. What do you think is the most dangerous part of re-entry? Explain why.

3. How does gravity affect the astronauts' bodies as they re-enter Earth's atmosphere?

4. Would you like to travel to outer space? Write a paragraph explaining why or why not

5. If you had the opportunity to interview Sally Ride about her trip to space and back, what questions would you ask her?

 Books to Enjoy

To Space & Back by Sally Ride with Susan Okie
Spend time on a spaceplane with Sally Ride and the rest of the crew. Learn how they eat, sleep, bathe, work, and play in zero gravity.

101 Questions and Answers About the Universe by Roy Gallant
A scientist answers 101 questions about the universe that were asked by students your age.

Journey to the Planets by Patricia Lauber
This book tells interesting facts about the planets, the sun, and the moon.

HUMAN BODY

Chapter 14

Support and Movement

Spare Parts

What would it be like to meet a bionic (bye AHN ihk) man or woman? Does the idea of bionic people sound like a part of a science-fiction story? You may know some-one who can be called bionic. To a doctor, the word bionic refers to artificial body parts that replace real but damaged ones.

When a part of the human body is dam-aged, the damaged part will often heal. For example, a broken leg bone can heal. But if the damage is great, doctors may have to re-place the body part. There are artificial arms, wrists, hands, hips, knees, feet, and so on.

Artificial legs and feet have been used for hundreds of years. These parts have replaced real legs and feet that were lost due to an accident or a disease. The very first artificial feet were made of carved wood. Later ones were made of molded plastic. Both types of feet—wood and plastic—were stiff. Try to walk without bending your foot. This is what it was like to walk with a wooden or a plastic foot.

A doctor and an engineer worked to-gether to make a new kind of artificial foot. They call it the Seattle foot, because Seattle is where it was invented. This foot can bend as a person walks. It is also springy. So it can act like a shock absorber, much as a real foot does. As the wearer steps down and begins to lift the leg, this foot gives a little push forward, as a real foot does.

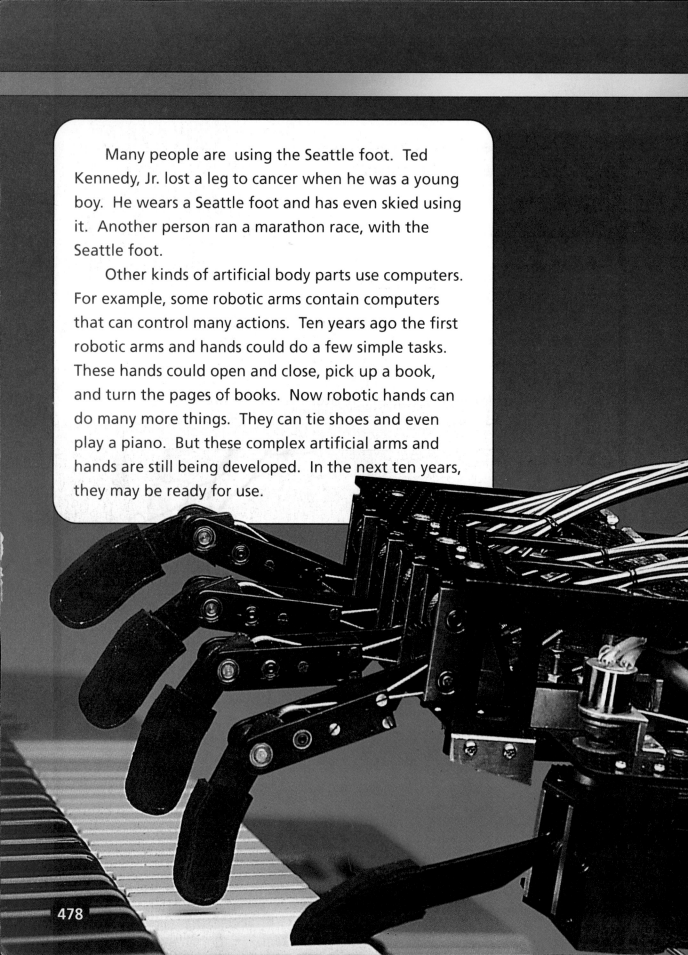

Many people are using the Seattle foot. Ted Kennedy, Jr. lost a leg to cancer when he was a young boy. He wears a Seattle foot and has even skied using it. Another person ran a marathon race, with the Seattle foot.

Other kinds of artificial body parts use computers. For example, some robotic arms contain computers that can control many actions. Ten years ago the first robotic arms and hands could do a few simple tasks. These hands could open and close, pick up a book, and turn the pages of books. Now robotic hands can do many more things. They can tie shoes and even play a piano. But these complex artificial arms and hands are still being developed. In the next ten years, they may be ready for use.

Discover

What is it like to have an artificial hand?

Materials   tweezers · pencil · paper

Procedure

The first artificial hands could not move in many ways. Experiment to see what it might be like to use such a hand. Use tweezers to do the tasks you usually do with your fingers and hands. First make a list of tasks that you think you could do easily using tweezers. Then make a list of things that would be hard to do. Try some of these tasks. Were your predictions correct?

In this chapter you will learn about the muscles and bones that support your body and help it to move. You will also learn how to keep these body parts healthy.

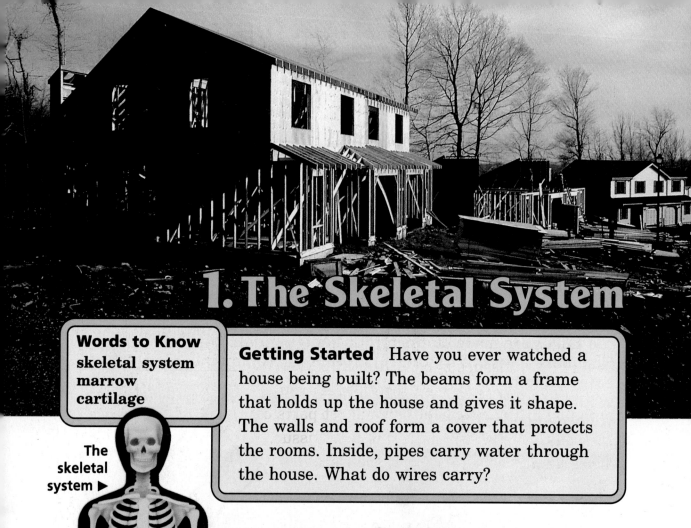

1. The Skeletal System

The
skeletal
system ▶

Getting Started Have you ever watched a house being built? The beams form a frame that holds up the house and gives it shape. The walls and roof form a cover that protects the rooms. Inside, pipes carry water through the house. What do wires carry?

What does the skeletal system do?

A house is made up of parts that work together. The wires work together carrying electricity through the house. The beams work together and support the house.

Like the house, your body is made up of parts that work together. These parts are called organs. A group of organs that work together is called an organ system. The body has many organ systems. One of these systems is the skeletal (SKEL uh tul) system. The **skeletal system** is the frame of bones that supports the body. Look at the drawing of the skeletal system. How are bones like the beams of a house?

The skeletal system does more than just support the body. It also gives the body shape, protects organs inside the body, and helps the body move.

The organs of the skeletal system are the bones. There are over 200 bones in the body. These bones work together and help support, protect, and move the body. The bones in your legs work together and help you move. Think about the bones that make up your skull. How do you think these bones work together?

Bones are made of different kinds of tissues. One of these tissues is bone tissue. A tissue is a group of cells that work together. As you probably know, cells are the smallest parts of the body. Look at the picture of bone tissue. What kind of cells make up bone tissue?

▼ **Bone tissue**

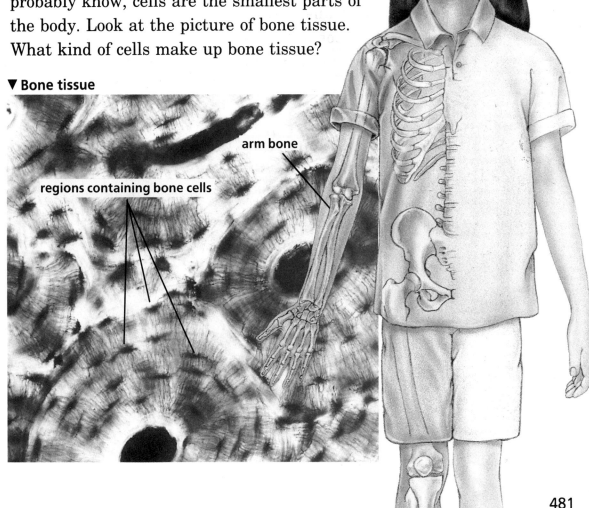

arm bone

regions containing bone cells

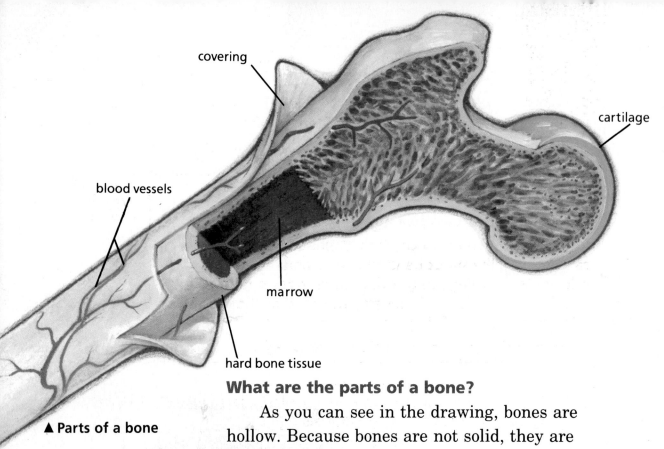

covering

cartilage

blood vessels

marrow

hard bone tissue

▲ Parts of a bone

What are the parts of a bone?

As you can see in the drawing, bones are hollow. Because bones are not solid, they are strong but light. The outer part of a bone is made of hard bone tissue. The hardness comes from tiny crystals of minerals, such as calcium, that surround the living bone cells.

In the center of a bone, there is a space filled with marrow (MAR oh). **Marrow** is a soft tissue inside bones. Some marrow produces new blood cells. This is another important thing that the skeletal system does. Notice that blood vessels run into the marrow through holes in the outside of the bone. These vessels carry food and oxygen to the bone cells. Why is this important?[5]

Notice that the outside of the bone has a thin covering. This covering protects the bone and helps repair damaged bone tissue. Now look at the end of the bone. The ends of bones are covered and protected with pads of tissue called cartilage (KAHRT ul ihj).

Explore

What happens when calcium is removed from bones?

Have you ever read the label on a carton of milk? If so, you have probably noticed that vitamin D is added to milk. Vitamin D is needed by children. Without vitamin D the calcium in milk cannot be used by the body. Without calcium the cartilage in growing bones does not harden and form bone tissue. Bones stay so soft that they can bend or twist out of shape.

Materials

2 chicken bones with meat removed · 2 plastic jars with lids · water · masking tape · vinegar · paper towels

Procedure

A. Examine each bone.
   1. Do the bones feel hard or soft?
   2. Do the bones bend?

B. Half fill a jar with water. Add one bone, and then place the lid tightly on the jar. Use masking tape to label the jar *water*.

C. Repeat step **B**, using vinegar instead of water.

D. After 5 days, remove the bone from the jar of water. Rinse the bone in water and dry the bone with a paper towel. Examine the bone again.
   3. Does the bone bend?

E. Remove the bone from the vinegar. Rinse the bone in water and dry the bone with a paper

towel. Examine the bone again.
   4. Does the bone bend?

Writing and Sharing Results and Conclusions

1. Describe any changes in the bone that had been in water for 5 days.

2. Describe any changes in the bone that had been in vinegar for 5 days.

3. What happens to a bone when a chemical like vinegar removes the calcium from the bone?

483

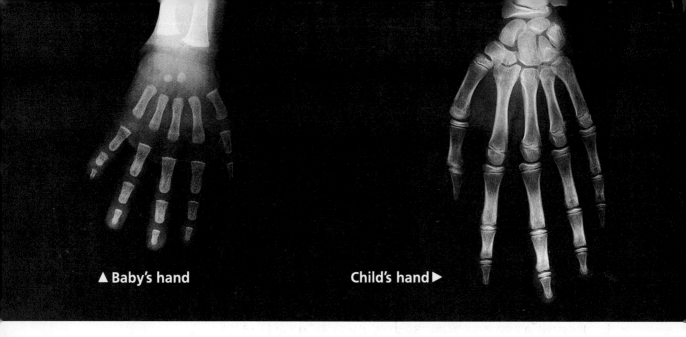

▲ Baby's hand   Child's hand ▶

Cartilage is a strong, elastic tissue in the skeletal system. Cartilage is found in places where bones come together. Cartilage also forms your outer ears and the tip of your nose.

Feel the tip of your nose. This is how your bones felt when you were born. A baby's bones are soft and bendable because they are made mostly of cartilage. As you grow, your bones become harder and stronger as calcium passes into them. Compare the X-ray pictures of a baby's bones and the bones of someone about your age. As you may know, an X-ray is a kind of picture of parts inside the body. In the X-ray of the baby, parts of the bones seem to be missing. This is because hard bone shows up better on an X-ray than does cartilage.

Physical Science
CONNECTION

X-rays are one part of the electromagnetic spectrum. Find out about other uses for X-rays.

Lesson Review

1. List three things the skeletal system does.
2. What are the organs of the skeletal system?
3. What kind of tissue is found inside a bone?

Think! What might happen if your bones did not contain enough calcium?

THINKING

Skills

Using the senses

You can learn about body systems, such as the skeletal system, by reading about them. But you can also learn by making your own observations. To do this you use such senses as sight, hearing, and touch. By making exact and complete observations, you will learn more.

Practicing the skill

1. Observe a chicken bone as described in the steps that follow. As you make observations, write them down.

2. Begin by measuring the bone. How long is it?

3. What words would you use to describe the shape of the bone? Be as exact and complete as you can.

4. Notice the color of the bone. Describe how the color changes from one part to another.

5. Draw a sketch of the chicken bone.

6. Use your finger to feel the bone carefully. How does it feel?

7. Tap the bone on a table. What kind of sound is made?

Thinking about the skill

You recorded your observations in two ways—by writing words and drawing a picture. What observations can you record in each way?

Applying the skill

Carefully observe the broken chicken bone that your teacher gives you. Use a hand lens to study the inside of the bone closely. How is the inside of the bone different from the outside?

2. Parts of The Skeleton

Words to Know
backbone
vertebrae
pelvis
joint
ligaments

Getting Started Hold a plastic straw between your fingers and try to bend it. Cut a second straw into ten pieces and string them together on a shoelace. Hold the ends of the shoelace so that the pieces stay together. Try to bend this straw. Which straw bends more easily?

What do the bones of the skeleton do?
The skeletal system is also called the skeleton. Some important bones of the skeleton are shown here. Look at the drawings as you read about how these bones support and protect the body.

The main part of the skeleton that holds up the body is the backbone, or spine. The **backbone** is a long row of connected bones in the middle of the back. As you may know, the backbone is curved and shaped somewhat like the letter *S*.

The bones of the backbone are called **vertebrae** (VER tuh bray). Try to count these bones. There are more than 30 vertebrae in the backbone. Having many vertebrae helps the backbone bend easily in almost all directions.

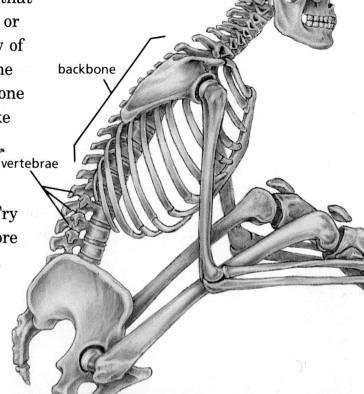

backbone

vertebrae

Notice that the skull is attached to the top of the backbone. The skull is made up of many bones. Some bones form the face. The rest of the bones form a case that covers and protects the brain.

Farther down, the backbone is attached to bones called ribs. The ribs form a cage around the chest. As you can see, this rib cage protects important organs inside the body. Which organs do the ribs protect?

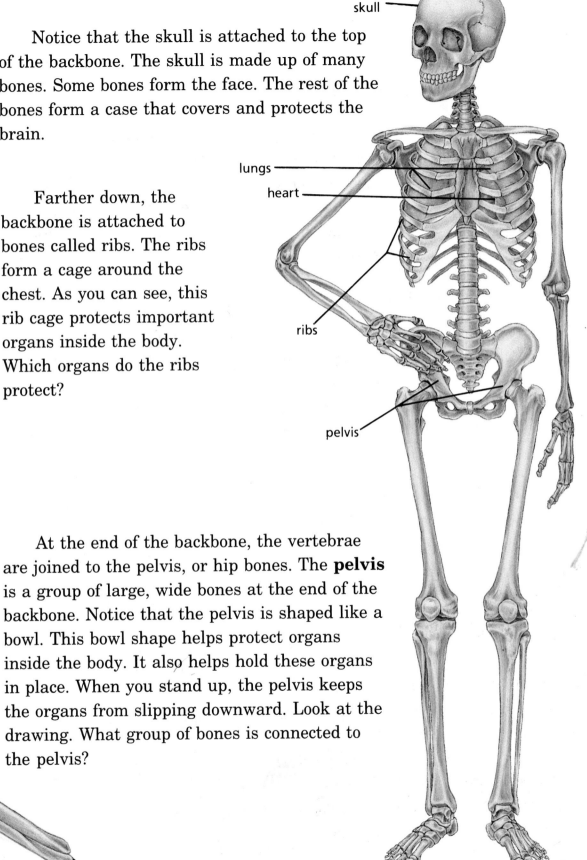

skull

lungs

heart

ribs

pelvis

At the end of the backbone, the vertebrae are joined to the pelvis, or hip bones. The **pelvis** is a group of large, wide bones at the end of the backbone. Notice that the pelvis is shaped like a bowl. This bowl shape helps protect organs inside the body. It also helps hold these organs in place. When you stand up, the pelvis keeps the organs from slipping downward. Look at the drawing. What group of bones is connected to the pelvis?

How are the bones of the skeleton connected?

As you learned, bones help the body move. Bones can move because of the way they are joined together. The place where two or more bones come together is called a **joint.** Four kinds of joints allow bones to move in different ways. Look at the drawings as you read about these joints.

SLIDING JOINT The sliding joint is a joint that allows small sliding movements. The bones of the backbone are connected at sliding joints. Notice that these bones have pads of cartilage between them. The bones slide a little over these pads, allowing the backbone to bend and twist.

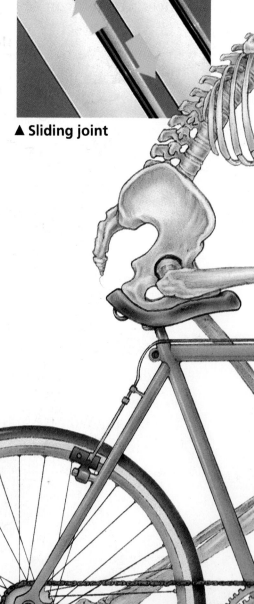

▲ Sliding joint

BALL-AND-SOCKET JOINT The ball-and-socket joint allows the most movement of bones. Your leg can move in many directions because a ball-and-socket joint connects the upper leg to the hip bone. How does a ball-and-socket joint work? Make a fist with one hand and cup your other hand around it. Now turn the ball of your fist in all directions in the cup of your hand.

Ball-and-socket joint ▶

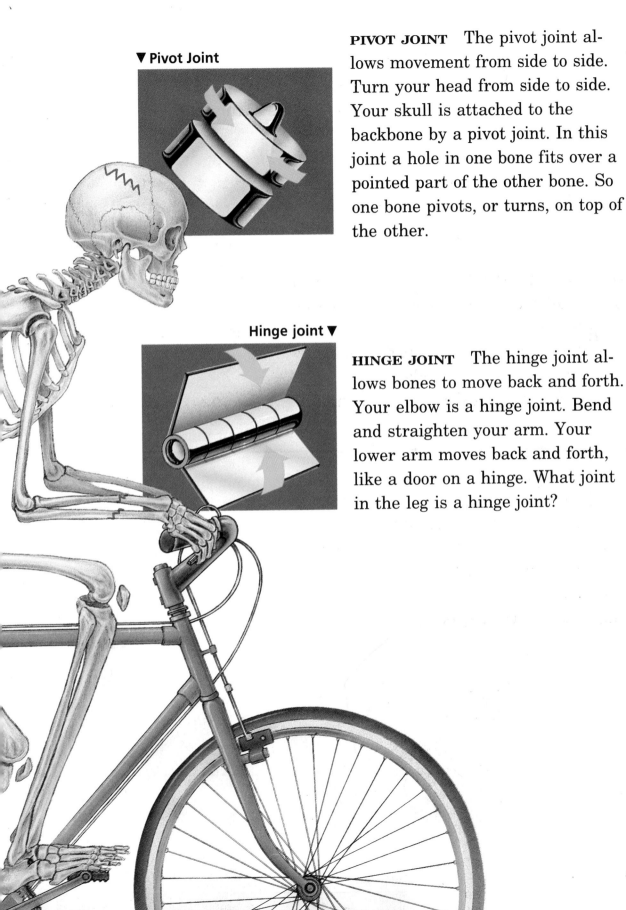

▼ Pivot Joint

PIVOT JOINT The pivot joint allows movement from side to side. Turn your head from side to side. Your skull is attached to the backbone by a pivot joint. In this joint a hole in one bone fits over a pointed part of the other bone. So one bone pivots, or turns, on top of the other.

Hinge joint ▼

HINGE JOINT The hinge joint allows bones to move back and forth. Your elbow is a hinge joint. Bend and straighten your arm. Your lower arm moves back and forth, like a door on a hinge. What joint in the leg is a hinge joint?

Problem Solving

Rolling Along!

Can you imagine moving about on wheels instead of on legs? Suppose the trunk of your body were attached to bonelike wheels instead of to legs and feet.

Would bonelike wheels be helpful to humans?

Make a list of all the ways you move about each day. Which movements would be easier on wheels? Which movements would be harder? Decide whether wheels or legs are more useful to humans. Then draw or build a model of a skeleton with wheels attached to the backbone. Include joints in your model.

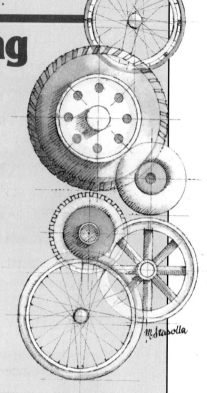

FIXED JOINT   You have read about four kinds of joints that allow many kinds of movements. But one kind of joint allows no movement at all. A joint between bones that do not move is called a fixed joint. The joints between the bones of the skull are fixed joints. These bones are locked together tightly. Why is it important that the skull bones do not move?

Fixed joint ▼

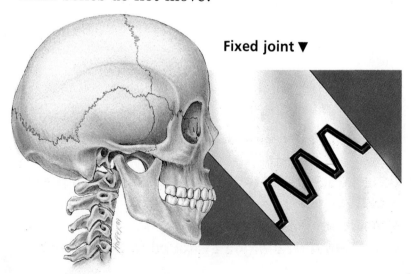

490

What are the parts of a joint?

As you learned, most joints allow bones to move. In these joints, pads of cartilage cover the ends of the bones. Cartilage is smooth and slippery. This allows the bones to move easily over one another. But what stops the bones from moving too far apart? The bones at a joint are held together by strong bands of tissue called **ligaments** (LIHG uh munts). Look at the drawing of the knee joint. What bones do these ligaments hold together?

▼ **Parts of the knee joint**

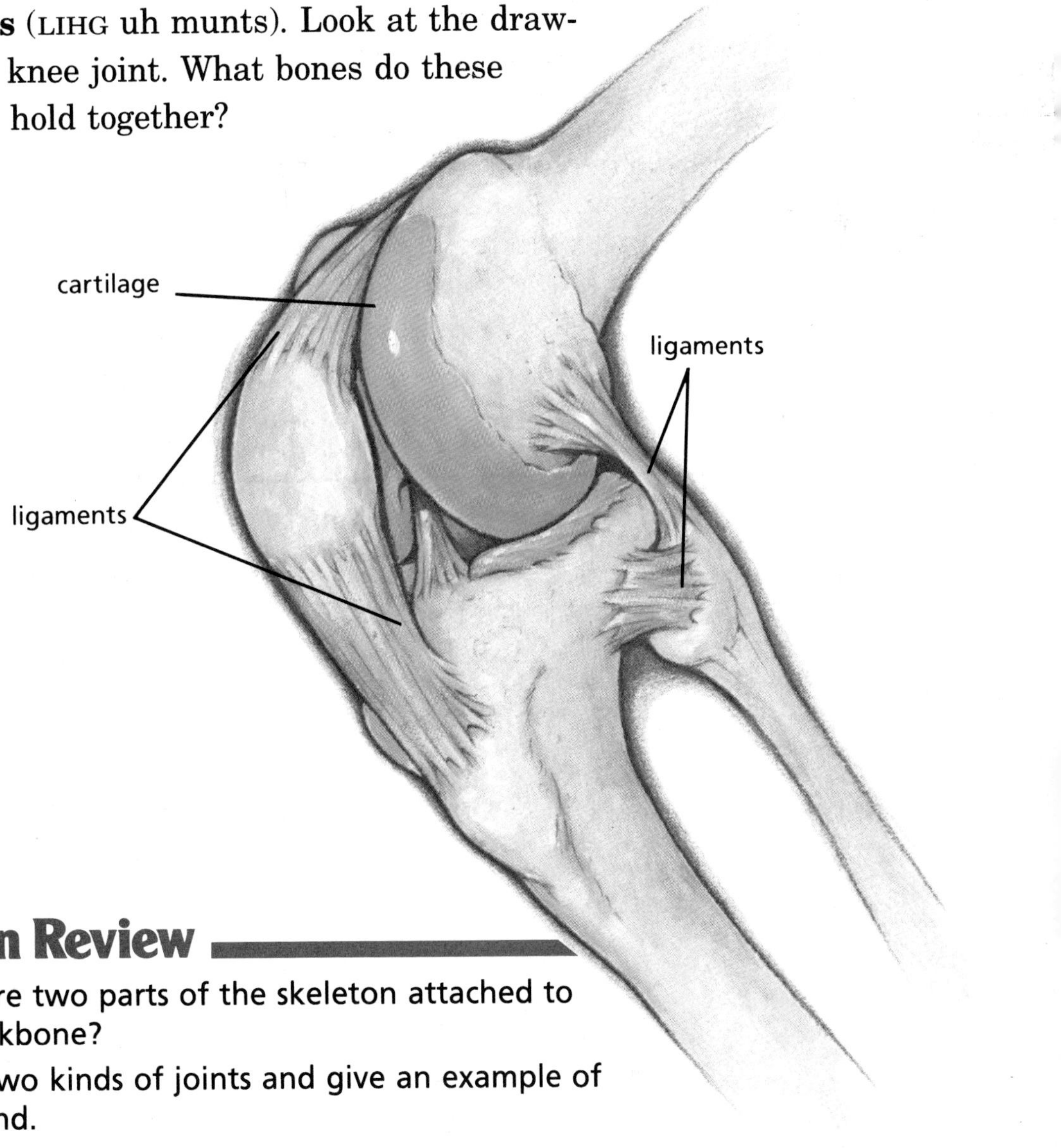

cartilage

ligaments

ligaments

Lesson Review

1. What are two parts of the skeleton attached to the backbone?
2. Name two kinds of joints and give an example of each kind.
3. What are ligaments?

Think! What kind of joint is found in the fingers?

How can electric current be used for healing bones?

Each year about 2 million people in America break bones. Most broken bones heal well. But in more than 100,000 cases, the broken bones do not heal. For these patients, some doctors use a special treatment to heal the bones.

The bodies of living things have weak electric currents inside them. These currents are caused by charged particles that move around and through cells. Now, doctors have found a way to cause currents inside the body— currents that help bones to heal.

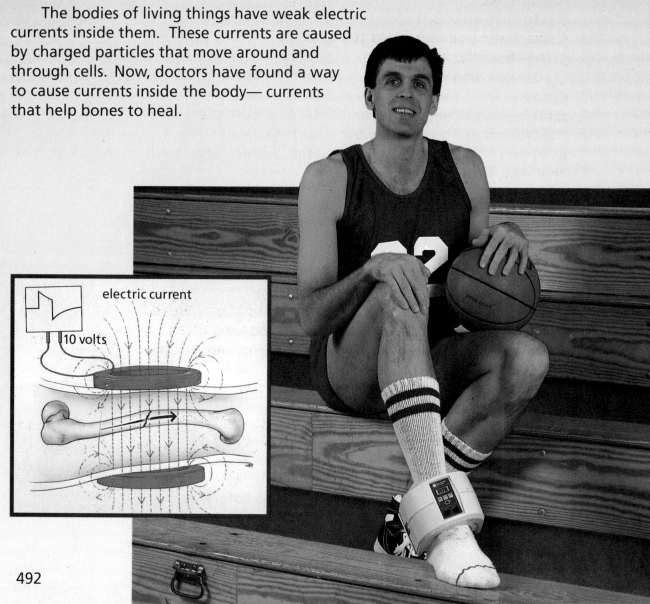

electric current

10 volts

In this new treatment the patient wears a plastic disk over the broken bone. Inside the disk is a coil of wire. The wire is connected to a source of electric current. When electric current flows through the wire, the wire acts like a magnet. The wire magnet outside the body causes a weak electric current in the bone.

The patient wears the disk for a few months. During this time the disk sends a very weak electric current through the body for up to 10 hours a day. Most people do not feel it at all.

Some doctors think that this treatment needs to be tested more. They say it might cause the growth of harmful cells. But other doctors point out that more than 200,000 bones have already been healed safely with this treatment. These doctors hope that more new ways to heal body tissues can be found.

Critical thinking

1. How can scientists tell how safe electric current is for healing bones?

2. A law says that medical treatments must be approved by the government before they can be used on patients. How does this law protect people? How can this law cause problems for people?

Using what you learned

When people are ill, doctors give them treatments or medicines. Sometimes a treatment is new, and people may not know much about it. They would be wise to get information about the treatment first. Write a list of questions that people should ask doctors before having a new kind of treatment.

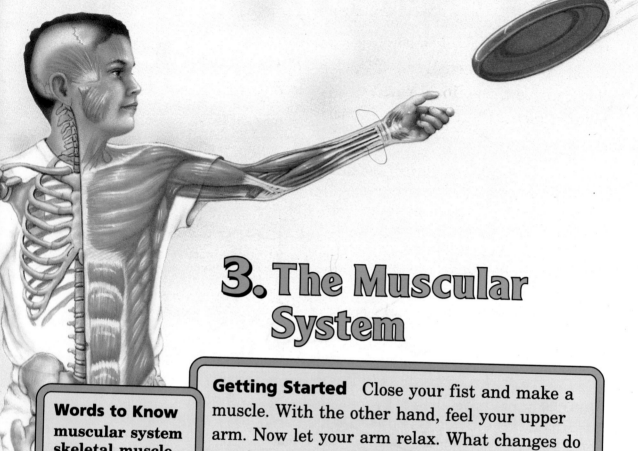

3. The Muscular System

Getting Started   Close your fist and make a muscle. With the other hand, feel your upper arm. Now let your arm relax. What changes do you feel in your upper arm?

Words to Know
muscular system
skeletal muscle
smooth muscle
heart muscle
tendon

What does the muscular system do?

You have learned that the skeletal system helps the body move. But the skeletal system does not work alone. The whole skeletal system is covered with muscles. Without muscles, bones could not move. The muscles that move the parts of the body make up the organ system called the **muscular** (MUS kyoo lur) **system**.

The organs of the muscular system are the muscles. There are over 600 muscles in the body. Muscles do more than just move bones. Muscles also move other organs, such as the heart and the stomach.

494

Muscles are made of soft but strong muscle tissue. As the drawing shows, muscle tissue is made up of bundles of long, threadlike fibers. You can see these fibers when you cut into a piece of meat. Each fiber is a muscle cell.

muscle fiber

bundle of fibers

muscle

What are three kinds of muscle tissue?

There are three different kinds of muscle tissue. The pictures show what these tissues look like when seen through a microscope.

Skeletal muscle is the muscle that is attached to the bones of the skeleton. These muscles move the bones of the body. You can control the movement of skeletal muscles. For example, the muscles in your fingers move whenever you think about moving them. Muscles that you control are called voluntary muscles. Name an action you do with voluntary skeletal muscles.

▼ Skeletal muscle

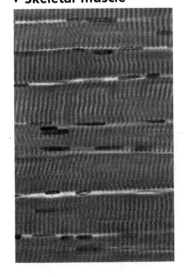

Smooth muscle is the muscle that makes up the walls of many organs of the body. Have you ever felt your stomach rumble? This is caused by movements of smooth muscle in the stomach. These muscles squeeze and mix the food inside the stomach. As you know, you cannot make the muscles inside your stomach move. Smooth muscle is involuntary muscle, or muscle you cannot control.

▼ **Smooth muscle**

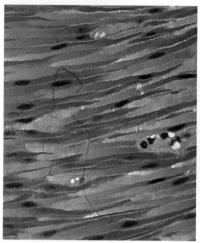

▼ **Heart muscle**

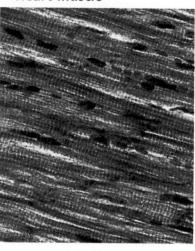

Heart muscle is muscle found only in the heart. Like smooth muscle, heart muscle is involuntary. Suppose you had to control your heartbeat. Then you would also have to think about moving your heart muscle about 80 times each minute!

How do skeletal muscles move bones?

▼ **Marionette**

Look at the picture of the marionette. As you can see, a marionette is a puppet held up by strings. The strings move the marionette by pulling on it. Strings can only pull; they cannot push.

Skeletal muscles work like marionette strings. They move the body by pulling on the bones of the skeleton. Muscles are not connected directly to bones. A strong band of tissue called a **tendon** (TEN dun) connects a muscle to a bone. Find the tendon in the drawing. This big tendon connects the heel bone with the large muscle in the calf of your leg. Now find this tendon in your leg.

How a muscle is attached to a bone
▼

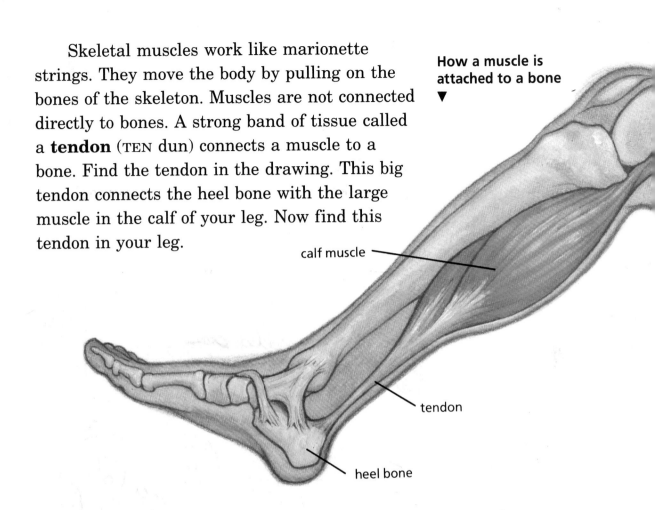

calf muscle

tendon

heel bone

Like marionette strings, muscles can pull, but they cannot push. When a muscle contracts, it gets shorter and thicker. This pulls the bone and moves it. Muscles also relax. When a muscle relaxes, it gets longer and thinner. A relaxing muscle does not pull on the bone connected to it.

Place your left hand over the muscle on the top of your upper right arm. Raise your lower arm. You should feel the muscle in your right arm bulge. This muscle bulges because it is contracting. As it contracts, it pulls the bones in your lower arm upward.

ACTIVITY

Explore Together

What happens when you overwork your muscles?

Organizer

Materials

clothespin · timer · paper

A

Investigator

Procedure

A. Count how many times you can open and close the clothespin in 30 seconds. Each open-and-close movement counts as one action.

Manager

B. Use the timer to tell the Investigator when to start counting and when to stop counting.

Recorder

C. Record the number in a table like the one shown.

Investigator,
Manager
Recorder

D. Repeat steps **A**, **B**, and **C** four more times.

Group

1. Did the number of openings and closings change as the procedure was repeated?

Trials	Number of Actions
1	
2	
3	
4	
5	

2. How did the muscles in the hand feel as the procedure was repeated?

Writing and Sharing Results and Conclusions

Group,
Recorder

1. How does repeating an action change the way muscles feel?

2. How does repeating an action change the way muscles can carry out a task?

Reporter

3. How do your results and conclusions compare with those of your classmates?

498

Now feel the muscle on the underside of your upper arm. This muscle should feel soft. It is soft because it is relaxed.

When you raise your lower arm, a pair of muscles works together. Most skeletal muscles work in pairs. When a bone moves, one muscle of the pair contracts. The other muscle of the pair relaxes. One muscle pulls a bone in one direction. The other pulls the bone in the opposite direction.

Now lower your arm. Again feel the pair of muscles. Which one contracts? Which one relaxes? The drawings show what these muscles look like as you raise and lower your arm.

How muscles move bones of the lower arm ▼

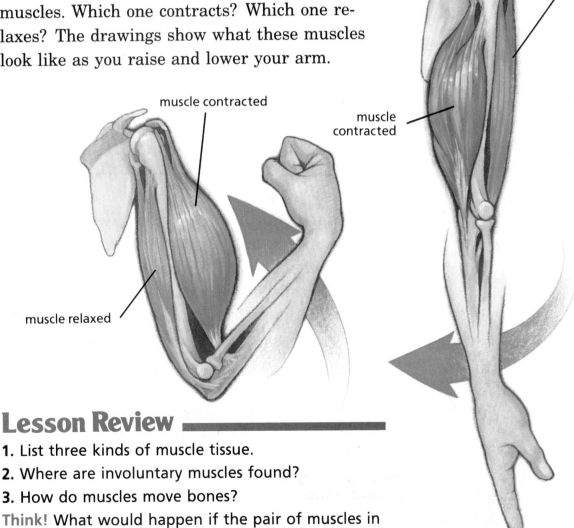

muscle relaxed

muscle contracted

muscle contracted

muscle relaxed

Lesson Review

1. List three kinds of muscle tissue.

2. Where are involuntary muscles found?

3. How do muscles move bones?

Think! What would happen if the pair of muscles in your upper arm contracted at the same time?

499

4. Keeping Bones and Muscles Healthy

Getting Started Raise your hand above your head. As you do this, dozens of muscles move many bones. Where are these bones and muscles? Suppose one of them is injured. How might this change the way your arm moves?

How can you keep bones and muscles healthy?

Without healthy bones and muscles, even simple actions would not be possible. One way to keep bones and muscles healthy is to eat the foods shown here. Dairy products, fruits, and vegetables contain calcium and other minerals. Remember that calcium helps make bones hard and strong. Calcium is also used by muscles when they contract. Milk, meat, fish, and eggs contain proteins. Proteins help build muscle tissue. Breads and cereals provide energy that muscles need to move bones. Which of these foods have you eaten today?

A second way to keep bones and muscles healthy is to exercise. Exercise helps bones and muscles become stronger. Strong skeletal muscles move bones more easily. Exercise also helps make heart muscle stronger. Many kinds of sports and play are good exercise. These children are getting another kind of exercise that helps keep bones and muscles healthy. What kinds of exercise have you done today?

A third way to keep bones and muscles healthy is to rest and sleep. When you exercise, muscles use energy that is released from food. As this energy is released, waste materials are formed. These wastes build up in muscles and make muscles feel tired. When you rest, the

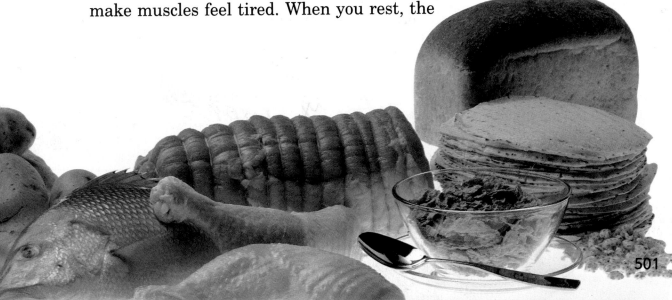

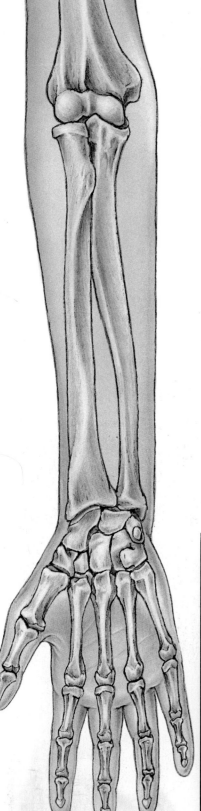

wastes are carried away from the muscles by the blood. Rest also gives the body time to make and repair bone and muscle tissue.

What are some problems with bones?

Although bones are strong, they can be injured. Have you ever broken a bone? Because most young people are very active, they may break bones. A crack or break in a bone is called a **fracture** (FRAK chur).

As the X-ray pictures show, bones can fracture in two different ways. In an open fracture the ends of the broken bone stick out through a break in the skin. In a closed fracture the bone is broken, but the ends of the bone do not go through the skin. Which kind of fracture is probably more dangerous?

Because bones are made of living tissue, they can repair themselves. The parts of broken

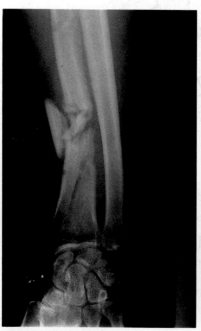

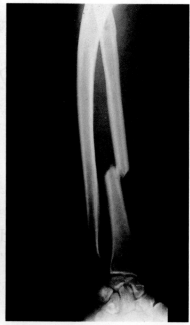

▲ Healthy arm bones   ▲ Open fracture   ▲ Closed fracture

bones are put back in place, or set, by a doctor. Then the broken parts will grow back together.

While new bone cells grow, a cast holds the broken ends in place. As the picture shows, a cast is a stiff covering around a broken bone.

The ligaments that connect bones can also be injured. A sprain is an injury in which a ligament is stretched or torn. This happens when the bones at a joint move in the wrong direction. Sprains often occur at the knee, wrist, and ankle joints. In the picture a doctor is wrapping a bandage around a sprained knee. How might this help heal the sprain?

▼ Plaster cast on a broken bone

▼ Wrapping a sprain

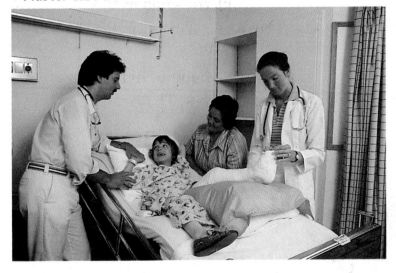
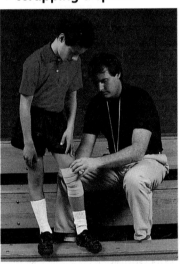

Another problem of the skeletal system affects the backbone. The backbone curves from front to back. But the backbone may also curve to one side. A side to side curve of the backbone is called scoliosis (skoh lee OH sihs). Many children have mild forms of scoliosis. They may need doctors' checkups to make sure the curve does not get worse as they grow.

What are some problems with muscles?

Muscles may become injured and sore when you exercise too hard or too long. If a muscle or tendon is overused, it can stretch or tear. A strain is an injury caused by stretching a muscle or tendon too far.

Too much exercise can also cause a muscle to cramp, or contract strongly and painfully. Did you ever wake up at night with a cramp in your leg or foot? If so, do you think a cramp is a voluntary or involuntary action? The pictures show ways to treat injured muscles.

▼ Rubbing a cramped muscle

▲ Putting ice on a strained tendon

Lesson Review

1. List three ways to keep your bones and muscles healthy.

2. Name two kinds of fractures.

3. How does a sprain differ from a strain?

Think! Suppose you wanted to invent an artificial thumb. What kinds of movements would you want the thumb to be able to do?

Chapter Connections

Write five questions based on the graphic organizer.
Exchange papers with a partner. Answer the questions,
and then check.

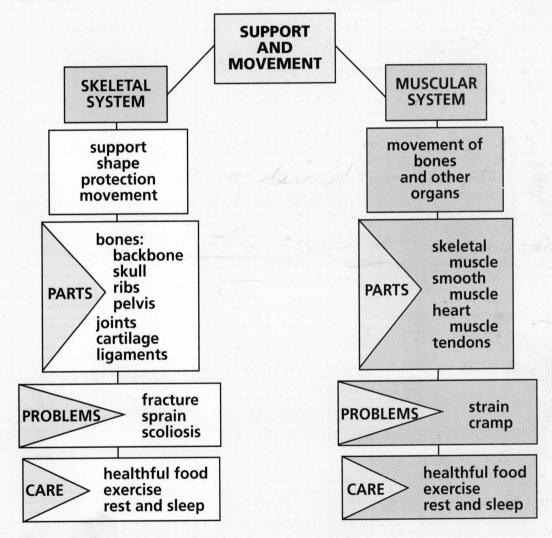

Writing About Science • Persuade

Why is it important to include warm-up and cool-down
time when you exercise? Find out why and write a
paragraph to persuade someone who does not agree.

Science Terms

A. Number your paper from 1 to 5. Use the terms below to complete the sentences. Write the correct term next to each number.

heart muscle   muscular system   skeletal muscle
smooth muscle   tendon

The ___(1)___ is the system of muscles that move the parts of the body. There are three kinds of muscles. The muscle that moves bones is ___(2)___. A skeletal muscle is attached to a bone by a ___(3)___. The involuntary muscle found inside most organs is ___(4)___. Muscle that pumps blood through the body is ___(5)___.

B. Copy the sentences below. Use the terms listed to complete the sentences.

backbone   cartilage   fracture   joint   ligaments
marrow   pelvis   skeletal system   vertebrae

1. A broken bone is called a _____.

2. A soft tissue inside bones is _____.

3. The long row of connected bones that is the main support of the body is the _____.

4. The bones of the backbone are called _____.

5. The group of bones joined to the lower end of the backbone is the _____.

6. The frame of bones that supports the body is the _____.

7. Strong, elastic tissue found at the ends of bones and in the ears and nose is _____.

8. The place where two bones are joined together is a _____.

9. Strong bands of tissue called _____ hold bones together at a joint.

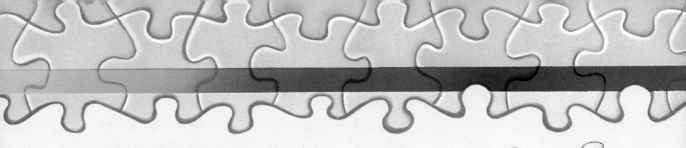

Science Ideas

Use complete sentences to answer the following.

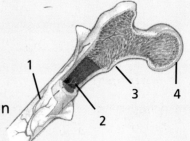

1. Write the correct term for each number in the drawing of the bone.
2. What parts of the skeletal system protect the brain and the heart?
3. What joints in the body work in the ways shown below?

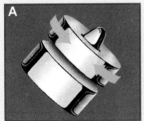
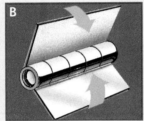
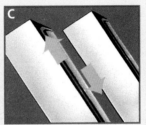
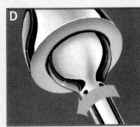

4. How does voluntary muscle differ from involuntary muscle? Give an example of each kind.
5. Explain how pairs of muscles move bones.
6. How does rest help keep muscles healthy?
7. What is scoliosis?

Applying Science Ideas

Use complete sentences to answer the following.

1. Suppose your fingers had ball-and-socket joints instead of hinge joints. How would the movements of your fingers be different? Would it be easier or harder to pick up objects?
2. What would happen on long space missions if astronauts did not exercise?
3. Some broken bones do not heal. What new treatment can be used to help heal these bones?

Using Science Skills

Take a few steps. Think about how your bones are moving with each step. Write a description of how the bones move when you take a step. What kinds of joints are used?

507

15

Control Systems

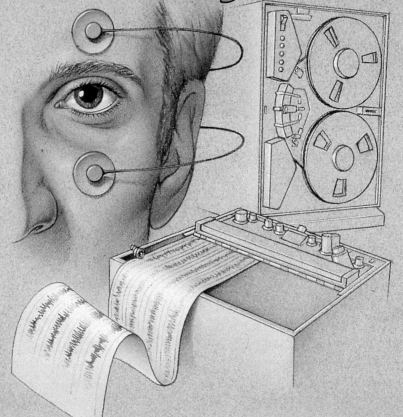

An Eye Opener

Can someone look into your eyes and know what you are thinking? No one can tell what you are thinking just by looking at you. But psychologist John Stern can see much in your eyes. He can tell whether you are nervous, excited, or tired. He can even see whether you are thinking hard or just daydreaming.

Dr. Stern made a startling discovery. He found that blinking is linked to what is going on in the mind. He began to study blinking over 20 years ago. Dr. Stern observed that people who were anxious seemed to blink more often than those who were not.

How does Dr. Stern study blinking? He begins with careful observations. A volunteer is fitted with tiny devices that detect movements of the eyelid. The devices are placed on the person's cheek and forehead, and are wired to a printer. The printer records when each blink starts and stops. In this way, Dr. Stern knows when the person blinks and how long each blink lasts.

After observing hundreds of people, Dr. Stern has learned much about blinking. He has found that people seldom blink when they are learning or getting facts. For example, volunteers were asked to learn a series of six numbers. They did not blink until they had finished listening to the numbers and memorizing them. Dr. Stern compares blinks to punctuation marks: "You have listened to a question. You understand it; now you can take time out for a blink."

Dr. Stern has also found that people blink less often when they are concentrating than when they are relaxed. They blink more slowly when they are tired.

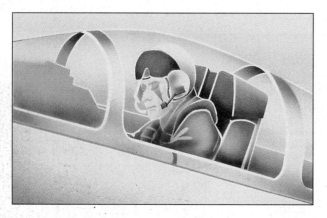

How can these discoveries be useful? Think of some times—such as flying an airplane—when concentration is necessary. A device that measures blinking could sound an alarm if the pilot became drowsy or stopped paying attention. And just think—someday teachers may even use a blinkometer on their students, to make sure they are paying attention!

Discover

What does blinking tell us?

Materials television · timer · pencil · paper

Procedure

When people are relaxed, they may blink as much as 10 to 20 times each minute. Or they may blink as little as once every 2 minutes.

Now make your own observations of blinking. Watch a news broadcast, interview show, or game show on television. Count the number of times one person blinks in 30 seconds. Have someone keep time for you. Then record what that person was saying during the 30 seconds. Get five samples of blinking from the same person. Does the rate of blinking change with the material being discussed? What conclusions about blinking can you draw from your observations?

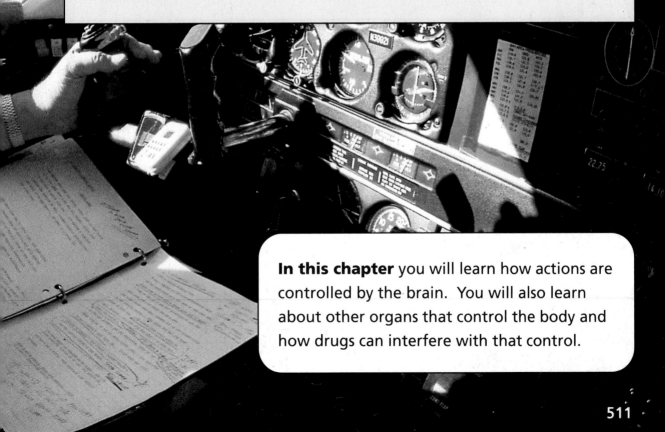

In this chapter you will learn how actions are controlled by the brain. You will also learn about other organs that control the body and how drugs can interfere with that control.

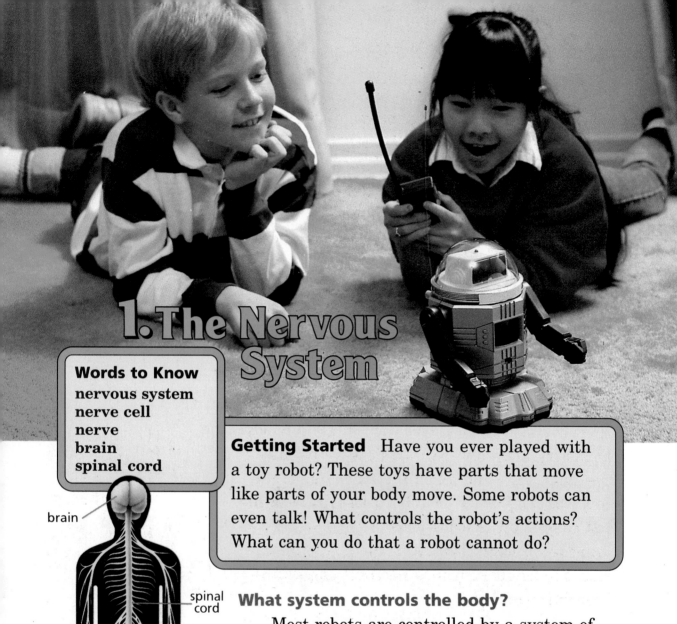

1. The Nervous System

Words to Know
nervous system
nerve cell
nerve
brain
spinal cord

brain

spinal cord

nerves

The nervous system ▲

Getting Started Have you ever played with a toy robot? These toys have parts that move like parts of your body move. Some robots can even talk! What controls the robot's actions? What can you do that a robot cannot do?

What system controls the body?

Most robots are controlled by a system of wires connected to a computer. The wires carry messages to and from the computer. These messages can make a robot do many things.

Like the robot, your body has a system that controls its actions. Most of the actions of the body are controlled by the nervous system. The **nervous system** is a control system made up of the brain, the spinal cord, and the nerves. Find these three parts in the drawing. Which part is found inside the head?

512

How does the nervous system control actions?

The nervous system carries messages to and from all parts of the body. These messages control the actions of parts of the body.

Messages travel through the nervous system along nerve cells. A **nerve cell** is a cell that can receive and send messages. Most nerve cells are arranged end to end. In this way, messages travel from one cell to the next.

Look at the drawing of nerve cells. Notice that branches stretch out from the cell body, or central part. These branches carry messages into and out of the nerve cell. Find the many short branches that look like tree branches. The short branches receive messages from other nerve cells and carry them toward the cell body. Now find the single long branch on the other side of the cell. The long branch carries messages from the cell body to other nerve cells. Some long branches are very long. A single long branch runs the length of your arm. How long is this branch in your arm?

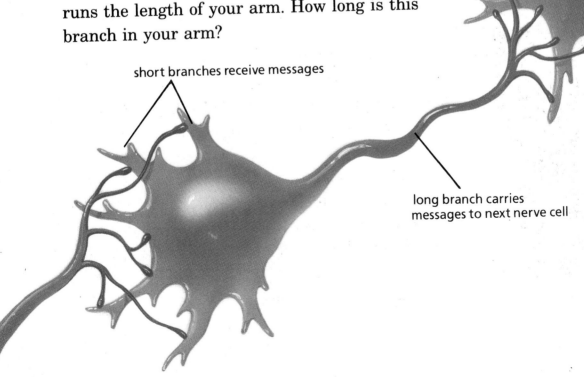

Nerve cells ▶

cell body

short branches receive messages

long branch carries messages to next nerve cell

513

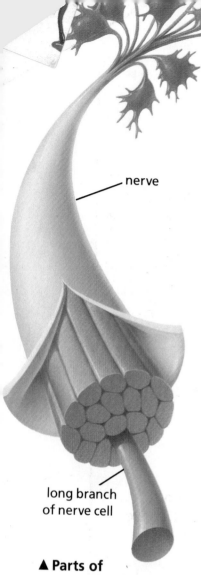

nerve

long branch
of nerve cell

**▲ Parts of
a nerve**

Most nerve cells are found in bundles. A bundle of nerve cells is called a **nerve**. Some nerves are very small. Others are as big around as a pencil or your little finger. You can compare a nerve to an electric cable, which is made up of many small wires. To what parts of the nerve would you compare the small wires?

What are the three parts of the brain?

The main organ of the nervous system is the **brain.** The brain is the control center of the body. Most of the messages that move through the nervous system enter and leave the brain. In what way is the brain like the computer in a robot?

As the drawing shows, the brain has three parts. They are the cerebrum (se REE brum), the cerebellum (ser uh BEL um), and the brainstem. Each part of the brain controls certain activities.

**Parts of
the brain ▶**

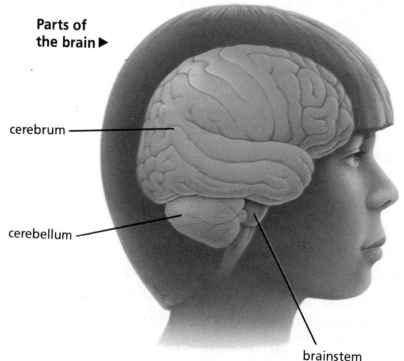

cerebrum

cerebellum

brainstem

Problem Solving

Choosing Up Sides

Quick! Without thinking about it, fold your arms across your chest. Which arm is on top? The answer might tell which side of your brain—left or right—has dominance (DAHM uh nuns). *Dominance* means "having control over." Suppose your right arm was on top. Then the left side of your brain probably has dominance.

Right-brain dominance or left-brain dominance may be shown in other body parts besides your arms. It may also be shown in your legs, hands, feet, eyes, and ears.

How can you test for dominance?

Design a test to show which part of a person's brain might have dominance. The test should include two of the body parts named above. Test five of your classmates. Compare your results with those of other classmates.

The largest part of the brain is the cerebrum. Notice that its surface is folded and wrinkled. The cerebrum's folds and wrinkles enable its huge surface area to fit within the skull. If the surface folds and wrinkles were stretched out, they would take up an area of 2,500 cm² (400 square inches).

The cerebrum has a right half and a left half. A person who has seriously injured the left side of the brain may suffer loss of speech. A person who has seriously injured the right side of the brain may have trouble recognizing familiar faces.

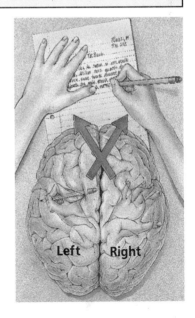

Left   Right

The cerebrum controls all your thinking. It also controls the movements of many muscles. Look at the "map" of the cerebrum. Notice that different regions control different activities. Find the regions that control what you see, hear, smell, and feel.

Map of the cerebrum ▶

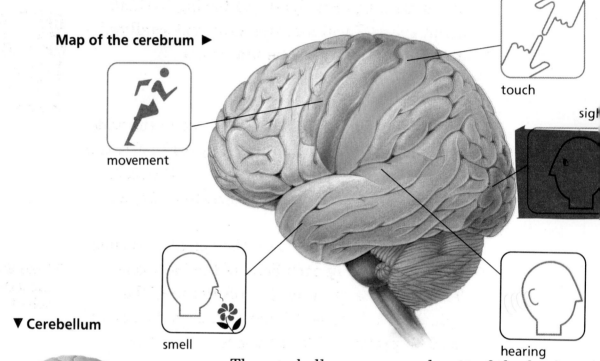

touch

sigh

movement

smell

hearing

▼ Cerebellum

The cerebellum, or second part of the brain, lies just under the back part of the cerebrum. Like the cerebrum, the cerebellum has many deep folds. But it is much smaller than the cerebrum. The cerebellum helps muscles work together. The cerebellum also helps the body keep its balance.

balance

movement

Without the cerebellum, movements would be clumsy instead of smooth. You would not be able to pick up a pencil without dropping it. To pick up a pencil, muscles in the eyes, arm, and fingers must work together. The cerebellum controls these muscles so they work together smoothly.

516

The brainstem is the third and smallest part of the brain. Find this part in the drawing. The brainstem controls many actions that help keep you alive. For example, the brainstem controls the heartbeat, breathing, and the digestion of food. The brainstem controls these actions automatically, or without you having to think about them. Coughing, sneezing, and swallowing are also controlled by the brainstem.

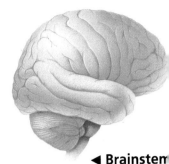

◀ **Brainstem**

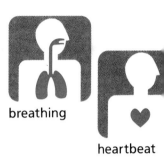

breathing

heartbeat

What does the spinal cord do?

Notice that the brainstem is really the wide top part of the spinal cord. The **spinal cord** is a thick cord of nerves in the middle of the back. The spinal cord carries messages to and from the brain.

As the drawing shows, the spinal cord runs through a hole in each bone of the backbone. The backbone protects the soft tissue of the spinal cord. Why is it important that the spinal cord be protected? What bones protect the brain?

▼ **How the backbone protects the spinal cord**

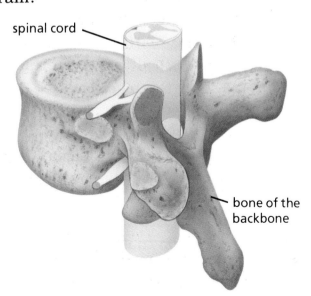

spinal cord

bone of the backbone

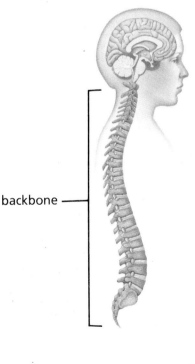

backbone

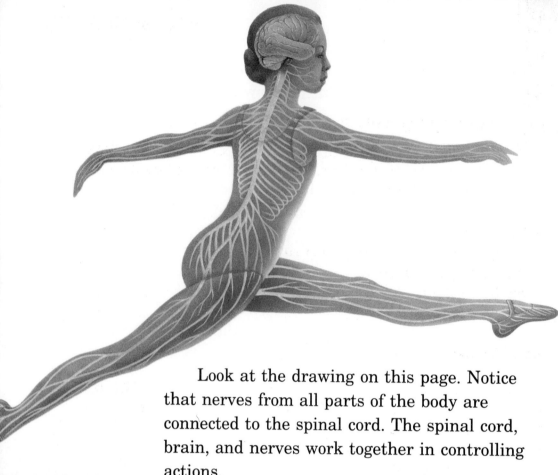

How messages travel through the parts of the nervous system

Look at the drawing on this page. Notice that nerves from all parts of the body are connected to the spinal cord. The spinal cord, brain, and nerves work together in controlling actions.

Messages from the brain travel down the spinal cord to the nerves. Then the nerves carry the messages to all parts of the body. Messages from all parts of the body travel from the nerves into the spinal cord. Then the spinal cord carries the messages up to the brain. In the next section, you will learn more about how the brain, spinal cord, and nerves work together.

Lesson Review ⎯⎯⎯⎯

1. List the three parts of the nervous system.

2. What are the three parts of the brain? Name one thing that each part controls.

3. What does the spinal cord do?

Think! Do you think a person could live for very long with a damaged brainstem? Explain your answer.

8

THINKING

Skills

Identifying useful data

When you do an experiment, you do not always use all the data you obtain. It is important to know which data you need and which you do not need.

Practicing the skill

1. The brain gets energy from a sugar called glucose. Scientists gave a group of people a written test. At the same time, they measured the sugar that these people's brains used. The table shows the results.

Brain's Use of Energy

Person's initials	Age	Correct answers	Units of sugar used
E.K.	18	11	50
R.D.	25	15	42
L.N.	19	19	40
S.E.	22	21	36
C.W.	23	23	34
S.B.	24	26	30
D.M.	20	30	28
B.G.	21	33	25

2. Which data in the table would you use to answer this question: Did the brains of people with high test scores use more sugar than the brains of people with low scores?

Thinking about the skill

Tell about another time when you had to choose which information you needed and which you did not.

Applying the skill

Suppose you wanted to learn if people's age affected their test scores. Which data would you look at?

2. Actions of the Nervous System

Getting Started   Cross your legs at the knees. With the edge of your hand, firmly tap the top leg just below the knee. What happens? Think about the part of the nervous system that might control this action.

What actions does the nervous system control?

When you tap your knee with your hand, your leg jerks forward automatically. Many of the actions controlled by the nervous system happen without your thinking about it. Actions that are controlled without having to think about them are involuntary actions. The activities of the heart and lungs are involuntary actions. Why is it important that heartbeat and breathing be controlled automatically?

▼ Voluntary actions

Now think about actions that you decide to do. You might decide to pick up a pencil or open a book. Actions that are controlled by thinking about them are voluntary actions. Like involuntary actions, voluntary actions are controlled by the nervous system. The actions of the muscles of your skeletal system are voluntary. Some of these voluntary actions are shown here.

How does the nervous system control actions?

As you learned, nerve cells carry messages that control the actions of the body. Nerve cells can be divided into three groups.

The first group is the sensory nerve cells. **Sensory nerve cells** are nerve cells that carry messages to the spinal cord and brain. Some sensory nerve cells pick up messages from inside your body. Many others pick up messages from outside your body. These sensory nerve cells are found in the sense organs—your eyes, ears, nose, tongue, and skin. For example, sensory nerve cells in your skin pick up messages about heat, cold, pain, and pressure.

*"When the going gets tough, the tough get going!" Meet a very tough young girl and her family in **Mine for Keeps**, page 542.*

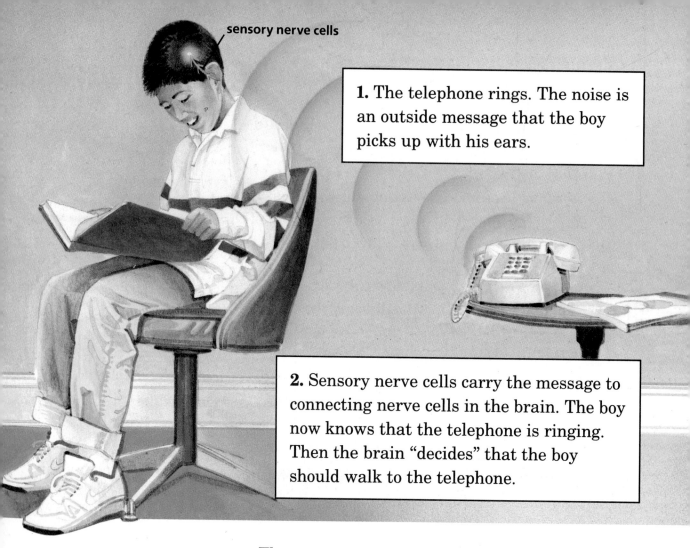

sensory nerve cells

1. The telephone rings. The noise is an outside message that the boy picks up with his ears.

2. Sensory nerve cells carry the message to connecting nerve cells in the brain. The boy now knows that the telephone is ringing. Then the brain "decides" that the boy should walk to the telephone.

▲ How the three kinds of nerve cells control actions

The second group of nerve cells is the motor nerve cells. **Motor nerve cells** are nerve cells that carry messages away from the brain and spinal cord. Many motor nerve cells carry messages that make your muscles move.

The third group of nerve cells is the connecting nerve cells. **Connecting nerve cells** are nerve cells that connect sensory nerve cells with motor nerve cells. Connecting nerve cells are found within the brain and spinal cord. Look at the drawing to see how the three kinds of nerve cells work together.

Sometimes messages take shortcuts. They may travel from sensory to motor nerve cells

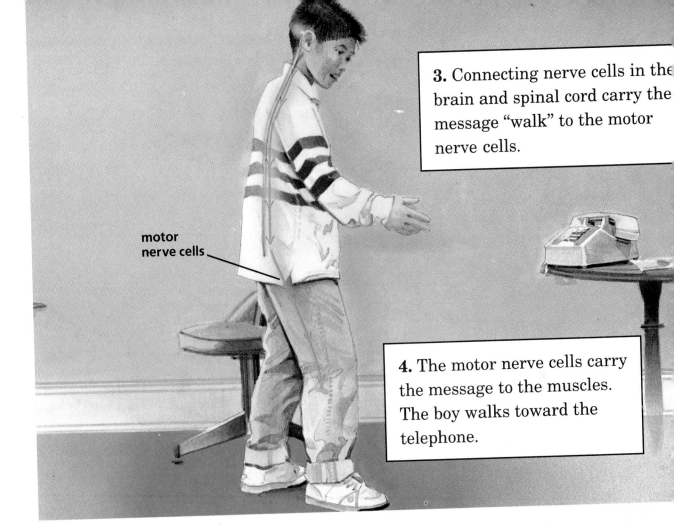

3. Connecting nerve cells in the brain and spinal cord carry the message "walk" to the motor nerve cells.

motor nerve cells

4. The motor nerve cells carry the message to the muscles. The boy walks toward the telephone.

without going to the brain. Suppose, for example, that you touch something hot. Without thinking about it, you pull your hand away quickly. The muscles in your hand act before your brain gets the message about what is happening.

Now think about what happened when you tapped your knee. Remember that your leg jerked forward automatically. Both of these actions are examples of reflexes (REE fleks ihz). A **reflex** is a quick, automatic action. Because reflexes are very fast, they help protect the body from harm. How does pulling away quickly from something hot protect your hand?

Explore

Where are nerve cells close together in the skin?

Imagine you are watching a father prepare a baby's bottle. After he heats the milk, he tests its temperature by sprinkling a few drops on the inside of his wrist. He wants to make sure that the milk is not too hot.

Materials

paper clip · metric ruler

Procedure

. Open a paper clip and bend it into a U shape. Bring the ends together until they touch.

Prepare a table like the one shown.

Body Part	Distance between points	Number of points felt
wrist	0.0	
	0.5	
	1.0	
	1.5	
fingertip	0.0	
	0.5	

Work with a partner. While your partner's eyes are closed, gently touch the inside of his or her wrist with the points of the paper clip. Ask whether your partner feels one point or two. Record this number in the table.

Move the points 0.5 cm apart and repeat step **C**. Next open the

points by 1.0 cm and then by 1.5 cm. Repeat step **C** for each amount.

E. Repeat steps **C** and **D** for the following body parts: fingertip, back of hand, back of neck.

Writing and Sharing Results and Conclusions

1. For each body part tested, what was the smallest distance between the points when both were first felt?

2. Of the body parts tested, where are nerve cells closest together? How do you know?

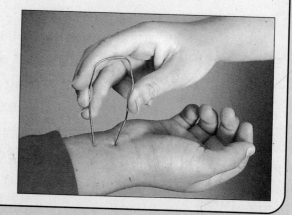

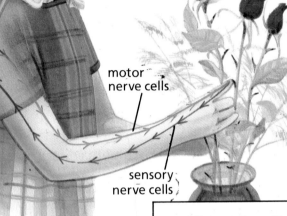

1. When the girl touches the sharp thorn, sensory nerve cells receive the pain message. These nerve cells carry the message to the spinal cord.

3. The motor nerve cells carry the message to muscles in the hand.

2. Connecting nerve cells in the spinal cord carry the message to motor nerve cells.

motor nerve cells

sensory nerve cells

4. The girl pulls her hand away.

The drawing shows what happens during a reflex. Follow the path of the message as you read.

Notice that the path of the reflex message is short, because it does not include the brain. So reflexes take less time than other actions. A reflex may happen in as little as 1/100 second.

Lesson Review

1. How do involuntary actions differ from voluntary actions?
2. List the three groups of nerve cells and tell what each group does.

Think! Trace the path of the reflex message that begins when your knee is tapped and ends when your leg jerks forward.

Physical Science
CONNECTION

How can the nervous system be compared with a telephone network?

3. The Endocrine System

Getting Started Do you ever get "nervous" before a big test? Perhaps your stomach feels upset or your mouth gets dry. What else happens to your body when you are frightened? Do you think your nervous system controls these actions?

Words to Know
endocrine system
glands
hormones

What other system controls the body?

You have learned that most of your actions are controlled by the nervous system. But some activities are controlled by a second system. The **endocrine** (EN doh krihn) **system** is a control system made up of glands. **Glands** are organs or tissues that make and release chemicals. As the drawing shows, the endocrine glands are not connected to one another. How is this different from the parts of the nervous system?

▼ The endocrine system

hypothalamus

pituitary gland

thyroid gland

parathyroid glands

adrenal glands

pancreas

female reproductive organs

male reproductive organs

526

The chemicals made by the endocrine glands are called **hormones** (HOR mohnz). Hormones are like messages. They travel through the body and help control the activities of certain body parts.

The endocrine glands may be far from the body parts they control. How, then, do hormones reach those parts? The glands release hormones into the blood. Then the hormones are carried by the blood to the places where they are used.

What are two glands that control other glands?

HYPOTHALAMUS   One part of the brain acts like a bridge between the nervous system and the endocrine system. This part of the brain, the hypothalamus (hye poh THAL uh mus), releases many hormones.

Two glands that control other glands ▼

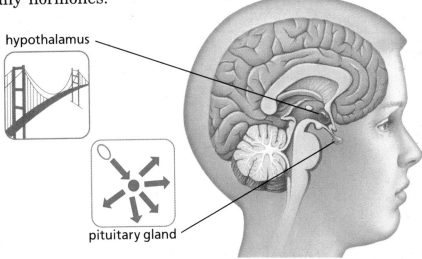

hypothalamus

pituitary gland

PITUITARY GLAND   Some hormones made by the hypothalamus control the pituitary (pih TOO-uh tair ee) gland. In turn, the pituitary gland makes hormones that control other glands. Although the pituitary gland is very small, it makes many hormones.

▲ Growth hormone controls muscle and bone growth

One of these hormones is growth hormone. As you grow up, growth hormone helps form muscle tissue and makes bones grow. As muscles and bones grow, you gain weight and grow taller. When this baby is grown up, he may weigh 20 times as much as when he was born! And he will probably be about 4 times as tall.

What are some other endocrine glands?

thyroid gland

THYROID GLAND Two types of glands are found in the neck. Can you feel your Adam's apple, or voice box? The thyroid (THYE roid) gland is just below and in front of the voice box. Find the thyroid gland in the drawing. How would you describe its shape?

Thyroid hormone controls how fast the body releases the energy stored in food. Too much of this hormone causes the body to use food too quickly. Then a person might have a lot of energy for body activities. He or she might have to eat a lot to keep from losing weight. Suppose a person's thyroid gland makes too little hormone. Why might this person feel tired?

PARATHYROID GLANDS   Four small parathyroid (par uh THYE roid) glands are attached to the thyroid gland. They make a hormone that controls the amount of calcium in the blood. Calcium helps make bones and teeth strong. It also helps nerves and muscles work properly.

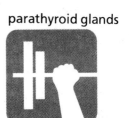

parathyroid glands

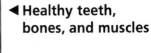

◄ Healthy teeth, bones, and muscles

PANCREAS   The pancreas (PAN kree us) is a large gland found under the stomach. One hormone made by this gland is insulin (IHN se lihn). Insulin causes sugar to move from the blood to the cells of the body. Sugar is a food used by cells. Without the right amount of sugar, cells cannot work properly.

pancreas

  In some people the pancreas does not make enough insulin. These people have a condition called diabetes (dye uh BEET eez). Without insulin, sugar cannot enter cells. Instead, sugar collects in the blood. People with diabetes must control the foods they eat. They may also need to take medicine that contains insulin.

ADRENAL GLANDS The two adrenal (uh DREE nul) glands look like little caps, one on top of each kidney. One hormone made by these glands is adrenaline (un DREN uh lihn), the emergency hormone. Adrenaline is released when you are frightened or in danger. This hormone prepares the body to act quickly, for you may have to protect yourself in some way. Your eyes open wider, your heart beats faster, and you breathe faster. More blood is sent to the brain and muscles so that you can think and act more quickly. How might adrenaline help prepare the body for the emergency shown here?

adrenal glands

An emergency ▶

Adrenaline is often released for "false alarms." Suppose you watch a scary movie. Adrenaline is sent through your blood, even though there is really no danger. What other "false alarms" might make your heart beat faster?

reproductive glands

REPRODUCTIVE GLANDS Males and females have a pair of reproductive organs. In males,

▲ Group of fifth-grade children

these organs are the testes (TES teez). In females, these organs are the ovaries (OH vuh reez).

The reproductive organs produce sperm and egg cells—the male and female sex cells. But these organs are also endocrine glands that release sex hormones. Sex hormones cause changes in the body as you mature, or grow up.

As boys mature, their voices get lower, their shoulders get broader, and their muscles get larger. When girls mature, their body shape becomes more like that of a woman. Other changes take place inside their body. As the picture shows, these changes happen more quickly in some children than in others.

Lesson Review

1. Name three glands of the endocrine system.
2. List two hormones and describe how they control the body.
3. What condition is caused by too little insulin?

Think! Why might doctors inject adrenaline into someone whose heart is beating too slowly?

4. Keeping the Control Systems Healthy

Getting Started Do you have a bicycle? If so, you know how to take care of it. Make a list of things a bicycle needs to keep it running well. What things does your body need to keep it healthy?

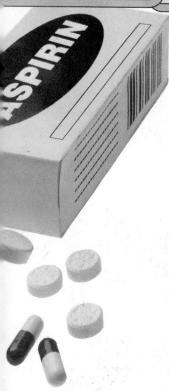

How can drugs be helpful?

To stay healthy, you need certain things, such as food, exercise, and sleep. But suppose you get sick. Then you may need medicine to help you feel better and get well. When you have a cold, for example, medicine may stop your sneezing and coughing. But medicine may also cause side effects, or changes that are not needed. What might be a side effect of cold medicine?

Medicines are a kind of drug. A **drug** is a chemical taken into the body. Drugs cause changes in the body. Many drugs, such as these medicines, help cure diseases, fight infections, and get rid of pain.

How can drugs harm the body?

There are proper and improper ways to use drugs. People can use drugs properly in two ways. First, they can follow the directions on the label of the drug container. Second, they can follow a doctor's instructions for taking a drug. In fact, many drugs can be taken only with a prescription, or doctor's order.

When drugs are taken as directed, they are safe and helpful. But drugs can also be misused, or used improperly. The misuse of drugs is called **drug abuse.** When they are abused, drugs can be dangerous and very harmful.

Many drugs harm the body by changing the way the control systems work. Some drugs speed up or slow down the messages that travel through the nervous system. Other drugs may harm the brain's ability to receive and send messages.

What kinds of drugs can be abused?

STIMULANTS   Drugs that speed up the actions of the nervous system are called stimulants (STIHM yoo lunts). The nervous system, in turn, causes the heart to beat faster and breathing to speed up. Stimulants make a person more active and alert than usual.

Caffeine (kaf EEN), a mild stimulant, is found in coffee, tea, cola drinks, and chocolate. Nicotine (NIHK uh teen), found in tobacco, is also a mild stimulant.

Cocaine (koh KAYN) is a strong stimulant. It can block the brain's control of the heart and breathing. How would this harm the body? One form of cocaine is crack. Crack is one of the most dangerous drugs that people use.

*Something is wrong with Roboman. He never acted this strangely before. Can you figure out what is wrong? Read about it in **Roboman's Problem** in Horizons Plus.*

DEPRESSANTS Drugs that slow down the nervous system are called depressants (dee PRES-unts). The nervous system, in turn, slows down the heartbeat and breathing. A person using depressants may feel confused and sleepy.

The most abused depressant is alcohol (AL-kuh hawl), which is found in wine, beer, and whiskey. Alcohol slows a person's reaction time. The reaction time is the time it takes for an action to take place. How would this affect a person's ability to drive a car?

Quick thinking and ▶ acting is important.

NARCOTICS Narcotics (nahr KAHT ihks) are another group of drugs that slow down the actions of the nervous system. Narcotics are used as painkillers. But these drugs are often abused. People inject narcotics into their blood with needles. If they share the needles, they can spread diseases, such as AIDS.

ACTIVITY

Explore Together

How can you measure reaction time?

Materials

Organizer
activity sheet "Reaction-Time Scale" · scissors · meter stick · tape · graph paper

Procedure

Investigator
A. Cut out the reaction-time scale. Center the scale along the length of the meter stick. Line up the marks for 0.17 sec and 50 cm. Tape the scale in place. Notice that the marks on the scale are not evenly spaced. These marks stand for parts of a second.

Investigator
B. Stand facing the Manager. Hold the meter stick near the top end.

Manager
C. As the Investigator holds the meter stick, place your thumb and forefinger around the meter stick at the 0.00 mark on the scale. Do not touch the meter stick yet. Be prepared to catch the meter stick when the Investigator drops it.

Investigator
D. Tell the Manager to catch the meter stick when you drop it. Drop the meter stick without warning.

Group, Recorder
1. Record the Manager's reaction time in seconds.

Investigator, Recorder
E. Repeat steps **B** through **D** for five more trials, or times.

Group, Recorder
2. How did reaction time change with each trial?

Writing and Sharing Results and Conclusions

Group, Recorder
1. On a sheet of graph paper, graph the reaction times against the number of trials.

Reporter
2. How do your results and conclusions compare with those of your classmates?

HALLUCINOGENS Hallucinogens (huh LOO sih-nuh jenz) are drugs that cause a person to see, hear, or feel things that do not exist. A mild hallucinogen is marijuana (mar ih WAH nuh), or pot. Like alcohol, marijuana can slow down a person's reaction time. Strong hallucinogens include PCP, or angel dust, and LSD, or acid. These drugs often cause brain damage.

Some Abused Drugs and Their Effects		
Types of Drugs	**Examples**	**Effects of Drugs**
Stimulants	Caffeine Nicotine Cocaine	Speed up actions of nervous system; speed up heartbeat and breathing.
Depressants	Alcohol	Slow down actions of nervous system; slow heartbeat and breathing; cause sleepiness and confusion.
Narcotics	Morphine Heroin Codeine	Slow down actions of nervous system; slow heartbeat and breathing; cause sleepiness and confusion.
Hallucinogens	Marijuana PCP LSD	Cause user to see, hear, and feel things that are not real; slow reaction time.

Lesson Review

1. List two ways that people use drugs properly.
2. Compare the effects of stimulants and depressants on the nervous system.
3. Give an example of a drug that is a hallucinogen.

Think! What do you think might be the effect of using alcohol with another depressant?

Chapter Connections

Explain the main ideas in this chapter to a partner. Use the graphic organizer to help you. Have your partner take notes. Compare the notes with other classmates.

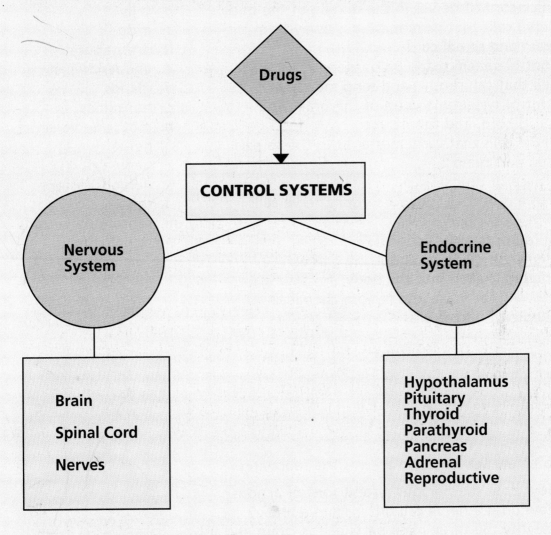

Writing About Science • Inform

Research the effects of drugs on all parts of the body. Write a paragraph as a news reporter. Tell your audience about the dangers of drugs.

Science Terms

Write the letter of the term that best matches the definition.

1. Main organ and control center of the nervous system
2. Thick cord of nerves in the middle of the back
3. Nerve cells that carry messages away from the brain and spinal cord
4. Control system made up of glands
5. Cell that can receive and send messages
6. Control system made up of the brain, the spinal cord, and the nerves
7. Nerve cells that carry messages to the spinal cord and brain
8. Misuse of drugs
9. Nerve cells that connect sensory nerve cells with motor nerve cells
10. Quick, automatic action
11. Chemicals made by endocrine glands
12. Chemical taken into the body
13. Organs that make and release chemicals
14. Bundle of nerve cells

a. brain
b. connecting nerve cells
c. drug
d. drug abuse
e. endocrine system
f. glands
g. hormones
h. motor nerve cells
i. nerve
j. nerve cell
k. nervous system
l. reflex
m. sensory nerve cells
n. spinal cord

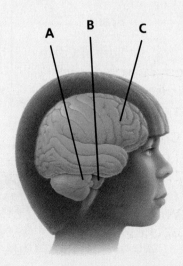

Science Ideas

Use complete sentences to answer the following.

1. How does the nervous system control actions?
2. How does a nerve cell differ from a nerve?
3. Identify the three main parts of the brain and list one thing each part does. Label your answers A–C.
4. Give an example of an involuntary action and an example of a voluntary action.
5. How do sensory nerve cells differ from motor nerve cells?

6. How does a hormone travel from the gland where it is produced to the body part it controls?
7. Identify each endocrine gland and tell how each gland controls the body.
8. How can some drugs be helpful?
9. List two kinds of abused drugs and give an example of each kind.

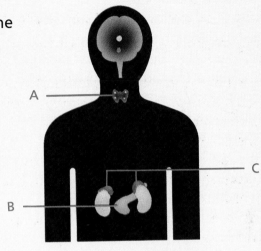

Applying Science Ideas

1. What part of the brain helps you pick up a glass of milk without spilling it?
2. Why does your heart keep beating while you are asleep?
3. Why does an injury to the spinal cord often cause a person to be paralyzed?
4. Suppose you walk through the woods and step on something sharp. When you look down, you see a snake. Predict how your control systems would help you act quickly?

Using Science Skills

A woman with a cold went to a drugstore to find medicine. One bottle of pills had the following information on its label:

A. Do not take this medicine if you are allergic to aspirin.
B. This medicine is manufactured in New York, NY
C. This medicine relieves pain, stuffy nose, and fever.
D. This medicine may make you sleepy.
   What information would help the woman decide whether this drug is a good choice for her?

Careers in Health Science

Research Scientist

You are a scientist who has the chance to search for the cure of a serious disease. But you must pick just one disease to study. How would you choose? Ask Dr. Frank Douglas. Dr. Douglas is a **research scientist.** These questions are part of his job as the director of research at a large drug company in New Jersey. His company makes medicines that treat diseases such as cancer, arthritis, and heart disease.

Deciding which diseases to investigate is the first step in a long process. It can take up to 15 years till a medicine is ready for use. In that time, chemists make thousands of different drugs. Each one is checked and tested. Some may not work. Others may not be safe. After many experiments, Dr. Douglas and the hundreds of people he works with will have a drug that can treat, cure, or prevent a disease.

It is important to Frank Douglas that his work helps others. "Working with other scientists whose goal is to get important medicines to the people who need them makes the hard work worthwhile."

Frank Douglas was always interested in biology and medicine. When he was growing up, he liked to catch frogs and study them. And to Frank, the best part of school was science. In college, Frank learned more biology and chemistry. Now, Dr. Douglas has doctoral degrees in both chemistry and medicine.

Would you like to help develop a new medicine? You could be a **technician,** a **chemist,** a **biologist,** or one of many other specialists who do just that.

Connecting Science Ideas

1. Imagine that a drug researcher such as Dr. Douglas visited your school. What might he say to students about the benefits and problems of drugs? **Careers; Chapter 15**

2. In what two science subjects is Dr. Douglas an expert? You read about a cure for broken bones on pages 492–493. In what two science subjects might the scientist who worked on that cure be an expert? **Careers; Chapter 14**

3. How do the nervous system and the muscular system work together when you throw a ball? **Chapter 14; Chapter 15**

4. Think about a ballet dancer performing. Which of the body systems you read about are being used? Explain how they are being used. **Chapter 14; Chapter 15**

5. You read that the nervous system can be compared with a system of wires connected to a computer inside a robot. Comparing these two is called *using a model*. What is the model used to describe the skeleton in Chapter 14? What might be a good model to describe the endocrine system? **Chapter 14; Chapter 15**

6. The endocrine system affects other body systems. What systems of the body does a release of adrenalin affect? **Chapter 14; Chapter 15**

7. The skeleton provides support and protection for many organs. Name some bones and the organs they protect. Tell the system to which each organ belongs. **Chapter 14; Chapter 15**

8. On pages 476–479 you read about artificial body parts. In a robotic arm, what parts replace each of the following: the skeletal system, the muscular system, and the nervous system? **Chapter 14; Chapter 15**

Unit Project

In Chapter 14, you learned about four kinds of joints that move. Make a working model of each kind of joint. Decide what materials would work best for each joint. Label the parts of the joint on each model. .

from

Mine for Keeps

by Jean Little

Sal Copeland has cerebral palsy. For the last five years she has lived at the Allendale School for Handicapped Children. Now she's come home to live with her family. With their love and support, Sal comes to understand her illness and learns that she can become an independent adult.

"Have you really looked at the clothes I put out for you to wear this morning, Sal?"

Unable to speak, Sal only shook her head. Mother rose and reached for the clothes. One piece at a time, she spread them out across Sal's knees.

"Now show me those buttons you're so worried about!" With her head bent and her heart thumping uncomfortably, Sal inspected the clothing. The expression on her face grew more and more sheepish as she looked.

There were no buttons. Not a single button anywhere! In fact, the clothes on her lap were the simplest clothes to put on that Sal had ever seen. The skirt was full with an elasticized top. No zipper! No tricky fastening at all! And the soft yellow blouse had a wide boat neck with a rolled-over collar. No hooks and eyes! No skimpy little puffed sleeves! Even the underwear was specially made with generous openings for arms and legs. All the things that made dressing difficult were missing—and yet the clothes themselves looked lovely.

"Now guess who suggested those new clothes for you."

"You must have," Sal faltered.

"Wrong. Miss Jonas did."

"MISS JONAS!"

"Miss Jonas. When you left Allendale, she wrote us a long letter about you. You'd be surprised at some of the things she knows about you, Sarah Jane. Most important, she told us that if we all, including you, started working on it right away, there will come a day when you, Sal Copeland, will be an independent adult. An independent adult is a person who decides things for herself and does things for herself and for others. It would mean having your own job, your own friends, your own money, your freedom."

"But to be independent someday means beginning practicing independence *today*; and the first step is dressing yourself. Only, before you begin, I'm going to cut your hair."

Twenty minutes later, Mother stood back, looked over her handiwork one last time, and declared it was perfect. The floor was littered with long strands of wheat-colored familiar-looking hair. Gingerly, Sal put up a hand to feel what was left, but Mother batted her exploring fingers down.

"None of that," she ordered. "No looking in the mirror, either. Here are your clothes. Get yourself dressed. Then you can see your whole new self at once. Now get busy."

She hoisted Sal back to the bed, from the captain's chair where she had sat to have her hair cut, put her crutches within reach, and left.

For one long moment, Sal sat and stared down at the clothes beside her. Then she began to move. She hitched the short nightgown out from under her and hauled it over her head. For the first time, she noticed that it was new and different too, like the other clothes. Only the gay up and down stripes saved it from looking like a plain sack with holes in it for her head and arms.

But it was too cold in the room to sit in her bare skin and admire it. If she didn't get into something quickly, she'd freeze.

Just the same, frozen or thawed, it took a long time. Wriggling into and tugging at each garment in turn soon had her puffing and red in the face.

She looked down at herself and drew a sharp little breath of excitement. She had managed it! She was dressed. She wriggled forward until her feet were firmly on the floor and reached for her crutches. Leaning down, she got her braces locked and then put her weight solidly on the handgrips. After trying a couple of times, she was up. Holding her breath, she turned and started for the mirror.

Shyly, shakily, Sally approached the glass. As she caught sight of herself, she stopped in her tracks. Even though she had known she would be different, she was totally unprepared for this girl in the mirror.

This was a new Sally.

She was dressed in bright, soft colors. In place of the long braids she wore a smooth shining cap of hair with no part at all. It was almost as short as a boy's, but it had bangs straight across the front and it curved in just a little on the ends. From all her hard work, and excitement, her cheeks glowed like roses. In spite of herself, her mouth tipped up in a delighted smile and her blue eyes shone bluer than ever with wonder.

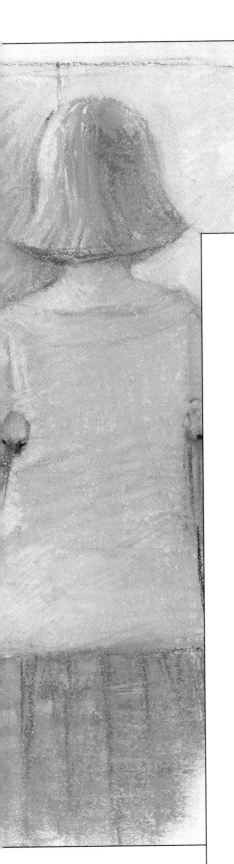

In the morning, Dad drove Mother, Sally and Meg to Toronto to see Dr. Eastman. Dr. Eastman was Sally's specialist. Their family doctor had referred them to him as soon as they had realized that Sal had cerebral palsy.

After he had checked her over, watched her walk and lifted her onto a table while he examined her to see she was "still working properly" as he put it, the doctor turned to find Meg standing at his elbow, her face one big question.

"What's the matter with her, do you know?" Meg asked him.

"Your brain is like a motor," he told them. "Part of this motor makes you walk. Part of it makes you talk. Part of it makes you able to use your hands easily. Another part helps you to see, another to hear, and so on. If you are going to be able to walk and use your hands well, you have to have the motor part of your brain in good working order besides having well-built arms and legs."

"I walk just on legs," Meg remarked, not believing a word of it.

"Sure you do—just as a car runs on its wheels. But if the motor wasn't in the car too, or if the motor in the car was broken, then what would happen?"

Meg thought about it.

"It wouldn't go," she admitted.

Dr. Eastman smiled. "You're right. It wouldn't," he said. "And it's the same with the brain. Most babies are born with the motor part of their brain all ready to go. But once in a while a baby is born with part of its motor broken—or injured, in other words."

Sal's eyes were bright with excitement. So that was why children with cerebral palsy were handicapped in so many different ways!

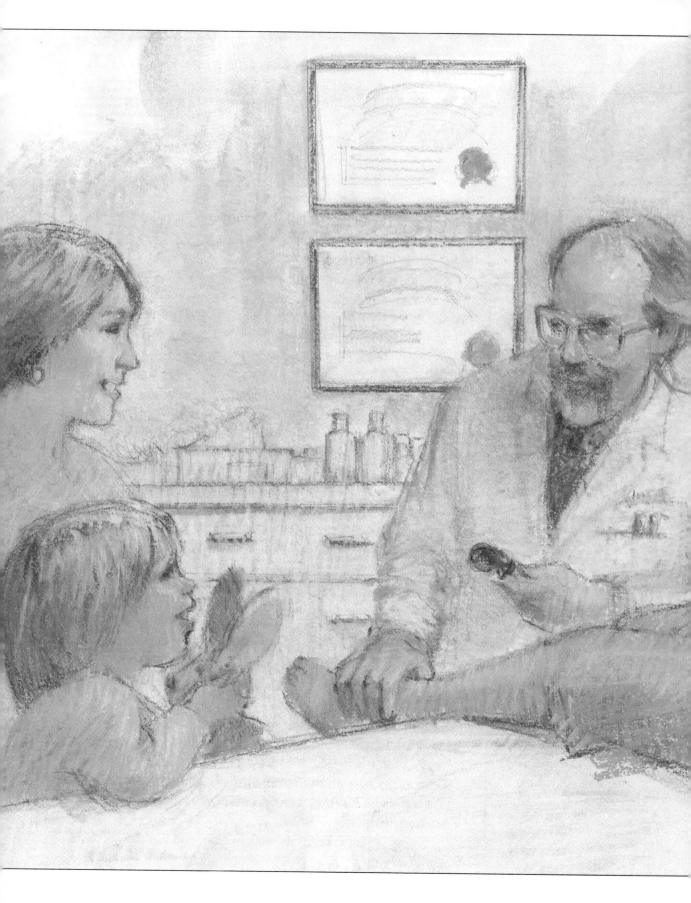

"Do you fix the broken parts or do you buy new parts?" Meg had more questions ready.

"I wish we could buy new parts," Dr. Eastman said. "We can't fix the broken or injured parts, Meg, and there isn't any place where you can buy new brains. But sometimes we can get other parts of the brain to do the work of the injured or broken part. It's as though you had to fix your car motor by getting another motor and working with it and trying it over and over until it worked—not as well as the right motor would have, but well enough to get the car moving. You learned how to drive the motor part of your brain when you learned to walk. Now Sally has to do that too—but she has to start off with the wrong motor and work a lot harder at it and teach it how to work.

"Who is the teacher?" Meg asked, looking Sal over as though she expected to see some special little person peeking out of her ear.

"The therapists who give her treatment help," he answered, "but the person who does most of it is, as I said, Sally herself."

Sal stared at him, sure he was mixed up, but he only nodded, smiling.

"Yes, you. Every time you do something yourself, getting yourself dressed maybe" (Sal blushed, thinking back) "or walking across a room, or anything that means putting the brain to work for you, it gets more used to its new job and does it a bit better. Mind you, it takes years and years for it to learn. Brains aren't too brainy, I guess," he finished.

Sal was still thinking about what he had said when they were out in the car. She wished somebody had told her about it years ago, but maybe it wouldn't have seemed so simple then.

Reader's Response

How do you think Sal felt when she dressed herself for the first time? What would you have said to her if you had been there?

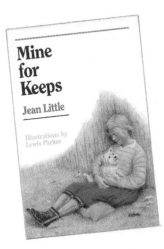

Mine for Keeps

 ## Responding to Literature

1. Explain how Dr. Eastman helps both Meg and Sal understand cerebral palsy.

2. Why did Mrs. Copeland cut Sal's hair and buy her new clothes?

3. Do you agree that it is important for Sal to become an independent adult? Explain why or why not.

4. There are many things that both Sal and you will have to learn to become independent adults. What are some of those things?

5. Sal feels better about herself and her disorder after talking with Dr. Eastman. What did she learn that made her feel better?

 ## Books to Enjoy

Mine for Keeps by Jean Little
Read the book to discover more about Sal, her family, and the new friends she makes. And find out what she grows to love so much that she announces it is "mine for keeps."

Why Does My Nose Run? by Joanne Settel and Nancy Baggett
This book answers this question and many others about the human body.

Your Wonderful Body! edited by Donald J. Crump
Full of color photographs, this book describes how the many systems in your body work.

Glossary

Some words in this book may be new to you or difficult to pronounce. Those words have been spelled phonetically in parentheses. The syllable that receives stress in a word is shown in small capital letters.

For example: **Chicago** (shuh KAH goh)

Most phonetic spellings are easy to read. In the following Pronunciation Key, you can see how letters are used to show different sounds.

PRONUNCIATION KEY

a	after	(AF tur)
ah	father	(FAH thur)
ai	care	(kair)
aw	dog	(dawg)
ay	paper	(PAY pur)
e	letter	(LET ur)
ee	eat	(eet)
ih	trip	(trihp)
eye	idea	(eye DEE uh)
y	hide	(hyd)
ye	lie	(lye)
oh	flow	(floh)
oi	boy	(boi)
oo	rule	(rool)
or	horse	(hors)
ou	cow	(kou)
yoo	few	(fyoo)
u	taken	(TAY kun)
	matter	(MAT ur)
uh	ago	(uh GOH)

ch	chicken	(CHIHK un)
g	game	(gaym)
ing	coming	(KUM ing)
j	job	(jahb)
k	came	(kaym)
ng	long	(lawng)
s	city	(SIH tee)
sh	ship	(shihp)
th	thin	(thihn)
thh	feather	(FETHH ur)
y	yard	(yahrd)
z	size	(syz)
zh	division	(duh VIHZH un)

A

abdomen (AB duh mun)   The rear part of an insect's body. p. 85

acid rain (AS ihd   rayn)   A mixture of acid and rainwater. p. 350

adaptation (ad up TAY shun)   A response or structure that helps a living thing survive. p. 112

air mass (air   mas)   A large body of air that has about the same temperature and moisture throughout. p. 314

annual rings (AN yoo ul   ringz) The rings of wood that are produced yearly in the stems of trees. p. 106

arthropod (AHR throh pahd) An animal with jointed legs, a segmented body, and a hard outer covering. p. 80

asteroids (AS tur oidz)   Chunks of rock found mainly in the region of space between Mars and Jupiter. p. 458

astronomy (us STRAHN uh mee) The science that deals with the study of objects in the sky. p. 442

atom (AT um)   The smallest particle of an element that has the chemical properties of the element. p. 186

atomic number (uh TAHM ihk   NUM-bur)   The number of protons in one atom of an element. p. 187

B

backbone (BAK bohn)   A long row of connected bones in the middle of the back. p. 486

bacteria (bak TIHR ee uh); *singular form,* bacterium (bak TIHR ee um) Another name for monerans. p. 48

bioconversion (bye oh kun VUR-zhun)   The process by which biomass is changed to a gas or liquid fuel. p. 393

biodegradable substance (bye oh-dih GRAY duh bul   SUB stuns)   A substance that can be broken down by microbes. p. 414

biomass (BYE oh mas)   Any kind of organic matter that can be used as a fuel. p. 393

biome (BYE ohm)   A large region on the earth that has a certain climate and certain kinds of organisms. p. 125

brain (brayn)   The main organ of the nervous system. p. 514

buoyant force (BOI unt   fors)   The upward force that water exerts on an object in the water; also known as buoyancy. p. 253

C

cartilage (KAHRT ul ihj)   A strong, elastic tissue in the skeletal system. p. 484

cell (sel)   The basic part of all living things. p. 32

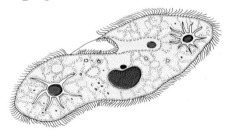

cell membrane (sel   MEM brayn) A structure that surrounds and protects a cell. p. 37

cell wall (sel   wawl)   A stiff structure outside the cell membrane of some cells. p. 40

chemical bond (KEM ih kul   bahnd) A force that holds two atoms together. p. 191

chemical change (KEM ih kul chaynj)   A change in which one or more new substances are formed. p. 220

chemical property (KEM ih kul PRAHP ur tee)   A trait that describes how one substance reacts with another substance. p. 175

chemical symbol (KEM ih kul SIHM bul)   One or two letters that stand for the name of an element. p. 192

climate (KLYE mut)   The average weather of a region over a long period of time. p. 124

comet (KAHM iht)   A body in space that is formed of rocks, frozen water, frozen gases, and dust. p. 459

compound (KAHM pound)   A substance made when two or more elements combine to form a new substance. p. 172

conductor (kun DUK tur)   A material through which electrons move easily. p. 274

connecting nerve cell (kuh NEK-ting   nurv   sel)   A nerve cell that connects sensory nerve cells with motor nerve cells. p. 522

conservation (kahn sur VAY shun) The careful use of natural resources. p. 404

corona (kuh ROH nuh)   The hot, outer atmosphere of the sun. p. 439

cytoplasm (SYT oh plaz um)   The jellylike material that surrounds the nucleus of a cell. p. 37

D

deciduous forest (dee SIHJ oo us FOR ihst)   A biome named for the broad-leaved trees found there. p. 134

deposition (dep uh ZIHSH un)   The dropping of sediment by agents of erosion. p. 358

desert (DEZ urt)   A biome that receives less than 25 cm (10 inches) of rainfall each year. p. 148

drug (drug)   A chemical taken into the body that causes changes in the body. p. 532

drug abuse (drug   uh BYOOS)   The misuse of drugs. p. 533

E

echinoderm (ee KYE noh durm)   A spiny-skinned invertebrate that lives in the ocean. p. 78

electric circuit (ee LEK trihk   SUR-kiht)   A path on which electrons move continuously. p. 276

electric current (ee LEK trihk KUR unt)   The continuous movement of electrons. p. 274

electric discharge (ee LEK trihk DIHS chahrj)   The movement of extra electrons from one object to another. p. 272

electromagnet (ee LEK troh mag-niht)   A magnet made when electrons move through a coil of wire wrapped around an iron core. p. 282

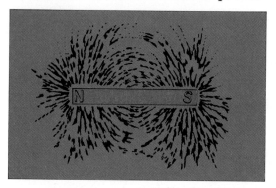

electron (ee LEK trahn)   A particle that has a negative electric charge. p. 187

element (EL uh munt)   A substance that cannot be broken down by simple means into any other substance. p. 172

endocrine system (EN doh krihn SIHS tum)   A control system made up of glands. p. 526

erosion (ee ROH zhun)   The picking up and moving away of weathered rock and soil. p. 358

exoskeleton (eks oh SKEL uh tun) The hard outer covering of an arthropod. p. 81

extinct (ek STINGKT)   A species of animal or plant that no longer has any living members. p. 115

F

fertilizer (FUR tuh lye zur)   A chemical used to enrich the soil with minerals. p. 421

filament (FIHL uh munt)   A thin wire inside the glass bulb of a light bulb. p. 275

flatworm (FLAT wurm)   A worm with a flattened body and only one body opening. p. 69

fluid (FLOO ihd)   Matter that flows. p. 252

force (fors)   A push or a pull on an object, caused by another object. p. 237

formula (FOR myoo luh)   A group of symbols that shows how many atoms of each element are in a molecule or in the smallest unit of a compound. p. 193

fossil fuel (FAHS ul   FYOO ul)   A fuel formed from decayed plants and animals that lived long ago. p. 371

fracture (FRAK chur)   A crack or break in a bone. p. 502

friction (FRIHK shun)   The force that resists the movement of one object against another when the objects touch. p. 242

front (frunt)   The boundary, or area of contact, between two air masses. p. 317

frost action (frawst   AK shun)   The weathering of rock by repeated freezing and melting of water. p. 344

fuel (FYOO ul)   A substance that is burned to release its stored energy. p. 370

fungus (FUNG gus)   A plantlike living thing that does not contain chlorophyll. p. 42

G

generator (JEN ur ayt ur)   A machine that changes the mechanical energy of a turbine to electrical energy. pp. 286, 373

geothermal energy (jee oh THUR-mul   EN ur jee)   Energy from the natural heat within the earth's crust. p. 391

glacier (GLAY shur)   A large body of moving ice. p. 361

gland (gland)   An organ or tissue that makes and releases chemicals. p. 526

grassland (GRAS land)   A biome that has cold winters, warm summers, and uneven precipitation, and that is found in temperate regions. p. 144

gravity (GRAV ih tee)   A force that pulls, or attracts, objects toward one another. p. 247

greenhouse effect (GREEN hous e FEKT)   The trapping and building up of heat in the atmosphere. p. 407

growth region (grohth REE jun)   A tissue in a plant in which growth occurs. p. 99

H
heart muscle (hahrt MUS ul)   Muscle found only in the heart. p. 496

hormones (HOR mohnz)   The chemicals made by the endocrine glands that help control activities of certain body parts. p. 527

humus (HYOO mus)   The decayed remains of plant and animal matter in soil. p. 354

hurricane (HUR ih kayn)   A large tropical storm that has very high winds and heavy rainfall. p. 322

hydroelectric energy (hye droh ee-LEK trihk EN ur jee)   Electrical energy produced by moving water. p. 386

I
incinerator (ihn SIHN ur ayt ur)   A huge furnace for burning garbage. p. 414

inertia (ihn UR shuh)   The resistance of matter to a change in its motion. p. 238

inner planets (IHN ur PLAN ihts) The four planets closest to the sun: Mercury, Venus, Earth, and Mars. p. 446

insulator (IHN suh layt ur)   A material through which electrons do not move easily. p. 275

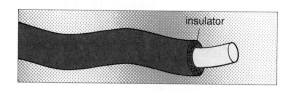

invertebrate (ihn VER tuh briht) An animal that has no backbone. p. 61

isobar (EYE soh bahr)   A line on a weather map that connects places that have the same air pressure. p. 327

J

joint (joint)   A place where two or more bones come together. p. 488

K

kingdom (KING dum)   One of five large groups into which scientists classify all organisms. p. 34

L

ligament (LIHG uh munt)   A strong band of tissue that holds bones together at a joint. p. 491

M

magnet (MAG niht)   Any object that is surrounded by magnetic lines of force. p. 249

magnetic field (mag NET ihk feeld)   The magnetic lines of force around a magnet. p. 249

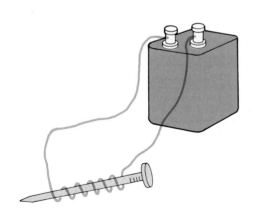

magnetic force (mag NET ihk fors)   A force between magnetic objects, such as iron, steel, nickel, and cobalt. p. 249

mantle (MAN tul)   A fleshy covering that protects the organs of a mollusk. p. 77

marrow (MAR oh)   A soft tissue inside bones. p. 482

matter (MAT ur)   Anything that has mass and takes up space. p. 170

metal (MET ul)   An element that is shiny and can be rolled or pounded into various shapes. p. 184

meteor (MEET ee ur)   The streak of light caused by a meteoroid passing through the earth's atmosphere. p. 456

meteorite (MEET ee uh ryt)   A meteoroid that lands on the earth. p. 457

meteoroid (MEET ee ur oid)   A mass of metal or stone moving through space. p. 456

meteorologist (meet ee ur AHL uh-jihst)   A scientist who studies weather. p. 326

mixture (MIHKS chur)   Matter that contains two or more different substances. p. 171

model (MAHD ul)   A way to describe how something looks or acts. p. 186

molecule (MAHL ih kyool)   A group of atoms held together by one type of chemical bond. p. 191

mollusk (MAHL usk)   An invertebrate that has a soft body. p. 76

molt (mohlt)   To shed the outer body covering. p. 81

moneran (moh NER un)   A one-celled organism that does not have a nucleus. p. 48

motion (MOH shun)   Any change in the position of an object. p. 232

motor nerve cell (MOHT ur nurv sel)   A nerve cell that carries messages away from the brain and spinal cord. p. 522

muscular system (MUS kyoo lur SIHS tum)   The muscles that move the parts of the body. p. 494

N

natural resource (NACH ur ul REE sors)   A useful material that is taken from the environment. p. 373

nerve (nurv)   A bundle of nerve cells. p. 514

nerve cell (nurv sel)   A cell that can receive and send messages. p. 513

nervous system (NUR vus SIHS-tum)   A control system made up of the brain, the spinal cord, and the nerves. p. 512

neutron (NOO trahn)   A particle that has no electric charge. p. 187

noble gas (NOH bul gas)   An element that is a gas and does not react readily with other elements. p. 185

nonmetal (nahn MET ul)   An element that has no shine and cannot be shaped. p. 185

nonrenewable resource (nahn-rih NOO uh bul REE sors)   A useful substance that cannot easily be replaced once it is used. p. 373

nuclear energy (NOO klee ur EN-ur jee)   The energy contained in the nucleus of an atom. p. 376

nuclear fission (NOO klee ur FIHSH un)   The splitting of the nucleus of an atom with the release of energy. p. 376

nuclear fusion (NOO klee ur FYOO-zhun)   A nuclear reaction in which the nuclei of atoms join together. p. 379

nucleus (NOO klee us)   **1.** The control center of a cell. p. 37. **2.** The dense central core of an atom. p. 187

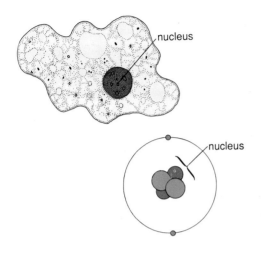

nucleus

nucleus

O

oil slick (oil   slihk)   A layer of oil floating on sea water. p. 425

orbit (OR biht)   An oval-shaped path on which an object travels as it moves around another body. p. 435

organism (OR guh nihz um)   Any single living thing. p. 32

outer planets (OUT ur PLAN ihts) The five planets farthest from the sun: Jupiter, Saturn, Uranus, Neptune, and Pluto. p. 446

oxidation (ahks ih DAY shun)   The process by which oxygen combines with another substance. p. 221

ozone layer (OH zohn LAY ur) A very thin layer of ozone gas high above the earth. p. 410

P

parasite (PAR uh syt)   A living thing that lives on or in another living thing and harms the living thing on which it lives. p. 69

pelvis (PEL vihs)   A group of large, wide bones at the end of the backbone. p. 487

pesticide (PES tuh syd)   A chemical used to kill insect pests that harm crops. p. 415

phloem (FLO em)   A tissue made of tubes that carry food through a plant. p. 104

physical change (FIHZ ih kul chaynj)   A change in the size, shape, or state of matter. p. 202

physical property (FIHZ ih kul PRAHP ur tee)   A trait that can be observed or measured without changing the identity of the substance. p. 175

planet (PLAN iht)   One of the nine large bodies that move around the sun. p. 434

poles (pohlz)   The parts of a magnet where the magnetic force is strongest. p. 251

pollutant (puh LOOT unt)   Harmful matter added to the environment. p. 406

pollution (puh LOO shun)   The addition of unwanted substances to the environment. p. 404

pore (por)   A small hole or opening in a sponge. p. 65

protist (PROHT ihst)   A one-celled organism. p. 36

proton (PROH tahn)   A particle with a positive electric charge. p. 187

R

radon (RAY dahn)   A gas produced by the decay of uranium in rocks and soil. p. 411

reflex (REE fleks)   A quick, automatic action. p. 523

relative humidity (REL uh tihv hyoo MIHD uh tee)   The amount of water vapor in the air compared with the total amount of water vapor that the air can hold at that temperature. p. 309

renewable resource (rih NOO uh-bul REE sors)   A useful substance that is fairly easy to replace if it is used. p. 373

repel (rih PEL)   To push away. p. 251

response (rih SPAHNS)   The reaction of a living thing to something in its environment. p. 108

revolution (rev uh LOO shun)   The movement of a planet along its orbit. p. 435

rotation (roh TAY shun)   The turning of a body on its axis. p. 436

roundworm (ROUND wurm)   A worm that has a round body and two body openings. p. 71

S

sanitary landfill (SAN uh ter ee LAND fihl)   A place on land in which wastes are dumped. p. 413

segmented worm (seg MENT ihd wurm)   A worm that has a body divided into sections. p. 71

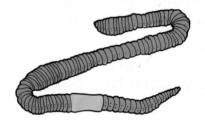

semimetal (sem ee MET ul)   An element that has properties of both a metal and a nonmetal. p. 185

sensory nerve cell (SEN sur ee nurv sel)   A nerve cell that carries messages to the spinal cord and brain. p. 521

skeletal muscle (SKEL uh tul MUS-ul)   The muscle that is attached to the bones of the skeleton. p. 495

skeletal system (SKEL uh tul   SIHS-tum)   The frame of bones that supports the body. p. 480

smog (smahg)   A mixture of smoke and fog in the air. p. 408

smooth muscle (smoothh   MUS ul) Muscle that makes up the walls of many organs of the body. p. 496

soil (soil)   The loose material on the earth's surface in which plants can grow. p. 352

solar cell (SOH lur   sel)   A device that changes solar energy directly to electrical energy. p. 384

solar collector (SOH lur   kuh LEK tur)   A device used to collect solar energy. p. 383

solar energy (SOH lur   EN ur jee) Energy from the sun. p. 382

solar flare (SOH lur   flair)   An eruption on the surface of the sun. p. 439

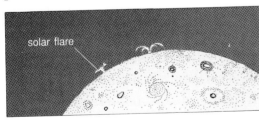

solar flare

solar system (SOH lur   SIHS tum) The sun and the bodies that move around it. p. 434

solute (SAHL yoot)   The material that is present in the smaller amount in a solution. p. 213

solution (suh LOO shun)   A mixture in which the different particles of matter are spread evenly throughout. p. 212

solvent (SAHL vunt)   The material that is present in the greater amount in a solution. p. 213

space probe (spays   prohb)   A spacecraft without humans aboard that gathers data about objects in space. p. 445

speed (speed)   The distance an object moves in a certain period of time. p. 233

spinal cord (SPYE nul   kord)   A thick cord of nerves in the middle of the back. p. 517

spore (spohr)   A single cell that can grow into a new organism. p. 44

static electricity (STAT ihk   ee lek-TRIHS ih tee)   An electric charge that collects on the surface of an object. p. 268

stimulus (STIHM yoo lus); *plural form*, stimuli (STIHM yoo lye)   An object or event that can cause a living thing to react. p. 108

stinging cell (STING ing sel)   A cell that contains a poisonous thread. p. 66

storm (storm)   A weather disturbance caused by unusual weather conditions. p. 320

subsoil (SUB soil)   The soil just below the topsoil. p. 355

substance (SUB stuns)   Something made of only one kind of matter. p. 171

sunspot (SUN spaht)   A dark region on the surface of the sun. p. 439

T

taiga (TYE guh)   A biome in which the main type of plant life is evergreen trees. p. 131

telescope (TEL uh skohp)   A device that makes some distant objects look brighter, clearer, and nearer. p. 442

tendon (TEN dun)   A strong band of tissue that connects a muscle to a bone. p. 497

tentacle (TEN tuh kul)   An armlike part around the mouth of a stinging-cell animal. p. 66

thermal pollution (THUR mul puh LOO shun)   A form of pollution caused by heat added to bodies of water. p. 422

thorax (THOR aks)   The middle part of an insect's body. p. 85

thunderstorm (THUN dur storm)   A small, local storm with tall clouds, heavy rain, and thunder and lightning. p. 321

tidal energy (TYD ul   EN ur jee)   The energy of the moving water of tides. p. 388

topsoil (TAHP soil)   The upper layer of soil. p. 354

tornado (tor NAY doh)   A small funnel of quickly spinning air. p. 324

tropical rain forest (TRAHP ih kul rayn   FOR ihst)   A biome that has high temperatures and a large amount of rain. p. 138

tropism (TROH pihz um)   A plant response that involves growth. p. 109

troposphere (TROH poh sfihr)   The layer of the atmosphere closest to the earth's surface. p. 307

tube foot   a hollow structure with a sucker at the end. p. 78

tundra (TUN druh)   A biome that is cold and receives little precipitation. p. 128

turbine (TUR bihn)   A machine with a wheel and blades that changes the energy in steam to mechanical energy. p. 373

V

vertebrae (VER tuh bray)   The bones of the backbone. p. 486

virus (VYE rus)   A thing that seems to be alive, but is not made of cells. p. 51

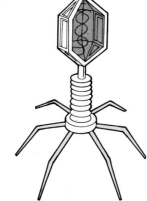

W

weather forecast (WETHH ur FOR-kast) A prediction of what future weather conditions will be. p. 326

weathering (WETHH ur ing)   The processes that break apart and change the chemical makeup of rocks. p. 341

weight (wayt)   The force between the earth and an object. p. 248

X

xylem (ZYE lum)   A tissue made of tubes that carry water and minerals through a plant from the roots to the leaves. p. 105

Index

Credits

Chapter 4 120–121: © Photo Researchers, Inc. 122–123: Grant Heilman/Grant Heilman Photography. 123: Bill Kontzias for SB&G. 124: *t.* David C. Fritts/Animals Animals; *b.* Laura Riley/Bruce Coleman. 128: *l.* Zig Leszczynski/Earth Scenes; *r.* © Photo Researchers, Inc. 130: *t.* © S.J. Krasemann/Photo Researchers, Inc.; *m.* © Tom McHugh/Photo Researchers, Inc. 131: Ken Lax for SB&G. 132: *l.* Keith Gunnar/Bruce Coleman; *t.r.* Robert Maier/Animals Animals; *b.r.* Wayne Lankinen/Bruce Coleman. 133: © G.C. Kelley/Photo Researchers, Inc. 134: © James Prince/Photo Researchers, Inc. 136: Ken Lax for SB&G. 137: Edgar T. Jones/Bruce Coleman. 140: *t.* Stephen Dalton/Oxford Scientific Films/Animals Animals; *b.l.* K. Fink/Bruce Coleman; *m.* E.R. Degginger/Animals, Animals. 141: *t.* © Gregory G. Dimijian, M.D./Photo Researchers, Inc.; *r.* © Tom McHugh/Photo Researchers, Inc. 142–143: © Gary Retherford/Photo Researchers, Inc. 142: *r.* Dr. Nigel Smith/Earth Scenes. 143: M.J. Balick/Peter Arnold, Inc. 144: John M. Burnley/Bruce Coleman. 146: © Francois Gohier/Photo Researchers, Inc. 147: Ken Lax for SB&G. 150: Carol Hughes/Bruce Coleman. 154: Doug Wilson for SB&G.

Unit 2 opener 165: E.R. Degginger.

Chapter 5 166–167: Peter Pearson/TSW. 167: Ginger Chin/Peter Arnold, Inc. 168–169: © Lawrence Migdale/Photo Researchers, Inc. 168: Stephan G. St. John. 170–171: Todd Haiman for SB&G. 172: *t.l.* E.R. Degginger. 172: *t.l., l to r.* E.R. Degginger; J. Cancalosi/Peter Arnold, Inc.; CBI Industries; Joe Sachs for SB&G; *b.* CBI Industries. 173: John Curtis/Offshoot for SB&G. 174: *t.l., t.m., b.l., b.r.* John Lei/OPC for SB&G; *t.r.* L.S. Stepanowicz/Pano Graphics. 176: *t., b.m.* Joe Sachs for SB&G; *l.* Ken Lax for SB&G. 177: Ken Lax for SB&G. 179: *t.* E.R. Degginger; *inset* L.S. Stepanowicz/Pano Graphics; *b.* Joe Sachs for SB&G. 182: E.R. Degginger. 183: *t.l.* Chip Clark; *b.l., b.r.* E.R. Degginger. 184: *t.* Ken Lax for SB&G; *b.* Breck P. Kent. 185: *t.* Barry Runk/Grant Heilman Photography, photo courtesy of North Museum, Franklin and Marshall College; *m.* John Cancalosi/Peter Arnold, Inc.; *b.* F. Stuart Westmorland/TOM STACK & ASSOCIATES. 186: Todd Haiman for SB&G. 188: Ken Lax for SB&G. 190: *t.l.* © 1983 Harold & Erica Van Pelt; *t.r.* Runk-Schoenberger/Grant Heilman Photography; *b.r.* E.R. Degginger. 191: Joe Sachs for SB&G. 192: E.R. Degginger. 193: *m.r.* E.R. Degginger; *b.* Todd Haiman for SB&G.

Chapter 6 198–199: Matthew Smith for SB&G. 200–201: John Feingersh/Stock, Boston. 200: Stacy Pick/Stock, Boston. 201: Ken Karp for SB&G. 202: Todd Haiman for SB&G. 204: Richard Choy/Peter Arnold, Inc. 205: © Richard Megna, 1988/Fundamental Photographs. 206: *t., l.* Todd Haiman for SB&G; *b.m., b.r.* E.R. Degginger. 207: *t.l.* © Kristen Brochmann, 1989/Fundamental Photographs; *b.r.* © Richard Megna/Fundamental Photographs. 208: *b.l.* © Farrell Grehan/Photo Researchers, Inc.; *b.r.* David Hiser/The Image Bank. 209: *t.* Ken Lax for SB&G; *b.* E.R. Degginger. 210: Air Products & Chemicals, Inc. 211: Light Mechanics for SB&G. 213: © Richard Megna, 1987/Fundamental Photographs. 214: Victoria Beller-Smith for SB&G. 216: *t.l.* Joe Sachs for SB&G; *b.l., b.m., b.r.* © Richard Megna, 1988/Fundamental Photographs. 218–219: Elgard Corporation. 218: *b.l.* Minkowski/Gamma-Liaison; *m.r.* Elgard Corporation. 220: *b.l.* Todd Haiman for SB&G. 221: Bill Ross/West Light. 222: Victoria Beller-Smith for SB&G. 223: Runk-Schoenberger/Grant Heilman Photography.

Chapter 7 228–229: Paul L. Ruben. 230–231: Ricardo Ferro/Black Star. 231: Elizabeth Hathon for SB&G. 234: Ken Lax for SB&G. 235: Gary Gladstone/The Image Bank. 236: © P Saloutos/The Stock Market. 237: *t.r.* John Iacono/© *Sports Illustrated,* © Time, Inc.; *b.r.* Ronald C. Modra/© *Sports Illustrated,* © Time, Inc.; *b.l.* V.J. Lovero/© *Sports Illustrated,* © Time, Inc. 240: *l.* © George Jones III/Photo Researchers, Inc.; *r.* ESTO Photographics, Inc. 241: © David R. Frazier/Photo Researchers, Inc. 242: Brian Parker/TOM STACK & ASSOCIATES. 243: Todd Haiman for SB&G. 244: Gerhard Gscheidle/The Image Bank. 245: *l.* Todd Haiman for SB&G; *r.* Gary Bublitz/M.L. Dembinsky, Jr. Photography Associates. 246: Bruce Coleman. 248: John Lei/OPC for SB&G. 249: © Richard Megna, 1986/Fundamental Photographs. 250: John Lei/OPC for SB&G. 251: © Richard Megna/Fundamental Photographs. 252: *t.* Comstock; *b.* © Richard Megna/Fundamental Photographs. 255: *t.* Gregory Heisler/The Image Bank; *b.r.* © Ed Bohon/The Stock Market. 256: John Lei/OPC for SB&G.

Chapter 8 260–261: Bob Thomason/Picturesque. 260: Mike Borum. 262–263: Bill Kontzias for SB&G. 263: Dan DeWilde for SB&G. 264: © Louis Goldman/Photo Researchers, Inc. 267: Ken O'Donoghue for SB&G. 268: Hank Morgan/Rainbow. 269: Ken Lax for SB&G. 270: *t.* © Richard Megna/Fundamental Photographs; *b.* Roger Ressmeyer/Starlight. 271: *t.r.* John Lei/OPC for SB&G; *m.r.* © Science Source/Photo Researchers, Inc. 272: Ken Lax for SB&G. 273: Steve Lissau/Rainbow. 274–275, 276: © Richard Megna/Fundamental Photographs. 277: John Lei/OPC for SB&G. 280, 282: © Richard Megna/Fundamental Photographs. 283: John Lei/OPC for SB&G. 284: *t.* Flip Chalfant/The Image Bank. 286: © 1991 Chuck O'Rear/Woodfin Camp & Associates. 290: Caltrans Photo.

Unit 3 opener 301: C.A. Morgan/Peter Arnold, Inc.

Chapter 9 302–303: Edi Ann Otto. 303: *l., r.* Unisys. 304–305: © Jed Share/The Stock Market. 304: Unisys. 309: E.R. Degginger/Bruce Coleman. 314: © R. Bierregaard/Photo Researchers, Inc. 316: Ken Lax for SB&G. 320: © Jerry Irwin/Photo Researchers, Inc. 323: Johnson Space Center, NASA, Houston, Texas. 324: © 1991 Odyssey/Woodfin Camp & Associates. 325: Edi Ann Otto. 326: *t.* Jet Propulsion Laboratory; *b.* © Lawrence Migdale/Photo Researchers, Inc.

Chapter 10 334–335: © Charles E. Mohr/Photo Researchers, Inc. 336–337: Superstock. 337: Dan DeWilde for SB&G. 338: Gene Ahrens/Bruce Coleman. 340: © Francois Gohier/Photo Researchers, Inc. 341: *t.* © Jerry L. Ferrara/Photo Researchers, Inc.; *b.r.* E.R. Degginger. 342: *l.* Mitchell Bleier/Peter Arnold, Inc.; *m.* Townsend P. Dickinson/Photo Researchers, Inc.; *r.* © Farrell Grehan/Photo Researchers, Inc. 343: Light Mechanics for SB&G. 344: © Caroline W. Coleman/William E. Ferguson. 345: © William E. Ferguson. 346: *l.* Ken Stepnell/Bruce Coleman; *r.* © 1991 Robert Frerck/Woodfin Camp & Associates. 348: Ken Lax for SB&G. 349: *b.l.* Bruce Coleman; *b.r.* © William E. Ferguson; *t.r. inset* Michael S. Renner/Bruce Coleman. 350: D. & J. McClure/Bruce Coleman. 351: *l.* 1991 Dan Budnik/Woodfin Camp & Associates; *b.r.* © William E. Ferguson. 352–353: Todd Haiman for SB&G. 356: Ken Lax for SB&G. 357: *t.l.* Richard Kolar/Earth Scenes; *b.r.* © William E. Ferguson; *t.r.* John Lei/OPC for SB&G. 358: G.I. Bernhard/Earth Scenes. 359: © Dan Guravich/Photo Researchers, Inc. 360: *t.r.* Joe Sachs for SB&G; *b.* Zig Leszczynski/Animals Animals/Earth Scenes. 361: *t.r.* Grant Heilman/Grant Heilman Photography; *b.* S.J. Krasemann/Peter Arnold, Inc. 362: *l.* © William E. Ferguson.

Chapter 11 367–369: Institute for Aerospace Studies/University of Toronto. 372: Joe Sachs for SB&G. 376: David Madison/Bruce Coleman. 378: *l.* Dan McCoy/Rainbow; *r.* © Bertrand-Explorer/Photo Researchers, Inc. 380: Mark

Sherman/Bruce Coleman. 384: *t.r.* Peter Ward/Bruce Coleman; *b.l.* © John Keating/Photo Researchers, Inc. 385 *t.r.* David Austin/Black Star; *m.* Gamma-Liaison. 386: © Earl Roberge/Photo Researchers, Inc. 389: *l.* Miller/Comstock; *r.* Bierwagen-Miller/Comstock. 390: *t.* © Lowell Georgia/Photo Researchers, Inc.; *b.* © Jan Halaska/Photo Researchers, Inc. 391: *l.* Phil Degginger/Bruce Coleman; *r.* © Leonard Lee Rue III/Photo Researchers, Inc. 393: *l.* © N.L. Brown; *r.* © 1991 Jonathan Blair/Woodfin Camp & Associates.

Chapter 12   398–399: Ron Levy/Gamma-Liaison. 399: Sygma. 400–401: Ron Levy/Gamma-Liaison. 400: *t.* B. Nation/Sygma; *b.* Charles Mason/Black Star. 401: Dan DeWilde for SB&G. 402: *b.m.* © Tom Hollyman/Photo Researchers, Inc. 404: *t.* Ken Lax for SB&G; *l.m.* Victoria Beller-Smith for SB&G; *b.l.* Norman Owen Tomalin/Bruce Coleman. 405: Ken O'Donoghue for SB&G. 406: *t.* © Mark Boulton/Photo Researchers, Inc. 407: *t.* Ted Spiegel/Black Star; *b.* Jon Reis/The Stock Market. 408: Ted Spiegel/Black Star. 409: Ken Lax for SB&G. 410: *t.* Joe Sachs for SB&G; *m.* © NASA/Science Photo Library/Photo Researchers, Inc. 411: *t.r.* Sal Di Marco, Jr./Black Star; *b.r.* Marketing Support, Inc., Chicago. 413: Larry Lefever/Grant Heilman Photography. 414: Ken Lax for SB&G. 416: Fred Ward/Black Star; *inset* © Joe Baraban. 417: *t.l.* Irwin & Peggy Bauer/Bruce Coleman; *t.r.* © Richard Hutchings/Photo Researchers, Inc.; *m.* Peter Cole/Bruce Coleman; *b.l.* © Alexander Lowry/Photo Researchers, Inc.; *b.r.* E.R. Degginger. 418: © 1991 Jeffrey D. Smith/Woodfin Camp & Associates. 419: The U.S. Department of Energy's Pacific Northwest Laboratory. 420: NASA. 421: John E. Swedberg/Bruce Coleman. 422: Lee Foster/Bruce Coleman. 423: Patti Murray/Animals Animals. 425: *t.* © 1991 Jim E. Calle/Woodfin Camp & Associates; *m.r.* Michael Baytoff/Black Star.

Chapter 13   430–431: © NASA/Science Source/Photo Researchers, Inc. 432–433: NASA. 432: © Bruce H. Frisch/Science Source/Photo Researchers, Inc. 433: © Will & Deni McIntyre/Photo Researchers, Inc. 436: L.S. Stepanowicz/Pano Graphics. 437: Light Mechanics for SB&G. 439: *t.* © George East/Dennis Milon; *b.* National Optical Astronomy Observatories. 442: *t.* E.R. Degginger; *b.* © John Bova/Photo Researchers, Inc. 443: *t.r.* Courtesy of Edmund Scientific Company; *m.r.* California Institute of Technology & Carnegie Institution of Washington; *b.* NASA. 444: The Bettmann Archive. 445: *l.* Lick Observatory; *m.* NASA. 447–452: NASA. 454–455: Peter Menzel; except 454 *t.l.* NASA/Grant Heilman Photography. 456: © James W. Baker/Dennis Milon. 457: *t.* D.P. Hershkowitz; *b.* © Francois Gohier/Photo Researchers, Inc. 458: Ken Lax for SB&G. 460: TERSCH ENTERPRISES. 464: Dan DeWilde for SB&G.

Unit 4 opener   475: Roger Tully/After Image, Inc.

Chapter 14   476: © Catherine Ursillo/Photo Researchers, Inc. 477: Model & Instrument Development. 478–479: Gregory Heisler/The Image Bank. 479: Ken Karp for SB&G. 480: © Gary Guisinger/Photo Researchers, Inc. 481: © Ray Simons/Photo Researchers, Inc. 483: Ken Karp/OPC for SB&G. 484: Lester V. Bergman & Associates. 485: Ken O'Donoghue for SB&G. 492: Jim Wilson. 495: © Eric V. Grave/Photo Researchers, Inc. 496: *b.* Ken Karp/OPC for SB&G; *t.l.* © M.I. Walker/Science Source/Photo Researchers, Inc.; *t.r.* © Biophoto Associates/Photo Researchers, Inc. 498: Ken Lax for SB&G. 500: Todd Haiman for SB&G. 501: Victoria Beller-Smith for SB&G. 502: *b.m.* © James Stevenson/Science Photo Library/Photo Researchers, Inc.; *b.r.* © Russ Kinne/Comstock. 503: *m.* © Yoav/Phototake; *m.r.* Victoria Beller-Smith for SB&G. 504: *t.l., m.l.* Rick Brown for SB&G; *r.* Brian Parker/TOM STACK & ASSOCIATES.

Chapter 15   508: John Karapelou/*Discover Magazine*/Family Media. 509: Herb Weitman/Washington University. 510–511: © Renee Lynn/Photo Researchers, Inc. 510: Jana Brenning/*Discover Magazine*. 511: Dan DeWilde for SB&G. 512–515: Ken Lax for SB&G. 520–521: Globus Brothers/The Stock Market. 524: Victoria Beller-Smith for SB&G. 528: *l.* © Lea/OPC; *m.* © Wil Blanche/OPC; *r.* © Maryanne Russell/OPC. 529: Ken Lax for SB&G. 530: © Richard Folwell/Photo Science Library/Photo Researchers, Inc. 531: Ken Lax for SB&G. 532, 533: Todd Haiman for SB&G. 534: Victoria Beller-Smith for SB&G. 535: Ken Lax for SB&G. 540: Courtesy of Ciba-Geigy.

ACKNOWLEDGMENTS

Grateful acknowledgment is made to the following publishers, authors, and agents for their permission to reprint copyrighted material. Any adaptations are noted in the individual acknowledgments and are made with the full knowledge and approval of the authors or their representatives. Every effort has been made to locate all copyright proprietors; any errors or omissions in copyright notice are inadvertent and will be corrected in future printings as they are discovered.

p. 14:   From "A Long Last Look at *Titanic*" by Robert D. Ballard, in *National Geographic* magazine, December 1986. Courtesy of National Geographic Society.

p. 15:   From "A Long Last Look at *Titanic*" by Robert D. Ballard, in *National Geographic* magazine, December 1986. Courtesy of National Geographic Society.

p. 16:   From "A Long Last Look at *Titanic*" by Robert D. Ballard, in *National Geographic* magazine, December 1986. Courtesy of National Geographic Society.

p. 22:   From "A Long Last Look at *Titanic*" by Robert D. Ballard, in *National Geographic* magazine, December 1986. Courtesy of National Geographic Society.

p. 24:   Quote by Dr. Robert D. Ballard in *Jason* Project information paper, August 1989. Used courtesy of the Woods Hole Oceanographic Institution.

pp. 156–164:   From *One Day in the Desert* by Jean Craighead George, illustrated by Fred Brenner (Crowell). Text Copyright © 1983 by Jean Craighead George. Illustrations Copyright © 1983 by Fred Brenner. Reprinted by permission of Harper & Row, Publishers, Inc., and of Curtis Brown, Ltd.

pp. 292–300:   From *What's the Big Idea, Ben Franklin?*, text copyright © 1976 by Jean Fritz, illustrations copyright © 1976 by Margot Tomes. Reprinted by permission of The Putnam Publishing Group and of Gina Maccoby Literary Agency.

pp. 446–474:   From *To Space & Back* by Sally Ride and Susan Okie. Text Copyright © 1986 by the authors. By permission of Lothrop Lee & Shepard (A Division of William Morrow & Co.) and of International Creative Management.

pp. 542–550:   From *Mine for Keeps* by Jean Little. © 1962 by Jean Little. By permission of Little, Brown and Company.